EXILE WITHIN EXILES

FRONTIS Herbert Daniel in Paris, c. 1979. COURTESY OF GENY BRUNELLI DE CARVALHO.

DUKE UNIVERSITY PRESS *Durham and London* 2018

EXILE WITHIN EXILES

Herbert Daniel, Gay Brazilian Revolutionary

JAMES N. GREEN

© 2018 DUKE UNIVERSITY PRESS
All rights reserved

Designed by Matthew Tauch
Typeset in Whitman by Westchester Book Group

Library of Congress Cataloging-in-Publication Data
Names: Green, James Naylor, [date] author.
Title: Exile within exiles : Herbert Daniel, gay Brazilian revolutionary / James N. Green.
Description: Durham : Duke University Press, 2018. | Includes bibliographical references and index.
Identifiers: LCCN 2018008227 (print)
LCCN 2018009566 (ebook)
ISBN 9781478002352 (ebook)
ISBN 9781478000679 (hardcover : alk. paper)
ISBN 9781478000860 (pbk. : alk. paper)
Subjects: LCSH: Daniel, Herbert. | Gays—Brazil—Biography. | Revolutionaries—Brazil—Biography. | AIDS activists—Brazil—Biography.
Classification: LCC HQ76.3.B6 (ebook) | LCC HQ76.3.B6 G74 2018 (print) | DDC 306.76/6092 [B]—dc23
LC record available at https://lccn.loc.gov/2018008227

Cover art: Herbert Daniel in Paris. Photo courtesy of Geny Brunelli de Carvalho.

FOR MOSHÉ SLUHOVSKY, SONYA KRAHULIK ALLEE,

AND MARYCAROLYN G. FRANCE

The time has not yet arrived for autobiographies;

we are preparing hypotheses for self-criticisms,

above all else, avoiding writing artificial memoirs

in which one proves, even without wanting to,

that one was right.

I don't want to be right.

I want to conserve clarity.

—HERBERT DANIEL
Passagem para o próximo sonho (1982)

CONTENTS

Acknowledgments ix

List of Abbreviations xiii

	INTRODUCTION		1
1	Dare to Struggle, Dare to Win	1992	7
2	He Loved to Read	1946–1964	11
3	Medical School	1965–1967	26
4	The O.	1967–1968	41
5	Ângelo	1968	55
6	Underground	1969	68
7	Unity and Disunity	1969	84
8	To the Countryside!	1970	99
9	40 + 70 = 110	1970–1971	113
10	Falling Apart	1971	128
11	Cláudio	1972–1974	139
12	Red Carnations	1974–1975	154

13	Marginalia	1976–1981	171
14	Returning to Rio	1981–1982	187
15	Words, Words, Words	1983–1985	206
16	The Politics of Pleasure	1986–1988	223
17	Forty Seconds	1989–1992	241
	EPILOGUE. Remnants		259
	Chronology		265
	Notes		273
	Bibliography		299
	Index		315

ACKNOWLEDGMENTS

This book would not have been possible without the editorial, intellectual, and moral support of Moshé Sluhovsky, my lifetime partner. He continues to put up with my quirks, misplaced enthusiasm, and harebrained ideas. I am grateful for his love and patience.

A long chain of people is linked to this project, starting with Jeffrey Escoffier, who in 1974 joined me in a rather unsuccessful gay socialist study group in Philadelphia. My colleagues in the June 28 Union in the San Francisco Bay Area the following year, now dispersed and mostly deceased, offered a supportive group as we organized the "Gay Solidarity with the Chilean Resistance" event in September 1975 and tried to integrate the complexities of the personal and the political. Likewise, I am thankful to those who joined me in São Paulo in forming the first LGBT group within a South American left-wing party, especially Hiro Okita and Carlos Ricardo da Silva, as well as those members of Somos, Brazil's first gay and lesbian rights organization, who marched on May 1, 1980, under the banner "Down with the Discrimination of Homosexual Workers." Many years later, when I returned to graduate school, John D'Emilio was a loyal sponsor of my work, and I greatly appreciate his confidence in me.

Ângela Pezzuti, Beto Vasconcelos, Cristina Montenegro, Denise Rollemberg, Jessie Jane Vieira de Sousa, Ivan Seixas, Lúcia Velloso Maurício, Maria do Carmo Brito, Monica Arruda, Sérgio Xavier Ferreira, Veriano Terto, and Zenaide Machado offered me contacts that were essential in tracking down this story. I also wish to thank Isabel Leite and Yama Arruda for patiently transcribing dozens of interviews, António J. Ramalho for doing research and conducting an interview for me in Portugal, and Américio Oscar Guichard Freire for supplying me with copies of Portuguese police records.

Many people, including the anonymous readers, offered helpful suggestions for versions of the manuscript: thank you to Andre Pagliarini, Barbara Weinstein, Ben Cowan, Caroline Landau, Claudia Kedar, Isadora Mota, Javier Fernandez, Justina Hwang, Kenneth Serbin, Luke Smith, Marc Hertzman, Márcia Bassettos Paes, Michael Gale, Michele Mericle, Natan Zeichner, Pablo Ben, Ryan Jones, Sandra Hardy, and Yesenia Barrigan. Equally important to recognize are my colleagues Amy Remensnyder and Nancy Jacobs at Brown University, and especially the Latin American historians Daniel Rodriguez, Doug Cope, Evelyn Hu-DeHart, Jennifer Lambe, Jeremy Mumford, Neil Safier, and Roquinaldo Ferreira. I am grateful for the assistance of Mary Beth Bryson, Julissa Bautista, and Cherrie Guerzon from the history department while I was working on this text. Michael Gale and Dylan Blau Edelstein are to be thanked for the research that they did for me in Brazil. Ramon Stern, the administrative manager of Brown's Brazil Initiative, was quite patient with me as I completed the manuscript. I regret that Thomas E. Skidmore did not live to read the completed manuscript, as he had enthusiastically encouraged the project, but I appreciate the support that Felicity Skidmore has given me since I arrived at Brown.

My Brazilian colleagues continue to show their limitless friendship. They include Amélia Teles, Beatriz Kushnir, Carlos Fico, Daria Jaremtchuk, Durval Muniz de Albuquerque, Henrique Carneiro, Janaina Teles, João Moreira Salles, João Roberto Martins Júnior, Lilia Schwarcz, Lula Ramires, Luiz Morando, Marcelo Torelly, Márcio Caetano, Marisa Fernandes, Marlon Weichert, Monica Schpun, Nadia Nogueira, Paulo Abrão, Paulo Roberto Pepe, Renan Quinalha, Ronaldo Trindade, Silvia Miskulin, Tânia Pellegrini, and Wilson da Silva. Ruth Fine, Claudia Kedar, and Manuela Consonni at Hebrew University of Jerusalem generously welcomed me into their program during these years as I balanced working on the manuscript and building a Brazil program there. Michel Gherman has been a loyal collaborator in many academic and other endeavors and has helped me think about ways the Brazilian Left has failed to address multiple forms of discrimination.

As always, Lauro Ávila Pereira has been a faithful backer of my research, especially when he led a dedicated staff at the State Archive of São Paulo. Likewise, Sátiro Nunes of the Brazilian National Archive diligently helped me find valuable archival material, as did Elaine Zanatta from the Edgard Leuenroth Arquive at the Universidade Estadual de Campinas. Vicente Arruda Camara Rodrigues and Inez Terezinha Stampa of the Memórias Reveladas Project at the National Archive were generous in securing images for this volume, as were Almir Martins, Beatriz Kushnir, Cristina Montenegro,

Ethel Mizrahy, Fabiano Carnevale, Fernando Nogueira, Geny Brunelli de Carvalho, Isabel Leite, Magaly Mesquita, Martina Spohr Gonçalves, Miguel Mesquita, Sérgio Ferreira, Veriano Terto, and Vladmir Sacchetta.

Martinha Arruda and Edméa Jafet continue to offer their generous hospitality during my visits to Rio and São Paulo. In Belo Horizonte, Andrea Moreira Lima, Carlos Magno, Elizabeth Maria Leite, and Vitor Santana graciously opened up their homes to while I was doing research. Similarly Marcelo Torelly was a warm host in Brasília.

Special thanks go to Karen Krahulik and Susan Allee for allowing me to be a part of their lives and that of their daughter, Sonya.

A research and writing fellowship from the American Council of Learned Societies, a summer grant from the American Philosophical Society, a Brown University Humanities Research Fellowship, and a Visiting Scholars Fellowship at Princeton University's Program in Latin American Studies gave me the opportunity to work on the first draft.

Particular gratitude goes to my sister, Marycarolyn G. France, who told me bedtime stories when I was a child that engendered a love for seductive narratives and enticed me to write my own (historical) tales. Her multiple rounds of editing helped improve the manuscript immensely.

Finally, I am especially indebted to Herbert's family for allowing me to write this biography of their beloved son and brother, Bete.

ABBREVIATIONS

ABIA	Associação Brasileira Interdisciplinar de AIDS / Brazilian Interdisciplinary AIDS Association
AI-5	Ato Institucional Número 5 / Institutional Act No. 5
ALN	Ação Libertadora Nacional / National Liberating Action
AP	Ação Popular / Popular Action
ARENA	Aliança Renovadora Nacional / National Renovating Alliance
CBA	Comitê Brasileiro de Anistia / Brazilian Amnesty Committee
CEM	Centro de Estudos de Medicina / Center for the Study of Medicine
COLINA	Comandos de Libertação Nacional / National Liberation Commandos
COSEC	Comando de Estudantes Secundaristas / High School Students' Command
DCE	Diretório Central de Estudantes / Central Student Directorate

DDD	Dissidência da Dissidência / Dissidence of the Dissidence
DVP	Dissidência de VAR-Palmares / VAR-Palmares Dissidence
FHAR	Front Homosexuel d'Action Révolutionnaire / Homosexual Front for Revolutionary Action
GAPA	Grupo de Apoio à Prevenção à AIDS / Support Group for AIDS Prevention
GGB	Grupo Gay da Bahia / Gay Group of Bahia
GLH—P&Q	Groupe de Libération Homosexuelle—Politique et Quotidien / Homosexual Liberation Group—Politics and Daily Life
GPV	Grupo Pela VIDDA (Valorização, Integração, e Dignidade do Doente de AIDS) / Pela VIDDA Group (The Valuing, Integration, and Dignity of Those Sick with AIDS)
MDB	Movimento Democrático Brasileiro / Brazilian Democratic Movement
MFA	Movimento das Forças Armadas / Movement of the Armed Forces
MNR	Movimento Nacional Revolucionário / National Revolutionary Movement
MR-8	Movimento Revolucionário 8 de Outubro / October 8th Revolutionary Movement
MRP	Movimento de Resistencia Popular / Movement of Popular Resistance
MRT	Movimento Revolucionário Tiradentes / Tiradentes Revolutionary Movement

PCB	Partido Comunista Brasileira / Brazilian Communist Party
PDS	Partido Democrático Social / Social Democratic Party
PDT	Partido Democrático Trabalhista / Democratic Labor Party
PMDB	Partido do Movimento Democrático Brasileiro / Party of the Brazilian Democratic Movement
POLOP	Organização Revolucionária Marxista—Política Operária / Revolutionary Marxist Organization—Workers' Politics
PT	Partido dos Trabalhadores / Workers' Party
PTB	Partido Trabalhista Brasileira / Brazilian Labor Party
PV	Partido Verde / Green Party
REDE	Resistência Democrática / Democratic Resistance
SOMOS	Somos: Grupo de Afirmação Homossexual / We Are: Group of Homosexual Affirmation
UFMG	Universidade Federal de Minas Gerais / Federal University of Minas Gerais
UNE	União Nacional de Estudantes / National Union of Students
VAR-Palmares	Vanguarda Armada Revolucionária—Palmares / Revolutionary Armed Vanguard—Palmares
VPR	Vanguarda Popular Revolucionária / People's Revolutionary Vanguard

INTRODUCTION

I am very proud of my generation and that we fought and participated fully in the fight to build a better Brazil. We learned a lot. We did much that was foolish, but that is not what characterizes us. What characterizes us is to have been bold enough to want a better country.

— DILMA ROUSSEFF

I never met Herbert Daniel, but our paths almost crossed in late 1981. He had returned from seven years of European exile in October and was living in Rio de Janeiro. I was preparing to leave Brazil after a six-month visit that had turned into a six-year stay. I thought of traveling from São Paulo, where I lived, to Rio to say goodbye to friends. I imagined trying to meet him. Somehow my trip never happened.

I had first heard of Herbert Daniel a year and a half earlier. One of the thousands of Brazilians who engaged in the armed resistance to the military dictatorship (1964–1985), he was convicted *in absentia* for having violated the National Security Act and was sentenced to several lifetimes in prison for abducting the German and Swiss ambassadors and demanding freedom for 110 political prisoners in exchange for the diplomats' release. Never arrested, he slipped out of the country in September 1974 and had been living in European exile.

In October 1979, Daniel wrote an open letter to the Brazilian Left about the Amnesty Law, passed the previous month, that pardoned most political prisoners and allowed almost all exiles to return to Brazil, but it didn't include those involved in violent acts in which someone had died. Defiantly he declared: "The dictatorship has nothing to pardon or grant me. Being granted amnesty does not mean repenting to the dictatorship; rather it allows [the dictatorship] to recognize some of its errors. It is not we, those exiled and imprisoned, who should criticize ourselves to the dictatorship, rather it is the current popular democratic movement that has forced the government to make amends for its abuses."[1] Daniel lingered abroad, unable to get a passport and fearful of incarceration when and if he were to step off a plane in Brazil.

Daniel's intransigent attitude toward the military regime was not the only reason he remained a castaway. By late 1979, it was widely known among the Brazilian revolutionary Left that Herbert Daniel was gay. In fact, the former leader of the (by-then dismantled) guerrilla group People's Revolutionary Vanguard (VPR) was unabashedly living in Paris with his partner, Cláudio Mesquita. His announced homosexuality had created anxiety and revulsion among some of the exiled Left, while others tranquilly accepted his sexual orientation.

Daniel's open letter was an appeal to antidictatorship forces to support his attempts to return home. In Brazil, the emergent Homosexual Movement, as it called itself at the time, came to Daniel's aid. The alternative newspaper *Lampião da Esquina* published his appeal in its entirety. The tabloid-sized monthly first came out in April 1978, as the political climate in Brazil opened up and the ruling generals initiated a gradual liberalization. This new political space offered opportunities for circulating innovative ways of thinking, and *Lampião* advocated for the defense of homosexuals, blacks, women, Indians, and the environment, which was quite a novelty in Brazil at the time.

According to a comment penned by Aguinaldo Silva, a leading member of the journal's editorial board, Daniel's letter had not been read at a national meeting of the Brazilian Amnesty Committee (CBA) the previous year because Daniel was gay. "We homosexuals of *Lampião*," Silva wrote, "are in solidarity with him, as we would be—pay attention, those in the CBA—with any heterosexual in the same situation."[2] Reprimanding the amnesty movement over its alleged mistreatment of Herbert Daniel also represented a larger critique about homophobia within the Brazilian Left.

Living in Brazil at the time and being involved in gay and lesbian activism, I wanted to know more about this figure, who seemed to have lived a life similar to my own. I thought a conversation with him might help me sort out my own ambivalences about participating in the Left while observing and experiencing its homophobia. Although Herbert Daniel was a few years older, we had both embraced the revolutionary wave that swept Latin America in the 1960s. Almost simultaneously, we had also become critical of the lingering prejudice against homosexuality within the international Marxist movement. In different ways and in different places, but at about the same time, we had challenged its conservative notions of morality and propriety.

Herbert Daniel's story, however, was certainly much more dramatic than my own. As a medical student in the mid-1960s, he was a founding member of the National Liberation Commandos (COLINA). In early 1970, he engaged in rural guerrilla training, escaping imprisonment when several thousand soldiers surrounded the area. A few months later, he participated first in the abduction of the German ambassador and then, at the end of the year, the sequestering of the Swiss ambassador to gain the release of a total of 110 political prisoners who lingered in Brazilian jails. While in exile in the late 1970s, Daniel openly announced his homosexuality and stubbornly questioned the revolutionary Left's reluctance to address issues related to sexuality and the body.

My revolutionary credentials were much more modest.[3] I had participated actively in the anti–Vietnam War movement while in college in the late 1960s. A summer sojourn in Mexico to learn the fundamentals of Spanish took me down an unexpected path. I became determined to understand the revolutionary upheavals taking place throughout the continent. Quite by chance, in early 1973, I became involved in a campaign against torture in Brazil. My political thinking was evolving rapidly, as was my personal life, for it was at this juncture that I openly declared myself gay, feeling great relief that I could finally accept my sexuality.

The overthrow of the socialist government of Chilean President Salvador Allende on September 11, 1973, and the ensuing repression led me and many others to engage in round-the-clock efforts to denounce the Nixon administration's support of the Pinochet dictatorship. In 1975, on the second anniversary of the coup, I organized an event, "Gay Solidarity with the Chilean Resistance," designed to educate members of the San Francisco gay and lesbian communities about the Chilean situation. In early 1976, I journeyed through Central America and Colombia to Brazil. There I joined a semi-underground revolutionary organization, while simultaneously participating as a left-wing activist in the emergent gay and lesbian movement.

As if we had managed to coordinate our timing, Daniel in Paris and I in São Paulo confronted the Brazilian Left's backward attitudes toward homosexuality, feminism, and comportment. He was moving away from the organized Left; I remained active for another decade.

Years later, Herbert Daniel reappeared in my life while I was writing an article on homosexuality and the Brazilian revolutionary Left.[4] In seeking firsthand testimonies, I read Daniel's memoir *Passagem para o próximo sonho* (Ticket to the next dream), which he had written during his European exile while working in a gay Parisian sauna. His reminiscences of his time as a revolutionary, fugitive on the run, and exile were published in March 1982, soon after his safe return to Brazil. Daniel's insights were self-critical and perceptive. They touched me profoundly, both intellectually and emotionally.

I wanted to know more about this complex figure. Periodically I considered writing his biography. Then, by chance, Denise Rollemberg, a Brazilian historian, mentioned that Daniel's mother was living in Belo Horizonte. She gave me Dona Geny's telephone number, and I called her from Rio.[5] When I told her that I wanted to write a biography of her son, she immediately agreed to an interview.

Sitting in a modest living room in a tidy house, we spent several hours talking as she generously supplied me with coffee and cakes. She nostalgically showed me a photo album with pictures of Bete, as the family affectionately called him, as a baby, toddler, and young boy. Dona Geny also shared newspaper and magazine clippings and a few postcards that he had written from Paris, which she had saved as mementos of her beloved first-born child.

During our conversation, Hamilton, one of Daniel's younger brothers, called to find out how the interview with this curious U.S. historian was going. "What was the name of Bete's girlfriend?" she asked him, trying to dredge up memories of a distant past. "Laís," Hamilton responded. Her query surprised me, because Daniel's memoir had not mentioned a high school or college sweetheart. On the contrary, he had written about his frustrated love for a male member of the underground revolutionary organization that he had joined in 1967.

As we parted, I saw in her eyes a deep longing for her departed son. "Write the book," she insisted. "People have forgotten about him. He needs to be remembered."

With his childhood friend's name in hand, I tracked down Laís Pereira. We met in a bookstore café. "I only agreed to see you because you mentioned that you had spoken with Dona Geny," she confessed. Two hours, and many anecdotes later, I realized that I had enough material to start working on a book.

Never having written a biography, I was puzzled about how to proceed. There are few biographies of Brazilians in English, and those written for a Portuguese-language audience tend to focus on people who are famous, and the reader already has a general notion of the person's life trajectory. Historians have also produced biographies of obscure individuals from humble origins whose life histories are seen as emblematic representations of people from a specific social sector. A third genre, the recuperative biography, focuses on a person who was important but has not been recognized as such or even known to many people.

Such is the case of Herbert Daniel. Today, few Brazilians have heard of him. He has been all but forgotten except by his family, friends, former comrades in arms, and those who remember how he had courageously declared that he had AIDS in 1989. His literary legacy has been mostly overlooked, except among a handful of scholars seeking examples of early "queer" authors or graduate students examining his literary or AIDS work.[6] Some Brazilians confuse him with Herbert de Souza, another Brazilian revolutionary, who cofounded the AIDS organization where Herbert Daniel worked in the late 1980s.

Daniel's first book, *Passagem*, a semiautobiographical account of his life as a revolutionary and exile, published a decade before his death from AIDS in 1992, did not have a large readership. As I will argue in later chapters, most written remembrances by survivors of the armed struggle are tales of heroic deeds accomplished by noble warriors. In contrast, Daniel's story is a meditation on revolution, offering a critical assessment of the Left's attempt to overthrow the dictatorship through guerrilla warfare. It is as original in its honesty as it is experimental in its literary style. His detailed descriptions of promiscuous gay sex in Paris no doubt puzzled his readers and perhaps distanced many from his text. Because he had written the work half a decade before the Brazilian generals relinquished state power, many people and events were purposely portrayed in obscure ways to protect the identity of comrades who had been involved in the underground. His memoir offers a vast array of clues about details of his life that beg to be unveiled, but it also wraps a shroud of mystery around others. In this work, I have filled in some lacunas. Other questions about Daniel's life remain unanswered.

How then to tell the story of his life and times? As I dug up details of this story in dozens of interviews, scattered documents in diverse archives, numerous newspaper and magazine articles, and a cluster of video clips, I constantly confronted uncertainties and ambiguities in reconstructing Daniel's life. Living underground for nearly six years and deceiving the repressive apparatus mounted to dismantle the revolutionary Left meant revealing as little as possible about his activities to others. Even the name Herbert Daniel is a composite construction of his given first name and an assumed patronymic, "Daniel." It is one of more than a dozen noms de guerre he adopted casually and then as easily cast aside, as he moved in the shadows of urban centers and eluded police, acutely conscious of being on the generals' most-wanted list.

Many people who shared those dangerous moments with him and have survived those times simply did not know about or remember details of his life underground. Others have died, leaving no letters, diaries, or other traces of their revolutionary activities. Some were hesitant to refer to certain events, perhaps as a lingering reflex against revealing information that might in some way harm others. One person confessed after a long conversation that she had been reluctant to grant an interview for fear that I would create an incomplete and partial portraiture of their organization and its activities. Some of those I interviewed shared Daniel's hindsight about the limitations of the revolutionary Left's attempts to overthrow the dictatorship, while others were less critical of their former militancy. Few regretted, however, their decision to engage in radical resistance to the military regime, and this obviously colors their own narratives and their recollections of Daniel. Often, I had no additional source to check a fact or a remembrance and had to rely on my own intuition and contextualization of events to determine the veracity of someone's memory. In attempting to complete this book, I came to know Herbert Eustáquio de Carvalho, as he was baptized, slowly and unevenly, in bits and pieces. Only gradually did he become a living being in my mind's eye, and I am conscious that the version of his life I am creating is inevitably partial and incomplete.

As I have suggested in a brief mention of my own political activities, I identify with the protagonist of this biography, a fact that no doubt influences the ways I have chosen to tell his story. By all accounts Herbert Daniel was an exceptional figure, but certainly not representative of his generation. Yet by examining a person at the margins, both because of his sexuality and due to his radical militancy against the dictatorship and in defense of those with HIV/AIDS, we can learn much about the complexities of Brazilian politics, society, and culture; the nature of the Brazilian Left as it changed over time; and the constraints and options of those with nonnormative sexuality who lived during the second half of the twentieth century. His confrontation with the Left's conservative attitudes toward homosexuality in the 1970s and 1980s helped lay the groundwork for the LGBT movement's interactions with progressive politicians and the government in the late twentieth and early twenty-first centuries. His innovative and creative contributions to fighting discrimination against those with HIV/AIDS have been fundamental in shaping both official policies and grassroots activism. His life didn't just reflect the changes taking place in Brazil, but he himself was an agent in those changes. Daniel's biography, I argue, is not merely a rescue operation of a somewhat unique figure in the history of contemporary Brazil. It is also a vehicle for rethinking the entire narrative.[7]

1

Dare to Struggle, Dare to Win

(1992)

> He was the first to make it clear that this struggle [about AIDS] was not a personal one, but a question of human rights.
>
> — JOSÉ STALIN PEDROSO

At the end of my first visit with Dona Geny, Hamilton came over to meet me. He wanted to show me a family video, filmed during Christmas celebrations in December 1991, three months before his brother died. In the home movie, the family is sitting around a large table eating a hearty meal that Dona Geny has prepared. Cláudio, Herbert's partner of nearly twenty years, is clearly an integral family member, joking with Geraldo, Herbert's father, and playing with Herbert's nieces and nephews. It is a touching scene. AIDS had taken a toll on Herbert's body, and he appears thin and tired. At one point, he turns to his younger brother Hélder, the amateur filmmaker, lifts a glass, smiles into the camera, and states emphatically, "*Eu estou vivo.*" I am alive.

In early 1992, Dona Geny spent a month in Rio taking care of her son. She recalled, "Cláudio would come home from work and give him a bath. Cláudio

FIGURE 1.1 Herbert Daniel and his mother, Dona Geny, December 1991. COURTESY OF GENY BRUNELLI DE CARVALHO.

was very affectionate with him.... He would give him medicine, but Bete would throw it all up.... They had a twenty-year friendship, and I'll tell you, no woman would have taken care of my son as he did. Cláudio was a special person for him. If he had married a woman, she wouldn't have taken care of him in that way.... [Cláudio] took care of him as if he were a [delicate] flower."[1]

As Herbert neared death, Cláudio, his sister Magaly, and his close friends living in Rio de Janeiro looked after him around the clock. On a Sunday afternoon in late March, Válber Vieira, Daniel's doctor, was summoned to the apartment. With only his doctor and his partner Cláudio by his side, Herbert Daniel passed away.

A wake and burial were quickly organized. A hundred or more people gathered at the São João Batista Cemetery to mourn his passing. Cláudio could barely keep his composure. When pallbearers finally removed the coffin so that it could be transported to Belo Horizonte, those present broke out in applause in homage to their departed friend and comrade.

Cláudio and close friends accompanied the body on the plane. Unexpected delays caused the burial to be postponed until the following morning. Sixty or more friends and family gathered at the Cemitério Parque da Colina. A funeral cortege accompanied the body to the gravesite. People carried signs that stated "Long live life" and "Herbert Daniel: Freedom and Struggle."[2]

The burial ceremony was laced with ironies. Although Herbert had become an atheist, a mass was celebrated in his memory. Dona Geny would have it no other way. Part of the cemetery's name, Colina (Hill), was also the acronym of the revolutionary organization that Herbert had joined so enthusiastically twenty-five years previously as a medical student. A military honor guard accompanied the coffin as an act of solidarity with Herbert's brother, Major Hamilton Brunelli de Carvalho, as if Herbert's subversive activities against the armed forces no longer had any controversial meaning.

Herbert's father, Geraldo, Dona Geny, and Cláudio clutched each other in support as they slowly followed the coffin. After the funeral procession reached the gravesite, Helena Greco, president of the Belo Horizonte City Council Human Rights Commission, spoke about Daniel's fight against the dictatorship. Apolo Herlinger Lisboa, his former comrade in the revolutionary struggle, remembered his courage while underground, when their images shared space on a "Terrorists Wanted" poster. Cláudio, who had not slept for the last three days, was barely able to hold back convulsive sobs as he read from Herbert's writings: "I've had AIDS a long time. Perhaps for decades. My main discovery, however, is that I am alive. I have lived well with AIDS, and I have suffered. It is only a disease. I hope one day, when death takes me, no one will say that AIDS defeated me."[3]

When the coffin was lowered into the ground, mourners repeated the phrases "Life before death, not after it, is what is important," and "I don't want to be right; I want to be clear." The former had become his mantra for AIDS activism; the latter had been a phrase from Daniel's first book.

Local television stations showed brief scenes of the funeral on the midday and evening news. They mentioned his revolutionary trajectory, literary accomplishments, and openness about having AIDS. Obituaries and other news reports also emphasized his guerrilla past, especially his involvement in abducting the German and Swiss ambassadors, his European exile, and his career as a writer and AIDS activist after he returned to Brazil. One newspaper described the burial as a "protest act." Several mentioned that he was survived by Cláudio, his partner of twenty years, a personal fact about a same-sex couple, which, at the time, was rather unusual in the press.[4]

Newspaper clippings of the funeral are carefully preserved in the album that Dona Geny shared with me during my first visit. At some point during our conversations, she suddenly got up and shuffled into the back rooms of her house. After a minute or two, she reappeared with a 3.4-ounce bottle of

Chanel No. 5 Classic Perfume Spray clutched in her hand. "Bete brought this to me when he came back from France," she explained, with a deep sigh. Very little of the magical amber-colored fragrance was left in the crystal container. "Every time I want to think about him, I put on just a little bit. It helps me to remember."[5]

2

He Loved to Read

(1946–1964)

> Herbert studied all of the time. He was always first in his class. He was never number two. That made us very proud of him.
>
> — GENY BRUNELLI DE CARVALHO

Nearing ninety when I last interviewed her, Dona Geny Brunelli de Carvalho possessed a quiet, simple, and humble demeanor, combined with persistent energy and an inner strength that comes from a long life of unending work. In our first conversation, she told me that her own personal history influenced her firstborn son's choice to commit his life to political struggle. "He inherited it from me because I've been a fighter all of my life." Raising a family on a limited income and taking care of sick in-laws required vitality and perseverance. In our interviews, she rarely complained about her hardships. In part, her Catholic upbringing, she explained, sustained her, and she claimed to have experienced special favor from God in obtaining answers to her prayers.

"I was born in Barbacena [in Minas Gerais]," she recalled. "Until I was nine, it was the most marvelous place in the world because I had a father who adored me, and life was beautiful. Then he was in an accident and died." Dona Geny was the seventh of eleven children in a family of second-generation immigrants from southern Italy. Her father, Adolpho Brunelli, had labored diligently, managed to set up a nice home, and eventually owned one of the town's best bakeries. With his sudden death, the world collapsed around Carmelita Delben Brunelli and her children. "We were all minors. My uncle sold the house and left my mother with nothing, so we all had to work." Geny helped her mother at home until she was thirteen. Then her uncle got her a fake work permit, and she went to toil in a textile factory. Not protected by labor legislation, she worked a twelve-hour shift. "I only started earning the minimum wage a month before I got married at age nineteen."

It was love at first sight. "I was at a neighbor's birthday party. Geraldo was playing the tambourine for the dance, and we started flirting, that sort of thing. . . . We dated for a year, and then we got married. I was nineteen. Geraldo was very intelligent. He played music and drew a lot. He was completely different from my brothers. I loved him a lot, so much so that we lived sixty-three years together. Herbert was born one year after we were married."

At the time of their marriage Geraldo was a corporal in the military police. He was a distinguished-looking young man, partially descended from African slaves. Because his ailing mother was living in Belo Horizonte, he and his new bride moved to the state's capital so that Geny could take care of her, as was expected of dutiful daughters-in-law. The newlyweds settled into the Prado neighborhood close to the military police headquarters.

In 1946, Geraldo was posted to Bom Despacho, a tiny town one hundred miles from the capital, where his father, a captain in the military police, was also stationed. In the eighteenth century, residents had named the location after Our Lady of the Bom Despacho in honor of the Virgin Mary's benevolence in ensuring successful deliveries of newborns. Dona Geny, who was now pregnant, and her mother-in-law soon joined their husbands. Bom Despacho was, in Dona Geny's words, a "horrible place" with a single church, the barracks, and modest housing where the military families lived. "They didn't have a doctor; they didn't have a hospital. I had Herbert at home. It was a difficult delivery. He weighed 10.4 pounds and was my first child. There was no midwife or medicine, no anesthesia, nothing."

Born on December 14, 1946, he was baptized Herbert Eustáquio de Carvalho. His middle name was the result of a religious promise. Humberto van

FIGURE 2.1 Geny Brunelli and Geraldo Feliciano de Carvalho, December 8, 1945. COURTESY OF GENY BRUNELLI DE CARVALHO.

Lieshout, known as Father Eustáquio, was a Dutch priest who had come to Brazil in 1925 with the Congregation of Sacred Hearts. He quickly built a reputation for being able to summon up miracles to cure the sick. By the late 1940s, already a nationally known holy figure, he was en route to beatification. "At the time that I got married all of that was beginning, and everyone was talking about him. My mother-in-law said, 'Let's light a candle here for Padre Eustáquio. If he helps in the birth, then we will give the child the name Eustáquio.' But my husband didn't want to give him the name Eustáquio." They compromised on Herbert Eustáquio. Their son's first name honored a close friend of Geraldo's, who had been the best man at their wedding. His middle name fulfilled the pledge to the priest whose powers, Dona Geny was convinced, had guaranteed a healthy delivery. According to Dona Geny, Herbert always hated the name Eustáquio. He definitively cast it aside many years later when he went underground.

After a year in the backlands, the family returned to Belo Horizonte to the same downtown neighborhood. A cluster of photos in the family album attests to the fact that, as the firstborn, Herbert received considerable

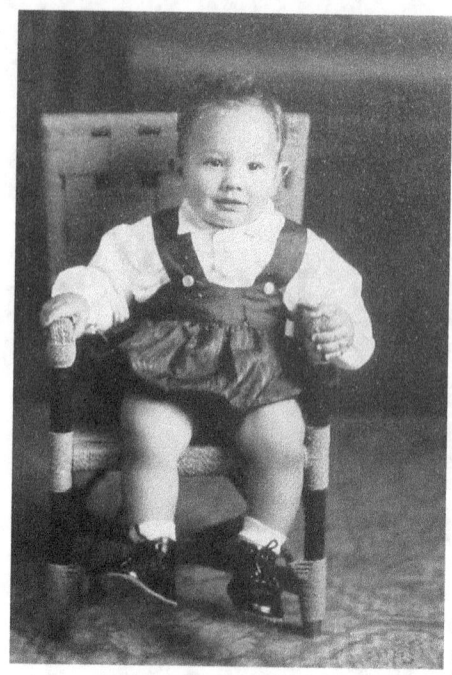

FIGURE 2.2 Herbert, one year old. COURTESY OF GENY BRUNELLI DE CARVALHO.

FIGURE 2.3 Herbert, three years old. COURTESY OF GENY BRUNELLI DE CARVALHO.

FIGURE 2.4 Herbert at five years old (left), and Hamilton (age three). COURTESY OF GENY BRUNELLI DE CARVALHO.

attention. "When Bete was only a three-year-old child, if you sat down next to him, he wouldn't stop talking. . . . After he entered school at age six, he would sit with a neighbor and talk for two or three hours. He read a lot. If he got a present, it had to be a book."

Living on the wages of a military police corporal was no easy task, but Geny was always good at improvising to make ends meet. "Someone gave me a wooden box that had been used for shipping codfish. I pasted paper onto it and turned it into a bookcase for his books." Herbert was a voracious reader who learned to decipher words before he was six. He devoured everything he could get his hands on: religious books, history of all kinds, fantasy tales, and stories penned by Brazilian authors of children's books. "We were poor, but we weren't totally destitute," Dona Geny explained. "Every time he asked for a book, we'd get it for him, or my sisters would give him books for his birthday."

Hamilton Brunelli, Geraldo and Geny's second child, was born two years and one month after Herbert. Herbert and Hamilton were as different as night and day. Herbert's early vocation for reading turned him inward, and he had few friends. While Hamilton spent endless hours playing soccer or games of guns and soldiers, Herbert quietly sat at home with a book in hand. "He was a peaceful child," his mother remembered. Later Herbert would engage in reading marathons into the night, sneaking into the kitchen to get something to eat while he continued to read. "I would fight with him the next morning," Dona Geny recalled, scolding him for leaving banana peels and orange skins strewn all over his room.

Hamilton affectionately recalled his older brother's lethargic tendencies. "He was lazy. He didn't like to walk. I remember when we were young, we took turns having to go get milk in the morning. One day it was Herbert's turn, the next day mine."[1] Although it was only a short distance to the bakery that sold bread and milk for the family's breakfast, Herbert always came up with excuses not to go. "He had to study or whatever. I ended up doing this chore for him. His laziness about walking was terrible. He really didn't like to do it." Their two-year age gap and different interests meant that they rarely played together and grew up with different circles of friends.

Even though young Herbert avoided walking when he didn't have to and seldom participated in sports or any hard physical activity, he excelled at school. "That lad consumed books, read, and [later] watched television. He wanted to know everything," Dona Geny boasted to me.

Mapping the constellation of family relations, dissecting the particular personalities of parents, or speculating about the legacies of heredity and genetics may seem to explain who and what a given child becomes. But many questions remain. How did Herbert, who hated walking, manage to endure the rough mountainous terrain during guerrilla training in a tropical rain forest in early 1970? If he was such a quiet, reserved child who disdained unnecessary physical activity, why had he opted to be a revolutionary fighter, an endeavor that required such corporal effort? One could point to a grandfather, father, uncles, and a brother who opted for the military or the police to explain a possible inclination, enlarged by family tradition, that led to his participation in the armed struggle, but as a young child he never indicated an interest in following what was almost a family profession. He certainly never showed any predisposition for armed violence by joining in the war games so common among young boys. Nor did his father ever insist that he pursue a career in the military.

Ideas, not violent acts, were at the heart of his later political commitment. His decision to pick up a gun was, no doubt, prompted by a firm conviction that it was the only path to overthrow the military regime. Politics and the dynamics of participating in a collective cause loomed larger than his own personal disdain for the physical effort required for the profession of many males in his family. On the other hand, military matters were not foreign to his upbringing, and there must have been something strangely familiar, as well as extremely ironic, about his later activities, if Herbert ever paused to consider the matter while robbing a bank or abducting a diplomat.

From an early age, his mother remembered, Herbert had wanted to be a doctor. That required hard mental work and disciplined study, both of which came naturally to him. In addition to his stellar performance in school, Hamilton recalled that as a child his brother also loved to dissect lizards and other small animals. His mother attributed her son's desire to be a physician to a general willingness to help others.

Like many among the Brazilian working and lower middle classes, Herbert's parents believed that a good education was the ladder to a respectable profession and a solid middle-class life. Although Dona Geny insists that her husband didn't push his sons in any professional direction, the family did try to give them good schooling. Brazilian public schools offered an adequate education, but private institutions promised to provide more discipline and attention to their students, and so the family enrolled first Herbert and then Hamilton in the Escola Chopin (the Chopin School). Herbert's grandfather paid the tuition for Bete, and later Geny and Geraldo scrimped and saved to make sure that Hamilton could attend the small private primary school near their house. "It was a very strict school," Hamilton remembered. It had the same type of discipline that he would later find in the military barracks, but the teaching was satisfactory. It allowed both boys to pass the rigorous test to gain entrance to the Colégio Tiradentes, the military school for sons and daughters of the armed forces and the police.

Pitágoras dos Santos was one of Herbert's classmates at the Chopin School starting in the third grade. Pitágoras remembered their time together in primary school: "Boys and girls were in the same classroom. It was a modest school, really a house."[2] Schooling took place in the morning, with lots of repetition, tedious exercises, and compositions that seemed more designed to fill the time than teach anything, he recalled.

Around midday pupils went home for lunch. Afternoons were busied with school lessons or playing near the house. "We didn't have much help from our parents or anyone else, so we learned to study on our own." It was a simple life. Pitágoras recalled, "Our dreams of consumption were completely different from today. At times even getting a soft drink was difficult." Yet Herbert's family possessed one item that set it apart. In 1956, Herbert's grandfather bought his son and daughter-in-law a television, so that his grandchildren would not become *televizinhos* (television neighbors), spending all their time in other people's houses. It was a novelty for the lower middle-class neighborhood where they lived, and as Herbert recalled in his memoir, it had much more status, social importance, and influences with friends than owning a soccer ball.³

Herbert and Pitágoras were both shy children and their friendship started as they shared an eraser and colored pencils. "Herbert and I were very well behaved, which was a sort of problem since at the time, good little boys were called sissies [*florzinhas*] or faggots [*maricas*]. . . . You had to be very careful not to get considered a sissy or a faggot." Since both boys were quiet, polite, hardworking students who got good grades and didn't cause trouble in the classroom, they ran the risk of being teased by their classmates. Pitágoras believes that the two identified with each other because they shared the same sensitivity about their personal situation. Reflecting back on his childhood, he described his and Herbert's reactions to the classroom climate: "We knew, that is, we had the intuition that there was something different from that everyday life that we were living." Doing well in school was the easiest way to get by for well-mannered and sensitive boys. Yet they lived a delicate balance between pleasing their teachers and becoming objects of ridicule. The boys' hard work and good grades paid off, and they both passed the entrance exam for the Colégio Tiradentes.

In 1960, when Herbert was fourteen, Geny became pregnant again. "My husband said that it might be a girl, but another boy came, so I said, 'That's it; no more.' I was afraid that we would fill the house with boys, and I couldn't manage it." With an affinity for alliteration, Geny and Geraldo named their third child Hélder Nazareno, so as to match the monikers of their first and second sons. His given name was his mother's homage to Dom Hélder Câmara, the charismatic archbishop.⁴ Hélder's middle name, Nazareno, paid tribute to his father's father. Having a third child made life more difficult for Dona Geny. Her mother-in-law, who had severe arthritis, could barely walk. "There was no way that we could afford to hire help, so I was the maid. Three boys, a husband, and a father and mother-in-law. . . . They lived across the street, so I had to take care of two households."

Geraldo was a good husband and father, but Dona Geny admitted that his true passion was the radio. "He loved to sing and to make jokes." Herbert inherited his father's humor, loquaciousness, and the gift of being a talented writer. Unlike his precocious son, however, Geraldo had few intellectual ambitions. "Geraldo didn't like to study," Dona Geny recalled. "He moved up the ranks and retired as a major, but he didn't put a lot of effort into his career."

Leafing through the scrapbook that Dona Geny has kept with clippings about her husband's second vocation as a radio personality, it quickly becomes clear that Geraldo's love for public performance was more important to him than his military career. After the family returned to Belo Horizonte, Geraldo got a spot as a singer on a radio program for amateur performers and caught the eye of the producers. He eventually landed a job playing the role of a journalist in a detective serial. One day, while watching a comedy skit, he asked if he could try his hand at humor and immediately revealed a natural talent for slapstick, jesting, and unscripted wit. So as not to be confused with Geraldo Tavares, another radio actor in the same studio, he was quickly baptized Gê de Carvalho, a professional name that stuck for the rest of his career. He was already a talented musician who could rearrange a song on a moment's notice, so Gê de Carvalho's wittiness and his nimble creation of oddball characters quickly consolidated a loyal radio audience for his madcap comedy routines.[5]

When Herbert was five and Hamilton still a toddler, their father joined Radio Inconfidência, known as the "Voice of Minas to the World," where he performed on comedy programs. At that time the capital of Minas Gerais had an estimated 365,000 inhabitants and was the nation's fourth largest city. Radio was the most accessible and popular form of mass entertainment. Gê de Carvalho maintained his nighttime radio career while continuing his daytime job in the military police as an artist in the audiovisual department. A picture in the family photo album shows him standing tall and erect in full military uniform, next to Herbert, who is attired in the crisply starched white dress uniform of the Colégio Tiradentes.

Herbert was a success in his studies at Colégio Tiradentes, excelling in all subjects, from math to science and literature. And then, one auspicious day, a young girl walked into Herbert's classroom. Before long she had become his best friend. Laís Soares Pereira still has vivid memories of the first time she met Herbert. She was fifteen and had just entered the first year of high school. "I sat down next to him, and we began to talk. People around us decided to have some fun. I began to sing, and they tapped out rhythms to accompany the music's beat." Suddenly their stern math teacher entered the classroom. "He was furious and said, 'The singer and her orchestra may step out of the room, and we'll see how you do on the next tests.'"[6]

Having had a strict upbringing, Laís was frightened by the threat. She was relieved when Herbert sought her out during recess. "He said, 'Don't be down about this. I'll study with you. You'll get the best grade, and he'll never bother you again.'" From that day on the two became faithful study partners, and Laís did, indeed, get top grades on the next tests. "He would come to my house in the afternoon or I would go to his. We lived somewhat near each other." Almost immediately a close friendship developed. "He was like my half-brother," she recalled. "His mother thought that we were dating. I never stopped to think what it was. It didn't have a name. It was a profound love, respect. . . . I think that I was his sister, a confidante."

In those adolescent years, Laís and Herbert were always together. On a typical Saturday, Herbert would stop by Laís's house, and they would sit for hours discussing all kinds of topics. "He would read a book and talk about it with me. If he thought that the book was a must, I would read a little, and we could talk about it." Saturday afternoon usually was spent going to a matinee show at the Pathé, the luxurious downtown movie theater. Afterward, Herbert and Laís would walk around Liberdade Plaza, passing in front of the governor's mansion, linger on a park bench to chat, and then go home. Although their friendship never took a romantic turn—no handholding or stolen kisses—Laís didn't seem to mind.

Their Saturday excursions were important to Herbert, Laís reminisced: "Herbert adored movies. He later wrote about them. When a given movie was marvelous, he would take me to see it, and we would talk about it. He would then write about the film, and I would read what he had written." Elaine, one of Herbert's classmates, also remembered that Herbert wrote about movies while in high school. Recollecting Herbert's talents, Elaine commented, "He wrote things that were funny, making puns about the titles of films or the names of songs. . . . It was the same style he used, I later realized, in his book."[7]

Herbert developed a tight-knit circle of friends in high school. Elaine summarized her impressions of Herbert. "He was timid and very, very intelligent, with a sense of humor, and a very good friend. But I thought he was very reserved; I didn't think that he opened up. That is, I realized this later, not at the time. I thought it was normal that he was so quiet."

The group would gather for parties in their parents' homes to celebrate birthdays or other special occasions. These were simple affairs, featuring snacks, soft drinks, a birthday cake, and music on a record player. "We really didn't like to dance," Nilton, Elaine's boyfriend, admitted. Instead, they would sit around and talk. Nilton remembered that he and Herbert liked to discuss movies, culture, and books. "He was very critical. He satirized things. He loved to talk, criticize, but he didn't talk a lot about politics."[8]

In the early 1960s, middle-class youth in Belo Horizonte, as in most of Brazil, still followed strict rules of "proper" moral behavior, implemented and regulated by observant parents, sanctioned by the ubiquitous influence of the Catholic Church, and reinforced by conservative social mores. Nilton, who later married Elaine, summarized the constraints imposed on them. First, couples were expected to spend a long time getting to know each other before dating, which usually meant simply holding hands. "You had to be officially dating to exchange kisses, but you could never let your parents know you were kissing." It took Nilton and Elaine six months to a year (they differ on the time) after they started "dating" to exchange their first kiss. Since physical expressions of love or sexual attraction were not encouraged, nobody was surprised that Herbert and Laís did not engage in displays of intimacy. Their obviously close friendship was enough to lead Elaine to assume that they were romantically involved.

It is likely that because society expected modesty and timidity in social interactions and caution in overtures to the opposite sex, Herbert was spared anxieties surrounding his latent but growing homosexual desires. Never pressured by Laís to move beyond their close friendship to "dating," Laís offered Herbert intellectual and emotional intimacy, as well as an appearance of heterosexual normalcy that shielded him from possible ridicule or ostracism.

While in high school, Herbert stayed away from sports that could have provoked teasing. Laís recalled, "Once there was a class of physical education or swimming, and Herbert refused to go. He didn't want to expose himself physically." Four decades after Herbert's adventures as a guerrilla fighter, it is still hard for Laís to imagine him in that role. "He was crazy, simply crazy, because he didn't know how to run. He didn't have endurance. He didn't swim, walk, climb, or bicycle. His exercise was carrying books and reading." In his memoir, Herbert readily admitted a hatred of his body. "My ugliness was in my skin. I became fat, bloated, evasive, rigid, graceless, slow moving, with a wild, primitive natural and deferential shyness that would not allow me to show myself in public."[9]

Many shy or unathletic boys growing up in Brazil in the 1960s who later assumed a gay identity were labeled effeminate or called *bicha*, a pejorative term for a homosexual. Herbert escaped this fate, even though he had a timid nature and lacked athletic prowess. Throughout high school he avoided activities that entailed traditional masculine displays of physical competence, but his exceptional intellectual talents compensated for what was expected of most boys and garnered him tremendous respect. As far as anyone can remember, Herbert's friends and classmates didn't think his behavior pointed toward inadequate masculinity or possibly homosexuality. Although Elaine lost contact with Herbert in 1968 as he moved closer to underground political activities, she was shocked to read a 1981 *Veja* magazine article about Herbert's exile that announced his homosexuality.[10] In her eyes, Herbert was never "suspect."

Yet as a teenager, Herbert experienced an inner turmoil about his body and his sexual attraction to other males. It might have gone unnoticed by his closest friends, but it left him in pain and confusion, for his latent erotic desires clashed with the ubiquitous imposition of a compulsory heterosexuality that was firmly embedded in Brazilian culture.

At some point in the early 1960s, during his perambulations through the streets of Belo Horizonte, Herbert found himself in the clandestine world of same-sex relations and learned the art of picking up an anonymous person for a furtive sexual encounter.[11] In his initial erotic experiences, he avoided acts that might have led him to question his own heterosexual masculinity. According to prescribed norms, only a passive person in a same-sex encounter was considered a homosexual. Therefore, as long as his role was to penetrate a partner, he was able to view himself as a "normal" heterosexual male. "There were no homosexual relationships," he wrote two decades later, "there were relationships *with* homosexuals." Separating himself from the homosexual "other," Herbert's remembrances of these years remained categorical: "I never admitted the possibility of being 'passive' or to wanting to be penetrated, which at the time I confused with passivity," which meant being feminine and a homosexual.[12]

Herbert's desperate nocturnal wanderings amid the shadows of the city's streets, public bathrooms, and municipal parks constituted a troubled aspect of his adolescence that he later ironically described as "half darkness, half promise."[13] The obscurity of the night was a challenge, but it offered many possibilities. In his second memoir, *Meu corpo daria um romance* (My body could be a novel), Herbert offers some vague details about these furtive liaisons: "I sought to preserve a meticulously clandestine sexual existence. My partners were always unknown individuals with whom I exchanged naïve lies and confusing fake names."[14] Allowing no anal contact was the barrier he initially erected to protect his assumed heterosexuality. However, over time his defenses dropped, and he finally succumbed. If his memoir is accurate, Herbert's "homosexual" initiation occurred when he was sixteen and finishing high school. His sexual partner was a young soldier whom he met on the street. The two went back to the modest apartment that the soldier shared with a cousin who also had sex with other men. The cousin seemed totally at ease when he met the two after their brief encounter. Herbert knew the soldier enjoyed their tryst and wanted to repeat the experience. Herbert, however, recalls that he panicked. In what would several years later become common practice in the revolutionary underground, he gave the young soldier a fake name, lied about his age and where he lived, and disappeared into the night.

The cover of darkness helped hide Herbert's secret from his family, his circle of friends, and even Laís, his confidante. However, at least once

Herbert's double life was almost exposed. Sometime in 1967, someone from the student movement approached Laís to inquire about Herbert, who had become increasingly involved in semi-underground activities against the regime. According to her best recollection, the person said that he had seen Herbert coming out of Municipal Park late at night, which he considered "strange."[15] Locating him in the city's central park at such a late hour was an indirect way of suggesting that Herbert was a faggot (*viado*) and had been seeking out a sexual partner in the shadows behind the shrubs. Belo Horizonte's Municipal Park had been notorious for decades as a place where homosexuals and hustlers congregated at night.[16] The coded reference was instantly clear.

As Laís recalls, she went to Herbert and asked him point-blank if it were true. Herbert's quick mind and fast tongue came to his rescue, and he rapidly offered an explanation. He was participating in a covert Marxist study group, he explained, having chosen the location because it was hidden and discreet. At a time when secrecy about the details of political activities prevailed and one avoided questions about meetings, Laís recalls that she accepted his explanation and eliminated from her mind the possibility that Herbert was a homosexual or sexually involved with other men. Laís's rather innocent, platonic love for Herbert may have blinded her from seeing the reality of his sexual inclinations. She likely did not know anyone who admitted that he or she had same-sex attractions. Moreover, Herbert had constructed a persona to hide his sexual life, even from his closest companion.

In many ways, this was Herbert's first exile, not to another country but to an inner world where he kept his sexual desires a secret from those around him. It was also his first experience living a clandestine life, using subterfuge to hide his sexual activities and creating a public image that gave others few clues about an important aspect of his life. Herbert's reluctance to admit his homosexual desires and the anguish that he experienced when he engaged in same-sex erotic activities precluded him from choosing other options. As Luiz Morando has meticulously documented, in the early 1960s an incipient semisecret world of gay sociability took shape in Belo Horizonte.[17] One of the downtown spaces appropriated by "sexual inverts" was Edifício Arcângelo Maletta, a towering apartment building complex with a large commercial center on the ground floor and mezzanine that included nightclubs and bars, some of which became places where homosexuals congregated. Throughout the decade, business proprietors, moralizing residents, and the police tried to eliminate the "city's meeting places of the *rapazes 'alegres'* [gay boys]" by making periodic arrests and charging those detained with violating public morality.[18] Herbert probably knew of these "notorious" places as they were located close to other popular eating and drinking facilities in the city center frequented by young people, but he likely avoided them so as hide from his peers any indications that he had homosexual desires.

There was certainly no suspicion at home about Herbert's secret sexual escapades. Indeed, life for the Carvalho family seems to have run smoothly in the early 1960s. Herbert studied hard and was en route to medical school. Hamilton managed to keep up with his studies. Young Hélder added extra chores for his already busy mother as she hurried back and forth across the street to tend to her in-laws, kept her own house clean and tidy, and made sure that her growing sons were properly nourished. The Carvalhos seemed to be a typical lower middle-class family, albeit with an unusually talented son, a father who loved performing on the radio, and a self-sacrificing mother who held the household together.

The routines of everyday activities in the Carvalho home were also undisturbed by the political turbulence that was boiling up throughout Brazil. As Herbert noted in his memoir, his father was quite disinterested in politics.[19] In August 1961, recently elected President Jânio Quadros, a maverick and eccentric politician, suddenly resigned after eight months in office in an inept attempt to blackmail the Congress into granting him more executive powers. Vice President João Goulart successfully mobilized his backers in the nationalist and populist Brazilian Labor Party, along with sectors of the

FIGURE 2.5 Graduation from Colégio Tiradentes, 1964. COURTESY OF GENY BRUNELLI DE CARVALHO.

armed forces and the trade unions, against an attempt by other military leaders to prevent him from taking office. However, Goulart assumed the presidency with reduced powers. Because he lacked a solid majority in Congress and was unable to control a dramatic rise in inflation over the following two and a half years, his popular support waned. Conservative civilian and military forces, with backing from the Kennedy and Johnson administrations, began a concerted effort to oust him from power.[20]

In 1964, the armed forces with civilian support overthrew Goulart, accusing him of being corrupt, radical, inept, and under communist influence. The military then installed an authoritarian regime, which lingered in power for two decades. This was a momentous event that was to change Herbert's life and have huge implications for all Brazilians. Yet Herbert seems to have largely ignored what was happening in politics. Instead, he focused on his studies, spending his mornings preparing to pass the difficult medical school entrance exam and his evenings finishing high school. Politics wasn't a priority; becoming a doctor was.

In March 1965, Herbert entered the publicly funded medical school where former President Jucelino Kubitschek had studied in the late 1920s. Hamilton remembered how proud their father had been when he heard the news. "He's going to be a doctor, a doctor in the family," he exalted. But Herbert's father was equally proud of Hamilton when he passed the competitive exam to enter the Military Police Academy. Geraldo told everyone in the neighborhood that his second son was going to be in the military police. "The day that I arrived in the barracks, he insisted that I use his uniform even though it was too big," Hamilton recalled.

Laís joined Herbert at the medical school the next year. By the time she started classes in 1966, Herbert, like so many students of his generation, had already plunged into the world of student politics. Laís cautiously followed her friend along that path, stopping short of joining the armed struggle. Today a physician who spends her mornings working in a clinic and her afternoons attending poor people in an outlying neighborhood, Laís confided to me, "I think I do this work among the poor because of Bete."

3

Medical School

(1965–1967)

> Herbert was very cultured. He wrote movie reviews for radio. It was hard to find anyone at the medical school with an intellectual range like his.
>
> — JORGE NAHAS

Medical school was paradise for Herbert. Suddenly he was in a world where ideas mattered, and people were engaged in serious debates. He embraced this new environment enthusiastically. The Federal University of Minas Gerais (UFMG) School of Medicine, founded in 1911, was an illustrious institution. When Herbert began studying there in 1965, it was housed in a large, modern ten-story structure located next to the Clinical Hospital in downtown Belo Horizonte, only a block away from the expansive Municipal Park, one of the sites of Herbert's nocturnal wanderings. From home, Herbert could hop on a bus and get to school in twenty minutes. He could also take advantage of a complex transportation network that crisscrossed the city and serviced its booming population, which by 1965 surpassed a million

FIGURE 3.1 School of Medicine, early 1960s. COURTESY OF THE CENTRO DE MEMÓRIA DE MEDICINA, UNIVERSIDADE FEDERAL DE MINAS GERAIS.

inhabitants. Commerce, government offices, culture, entertainment, and late-night sexual adventures were all concentrated in the region.

The School of Medicine was near other divisions within the UFMG—Law, Architecture, Economics, and Engineering. The School of Philosophy and Human Sciences was only slightly farther away. Catholic University, Belo Horizonte's other institution of higher education, was also situated downtown. Many young people who had moved to the capital to pursue a university education rented beds or rooms in nearby boarding houses or shared their living arrangements in student *repúblicas*. The university cafeteria offered inexpensive and mostly palatable food. To save money, however, Herbert usually went home for lunch.

Movie houses, theaters, and bars were close at hand. After classes, students congregated at corner lunch counters and small eating and drinking establishments to meet with friends, tease and flirt, talk about the latest film or freshest gossip, and, inevitably, discuss politics. The proximity to each other of these sites of leisure and entertainment, student residences, and the various schools of the Federal and Catholic universities provided an ideal environment for the development of a collective ethos among the city's youth.[1] In the aftermath of the 1964 military takeover, when the ruling generals passed the Suplicy Law that pushed the National Union of Students (UNE) underground and made it more difficult to organize local student entities in schools and departments, these constant interactions among students throughout the city facilitated the forging of a strong movement. It picked up steam in 1966 when students began organizing demonstrations against the regime. Herbert instantly became intrigued by the heated discussions over the political situation. He followed with great interest the arguments of political groups representing semiclandestine left-wing organizations as they debated how to respond to the generals in power.

When the armed forces took over in April 1964, they found themselves walking a political tightrope. They repressed radical nationalists, leftists, and other oppositionists, rounding up more than fifty thousand people in the first year after the coup.[2] At the same time the military believed it was necessary to appear to be on a course toward restoring democracy in order to satisfy Washington policymakers and appease the middle classes that had supported their actions. The Institutional Act of April 9, 1964, which among many authoritarian provisions suspended the rights of politicians who supported Goulart or were to his left, was premised on the promise of a hasty return to civilian rule. Yet when moderate opposition candidates won the gubernatorial elections in the states of Guanabara (which governed the city of Rio de Janeiro) and Minas Gerais in October 1965, the regime's leaders issued the Second Institutional Act. It abolished the political parties that had operated before 1965, established a new pro-government party with a guaranteed majority, and set up a new opposition party with a limited outlook for ever winning control of Congress. Subsequent measures eliminated direct presidential elections and took away the voters' rights to choose governors through the ballot box. Another decree gave the four-star general in charge of the national government the power to appoint mayors in the country's largest cities. By late 1965 it had become eminently clear that the armed forces were not planning to retreat to the barracks any time soon. With the possibility that the opposition might increase its strength through the ballot box, the armed forces set up new rules of the game that formally retained democratic institutions, such as political parties and regular elections, but guaranteed the military would continue to control the government. With the generals and their civilian allies deeply entrenched in power, left-wing currents debated what was to be done.

Even before April 1, 1964, the Brazilian Left had been in turmoil and in the process of multiple realignments. In the wake of Soviet Premier Nikita Khrushchev's indictments of the excesses of Stalinism in February 1956 and the failed Hungarian revolution in October of that year, the Central Committee of the Brazilian Communist Party (PCB) issued the Declaration of March 1958 that adopted a new political orientation. The Party leadership called for the support of radical nationalists, "progressive" industrialists, and sectors of the military. Brazil, so the analysis went, remained a backward country that had not yet transitioned from feudalism to capitalism. With a weak industrial base in a predominantly rural society, the conditions were not ripe for a socialist revolution, because capitalism remained underdeveloped and the proletariat was not large or strong enough to seize power. Communists, therefore, needed to support those political forces defending national sectors of the economy that had been marginalized by U.S. imperial, hegemonic control, including Brazilian industrialists weakened by competition with foreign firms. By the early 1960s, this meant building an alliance with the Brazilian Labor Party (PTB) under the leadership of President João Goulart, who had pledged to carry out a moderate land reform, legalize the Brazilian Communist Party, improve trade relations with the Soviet bloc, and expand benefits for workers. Rather than foment a socialist revolution, communists and other progressive forces needed to build strategic coalitions with other sectors of society to implement these reforms.[3]

Washington Cold Warriors, such as U.S. ambassador Lincoln Gordon, considered the apparently moderate turn of the PCB a ruse to hide its real intention to carry out another revolution similar to the one that had taken place in Cuba in 1959. Gordon, therefore, mobilized the State Department and the White House to back the ouster of Goulart. Working to unite the conspiracies being articulated among groups within the armed forces and secretly channeling funds to right-wing forces were among the efforts coordinated through the U.S. Embassy.[4]

Unlike Gordon, a sector of the Brazilian Left believed that the PCB really *had* abandoned its revolutionary heritage. In 1962, members of its Central Committee and their supporters split to form the Communist Party of Brazil, which backed the People's Republic of China. Initially weak and inexpressive, by the late 1960s, it began to implement a policy of preparing a prolonged popular war in the countryside where communist militants working among rural workers and peasants would build a people's army that would rise up, overthrow the military regime, and carry out a social revolution.[5]

In the early 1960s, two other political forces emerged to challenge the influence of the PCB, which until then had been the predominant left-wing force in unions, on campuses, and among artists and intellectuals. In January 1961, a sector of the youth wing of the Brazilian Socialist Party, left-wing dissidents within the PTB, and São Paulo supporters of the ideas of the German revolutionary Rosa Luxemburg founded the Revolutionary Marxist

Organization—Workers' Politics (POLOP). The new organization offered a radical critique of the PCB's reform-minded approach. It insisted that workers, who would lead any revolutionary movement, must remain politically independent from the bourgeoisie, and that the conditions were ripe for a socialist revolution. Under the intellectual guidance of Eric Sachs, the son of Austrian Marxists who had sought refuge from Nazism, POLOP quickly won adherents in São Paulo, Rio, and Minas Gerais.[6]

During the same period, another current of young radicals formed Ação Popular (Popular Action; AP), a group that also criticized the PCB's reformist stands. The organization emerged out of a long process in which sectors of the Catholic Church attempted to respond to social and economic inequality through engaging its young members in social action and establishing activities among young Catholic workers, high school pupils, and university students. Many participants in these programs began questioning the efficacy of Christian charity and good works alone in addressing Brazil's social and economic disparities. AP was founded in a Congress held in Belo Horizonte in June 1962 and evolved over the course of the 1960s from Marxist humanism to pro-Chinese Maoism. National in scope, the movement quickly became a potent force among student activists and won majority backing from UFMG students.[7]

In the aftermath of the 1964 coup, the military purged most radical labor leaders from union posts, allowing moderate pro-government forces to take over and control unions. In a defensive action, the PCB ordered its militants to go underground. With these political forces in retreat, students were the first coherent social group to protest systematically the regime's dictatorial power. Organized through local and statewide entities, as well as UNE, which at the time was led by AP, students mobilized against the severe curtailment of basic democratic rights. The middle-class background of most students, the tradition of having had autonomous organizations that were politically independent from the state, and the repressive measures against students: all were factors in the growth of support for activism. Even some who had clamored for Goulart's downfall soon realized that the military did not intend to restore democracy any time soon. Moreover, the conservative political character of the civilian-military coalition that overthrew Goulart and the authoritarian nature of the new regime, which had relied on significant middle-class support, now seemed to exclude most civilians from any important decision-making roles.

The military's repressive apparatus was particularly harsh in its dealings with the UFMG. In early 1966, police violently contained demonstrations by first-year students.[8] The right to protest publicly became an ongoing dispute between students and heavily armed police. Increasingly, these conflicts won public support, as bystanders in the congested downtown witnessed police beating up and arresting students or dispersing demonstrations with tear gas. Clandestine left-wing political groups led these mobilizations and actively attempted to recruit the most involved activists to their organizations.[9]

Although Herbert rarely talked about politics at home or among his friends during high school, when he reached the university the environment of ongoing discussions and debates engaged him completely. Through his passion for reading works that ranged from history to literature, Herbert had acquired a rich cultural capital that developed further and was refined as he absorbed new radical ideas at the university. Even though AP was the strongest political force among organized university students, the Catholic roots of many of their supporters likely alienated Herbert, who had dutifully taken first communion, as was expected of him, but then shunned further religious involvement, much to his mother's dismay.[10] The members and political ideas of POLOP seemed much more attractive than radical Catholicism. Known for their dedication to studying Marxism and for supporting the unorthodox ideas of Rosa Luxembourg and Leon Trotsky, among other European revolutionaries, POLOP militants were considered the most theoretically sophisticated student activists.[11] They also had won significant support among politicized students. In 1967, Jorge Batista Filho, served as president of the campus-wide student union (DCE) and João Batista Mares Guia was president of the statewide student association (UEE). Both were influential leaders and members of POLOP.[12]

Herbert immediately fell in with a new crowd of politicized students from his entering class at the medical school, among them Jorge Nahas, Maria José de Carvalho, and Maria Auxiliadora Lara Barcelos, affectionately called Dodora. Jorge Nahas quickly became a leader in the student movement. He participated in UNE's underground Congress, held in Belo Horizonte in 1966, and was a member of the leadership of the representative student body at the university.[13] Maria José de Carvalho, known as Zezé, met Jorge while studying in a preparatory course for the School of Medicine entrance exam and became politicized through student-run cultural activities at the university. Dodora, who became friends with Zezé, participated with her in these events.[14] All three joined POLOP within a year or so after entering medical school. Herbert, however, took longer to enter the organization.

As a way of extending their influence among other students in the School of Medicine and as a means of competing with their main political rival,

POLOP members formed the Center for the Study of Medicine (CEM), which organized public forums and debates around a plethora of topics. These events ranged from discussions about U.S. civil rights and anti–Vietnam War movements to talks on the influence of foreign companies in Brazil. Forty years later, CEM still evoked strong positive memories among those active in organizing or attending what was remembered as an exciting forum in which the students explored local, national, and international problems. Laís Pereira recalled that the events organized by the CEM didn't focus exclusively on political questions. They also emphasized issues that were important for the students' medical training. Among these was a discussion about how to prevent the transmission of rabies from canines to people.[15] Apolo Lisboa, a medical student and leader of POLOP on campus, reminisced that the CEM permitted the militants in POLOP to have a more public profile, which aided their recruitment. They debated Malthusian theories, brought leading scientists to discuss rural endemic diseases, and organized film shows and concerts, sometimes in conjunction with the official student representative body.[16] Zezé remembered how she got involved with politics at the university through the CEM. "I started making posters: 'Come to a lecture with a Black Power militant. . . . We debated the war in Vietnam, the pharmaceutical industry. . . . When [singer/composer] Vinicius de Moraes was in Belo Horizonte, we invited him to give a talk."[17]

Although it seems that no leaflets or posters announcing these events have survived, the intellectual vitality and excitement surrounding the CEM's activities remain sharply imprinted on the minds of these activists. And their idea worked: the CEM's innovative program attracted a new generation of students who entered school after the 1964 coup and were anxious to debate politics and social problems *and* find a way to oppose the dictatorship. Among them was Herbert.

POLOP itself was going through an internal debate between those who favored an orthodox Marxist perspective that privileged organizing the working class and others who saw a Cuban-style revolution and armed struggle as the means to defeat the dictatorship and establish socialism in Brazil. One of the main leaders of the pro-guerrilla wing of POLOP was Carlos Alberto Soares de Freitas, known to his friends as Beto, who later used the code name Breno when he went underground in 1967. (To avoid confusion with Herbert's nickname, Bete or Beto, I will refer to Carlos Alberto Soares de Freitas as Breno throughout this book). While an economics student, Breno had traveled to Cuba in 1962 representing POLOP at the Conference of the People, an international gathering of sympathizers with the recent revolution. He returned to Brazil energized about the possibilities of sweeping social change and became

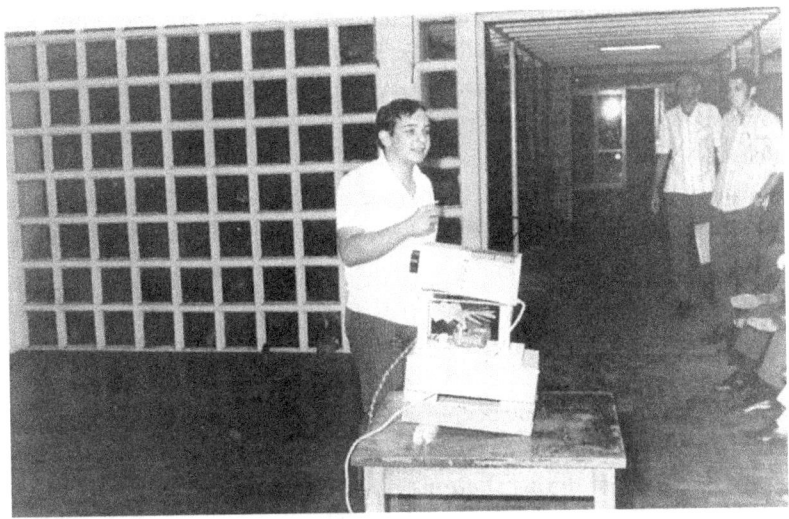

FIGURES 3.2 AND 3.3 Herbert giving a lecture during the orientation for first-year medical students, c. 1967. COURTESY OF GENY BRUNELLI DE CARVALHO.

active as a student agitator, helping POLOP to forge links between university activists and the labor and peasant movements that had radicalized in the period prior to the coup. He was arrested in 1964 for having posted fliers around town supporting the Cuban Revolution and criticizing the military takeover. Released after ninety days of incarceration, he eventually went underground and became a "veteran" leader of the organization.[18]

Among the many people whom Breno recruited to the organization was Apolo Lisboa. Raised in a Presbyterian household, Apolo saw his radicalization as a product of a Protestant upbringing from which he had acquired values of social justice that were inculcated as part of his religious education.[19] Even before entering medical school in 1963, he had led a spontaneous movement of young people who had passed the university entrance exams but could not enroll because there were a limited number of slots available. Arrested during the 1964 coup, he became friends with Breno while in prison. Through their political discussions, Breno convinced him to join POLOP. Apolo continued his activities in university student politics in 1964, becoming vice president and then president of the medical school's student organization. In July 1966, he was elected one of UNE's vice presidents during the organization's XXVIII Congress, held clandestinely in the basement of the São Francisco Church in downtown Belo Horizonte. Just as Breno had recruited Apolo to POLOP, he in turn recruited a cluster of the first- and second-year medical school students.[20]

Herbert seemed to thrive in this new environment of political debates on issues ranging from public health to international politics. He also dedicated himself to his studies. In his first year, he earned excellent grades (9 out of 10) in all of his courses: Psychology, Anatomy, Histology and Embryology, Biological Physics, and Preventative Medicine.[21] He embraced life as a student with energy and enthusiasm, dividing his time between school and a passion for theater and film. When Herbert was fourteen and still in high school, his father got him a job as a movie reviewer at the radio station where Geraldo worked in his off hours. Every week Herbert would compose a short critique of a film he had seen in one of the downtown movie houses. No one seems to have saved the scripts for this short broadcast item, entitled *On Cinema*, but his friends remember that Herbert was well versed in films of all kinds and added clever and humorous touches to his texts that made them enjoyable to hear on the radio.[22] Herbert earned very little for this work, but his mother made sure that he had at least enough money for bus transportation. As Herbert became more and more involved in politics in 1967 and 1968, he had less time to watch movies and write reviews. His brother Hamilton remembers that Herbert would come home late Friday night (he later understood that it was from political meetings) and dash something down that Hamilton would then pound off on the typewriter so it would be ready for the Saturday show.[23]

Herbert finished his second year of medical school in December 1966 with an outstanding record, receiving a perfect grade (10) in Biochemistry, Physiology, and General Pathology; a very good showing in Hygiene and Preventative Medicine (8.7) and Parasitology (8.0); and a decent mark in Microbiology (7.6).[24] His high standing in school promised a successful career in medicine. But, when he returned to classes after Carnival in March, both he and Brazil were changing all too rapidly. Over the course of 1967, performing well in school, which had always been so easy for him and a major focus, lost its importance. By December, he had failed to attend four of his science courses. He didn't take the final exam in Anatomy and Pathological Physiology and received a mediocre grade in Sociology. Slowly that year his studies took second place to his passion for politics and his love for the theater.

Mobilizations against the dictatorship, which had slowly stirred the year before, expanded significantly in early 1967, and Herbert was increasingly involved in student activism. In his memoir he recalled that after "devouring" the *Communist Manifesto*, he immediately considered himself a Marxist and wanted to put his newfound theories into practice.[25] Yet none of the activists participating in left-wing political groups tried to recruit him. Herbert didn't understand why. "I was perplexed: maybe I am inept," he reminisced.[26] At times he pondered that perhaps it was because he was a homosexual and therefore wouldn't be accepted into any of the groups. "But I didn't show it," he wrote more than a decade later, wondering at the time if anyone suspected that he had sex with guys he had met in Municipal Park or during casual strolls downtown. Even when he tried to have fewer sexual encounters and conduct himself more discreetly, he lamented in his memoir that none of the radical students seemed to think he was a good candidate for membership in their organization.

On his own, Herbert had already decided that the PCB's moderate policies didn't seem radical enough. So, when a member of that organization tried to pass him a copy of its underground publication, he simply wasn't interested. He had read a few of the documents that POLOP had circulated among student activists and thought that their forceful language about the proletarian revolution was much more engaging than that of the communists, but classmates and friends who supported the ideas of POLOP didn't return his interest.[27]

Then one day in March 1967, Ângelo Pezzuti, a fourth-year medical student and emerging leader of POLOP, observed by chance an incident when a friend of Herbert's who was a member of the Communist Party inconspicuously slipped him a document of some kind. Ângelo immediately took up the matter in a cell of POLOP in the School of Medicine, realizing that if they didn't move fast, Herbert would soon be recruited to another underground group. After three days of intensive political discussions with Ângelo, Herbert joined the organization. "March 28, 1967," Herbert wrote some thirteen years later, "I'll never forget that glorious day."[28]

One of the first rites of passage into an organization operating underground was to choose an assumed name to use in cell meetings or when signing political documents. False names theoretically served as a protection against police infiltrators. In addition, should a militant get arrested, he or she supposedly would not be able to reveal the identity of others. Of course, for those who knew each other at the university or through the student movement, this security procedure was somewhat ineffective. Nonetheless, it was common practice among left-wing organizations. Herbert chose the rather unusual name Olímpio. Aretuza Garibaldi offered an explanation of why he adopted this uncommon appellation. She remembered that she and Ângelo Pezzuti, whom she dated in 1968, along with Herbert and a couple of other friends would sometimes meet at the Cantina do Lucas, a restaurant and bar in the Maleta Building, a ten-minute walk from the medical school and a hangout that attracted artists, intellectuals, bohemians, and students. She described Olímpio, the restaurant's most famous waiter: "He was a crazy old man, who saved a bottle of wine for the day that Franco died, even though he wasn't from Spain. . . . All of the left-wing students knew and loved Olímpio. He was great. If you went there and ordered a beer, he would say, 'No, you have a test tomorrow. I'm not going to serve you.' And he wouldn't." Aretuza was certain that Herbert chose the underground code name Olímpio in homage to this beloved character.[29]

It's easy to assume that Herbert's dedication to his new life as a revolutionary was purely political. His commitment over the next seven years was so absolute that it might seem unfair to read anything else into his deep involvement. Yet it appears that the intense friendships that he forged in medical school and later in difficult conditions underground became as important as his ideological devotion to radical change. He shared a common cause with people who didn't seem to notice that he was a homosexual. The powerful bonds among comrades that were forged in the joint project against a common enemy created a sense of belonging that trumped the isolation he had felt due to his nonnormative sexual desires. Here was a chance to edge away from the feeling of being exiled from the activities of his contemporaries. Herbert still had issues about his self-image; he was somewhat overweight and considered himself unattractive. Being part of an organization that valued his brilliance must have meant a lot to him.

There is no doubt that 1967 was a watershed year. Ângelo Pezzuti, who was charming, brilliant, and gregarious, had replaced Laís Pereira as his best friend. The new relationship seems to have been consolidated in 1966, even before Herbert joined POLOP.[30] Ângelo became Herbert's confidant, political mentor, and co-conspirator. After he took the basic course in Marxism and revolutionary theory that was almost a rite of passage for all new members, the leadership asked Herbert to teach this same course to new recruits. Nahas, who also claims to have recruited Herbert to POLOP, summed up his assessment of Herbert succinctly: "He was brilliant."[31] Within a year Herbert rose to the leadership of the organization. At this same time, when Herbert's political life began to expand in new directions, additional opportunities emerged to engage the creative sensibilities he shared with his father.

The venue that channeled these artistic interests was the Show Medicina (Medicine Show), which had been an established cultural tradition among medical school students since José Geraldo Dângelo founded the theater group in 1954. The show featured humorous skits and political satire written and performed by students. It became an immediate success and an annual event. Ângelo Machado, another medical student, soon joined forces with the show's talented founder. Together they wrote and directed the performances held toward the end of each academic year. The show continued under their stewardship even after they graduated and became medical school professors.[32]

The year that Herbert entered medical school, the Show Medicina faced strict government censorship because of its political content. One skit that particularly bothered the censors was titled "007 vs. the Haunted Castle [castelo assombrado]," evidently a James Bond parody that poked fun at Humberto de Alencar Castelo Branco, the four-star general who assumed the presidency after the 1964 coup. Using a pun that played on his last name (castle) seemed to anger the guardians of political propriety. After intensive negotiations with the censors, the script was cut drastically.

During the show's first performance in that politically volatile year, there was a short, programmed blackout following the end of the skit that had been censored. This brief pause provided just enough time for someone to throw sulfuric acid onto the stage from the balcony. It splashed on a member of the audience. At first there was pandemonium, but after the victim of the attack received medical attention, order was restored. Mauro Filgueiras, that year's director, gave an emotional speech, and the performance was resumed, though there was considerable tension in the air.[33] The following day the police interviewed the entire cast, implying that they were responsible for the incident, rather than seeking the true perpetrators of the act, who were probably members of a right-wing organization that opposed the political criticisms embedded in the show's script.[34]

Ângelo participated in the show in 1965, his second year at the medical school. Similarly, Apolo, Dodora, and Laís, who were all involved in the CEM, also displayed their amateur thespian talents in their first years in medical school. It was a way of having fun while making a political statement against the current state of affairs.

Two years later Filgueiras asked Herbert to write the show's script and codirect the production. The offer was an exciting opportunity for Herbert, who had shown talent both for humor and writing since high school. Herbert's mother carefully saved a copy of the show's program, which is one of the few records that his family has of Herbert's years in medical school. The worn and stained memento of her son's brief artistic career is filled with scribbled messages offering congratulations, hugs, and kisses that reflect both the excitement of opening or perhaps closing night and the enthusiasm of friends and relatives who had enjoyed the show. "This is mine," Herbert wrote on the upper left-hand corner of the cover over his signed name, almost as a reminder that it should be saved and treasured.

The program's featured text offers witty prose, no doubt penned by Herbert, as the style is so similar to his later writings. "Once upon a time . . . a Medicine Show, that suddenly began to grow and could no longer remain restricted to the students of the school, became theater. Only seeing it [is believing it]! We are still traditional in only one thing, the price of admission (very cheap). But that is because we are very dear."[35] If the show's script still exists it is not to be found among the archives of the university. Herbert's surviving friends from that period have only vague memories of the actual content of the skits and jokes that were performed over four nights to packed audiences comprised of classmates, friends, relatives, and a wider public.[36]

The titles of the sketches only offer a suggestion of their actual political content. As had become the tradition, references were to current events: "Le rouge et le noir," with "F. Castro and Stokely C.," for example, is an allusion to Stendhal's French classic novel, as well as to the Cuban leader and the U.S. Black Power militant. Another skit, "Na frente não" (Not in the front), whose title has a second meaning with sexual overtones, seems to parody the attempt by the right-wing politician Carlos Lacerda to forge a broad antigovernment front that would include political opponents such as former presidents Kubitschek, Quadros, and Goulart. A disclaimer warns the audience: "Any similarity between this program and the show is mere

FIGURE 3.4 Program for 1965 show. COURTESY OF GENY BRUNELLI DE CARVALHO.

FIGURE 3.5 Program for 1967 show. COURTESY OF GENY BRUNELLI DE CARVALHO.

coincidence." A second note adds: "Any coincidence of this show with real people, places and events is a mere similarity."

Mauro and Herbert, like almost all Brazilian playwrights and theater directors of the time, had to play a clever cat-and-mouse game with government censors. In addition to having their scripts approved in Brasília, they had to convince the local censors that their show was innocuous, because even if the language seemed innocent, the actual stage performance might transform a superficially inoffensive text into something that the regime's watchdogs thought was subversive or immoral. The censors required a special pre–opening night rehearsal to make sure that the presentation conformed to the script. Usually, the cast would read their lines at a fast clip in a boring monotone, to lull the censor into thinking that the content was harmless and somewhat tedious. This tactic also was designed to discourage censors from actually attending the live show, though producers were required to reserve front-row seats for them. Just before the show began the director or scriptwriter would peek from behind the curtain to see if the "enemy" had decided to attend the performance. If no censor was present, then the cast could let loose and inject into the skits the political and risqué humor that they had practiced during rehearsals. If the censor was there, the actors knew they had to be careful to avoid getting the show shut down.[37] Herbert's likely bouts with government censors no doubt contributed to his disapprobation of a regime that was rigid and culturally unsophisticated, if not downright backward and reactionary.

Apparently in 1967, unlike in previous years, none of Herbert's new comrades from POLOP were in the show. However, Laís did join the cast. She had not become a member of POLOP, but she was close to people in the group and was active in the student movement. Laís's note to Herbert, scribbled into the program, conveys the tenderness of a long-term closeness: "Herbert: I only want to be a star if you are always the director. How far will you go? To my *best*, a hug 'this' big. From Laís."

Herbert's success that year offered the promise of a career in theater. Laís recalled that Herbert stopped by her house, beaming with pride soon after the production closed, to show her a note that Dângelo had written to him: "Words, words, words, you have them," she remembered it had said.[38] This praise of his literary talents was perhaps the greatest recognition Herbert had received as of that date. Yet, over the course of the next twelve months, there would be no time for script writing or show business; political activism took center stage. Moreover, Herbert had become distracted by an intense infatuation that overwhelmed him.

4

The O.

(1967–1968)

> Herbert was the organizer. . . . He was a person who could see situations, establish objectives, look ahead . . .
>
> — ERWIN RESENDE DUARTE

Erwin Resende Duarte entered the School of Medicine in 1967. He was young, extremely handsome, and already politicized. "A golden boy," remembered Zezé, who was two years his senior.[1] Aretuza Garibaldi, a friend of Erwin's sister Marilda, described him vividly: "He was the kind of boy that all of the girls desired as their boyfriend. You know, like the American athlete that all the girls wanted to date. That was Erwin. And Herbert was timid, short, overweight. . . . Herbert was completely enchanted by him."[2] Erwin had been a left-wing activist in high school and joined POLOP at the university at about the same time that Ângelo, perhaps along with Jorge Nahas, convinced Herbert to become a member.

Herbert fell hard and fast for Erwin. Forty years after they last saw each other, Erwin warmly remembered his best friend from that time: "Herbert was a person with a very solid and beautiful cultural background, principally weighted toward the performing arts, cinema, theater. We became close due to this cultural connection and developed a friendship." They began to spend endless hours together at each other's houses. At times Erwin would sleep over on the couch in Herbert's living room, or Herbert would spend the night at Erwin's. Everyone thought they were inseparable.[3]

There was, however, something almost excessive about the relationship, according to Erwin. "At times he would have a crisis in which he was almost hysterical about our friendship." Asked to offer an example, Erwin commented, "He would say: 'Damn, I'm your friend, cut it out,' or whatever, and he would start shouting and get upset, at times losing control."

Possibly it was his repressed attraction to Erwin that led him to expect so much of his friend and feel so upset when it seemed he was being treated unfairly. In Herbert's second semiautobiographical work, he tells the story of an evening when he and Erwin were killing time waiting for another comrade for a meeting. Sitting on the steps of a house, Herbert showed Erwin a love letter he had written to "a person" with whom he was in love. Conveniently, the word *uma pessoa*, with a feminine article but a gender-neutral meaning, masked the true identity of his object of love and desire. As Erwin slowly read the letter, Herbert noticed tears welling up in his friend's eyes. Erwin finally commented that the letter was simply beautiful and encouraged Herbert to show it to the "special person" and reveal his true feelings. Herbert implied that it was impossible for him to do so. Suddenly, someone interrupted the scene and told them to get off the steps. The comrade they were waiting for arrived, and the three went to find a quiet place to talk about a political matter. On the way, Herbert discreetly tore up the letter and let the tiny bits fall along the sidewalk as they walked to their destination. Herbert had managed to reveal his emotions and had seen how much his words could move Erwin, yet he didn't have the courage to tell him the truth. As a result of the incident, Herbert experienced excruciating emotional pain that led to a deep depression.[4]

While Erwin could not remember this incident when interviewed many years after it had taken place, he comfortably offered details about another interaction between the two. One evening sometime in 1967, Herbert and Erwin shared a room at Erwin's house, though they slept in separate beds. As they lay awake talking, Herbert began a rambling monologue that hinted at his passion for Erwin without explicitly stating it. Erwin cut off Herbert's roundabout discourse and asked directly: "Are you saying you are in love with me?" Herbert confessed that he was, and Erwin explained that although he didn't feel any attraction to other men, it didn't mean that they had to stop being friends. Erwin insists that the conversation didn't alter their companionship, and in fact, after that incident Herbert occasionally confided in him about very personal matters.

In spite of their continued friendship, Herbert took Erwin's rejection quite hard. Dilma Rousseff, who had first met Herbert in 1967 while they were both members of POLOP, remembers that he came to her the next day in tears. Previously, Herbert had confided in her about his homosexuality and about his love for an unidentified male member of the organization, and she encouraged him to tell that person his feelings. She remembers how distraught he was the day after he followed through on her advice. All she could do was patiently comfort him, as he sobbed endlessly. It was her first friendship with a gay man, and years later she confessed that she had been rather innocent about such matters of the heart.[5] It seems that Herbert also confided in Dodora, as she later told at least two other female members of the organization about his homosexuality and that he was in love with Erwin.[6]

Ângelo, however, was likely the only male member of the organization to offer Herbert solace. He had become a close confidant, acting in some ways as a sympathetic connective link between Herbert's romantic and sexual desires and his involvement in revolutionary politics. Other female members may have heard something about Herbert's infatuation with Erwin, but none of his former male comrades interviewed for this book stated that they knew at the time that Herbert was gay. Not even Laís suspected anything about his repressed sexual feelings (or she chose not to see them). A year behind Herbert in medical school, they crossed paths less and less, largely because she was working odd jobs to put herself through school.

As has been amply documented elsewhere, homosexuality was still considered immoral and perverse both inside and outside the Brazilian Left.[7] An interlocking set of ideas about same-sex sexuality drawn from many sources led to this characterization. Following traditional perspectives shared by the international communist movement, homosexuality was considered a product of bourgeois decadence and would disappear when capitalism was overthrown and a socialist or communist society established. The leaders of the Cuban Revolution also held this position, leading to repressive campaigns against homosexuals in the early 1960s.[8] Notions borrowed from pervasive medical and psychiatric circles considered homosexuality to be a physical and/or emotional degeneration. Traditional Christian teachings deemed homosexuality a moral abomination. Although most revolutionaries rejected their religious upbringing, they rarely questioned this supposition.

Moreover, most leftists echoed popular sentiments that rejected male homosexuality because it implied the feminization of masculinity and disrupted a construction of revolutionary masculinity that was at the core of militants' self-images. Vera Lígia Huebra, who had joined POLOP in 1966 and knew Herbert well, reflected on what it must have been like for him to deal with his homosexuality within the context of the Brazilian Left. "The men [in the organization] were very prejudiced. I don't know how Herbert managed to get around within that milieu. . . . People were very rigid and discriminated."[9]

How, then, do we understand Dilma's and Ângelo's attitudes toward Herbert's homosexuality? Although heterosexuality was the norm, minority views about sexuality circulated among Brazilian youth. While paradigms held by members of the Left considered homosexuality an aberration, some thought differently. Dilma's acceptance of Herbert's homosexuality seemed to stem from their close friendship, which led to her empathy. "He was the kind of friend that you could be with him without the need to talk about anything."[10]

At first glance, one might be surprised that Ângelo would have comprehended Herbert's personal dilemma. During the late 1960s Ângelo had a series of girlfriends in a manner that paralleled traditional male patterns of privileged sexual promiscuity. While such behavior in men had tacit societal approval, young middle-class women were constrained by strict notions of propriety, morality, and chastity. Although these codes were shifting in the mid-1960s, Ângelo's sexual comportment reflected the double standard that remained widespread and reinforced rigid patterns of gendered behavior and heteronormativity. Ângelo wanted to become a psychiatrist after finishing medical school. Even though the Brazilian medical profession still defined homosexuality as a sickness, Ângelo revealed a certain degree of openness and critical thinking about sex that was unlike that of many, if not most, of his peers.[11] Perhaps his empathy for Herbert's pain and suffering reflected lessons from his preliminary training in the field of psychiatry.

Herbert and Ângelo were also linked by intellectual affinities, as well as the complexities of their emotional lives. Like Herbert, Ângelo was also particularly close to his mother. Carmela Pezzuti's passionate attachment to her firstborn son was profoundly mutual, and Ângelo looked after her and closely protected her when she legally separated from his father. Moreover, Ângelo encouraged his mother to date, and it seems that he did not object to his mother's affair with a prominent right-wing politician, even though Ângelo himself was quickly moving toward revolutionary politics. His apparent open attitude toward homosexuality, however, did not mean that he represented the norm among those drawn to revolutionary politics.

Members of radical left-wing organizations, including Herbert's group, were influenced by the shift toward more permissive sexual relations among Brazilian middle-class youth in the 1960s. Yet at the same time most militants were still wed to orthodox Marxist language and ideology that involved personal struggles within the groups that challenged their members to "overcome" their social backgrounds as they disciplined themselves to engage in revolutionary action. Student activists who had absorbed the rudiments of left-wing ideology tended to imagine that the working class would be an integral part of any revolutionary upheaval, and this was particularly true for those schooled in POLOP's Marxist traditions. Most students came from middle-class backgrounds, and so rooting out the supposed deviations inherent in their upbringing became a fixation. As Herbert himself explained, in the ethos of the period, most members of his organization considered a preoccupation with sex a "petty bourgeois" self-indulgence. "My *petty bourgeois* problems," Herbert wrote in his memoir, "worried me as obstacles that prevented me from becoming a good revolutionary. Among them sexuality, and more explicitly, homosexuality. Ever since I began to engage in political activities, I felt as if I had to make a choice: either I would lead a regular sexual life—disturbed, secret and absurd, that is, purely petty bourgeois, if not reactionary—or I would make the revolution. I wanted to make the revolution. Conclusion: I had to 'forget' my sexuality."[12] The attempt to purify himself by purging alleged deviant class-based behavior through self-sacrifice led Daniel to suppress his personal and sexual desires from sometime in late 1967 until 1972. It was the only way he felt he could adapt to a group norm and find the acceptance for which he yearned.

Herbert's choice of politics over pleasure took place at a crucial moment in POLOP's history. At the same time that Herbert was giving classes on Marxism to potential or new recruits and writing and directing the Show Medicina, POLOP was going through an internal battle that would lead to an explosion in September 1967. A national debate had simmered over the previous year. In this process, the majority of POLOP members in Belo Horizonte concluded that it wasn't enough to argue with the PCB over the socialist nature of the Brazilian revolution or to debate with left-wing students about the primacy of the working class in any social upheaval. The success of the Cuban Revolution and the ideas of Régis Debray, a French Marxist journalist who had written a series of articles and books about guerrilla warfare, become their guiding light. That year Sandino Press in Montevideo,

Uruguay, published Spanish versions of two of his books, *Revolution in the Revolution?* and *Castroism: The Long March of Latin America*. Together they offered a blueprint for social revolution across the continent.[13]

Apolo remembered that this literature circulated covertly through João Lucas Alves, a former sergeant who had been expelled from the Air Force in 1964 for organizing among the rank and file. "He was a bookseller . . . [and] a member of POLOP. He was the head of the armed wing, which really only existed on paper. He came to sell books [in Belo Horizonte]. He spread the ideas of Régis Debray and Che Guevara to earn money, but then everyone adhered to those ideas and broke with POLOP."

Debray, who had been imprisoned in Bolivia after interviewing Che Guevara in 1967, offered a theoretical justification for the revolution embraced by POLOP members, who advocated for a strategy of armed struggle to defeat the Brazilian military regime. Pointing to the success of Fidel Castro and his band of revolutionaries fighting in the Sierra Maestra in the late 1950s, Debray's writings systematized the *foco* theory and argued that a small dedicated group of revolutionaries could establish a rural base, demoralize a dictatorial regime, inspire the peasant masses to rise up, and ultimately overthrow a reactionary government.[14] It was a small motor that would activate a larger one, several former militants recalled the phrase they used at the time.[15]

The political trajectory of Che Guevara, the Argentine medical student who had joined the Cuban insurgents and had become a leader in the post-revolutionary government, served as an additional inspiration. Leaving his post as the Minister of Industry in Cuba to support the revolutionary movement in the Congo and then, when that endeavor failed, relocating to Bolivia to build a revolutionary base in an area strategically located near Argentina and Brazil, Che Guevara offered a dashing and romantic model for would-be Brazilian revolutionaries. Such was the case for Fernando Pimentel, a high school student in 1967 (and many years later the governor of Minas Gerais), who remembered reading works by Debray and Guevara and, as a result, decided to choose the pro-Cuban students in POLOP rather than the militants of Ação Popular, which at the time was moving toward Maoism.[16]

In September 1967, Ângelo, Apolo, Breno, Dilma, and other leading members of the group in Belo Horizonte attended the Fourth National Congress of POLOP in a beach house on the coast of São Paulo. Delegates debated a document penned by Eric Sachs, entitled "Socialist Program for Brazil," that recognized that the Cuban Revolution had "broken the monopoly of U.S. domination" through a "socialist revolution" and reaffirmed the possibility of a similar revolution in Brazil.[17] Yet the effectiveness of guerrilla warfare depended on a revolutionary situation in which the insurgents could become the voice of a united front of workers from both the city and the countryside who were prepared to take power. Although optimistic about the potential of guerrilla foci that might unleash the political forces of a workers' revolution, the document recognized that there might be a long road ahead before those goals were achieved.[18]

The rhythm of the revolution and the immediacy of armed struggle polarized the thirty delegates representing groups in Minas Gerais, São Paulo, and Rio de Janeiro. As far as the delegates from Belo Horizonte were concerned, the revolution was imminent. When they and their political allies in Rio and São Paulo lost a crucial vote over the approval of the document by a count of sixteen to fourteen, it caused a schism.[19]

In a three-page declaration entitled "Open Letter to Revolutionaries" and signed by "the Revolutionaries that split from POLOP," the dissident delegates marked a clear position: a radicalization was taking place throughout the world, but especially in Latin America. Brazil and Latin America were different from Europe, the document insisted. "Whereas the national leadership [of POLOP] has a proposal that is based on the expectation of an urban insurrection, we consider that armed struggle, as a fundamental form of class struggle in the current situation, must take place in the countryside in the form of guerrilla warfare."[20]

The urgency of the manifesto and the criticism of the "immobility" of the POLOP leadership reflected sentiments pervasive among radicalized students throughout Brazil and around the world in 1967: revolution is at hand; the conditions are ripe; now is the time; we must seize the moment. The student movement across the country had taken to the streets in 1966 and 1967 to protest censorship, government educational policies, and the military regime's repressive nature. Those breaking with POLOP judged that the Brazilian economic situation and conditions in Latin America more generally proved that there was a deep crisis in Brazil. The news of Che Guevara's fate in Bolivia in October 1967 didn't seem to dampen their spirits. Herbert recalled in his memoir that it "was lived as a victory and its justification as the certainty of the inevitability of a victorious future. It was a death filled with hope."[21]

Two weeks after the international press released news about Guevara's demise, Herbert basked in the limelight of his success in producing the Show Medicina. For the time being, it seems, he had managed to balance two parts of his life—politics and culture—while coming to the conclusion that his sexuality had to be cast aside or at least deeply repressed so that he could "make the revolution." Many important tasks lay head. He and his comrades had to regroup and consolidate a new organization yet to be named, so its members simply called it "O. period," their code for "the Organization."

When Herbert began his fourth year of medical school, it is unlikely that he foresaw how tumultuous the year would be. He later wrote that 1968 was so intense that it was impossible to record events in any chronological order.[22] Virtually abandoning his studies, he plunged into a whirlwind of activities: attending endless meetings, teaching clandestine courses, participating in the student movement, founding a new underground organization, assuming leadership responsibilities in it, traveling to Rio de Janeiro and São Paulo to fortify contacts, and preparing for the armed struggle.[23] When his parents chided him for seemingly abandoning his studies, he simply ignored them.[24] At the same time, he struggled to repress his homosexual desires, while consolidating an important friendship with Ângelo Pezzuti, who became his closest comrade-in-arms.

Every day brought something new and unexpected. As the year proceeded, it seemed as if a revolutionary uprising might overthrow the dictatorship, and it was imperative that he and his colleagues were prepared for that eventuality. In March the death of a student in Rio sparked massive student mobilizations throughout the country. In April an unprecedented strike of nearly 20,000 workers in an industrial city near Belo Horizonte challenged the government's labor and wage policies. That same month, Herbert participated in a secret conference of like-minded revolutionaries that drafted a document orienting his group's political work toward the armed struggle. The next month, a militant May Day rally by the city's leading labor unions was followed by a two-day strike and sit-in at the School of Medicine. In July, Herbert joined others in a congress that formally established "the O." as a "national" entity. Even the arrest of more than eight hundred delegates and student leaders, including members and supporters of the O., at a national UNE meeting in October didn't seem to dampen the optimism of Herbert and his colleagues as they forged ahead in their preparations for confronting the dictatorship.

When 1968 began, a convergence of diverse political forces throughout Brazil was voicing its opposition to the dictatorship.[25] A growing number of Catholic priests, nuns, active laypeople, bishops, and even a few archbishops were distancing themselves from the regime and speaking out against arbitrary government policies.[26] Carlos Lacerda, the disaffected right-wing politician who had so vociferously supported the 1964 coup d'état, continued to make a concerted effort to unite former presidents in the Broad Front to confront the military that lingered in power.[27] Government policies that held down wages to control inflation were fueling working-class

FIGURE 4.1 Herbert at his parents' home in 1967 or 1968. COURTESY OF GENY BRUNELLI DE CARVALHO.

discontent, as families struggled to make ends meet. Purchasing power fell as prices continued to rise. Inflation, while diminishing, was not under control, and this also undermined middle-class trust in the government's economic policies. Although the military attempted to hide its authoritarian rule by retaining semblances of democracy, this strategy showed signs of weakness. Artists and intellectuals protested censorship, and students across the country defied bans on political organizing. During the previous two years and into 1968, student activists mobilized in favor of expanding the number of slots for admission to public universities. They also fought against new educational policies that were centered on criticizing a proposal to institute tuition fees at state-sponsored universities.[28] Even members of the legal opposition had been emboldened to stand up in Congress to denounce government crackdowns against students and the use of torture.[29]

It is important to point out that 1968 was not only a time characterized by widespread political opposition to the dictatorship. As scholars have documented, cultural contestations and sociological changes were occurring simultaneously, marking the period as a watershed moment.[30] Whereas in the early 1960s sexual relations among middle-class youth were closely monitored, by the middle of the decade easier access to contraceptives, along with a general loosening of the influence of the Catholic Church, created conditions for a more sexually liberated climate among young people.[31] More audacious sartorial fashions for women, such as the miniskirt, and more informal styles for men, such as the elimination of the everyday use of the tie and suit jacket, were part and parcel of changes in what had been considered appropriate behavior for middle-class youth. New musical currents such as Tropicália provoked hotly contested debates about the foreign influence on national cultural production.[32] Singers, such as Caetano Veloso, not only revolutionized pop music but also expanded notions of acceptable gender performance by pushing the boundaries of traditional representations of masculinity and femininity.[33] Experimentation and notions of "newness" were in the air. Although most of these shifts in cultural values reinforced heteronormativity, there were also potential spaces for difference. Herbert lived amid all of these crosscurrents of political, social and cultural contestations and debates. It is impossible to know to what extent these factors directly influenced him. Nonetheless, by the end of the year, the decision to "make the revolution" had become the central focus of his life. It continued to be the reason he gave himself to justify repressing his homosexual desires. Regardless of how much he might have followed the cultural shifts that took place that year or even identified with them, he had made a clear choice to become a revolutionary, whatever the cost. For Herbert there was no compromise or reconciliation among the lifestyle choices confronting him.

Re-creating the political intensity of 1968 as Herbert experienced it and as it contributed to his commitment to revolutionary change is no easy task. The surviving members of the O. who knew Herbert in the late 1960s have few detailed memories of his day-to-day activities. Police records and the documents compiled in 1969 to indict Herbert for violating the National Security Act note that he was a member of the O. without offering many specifics about what he did that year. Even those people who were close to Herbert but not involved in radical politics have difficulty recollecting the specifics of 1968. Herbert's mother, for example, only remembered that he was so busy that he rarely stopped at home except to get a bite to eat or to invite his friends over for what she thought were school-related study groups. She recalled they would hole themselves up in his bedroom for hours. She had no idea what was really going on in those endless meetings, as she served them coffee or a snack.[34]

It is as if Herbert had already moved out of the spotlight into the shadows. Although he participated in the student takeover of the medical school in May, he wasn't publicly known as a student leader. Thumbnail biographical notes about his political activities, written after his death, erroneously claim that he was a vice president of the Central Student Directorate (DCE).

However, he didn't play a visible or leadership role in the organization in 1967 or 1968.[35] Nor does it seem that he was involved in leafleting at factory gates or door-to-door in the working-class neighborhoods during or after the April strike or later that year when another wildcat strike took place. Several comrades, however, remembered his talented teaching of the O.'s courses on Marxism for newly recruited supporters and members. By the end of the year, he had abandoned writing movie reviews for the radio. He also did not follow through with his promising role as a writer and director for the Show Medicina. There simply wasn't time, and these activities had likely lost their sense of importance. Rather he was playing an important behind-the-scenes role in maintaining the day-to-day operations of the O. as it balanced a turn to armed actions with maintaining work in the student and labor movements. Making use of his strong writing skills, he spent some time elaborating documents about the revolutionary situation and perspectives for armed struggle in Brazil, and he was one of the editors of *América Latina*, a voluminous mimeographed journal published irregularly by the O. He also wrote copy for *O Piquete*, a small newsletter that the group produced and that was oriented toward the working class.[36]

But following this paper trail does not lead very far. None of the materials produced by the O. and seized by the police in successive raids (at least such materials that are currently in the Minas Gerais State Archive) give any clue to his authorship of any specific work. Neither Herbert's initials nor his code name, Olímpio, appears in the reams of confiscated documents produced by the O. So it is difficult to know exactly what he wrote or didn't write. The shift from a relatively open student-based association of friends and classmates to a clandestine organization, in which no one was supposed to know more than the minimum about another's political activities, meant that Jorge, Zezé, Dodora, Erwin, and Laís, who studied with Herbert at the School of Medicine and were engaged in other discreet political activities, did not know at that time and so can have no recollections now of exactly what he was doing. Moreover, Herbert was still recovering from his unrequited love for Erwin and closely guarded those passionate feelings, revealing them only to Ângelo and Dilma, and later to Ângelo's girlfriend, Artruza, and one or two other women in the organization. Thus, to understand Herbert's role in the events of 1968, we must step back and examine what was happening around him. Only in this way can we make sense of the optimism he and his comrades felt as the year came to a close.

In late March, the gathering oppositional storm coalesced around the killing of Edson Luís, a poor high school student who had gone to Rio to get an education. He was slain by the police during a demonstration about precarious student housing and the poor quality of food in a subsidized student cafeteria, and his death set off a wave of demonstrations that swept throughout the country. Belo Horizonte was among the state capitals where students organized street protests against the regime's policies and practices. The April 1 issue of *O Piquete* reported on the mobilizations. On a page titled "Protests All Over Brazil," the four-page mimeographed publication noted that "today more than 5,000 people marched down Afonso Pena Avenue, held a rally [in front of] São Jorge's Church, and then continued to the Legislative Assembly. The speeches of the leaders set a tone: 'We will no longer respond peacefully to the rifles and machine guns of the police.'"[37] The militant tenor of the words reported in the O.'s modest journal mirrored the arguments that Herbert and his comrades were making in their secret meetings and in student assemblies: only revolutionary violence could bring down the dictatorship. As the first half of the year progressed, student demonstrations increased nationwide. So did conflicts with the police.

Pitched battles with agents of the state, however, were not the only ways students expressed their opposition to the dictatorship. The March of 100,000 in Rio de Janeiro on June 26 remained calm and marked the largest demonstration against the government until the late 1970s. All of the left-wing clandestine organizations grew in 1968, and massive public demonstrations from the first half of the year fueled a sense that the dictatorship's power was waning and the opposition's strength was increasing. As the political situation intensified and radicalized, the O. in Minas Gerais and its allies in Rio expanded their circle of supporters and recruited more people to their ranks.

Since 1965, a new generation of (mostly) student activists had joined POLOP and then founded the O. in late 1967. Only a few dedicated militants from the precoup period survived the repression and dispersion in the aftermath of the military takeover. Some of these leaders, such as Breno and Apolo, had passed through the dictatorship's prisons, which earned them respect as veteran revolutionaries. Breno worked discreetly in Belo Horizonte and traveled extensively for the O. while living underground.[38] Apolo became an important student leader and a UNE vice president. Guido Rocha, another longtime POLOP member, was an artist and, many years later, would become a prominent Brazilian sculptor. He contributed to the O. as the graphic designer for *O Piquete*. Cláudio Galeno Magalhães Linhares worked for the daily opposition newspaper, *Última Hora*, and provided logistical support for the group. Dilma had been recruited by Breno while a student at the Central High School, and she studied economics at UFMG

FIGURE 4.2 Inês Etienne Romeu and Carlos Alberto Soares de Freitas (Breno) at a party in 1967.
COURTESY OF SÉRGIO FERREIRA.

while helping produce and distribute *O Piquete* to working-class supporters of the organization. In 1967 she married Cláudio Galeno, and their apartment became an important meeting place for the O.[39] They both adhered to the split that favored the armed struggle.[40] Fernando da Matta Pimental entered the O. as a result of his activism within the high school students' movement while at the State High School of Minas Gerais, at the time the largest public school in Belo Horizonte.[41] Another important member of POLOP and later the O. was Inês Etienne Romeu, who was enrolled in an undergraduate course in sociology and politics at UFMG and was also involved with the Bankworkers' Union.

These experienced activists from POLOP quickly recruited new blood as student radicalization expanded in 1966 and 1967. By early 1968, the O. probably had fifty or so members, with an equal number of close supporters dispersed throughout the student and labor movements in Belo Horizonte. Additionally, there were a scattering of contacts and allies in several towns in Minas Gerais and a core of like-minded revolutionaries in Rio. One of their members, Athos Magno Costa e Silva, was the president of the university-wide student union at the UFMG, and Maurício Paiva from the School of Engineering served as secretary of the same entity.[42] In fact, the O. had members in the most important schools within the university. Among their most strategic areas of support was in the School of Medicine, where Apolo, Jorge, and Ângelo led an active group of militants, among them Herbert, Dodora, Zezé, and Edwin.

Although Breno remained a key leader of the O., Ângelo increasingly assumed a more central role in 1968, leading the group on a course toward armed struggle. He also had become Herbert's best friend, a relationship emphasized in *Passagem*, which is dedicated to Ângelo.[43] As friends and confidants, the two shared intellectual and political affinities that bound them closely together. Herbert's rise to a leadership role in the O. by the end of the year was, in part, due to Ângelo's confidence in his abilities. These new responsibilities only deepened his commitment to the revolution.

5

Ângelo

(1968)

> Herbert was an introverted person. . . . I remember that he was always biting his nails.
>
> — MARIA JOSÉ DE CARVALHO NAHAS

Ângelo Pezzuti da Silva was born in 1946 in the town of Araxá, southwestern Minas Gerais. His father, Theofredo Pinto da Silva, was a successful businessman, and his mother, Carmela Pezzuti, was the daughter of a prominent doctor. In the late 1950s, his parents moved to Belo Horizonte, where Ângelo completed high school in the midst of the disintegration of his parents' marriage. When his mother legally separated from her husband, she had to look after Ângelo and his younger brother, Murilo, on her own, with some support from her brothers and sisters. At the time it was still unusual for a respectable middle-class woman to leave her husband, and no doubt living in a larger city spared Carmela the gossip and social stigma that would have been attached to her in Araxá. Ângelo was a brilliant student who manifested rebellious tendencies and a social conscience in high school. He entered medical school in 1964, where he specialized in psychiatry. Murilo, who didn't have the same academic talents, went to work for the State Lottery. Ângela Pezzuti, Ângelo's aunt, who was close to her nephews, remembered how much Ângelo loved classical music, poetry, theater, and books, especially ones written by regional Brazilian authors.[1]

Helvécio Ratton, a student of economics and a member of the O., loved to engage in conversations with Ângelo about intellectual questions. "We talked a lot about [Wilhelm] Reich, because he was a person with whom I could discuss this sort of thing. . . . He had broad cultural knowledge, which was something other militants didn't have."[2] Similarly Herbert identified with Ângelo's wide range of intellectual interests, which became an important basis of their friendship and was reflected in the political documents they drafted together and in the discussions in which they participated as leaders of their underground organization.

In addition to his intellectual capabilities, Ângelo was incredibly charismatic. Aretuza, his girlfriend in 1968, reflected decades later, "I think his profession was to seduce people in general. Old people, children, heterosexuals, homosexuals. He had that capacity to seduce people. I didn't know anyone who didn't like him."[3] But though his charm was undeniable, it was not enough to conquer everyone he met. Breno, who had been an important leader in the group since the days of POLOP and was living underground, was at odds with Ângelo. Their leadership rivalries seem to have had less to do about politics and more to do about conflicting personalities. A division of responsibilities—Ângelo taking charge of armed actions later in the year and Breno taking on the task of finding a location for guerrilla training—kept hostilities from breaking out between them.[4]

Although participating in public demonstrations was an essential activity for members of the O., consolidating a structure to carry out strategic revolutionary goals increasingly became a priority. In April the group held a conference in Contagem, near the state capital, in a small getaway country place. The meeting, which involved intense political discussions about the world political situation, the nature of the regime, and the tasks ahead, was a gathering of the new and the old. Some, like Herbert, had only recently embraced Marxism and the political perspectives that favored guerrilla warfare. Others only a few years older than the average age of those present at the meeting, which hovered around twenty-one or twenty-two, were veterans of radical politics through their participation in POLOP.

The attendees approved a document entitled "Conception of the Revolutionary Struggle."[5] It is difficult to attribute authorship of the document, but it seems likely that Ângelo and Herbert, as two of the more theoretically minded members of the O., were closely involved in its elaboration. The document confirmed the position held by former POLOP members that Brazil was ready for a socialist revolution. It also justified their split: "Today in Brazil the conditions are ripe for the unleashing of the armed struggle."[6] The treatise recognized that opposition to the dictatorship implied a fight against U.S. imperialism and the large landholding structures that dominated the countryside and argued that revolutionary violence could take place effectively only in rural Brazil.

These ideas, modeled on what members of the O. understood to be the strategies employed by Cuban revolutionaries, as interpreted by Régis Debray and Che Guevara, articulated remarkably optimistic prospects. Politically committed urban-based revolutionaries were decisive for offering logistical support for rural guerrilla fighters. This outlook made it all the more urgent to move from talking about revolution to taking concrete steps to set up guerrilla units, whether in the city or the countryside.

While the O. was consolidating its program, internal structure, and operations, and at the same time joining student mobilizations, another development took place in Contagem that caught the group largely by surprise.[7] On April 16, soon after beginning the morning shift at the Belgo-Mineira Iron and Steel Company, 1,600 workers stopped production and demanded a 25 percent wage increase in response to an intentional squeeze on workers' earning. The owners countered with a 10 percent wage hike, which the workers rejected.[8] Three days later, employees of the Brazilian Electricity Company stopped work. The following day 4,500 from Mannesman, the largest factory in the region, joined the labor stoppage. Others followed suit until more than 15,000 had participated in the shutdown.[9]

On the face of it, this first major labor action against the military regime since 1964 seemed reasonable. Yet the strikers' most important demand, a salary readjustment to make up for a 25 percent loss in their buying power due to government economic policies, immediately provoked a confrontation with both employers and the state.[10] A new generation of radical activists from the different Marxist currents to the left of the PCB that had developed a grassroots network in the factories, and the communities surrounding the Industrial Park provided an important core leadership of the strike. Among them were supporters of the O.

Although visions of an imminent guerrilla struggle shaped the O.'s immediate political outlook, most of its older members had cut their political teeth as members of POLOP, which emphasized more traditional Marxist theories about the primacy of the working class in any social revolution. Some veteran POLOP members had important contacts with union activists in the working-class regions near Belo Horizonte, and *O Piquete*, which POLOP had published irregularly since 1965, gave the O. a modest vehicle for communication with workers. In its early years Breno wrote much of the copy and Guido Rocha did the graphic design. Dilma recalls etching the line drawings on a mimeograph stencil and then bundling the bulletin in packages to distribute throughout the city.[11] In 1968, Herbert also wrote text, and Murilo ran the mimeograph machine that produced the modest publication.[12] *O Piquete* became an important instrument for presenting the O.'s ideas in factories and in neighborhoods, with the hope of recruiting workers. By April 1968, POLOP (and later the O.) had produced sixty-eight issues of *O Piquete*.

It is not clear how extensive the O.'s actual participation was in the strike. The organization had recruited few workers, but it had a scattering of supporters at the Belgo-Mineira installations, where the strike began, and at the electricity plant.[13] Even though the O. was moving away from focusing on radical solutions to the problems of the working class to a policy that favored armed struggle, the fact that there were actual workers among its circle of supporters offered its mostly middle-class student membership, who held rather abstract and romantic notions about the industrial proletariat, the comforting feeling that overall the O. was on the right track.

Faced with an unexpected action that undercut the government's wage policies, Minister of Labor Jarbas Passarinho flew to Belo Horizonte on April 20 to negotiate directly with the workers. Appearing before the strike committee and its supporters, the minister insisted that their monthly wages were sufficient to support their families. His arguments didn't win much sympathy among those assembled.[14] He left the meeting threatening to take drastic actions if the strikers didn't return to work. The next day, more factories stopped production.

The federal government responded by shutting down the union, arresting twenty strike leaders, and sending in 1,500 troops to occupy the city. These measures effectively ended the labor action, and workers slowly returned to work for fear of losing their jobs. Realizing that the situation in Minas Gerais was explosive, soon thereafter President Costa e Silva (1967–69) announced a 10 percent across-the-board pay hike for workers nationwide in time to coincide with official Workers' Day activities on May 1.

Any labor action can be interpreted in many ways. Did the Contagem workers lose the strike because their 25 percent wage increase was not met, or did they successfully force the government to overturn its own wage-freeze policy and, in a preemptory move, grant a modest hike to workers throughout the country to avoid further labor unrest? Regardless of how one answers that question, the fact that the Contagem strike occurred and, later in the year, another militant work stoppage happened in Osasco, an industrial suburb of São Paulo, suggested a rise in labor militancy that encouraged many people to make optimistic predictions about a revolutionary tide sweeping the country.[15] Yet in reality, the labor movement in Belo Horizonte had shifted to a defensive position.

The labor leaders who had organized the strike feared that they would lose their legitimacy among the rank and file when workers returned to their jobs, so they planned a militant May Day celebration sponsored by fourteen unions to consolidate their base of support. Newspaper accounts of the event, as well as police reports of the day's activities, note the large number of students among the two thousand people who attended the rally at the Department of Health building. For this occasion, the O. prepared a special issue of *O Piquete*, printed by a commercial press. It praises the general strike as the appropriate response to the wage squeeze, reviews the history of May Day, offers an analysis of the Brazilian labor movement, and presents an article asking the readers to consider "What is to be done?" (in an allusion to a famous pamphlet by the Russian revolutionary Vladimir Lenin).[16]

During the May Day event, the strike leaders spoke one after another, offering their evaluation of the strike and calling for unity to move forward. It was an optimistic moment for the left-wing leaders who headed the movement. Soon thereafter most would lose their jobs, some would be arrested, and a few would be forced into exile. Yet that day, the militant tone of the speeches conveyed a notion that Brazilian labor was on the move.

Although there is no record to fully substantiate the supposition, we can assume that Herbert attended the May Day rally along with his medical school colleagues. They likely would have agreed to meet on a street corner near the event and then participate as a group to applaud the radical speeches of the more militant labor leaders and cheer for the members or supporters of the O. who spoke during the public meeting.

At the event's conclusion, as workers and students flowed out into the streets to participate in an unauthorized march, they met 3,500 troops that had been deployed to prevent a street protest. Using tear gas and batons, government forces dispersed the crowd and arrested some of the protesters.[17] Among them were two important members of the O.: Afonso Celso Lana Leite, who had spoken at the May Day rally on behalf of the outlawed UNE, and Apolo Lisboa, who led the O.'s work at the School of Medicine.

While in custody, an engineering student, who had been charged with distributing "subversive literature," attempted to commit suicide rather than turn over names of fellow students. The incident sparked a series of actions that spread throughout UFMG and the Catholic University. Engineering students occupied the school's buildings, took the director hostage, and demanded that their colleagues be released from jail and charges against them dropped.[18] Thus, as the general strike of workers dissipated, students organized their own stoppage, which continued momentum for radical action in the state's capital.

Among the schools that shut down was the School of Medicine.[19] On May 3, students held a large meeting to decide how to respond to the arrests. The following day authorities dispatched a police squad to the main building to break up a gathering of students who were spray painting antidictatorship slogans on the front wall. Fleeing into the building, they barricaded the doors and prevented the director, several professors, and some employees from leaving. The students demanded a meeting of the faculty to address the fact that the police had invaded the school, breaking a long tradition that regarded the university as a zone free from military or police intervention. They also organized a massive sit-in at both the director's office and the area around the main exit. After negotiations failed, police surrounded the medical school. Late that night they entered the building and began arresting students, who responded by pelting police with stones and bottles and releasing ammonia to slow down the authorities' operations.[20] Laís Pereira, who participated in the student occupation, recalls fleeing to an upper floor to evade arrest and hiding in a closet until the early morning, when she slipped out of the building.[21] Most were not so fortunate. Approximately 150 students and some staff who supported the occupation were arrested. Among them was Herbert Eustáquio de Carvalho.

What Herbert actually did during the occupation remains unclear. His police record offers no clues. It merely notes that he was arrested on the day of the protest and released the following day.[22] It seems that the police did not know he had joined the group, which had split from POLOP to form the O. and had opted for armed struggle. In the eyes of the state police, he was merely another one of hundreds of protesting students. It is likely, however, that Herbert's arrest strengthened his conviction that the situation in Brazil had polarized and that militant actions were justified. Ironically, it was also the only time in his long career as a political activist that he ever spent time in jail.

The events of May Day and the student demonstrations that followed in Belo Horizonte were not isolated occurrences. In São Paulo, radical students and workers forced moderate union leaders off the stage of the government-sponsored May Day rally and pelted the indirectly elected governor with stones, an event widely reported in the national press.[23] And, as noted in the previous chapter, massive student protests took place throughout the country in early 1968. For those who had adopted a revolutionary worldview, the battle lines seemed clearly drawn. No doubt Herbert, like all of the other members of the O., slept very little the first half of the year. It must have seemed impossible to respond to so many things happening at the same time. There was an invigorating urgency about all of these events that propelled people forward.

By midyear, the O. appeared to be gaining strength. Recruits from the student movement had joined the organization, and it had some working-class support. More widely, there was a growing sense among opponents of the regime that the dictatorship's hold was weakening. This sentiment was reinforced by the fact that on June 26, 100,000 people participated in a massive peaceful protest march against the dictatorship in downtown Rio.

Activists in Brazil were further encouraged by events taking place beyond their shores. Protests seemed to be exploding everywhere. Hundreds of thousands of African Americans rioted after the assassination of Martin Luther King Jr. in April. Students and workers united in a general strike in France in May. The Vietnamese National Liberation Front defeated U.S. and South Vietnamese forces at Khe Sanh in June, signaling to Brazilian radicals that even the overwhelming power of the U.S. military was vulnerable. They actually might have a chance to break the hold of the Brazilian dictatorship.

Moreover, discussions with revolutionaries living in Rio pointed to expanding the O. beyond Minas Gerais. In July, a clandestine meeting in a beach-resort town brought together leaders of the O. and former POLOP members from Minas Gerais, who had scattered to other cities in the wake of post-1964 repression, as well as other revolutionaries operating in Rio, to discuss joining forces. Ângelo, Apolo, and Breno represented the O. Among those from Rio who agreed to merge with militants in Belo Horizonte were Maria do Carmo Brito and her husband, Juares Guimarães de Brito. Maria do Carmo and Juares had been involved in radical politics as members of POLOP in Belo Horizonte since the early 1960s. In 1963, POLOP assigned them to organize peasants in the central state of Goiás. After the 1964 coup, Juares was detained for five months in Recife. When he was released, the couple decided to move to Rio to continue their political activities where they were less known. Maria do Carmo became involved in student politics and won over a group of students while studying social sciences at the Fluminense Federal University. Juares had a stable job in a publishing house, which provided an excellent cover for his clandestine revolutionary activities.[24] Also present at the meeting representing Rio was João Lucas Alves, the former Air Force sergeant who had been expelled from the armed forces in April 1964 for his opposition to the coup. In subsequent years he had joined other former members of the military in a failed attempt to organize an armed insurrection. Circulating secretly through the region, he was also the person who supplied students with books and pamphlets about the Cuban Revolution. Representatives from a similar revolutionary formation in São Paulo also attended the meeting but did not agree to an immediate merger.

Within this context of intense radical fervor both at home and abroad, one might have expected the leadership to adopt a new exciting and revolutionary sounding name to replace the vague term "Organization," yet those gathered were reluctant to assume a new designation prematurely. Hoping to unite with other groups in São Paulo and the southernmost state of Rio Grande do Sul, they decided to continue to call themselves the O.

The group's new challenge was to proceed immediately in creating the conditions for the guerrilla struggle. To do so, it took measures to acquire weapons, train some of its members in the use of arms, and identify an appropriate place to establish a rural base. During the meeting, the O. created a new leadership body, known as the Command, composed of Breno, Ângelo, and Juares. Later that year Maria do Carmo and Herbert were incorporated into this body. While Ângelo began setting up the infrastructure for armed actions in Belo Horizonte and Juares did the same in Rio, Breno took charge of seeking a propitious place to establish rural guerrilla activities. Breno recruited Reinaldo José de Melo, a UFMG geography student, and Erwin Duarte to help him in this task. The three traveled throughout the country looking for appropriate locations. Traveling in a jeep that they bought for the excursion, they also investigated whether or not there were any social conflicts brewing that might lead to support for their efforts among peasants or rural workers. After they concluded their journey, the three sold the jeep and returned to Belo Horizonte. On another trip to the south, however, the leadership of the O. decided to buy another jeep, registered in Erwin's name, that they used for the excursion and then kept for other purposes. That decision would contribute to the demise of the O. in Belo Horizonte several months later.[25]

While Breno sought out the proper geographical site for guerrilla activities, Ângelo's task was to acquire funds. The O. had attempted to raise money through a small store that sold books, jewelry, and other items, but it brought in little income.[26] Bank robberies and other "expropriations" of private or government monies seemed a more efficient means to accumulate cash to purchase more arms and finance the O.'s operations. In this regard, the members of the group believed that any means were justified in challenging the military regime, overthrowing the dictatorship, and laying the groundwork for a socialist revolution.

Ângelo organized several autonomous teams to implement his plan. The intelligence unit comprised six members, who included Apolo Lisboa, Guido Rocha, Cláudio Galeno de Magalhães, and his mother, Carmela Pezzuti, who had been recruited into the organization. A second unit that focused on "sabotage" was made up of Apolo and his wife, Carmem, along with three other militants. Ângelo headed up a third team in charge of "expropriations," composed of approximately ten militants. Among them were Jorge Nahas and Irani Campos, an employee at the School of Medicine. All but one in this unit was male. Ângelo recruited a fellow medical student, Maria José, to join because he wanted an inconspicuous woman to carry out intelligence operations in preparation for bank robberies. Zezé, who characterized herself as a very shy person, thought that she had become a permanent part of the expropriations unit because of her keen skills of observation. "Before [an action] several people cased the same place, and then we discussed it. We came to the conclusion that when I did it, I gathered more information than everyone else."

Zezé and her boyfriend Jorge also helped the group obtain weapons. Originally the O. procured them in a haphazard way from anyone who had access to weapons. She explained, "I was dating Jorge, and we were going through the debate: get married, don't get married, get married, don't get married. What are we going to do? And then we decided to get married." Zezé continued: "I went to talk to my mother and told her that I needed money to buy the wedding trousseau. We used the money to buy arms."[27] To this day Zezé doesn't know how Ângelo managed to find the three Thompson submachine guns that the O. used in its actions, but she remembers that he stopped by her apartment with a heavy package, opened it up, and said, "Here's your trousseau."[28] The money also bought revolvers, pistols, and ammunition.[29]

Their first action, however, was a complete failure. The group's intelligence team had received information that a courier from the State Ministry of Finance would be transporting a significant amount of money from Belo Horizonte to a town about 150 miles to the northeast. The expropriations unit procured military police uniforms to disguise themselves. Armed with a Thompson machine gun, they flagged down the military courier jeep, informing the soldiers they were checking for subversive material. To their disappointment, they found nothing of any value in the vehicle.

Three days later, they decided to try their luck again. This time they chose the Commerce and Industry Bank of Minas Gerais, located in Belo

Horizonte.[30] On the day of the robbery, Ângelo, wearing a dark three-quarter-length coat, headed the group of nine young revolutionaries who took part in the assault. Toting two machine guns and two .45 caliber pistols, four of the participants entered the bank while five others stood guard outside with getaway cars. Within three minutes they subdued the manager (along with seventeen bank employees, workers, and clients) and fled in two stolen cars. They absconded with approximately 20,000 *cruzeiros novos* (US$66,000), a tidy sum for the organization's first successful "expropriation."[31] In his memoir Herbert wrote that the next day the School of Medicine was abuzz speculating about which new organization might have carried out the armed action.[32] Herbert remained silent but was extremely pleased with the O.'s first success. Although he had not participated in the robbery, he knew, at least in general terms, about the activities that Ângelo was masterminding.

In spite of the mystery around the identity of this new urban guerrilla organization, the O. had already become vulnerable. A week prior to the successful bank robbery, it suffered its first serious security breach. On August 20, police invaded the house of João Batista dos Mares Guia, one of the O.'s most prominent student leaders, and arrested him under the National Security Act. During the raid, they found documents of the O. that gave them clues about the structure of the organization and its activities.[33] Perhaps as a cautionary measure, the O. didn't carry out any other actions during the month of September.

Yet the organization's expenses were mounting as its militants quietly rented apartments and other locations, known as *aparelhos*, or safehouses, to hold clandestine meetings and store weapons, propaganda material, and other supplies needed for underground activities. In addition, Breno needed resources for his team's exploration of potential guerrilla sites. So, five weeks after their first successful robbery, Ângelo planned a second "expropriation" from the Banco do Brasil. Ten members of the organization participated in this operation, this time wearing masks, dark glasses, and berets to hide their identities. They carried four machine guns and two revolvers. The operation took less than eight minutes and netted 10,000 *cruzeiros novos* (US$33,000).[34]

The O's second successful action had taken place at the same time that industrial workers in Contagem attempted a second strike that year for annual wage adjustments to keep up with inflation. Bank employees joined the striking metalworkers. Since the end of the April strike, union militants and the left organizations supporting the labor movement had prepared for this new work stoppage to align with annual wage adjustments. But the strike was a dismal failure. The government declared it to be illegal, intervened in the unions, and appointed a member of the government's Regional Labor Board to oversee the metalworkers' and bankworkers' unions. Authorities also ordered the arrest of key leaders, including Ênio Seabra, who had led the April strike. They then signed a 17 percent pay increase that barely kept up with inflation.[35]

The failure of the strike probably diminished the O.'s area of influence within the labor movement. An issue of O Piquete produced right after the strike presented a bleak analysis of its inability to achieve a concrete result. Less than a week later, the O. suffered its second major security breach when the police arrested two members of the organization visiting João Anunciato, who had been involved in the April labor stoppage.[36] Along with copies of O Piquete, police officers confiscated internal documents of the organization.

Now there was additional positive proof that a new clandestine organization was operating in Belo Horizonte. A detailed report listed many of its members, outlined its structure, and pointed to its involvement in the recent bank assault, a fact confirmed by a manifesto left at the bank site but not published in the press.[37] The police were close on the trail of the O., but the leadership continued to operate as if they had avoided detection.

In response to the strike defeat, the O.'s leadership decided to carry out a radical symbolic act to show support for the metalworkers and bank employees by planting bombs in the homes of both the person who had taken over control of the two striking unions and the Labor Court judge who had ruled against the work action. Although the O.'s guiding document, "Conception of the Revolutionary Struggle," prioritized the preparation for rural guerrilla warfare, it left the door open for other radical actions: "Terrorism, such as execution (in the city and the countryside) of reactionary henchmen, should obey a rigid political criteria." Among those individuals whose actions justified execution were torturers, "traitors to the people," or symbolic figures of special importance to the regime.[38] On October 18, 1968, a team of five militants, led by Ângelo with the support of his brother, Murilo, tossed the bombs over the walls of the residences of the two "symbolic figures," causing minor property damage. Whether they intended to execute their targets or merely create a climate of "terror" is not clear, but no one was hurt in the action. According to Dilma Rousseff, the bombing later caused a heated debate within the O., as she and others sharply criticized the tactic.[39]

Before slipping away from the bombing sites unnoticed, the O. left leaflets announcing their new name: Comandos de Libertação Nacional (COLINA).[40]

The one-page manifesto, likely written by Ângelo, perhaps with Herbert's assistance, begins dramatically with the statement "The working people are tired of oppression." After outlining the fact that the recent strikes were defeats, the document announces that "this all has to end. Against this violence that the dictatorship and the bosses employ to oppress and exploit the people, [COLINA] will use revolutionary violence." The manifesto continued: "The next strike should be more organized so that the bosses don't know about our leaders, our meetings, and our slogans. Our organization in every factory, in every bank, should be more secure, more clandestine. We should begin to construct a people's army, the National Liberation Army. Only in this way will we free ourselves from exploitation, bringing down the dictatorship that is at the service of the bosses."

Why the O. acquired the name Comandos de Libertação Nacional is not entirely clear. The term "national liberation" reflected a political analysis that called for freeing the country from foreign, namely, U.S. oppression, much like the strategic program of the Vietnamese National Liberation Front that was fighting against American troops in Southeast Asia. A premise of this formulation was that any such organization would unite with different "democratic" forces, including sectors of the economic elites that might have financial conflicts with foreign companies. This was hardly the analysis contained in the documents that the O. had approved in its April conference, which emphasized the socialist rather than the national liberation content of their struggle. On the other hand, the word "Comandos" communicated the militaristic nature of the organization, which was more in line with its new orientation toward guerrilla actions. No doubt the emotional connection with the Cuban and Vietnamese revolutions inspired the coinage of the new name.

As the O. transmuted into COLINA in the second half of 1968 and Herbert assumed a leadership role, he continued to experience internal turmoil over his sexual desires. Even though close friends listened compassionately to his discreet confession about his homoerotic feelings, it seems to have offered him insufficient comfort, and he considered committing suicide several times. In August 1968, he even absconded with his father's pistol and went to a deserted part of the city, thinking that he would end his life. As he was trying to muster the courage to shoot himself, two policemen ran into him. One of them recognized Herbert and told him to leave the area, as it wasn't safe.[41] Although his plan was aborted, Herbert remained depressed. The only fulfillment that seemed available to him was the achievement of the O.'s revolutionary goals.

On the night of December 13, while returning to Belo Horizonte with three other comrades from a secret meeting in São Paulo with the leaders of the People's Revolutionary Vanguard (VPR) to discuss possible unification with COLINA, Herbert and his companions heard Minister of Justice Gama e Silva read Institutional Act No. 5 (AI-5) over the radio. The new decree gave President Costa e Silva the power to close down Congress, suspend habeas corpus, increase government censorship, and cancel any oppositionist's political rights for ten years. It also signaled to the repressive apparatus that the ruling generals had given them the green light to systematically arrest and torture anyone considered subversive.

That this draconian measure marked a sharp turn to the right in the dictatorship's rule didn't seem to worry Herbert or his colleagues. Following the logic of an argument, pervasive at the time, that considered AI-5 as a "coup within the coup," Herbert recounted in his memoir: "That genuine coup d'état wasn't a motive for reevaluating our tactics. We took it very seriously and understood it to be an outright weakness of a desperate dictatorship."[42] The optimism and excitement of that year had blinded Herbert and his group to a stark new reality descending on the country.

6

Underground

(1969)

> He was essentially a very extroverted and happy person, which is so much the opposite of the image of a terrorist.
>
> — LADISLAU DOWBOR

In spite of the inauspicious political climate in the wake of Institutional Act No. 5, COLINA's "National Report," issued in early January 1969, confidently assessed that the organization had implemented measures to carry out rural guerrilla actions.[1] Having successfully expropriated a significant amount of cash from two banks, the leadership decided on a double bank robbery in order to stockpile money. The operation required expanding participation within the expropriations unit. Herbert, who had not joined any armed action up to that point, was tapped for the assignment to replace a militant not in Belo Horizonte at the moment. "1969 started well," Herbert later wrote. "Carrying out my first armed action, with total enthusiasm and a little bit of ignorance. This time, we were happy—we're starting to 'do something.' The Organization, one among many, had begun the [armed] struggle."[2]

Yet, as Herbert readily acknowledged, the group was rather unprepared: "At the moment, the important thing was revolutionary willingness." Herbert captured the surrealistic precariousness of his training in a (possibly apocryphal) anecdote:

> On the eve of the first bank robbery in which I was to participate, I raised a question, which was totally secondary, with the comrade who commanded the operation.
> "Listen, a small problem. I've never fired a shot in my life . . ."
> "So what?" he asked me. After all, he himself, the commander of the group, had trained by firing a few shots from a rife in a small farm in the countryside.
> "And so, I argued, if I need to shoot. . . ."
> "What do you want? If you need to shoot, pull the trigger here and the bullet comes out there in the front."[3]

Herbert claimed this was the only military training he had received in his early days as a guerrilla fighter. That may have been a slight exaggeration to make his point or to add a humorous note to his entertaining memoir. Still, the dozen urban warriors who participated in the double heist managed to pull it off. Their inexperience, however, led to a breakdown in security procedures. The police's response revealed that the state had started to gain the upper hand.

On January 14, 1969, Ângelo Pezzuti led eleven COLINA militants who simultaneously entered the Lavoura and Mercantil de Minas Gerais banks in Sabará, a town neighboring Belo Horizonte. Their action netted US$25,000. Zezé was the lone woman in the group. Two teams of four people simultaneously entered the banks, while two others stood guard outside, and two drivers waited in getaway cars. Herbert toted a .38 revolver.[4] One member of each team carried a machine gun. Zezé, who later admitted she was incredibly nervous, approached a teller and pulled out a gun.[5] The team commanders ordered the bank manager to open the safe, while another herded customers, employees, and bank guards into bathrooms and locked the doors. The entire operation was over in minutes. Within an hour, the police had already recovered one of the getaway cars, but the "thieves," as they were described in the press, had gotten away.

As is to be expected, eyewitnesses offered contradictory versions of events. Journalists, for their part, took poetic license and invented a character that quickly became a trope in subsequent reporting on revolutionary armed actions.[6] According to newspaper accounts, one of the bank robbers was a beautiful blond guerrilla fighter wearing a miniskirt. The newspaper

Estado de Minas Gerais first circulated the romanticized image in a feature article. Under the subheading "Mini-Skirt," the journalist reported, "The young woman who was a part of the gang is light-skinned with blond hair." The story added, "She wore a black mini-skirt and a light checkered blouse" and was silent throughout the action.[7]

The fantasy, shaped by journalistic accounts, that the only female guerrilla was a gun-slinging blond, presumably in a sexy miniskirt, no doubt was influenced by the U.S. movie *Bonnie and Clyde*, released in 1967 and shown in Brazil soon thereafter as *Bonnie and Clyde: A Spray of Bullets*. The film was loosely based on the story of a working-class Depression-era gangster couple, and Hollywood heartthrob Warren Beatty played opposite a blond, daring, and cold-blooded Faye Dunaway. One promotional poster showed the couple driving a car, laughing, with bullet holes dotting the windshield. Other material portrayed the elegantly dressed couple, arms locked and revolver in hand, poised to rob a bank. Set in rural Texas in the 1930s, the movie featured a daredevil pair with their sidekick partners, who barely managed to keep ahead of the law and were finally mowed down by police in a bloody ambush in the film's finale. It was not the happy ending Brazilian filmgoers usually saw in Hollywood productions. Yet it might have seemed strangely similar to a new phenomenon in Brazil, namely, radical youth engaged in "expropriations" that the press and dictatorship called "terrorist acts." The movie's morally ambiguous plot glorified the freewheeling, violent escapades of the Texas gangsters while offering a cautionary tale about their ultimate destiny. The press and the military regime, on the other hand, did not extol the feats of young revolutionaries who participated in bank expropriations or, later, ambassadorial abductions, but rather portrayed them first as reckless robbers and then as dangerous terrorists, spending little time explaining the ideological reasons for the bank actions.[8] This press treatment likely left some readers puzzled over the actual motives of these youthful bank robbers.

In his memoir, Herbert observed that the "blond bank robber" was the perfect creation of reporters seeking exotic copy although he failed to mention that she echoed images of Faye Dunaway.[9] Herbert remembered that in 1969 during endless hours in their *aparelhos*, he and others loved to read descriptions of this revolutionary personality and laugh about journalistic exaggerations. He wrote, "She was blond, beautiful, with stunning legs, wearing a daring mini-skirt and bravely commanding the assault. She had a firm voice, a decided gesture, and quick trigger finger."[10] Compassionless, she showed no mercy. As Herbert noted, every revolutionary organization ended up having such a figure attributed to its ranks, whether or not its female militants actually donned blond wigs (or had light hair). Herbert saw the image as a masculine fantasy that turned this mythical character into a woman who was simultaneously devastatingly beautiful and extraordinarily powerful, and therefore a sexually desirable figure.

Marcelo Ridenti has calculated that 15 to 20 percent of participants in armed struggle organizations were women, although a much smaller number held leadership responsibilities.[11] Almost all student leaders, whose movement had shaken the country the year before, had been male, and, therefore, women were still a novelty as prominent activists in 1968 and 1969. However, rather than presenting the multiplicity of female personalities involved in the guerrilla movement, as Herbert argued should have been the case, the press made women fighters into Hollywood sex symbols to titillate readers and increase circulation.

Whether or not, as some have claimed, Zezé was the first female guerrilla fighter to be portrayed as an icy, yet sexy, revolutionary, she confessed that she was very nervous that day. Nonetheless, she had worked enough with the expropriations unit to proceed calmly. This was not how Herbert reacted to his first experience as a practicing urban guerrilla. Zezé recalled that she and Herbert were dropped off on a crowded downtown street. She was thirsty and wanted to stop and order a Coke, while Herbert was a ball of nerves. He couldn't stop biting his nails.[12]

No doubt the entire organization, even those not directly involved in the planned assault, was jubilant at the bold and apparently successful expropriation.[13] Ângelo, normally careful to remain discreet, couldn't contain his excitement. Aretuza recalls they met that evening. "If I had had any doubt about what he was doing, that night I was sure, because he was euphoric . . . and began telling details of the robbery, saying that he had heard it on the radio. But there were too many details to have been heard on the radio."[14]

The next day Aretuza stopped by Ângelo's *aparelho*. No one was there, and she had forgotten to bring the key, so she went to his mother's apartment. She thought Carmela might know his whereabouts. When they met, Carmela told Aretuza she assumed that her son had been arrested since she hadn't received word from him.

Indeed, the police had already tracked down Ângelo. He had parked a getaway car downtown, and the police discovered it soon after the robbery. Finding Ângelo's fingerprints on the rearview mirror and discovering that the jeep was registered in Erwin's name, both were quickly picked up. Torture immediately followed.[15]

Once the news spread that they were in jail, the members of the expropriations unit tried to erase their tracks. They abandoned two houses used

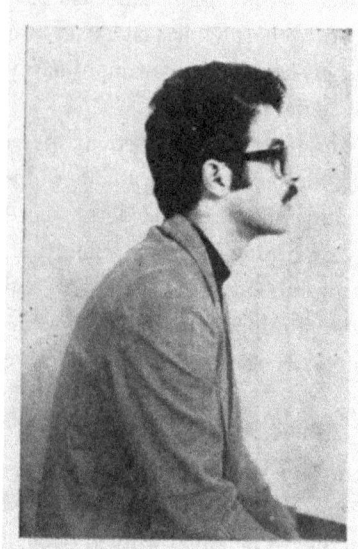

ÂNGELO PEZZUTI DA SILVA

FIGURE 6.1 Mug shot of Ângelo Pezzuti da Silva, January 1969. COURTESY OF THE ARQUIVO PÚBLICO DO ESTADO DE SÃO PAULO.

as hideaways, and Zezé rented a new *aparelho*, where the unit met to decide what to do next. They also sent someone to get rid of another car they had used. Instead of quickly selling it to a dealer, he bargained over the price. The manager became suspicious and reported the transaction to the police. The militant was eventually arrested, and after successive rounds of torture, he told the police about the new *aparelho*.[16]

On January 30, 1969, while the arrested members of COLINA were being tortured to obtain information, the expropriations unit was meeting to respond to successive security breaches. Throughout the night they discussed various possibilities for freeing their comrades. The meeting ended late, so they decided to sleep over rather than leave and arouse the neighbors' suspicions.

In the early morning, they were suddenly awakened when the police broke down the door and sprayed the house with bullets. Those inside resisted arrest. The crossfire killed the policeman Cecildes Moreira de Faria and the civil guard José Antunes Ferreira.

Seven members of the organization were arrested, including Zezé and her husband, Jorge.[17] Because Herbert wasn't an ongoing member of the unit, he hadn't attended the late-night meeting and was spared detention. It was the first of numerous times that he avoided incarceration by luck and happenstance.

Suddenly COLINA members not caught needed to disappear. Inês Etienne, a veteran of the student movement, POLOP, and the bankworkers' union, who had taken a leave of absence from the group, came to the rescue. Assuming charge of getting people out of the city, she arranged for Aretuza to hide in a house for several weeks, along with Vera Lígia Huebra, another member and student activist.[18] They slipped out of the city on a bus destined for Rio.[19] Many young *mineiros* were traveling to Rio for Carnival, so it was a perfect cover. Dilma Rousseff also used the holiday as a pretext to flee to Rio, staying with her aunt for a short time and then moving into a rental apartment.[20] Others, such as Helvécio Ratton, relied on friends and family for assistance. Hiding out at a farm for several weeks, he then traveled to Rio to contact the organization and continue political work. By the end of February 1969, COLINA had virtually ceased to exist in Minas Gerais.[21]

We don't know many details about Herbert's escape from Belo Horizonte. Nor does his family, as he managed to keep his clandestine political activities a secret, even as he fled his house in early February and eventually boarded a bus for Rio. Still living with his parents at the time, he calmly told his mother he planned to study with some friends, so he wouldn't be sleeping at home. Remembering that day decades later, Dona Geny lamented:

"He took a brown sweater that I had just knitted for him. 'Make sure that you don't lose that sweater,' I told him. I never imagined that he wouldn't come home."[22]

A week later the Carvalho family was surprised on returning from a weekend visit to Dona Geny's relatives in Barbacena to learn the police had surrounded the house in search of Herbert. Hamilton had just finished his military police training. He recalled that when neighbors informed officers that the family of Gê de Carvalho lived there and was traveling, they decided not to search the premises. The behavior of the police seems counterintuitive, but is unsurprising when taking into account Hamilton's and Geraldo's membership in the police corps. Loyalty and trust trumped an attempt to find clues of Herbert's whereabouts.[23] Moreover, Herbert's father was a local celebrity and as such was sheltered from the indignity of having his home searched. Six months later Herbert sent his family a telegram assuring them that they shouldn't worry.[24] After that communication, there was complete silence for three and a half years. Hamilton insists that, throughout the time Herbert was underground, authorities never interrogated him or his father about Herbert's whereabouts.

Maria do Carmo, Juares, and Breno now had the challenge of finding housing for several dozen people. Maria do Carmo's student-movement activities provided her with supporters who could help out. However, organizing hiding places for twenty or more people was no easy matter.[25] Called *os deslocados*, or the displaced ones, most had their names on police lists and were wanted for violating the National Security Act. They had to get fake identity cards, use code names when dealing with other members, and remain undetected by neighbors or landlords. Moreover, the police were quite publicly pursuing many of them. The government had initiated a national campaign, publishing posters with pictures of fugitive revolutionaries and the ominous slogan "Wanted Terrorists. Help Protect Your Life and That of Your Relatives. Tell the Police." These signs appeared in bus and train stations, banks, and other public places. Herbert and others had to proceed very cautiously so as not to arouse suspicion.

Abandoning the code name Olímpio was one of Herbert's first orders of business. Over the following years he took on over a dozen different assumed names—Daniel, David, Ezequiel, Formiga, Geraldo, Glauco, Isaac, Isaias, Marcelo, Noronha, Roberto, Ruivo, Tamoinha, and Tampinha—as a security measure within the organization. On the wanted poster, the names Daniel and Tampinha are listed as his code names, and at some point in 1969, the name Daniel stuck. In his memoir, he wrote a tongue-in-cheek introduction to an imagined novel. Referring to himself in the third person,

FIGURE 6.2 Wanted poster. Clockwise from top left: Apolo Herlinger Lisboa, Gilberto Faria Lima, Herbert Eustáquio de Carvalho, Carlos Alberto Soares de Freitas.

it began, "The contact, who gave him his first instructions, asked him to choose a new assumed name. Because of the title of the book that he had in his hand at the moment, he adopted the name of the author: Daniel. The contact told him that it wasn't possible because there was already another Daniel in the group. Another name? Because of the book he chose another name (from the novel's title): Robinson. Later there would be other names. But this one will remain forever. Almost his real name, or at least the name that was a part of his reality."[26] At the time there wasn't another comrade using Daniel as an assumed name, and there is no record that Herbert ever tried out Robinson during his clandestine life. Yet it seems possible that he might have been reading Daniel Defoe's *Robinson Crusoe* at the time he was required to invent a new name. Although his family still refers to him today as Bete, and his friends from Belo Horizonte as Herbert, those who lived with him underground and survived still remember him as Daniel.

One of the ways Daniel avoided raising suspicion was assuming the personality of a high school student, wearing the required white shirt and dark pants with a school insignia attached to the front shirt pocket. His young-looking face, short stature, and pudgy body created the image of an innocent pupil carrying a thick folder, presumably containing books and other school paraphernalia. An anecdote in his memoir illustrated how he incorporated this youthful persona. He had arranged a meeting at a predetermined place. Arriving slightly before the appointment, he realized the police had surrounded the area. Rather than panic, he casually walked through the ambush, kicking a can. Had they stopped to search him, they would have found a .45-caliber handgun rather than homework tucked away in his briefcase. On another occasion, simply offering a roll of bills to a policeman who wanted to see his identity papers prevented authorities from discovering he was armed and carrying incriminating political documents, not school assignments.[27]

In the mid- to late 1960s, Daniel had learned to hide the secret that he was attracted to other males and come up with alternative explanations about what he was doing in public places. Perhaps his skill in concealing his homosexuality became an aid in avoiding arrest. Peeking "out of the closet" and cautiously protecting himself from a hostile world regarding his sexual desires was, in many ways, similar to the talent he developed as a revolutionary to cloak his actions and intentions. Paradoxically, the symbolic closet that he constructed to cover up his erotic and emotional feelings seemed to serve him well underground.

Maria do Carmo can't recall the details of those hectic days when she, her husband, Juares, and Breno scrambled to find living quarters for comrades arriving from Minas Gerais and sites for clandestine activities. However, Daniel recounts that comrades in Rio arranged for him to stay with two homosexual artists, one of whom sympathized with the organization. "I was very excited and full of expectations. It was the first time that I had seen a couple of that kind who were accepted by all of their friends."[28] Hidden in a workshop for a period of time, he had occasional contact with one of the two. Although no erotic encounter took place, for months thereafter Daniel fantasized about having sex with the person who had hidden him, as he struggled to repress his sexuality and remain celibate.

Those who had fled Belo Horizonte lived a precarious life in Rio. They were fortunate, however, to have been assisted by Maria Nazareth Cunha da Rocha, a longtime supporter of the Left, who ran an agency that rented out vacation housing.[29] If Nazareth didn't have an available apartment, other agencies only required an identity document and a rental advance. False papers and money secured safe lodging. Tourists circulating through temporary rentals gave those living underground a convenient cover for their comings and goings, without raising suspicion among prying neighbors or inquisitive night porters. If these accommodations were unavailable, there was the option of a boarding house. Explaining that a person had come to Rio for a new job or to study for the university entrance exams was a perfect cover story for a *deslocado*, with the only drawback that one had to stay out on the street the entire day so as not to contradict one's fabrications. As a result, many militants spent endless hours in movie theaters watching films two or three times between arranged appointments, while others lingered in bookstores.[30] As Aretuza fondly remembered about Daniel and Vera Lígia, "Any free time that we got, we went to the beach. He [Daniel] would say: 'If the police want to find a *mineiro*, they should come to the beach. He's going to find the two of you.' We laughed a lot. He was very funny because, in the midst of all of that chaos, we had moments when it seemed that it was all a natural part of life."[31] Similarly Dilma Rousseff recalled spending time on the beach with Daniel and Iara Iavelberg, who had been sent from São Paulo to work with the organization.[32]

By 1969, the political police were well aware of how Brazil's revolutionary groups operated underground. State agents had begun to systematically use torture to extract information from those arrested in order to dismantle the regime's radical opposition. As a result, it had become dangerous to know where others lived; if someone was arrested they might reveal their housing address, leading to subsequent detentions. So rather than meeting secretly in apartments, encounters, known as *pontos*, were scheduled in public places at specific times to exchange information, pass on documents, or plan activities. Because the police knew about this practice, when a revolutionary was arrested, the repressive forces spent the first twenty-four hours using extreme methods of torture to extract information about upcoming *pontos*. Once a person missed an appointment and a previously agreed-upon alternative meeting time and place, an organization could be rather certain that the person had been arrested and could take necessary security precautions. Thus, the police needed to extract information about *pontos* immediately, before the organization realized that someone had been detained. Moreover, if a person shared lodgings and the housemate didn't come home by a certain hour, the rule was to evacuate the place under the supposition that she or he had been picked up and would only manage to withhold information for twenty-four to forty-eight hours. Although throughout 1969 and 1970 there were occasions when three or more militants shared housing, the leadership still had to find many separate locations where people could stay and was obliged to ensure that few in the organization knew where others lived.

These strict security measures required endless *pontos* throughout the week so that militants could maintain contact. These furtive encounters included both meetings to receive reports or get instructions, and occasional one-on-ones with other members of the small cells to which they were attached. When a longer meeting was required, the organization implemented additional security measures, including escorting people blindfolded (or with their eyes closed) to apartments or houses, presumably shielding knowledge of where the gathering had taken place. In addition to these complicated procedures, the organization needed funds to pay for the rent, food, and minimal expenses of those underground. It was all a logistical nightmare, and it had a severe psychological toll on militants.

Many former revolutionaries who lived clandestinely have difficulty remembering the sequences of their living arrangements, and they rarely knew about other comrades' accommodations. Thus, reconstructing where Herbert stayed that year is no easy task. At one point he lived with Maria do Carmo and Juares. At another moment he shared an apartment with Ladislau Dowbor, and they quite enjoyed each other's company and political discussions.[33] He also stayed with Breno for part of that year.[34] Dilma Rousseff remembered that in early 1969 she moved into an apartment in Copacabana with Iara Iavelberg and soon thereafter Daniel joined them. It was a small space with a single room, corridor, and kitchen, and the three slept on mattresses on the floor. Even in those tight quarters, Daniel was consistently upbeat and full of life. He also always woke up in a good mood. Dilma recalled that he would tie a kitchen towel around his waist and announce "Girls, coffee," and then serve them breakfast in bed.[35]

Daniel, however, didn't always have the best of luck with revolutionary roommates. Apolo Lisboa recounted that he also shared an apartment with his wife, Carmem, Daniel, and another comrade that year. Although he couldn't pinpoint the month, he remembered it was in Petrópolis, a mountainside town near Rio. He admitted he occasionally found Daniel annoying. "He hadn't declared his homosexuality, and he did things that I couldn't understand. For example, there was a double bed in the apartment. He argued that we were all individuals, and we had to choose lots to decide who would sleep in it. My wife and I would have to sleep in separate beds or on the floor, and he would sleep in the double bed in the bedroom with the other person. That was too much. . . . He disputed that bed with theoretical arguments of the greatest sophistication, citing the great philosophers."[36] Given Daniel's nimble tongue and sharp mind, one can imagine the kinds of arguments about individualism, private property, and the collective use of resources he might have employed to justify this arrangement. Apolo also noted: "Many times he protected a person that he liked. I think he lacked balanced judgment. . . . In day-to-day living, for example, when he had to carry out a task, he sometimes chose a person to go with him, and I think often times it was not the best person." Apolo referred to a specific moment: "There was a sixteen-year-old, a big guy . . . something really serious was at stake, but Herbert Daniel at times because of personal interests—and this is something that I say without being able to prove it—I think he did things not taking into consideration the political-military criteria in order to be with that person."

Perhaps, as Apolo speculated, spending time alone with certain male comrades was the only way that Daniel could cope with his repressed homosexuality. According to his memoir and letters that he sent to a close friend while living in European exile, Daniel maintained his resolve to remain celibate from some time in 1968 until 1972. It seems unlikely that he used democratic arguments about who should share the double mattress to actually seduce another comrade. Given the compulsory heteronormativity that surrounded him, if he indeed gave special preferences to some, it was most likely a way of maintaining a platonic relationship with those men to whom he felt attracted, whether sexually or otherwise.

Helvécio Ratton also noticed Daniel's focused interest in certain comrades. Soon after he escaped to Rio, Helvécio moved to a small fishing village along the coast, where he shared a small house with Severino Viana Colon, a former sergeant who had joined the armed struggle. There was a third member of the organization staying with them. Daniel was in charge of meeting with this three-person cell, and he took the two-hour trip from Rio at least twice while Helvécio was staying there in early 1969. Helvécio noticed the unusually close and intense attention that Daniel paid to the third person, and it confirmed a suspicion that Daniel might be gay. However, it was something that was not talked about, and Helvécio claims that, although the topic of Daniel's sexuality was discussed informally, he couldn't recall pejorative comments being made about him. Helvécio speculated that Daniel's prestige as a leader of the organization perhaps shielded him from being associated with the negative notions of homosexuality in the Left and Brazilian society.[37]

What seems clear is that, while living underground, one of the ways Daniel coped with his decision to repress (and hide) his homosexuality was through deep and intense friendships with certain militants. He may not have confided to them his suppressed sexual desires, but these friendships seemed to provide an intimacy that offered emotional support during tense times. It also followed a pattern established in his adolescence when he had few friends outside of a small circle of colleagues.

Apolo noted that Daniel was extremely close to Maria do Carmo. "In the middle of the armed struggle, they spent hours together laughing, while Juares, Maria do Carmo's husband, Breno, and I were very much worried about things." Apolo considered their behavior rather childish: "It was an infantilism of very intelligent people who had an intellectual education, especially about cinema, who knew about the most talked-about books. I, for example, much preferred to read a book about war by Clausewitz, Mao-Tse-Tung or the classics, Marx. They preferred to read comic books and laugh at the jokes in *Mad Magazine*, spending days upon end reading *Asterix*. He and Maria do Carmo dying of laughter and repression all around us; people dying while being tortured."

Maria do Carmo's recollections of those times underground coincide with those of Apolo regarding Daniel's and her favorite reading. Between revolutionary actions, they loved *Asterix* comic books, chuckling endlessly about the antics of the titular character and his friend Obelix. The Belgian comic book series, set in Gaul during the Roman Empire, tells the story of the residents of a village who resist their Roman occupiers by means of a magic Druid potion that gives them extraordinary strength. It must have been a comforting pastime to see the underdogs constantly outwitting the mighty Romans. Maria do Carmo remembered how much their giggling annoyed other comrades, but she saw it as a way to release tension in the midst of the repressive climate in which they lived. She and Daniel also loved science fiction stories and would read them voraciously during the lulls between the numerous *pontos* and the endless leadership meetings. She reminisced: "We spent hours discussing authors, reading everything. When we were on hard times financially, we would give up eating to buy science fiction books and then exchange them with each other." She readily admitted, "We maintained our mental sanity while underground by reading. I don't know how others did it, but we did it through reading."[38]

Dilma Rousseff has extremely fond memories of a profound friendship that flourished in Belo Horizonte in 1967 and 1968 and deepened in Rio. "He was a calm person, who was intelligent and creative. He was the kind of person who had an immense capacity to create personal relationships," she recalled. Dilma also remembered fun times together while living underground. On rainy days, they also bought *Asterix* comic books and bundled up together on a bed to read them while eating homemade guava-jelly cookie sandwiches. Like Maria do Carmo, she and Daniel liked to discuss science fiction, as a means to pass the time.[39]

Clearly Daniel, Maria do Carmo, and Dilma had found common outlets that permitted them to temporarily forget the enormous pressure constantly surrounding them. And Apolo admitted that their seeming frivolity didn't end up distracting Daniel from revolutionary duties: "At the same time he was able to then go out and kidnap an ambassador. I couldn't do that. I didn't have such courage, and I didn't have the ability to disconnect as much from the seriousness of what we were living through."[40]

Although Daniel had told Dilma that he had fallen in love with a male member of the organization when they were in Belo Horizonte, he was more cautious with Maria do Carmo. In spite of their intimacy, which Maria do Carmo confesses was greater than that with her husband, Juares, Daniel never confided in her about his homosexual desires. Asked if she suspected that he might have been gay, she answered, "I knew that Daniel was a homosexual because he fell in love with impossible people. . . . He never told me, but I felt it. For example he was in love with Marilyn Monroe. . . . Every homosexual who is not out [assumido] is in love with her."[41]

Daniel often impressed others as having qualities that didn't match the face he presented to the world. Maria do Carmo assumed that Daniel was a homosexual. Though he maintained the illusion of being a heterosexual, she had noticed that he had crushes on movie stars instead of female comrades. A slightly younger group of militants operating in Rio was also struck by the discrepancy between his outward appearance and his revolutionary capacities. On first impression, Daniel didn't conform to the image of the brave, bold urban guerrilla. Such was the experience of Alex Polari, who had been a high school student and joined COLINA in March 1969, around the time he first met Daniel. He and Alfredo Sirkis, another youthful recruit, were instructed to wait for a person on a bench at the beach. The comrade would carry a newspaper under his arm and identify himself by asking for the time. It took three attempts at inquiring the hour by a short, pudgy, young man wearing thick glasses, Bermuda shorts, and tacky sandals to convince Polari that Daniel was the person they were supposed to meet. Four decades after that first encounter, Sirkis remembered having similar thoughts: "It's not possible that this guy is the great revolutionary leader who is going to point us in the right direction."[42]

Daniel was simply a different kind of revolutionary leader. Rather than immediately dissecting a political document, discussing a revolutionary tactic, or offering a criticism of the Maoists, as Polari had expected, in their first conversation Daniel talked about Dostoevsky. Then he offered his opinion about the filmmaker Ingmar Bergman, followed by a discussion of the Colombian writer Gabriel García Márquez. Only after this did he finally touch on a document circulating in the organization. What should have been a brief encounter to comment on the latest political position or quickly decide practical matters turned into long intellectually pleasurable exchanges that excited these young revolutionaries. When there were only ten minutes left before Daniel's next clandestine meeting, Polari recalled, they quickly resolved organizational questions.[43]

Zé Gradel, who was in a combat unit of the organization, also remembered clandestine conversations with Daniel. "He began to schedule *pontos* with me in Niterói at the Icaraí beach, and we would sit there for hours talking. We would meet at the agreed-upon spot, exchange a couple of documents, and then spend the next four hours talking about cinema." This practice broke the organization's rules, as it was potentially dangerous for two militants to spend so much time together in public. But this didn't seem to bother Daniel. "We'd sit on a bench by the beach," Zé Gradel remembered, "and talk for two hours about Italian cinema, and then we'd get up, walk a half mile and then sit on another bench and chat for two more hours about French films."[44] Paulo Brandi de Barros Cachapuz, who also came from the high school movement, recalled his impressions of Daniel: "We were ready to become hardened regarding discipline, and Daniel didn't have the image of a hardened revolutionary. Daniel was irreverent, a figure that was interested in culture; he could talk about music, literature."[45]

Although Polari, Sirkis, Gradel, and Brandi all remembered stimulating intellectual conversations during their covert meetings, Aretuza Garibaldi recalled the emotional reconnections she experienced when they first met after she had abandoned Belo Horizonte. "It was a powerful meeting because we were both painfully sad. I was too young to fully understand what was happening, since it was a really radical change in my life."[46] She had never had the chance to say goodbye to Ângelo, and she felt tremendously lost and isolated in Rio. Daniel was suffering as well. He had received the news of Erwin's treatment in prison and feared that he was to blame for Erwin's arrest because he had pushed Ângelo to promote him within the organization. "He questioned whether he had demanded too much of Erwin; if he had given him too many responsibilities. Erwin's participation in the organization was meteoric. He had very quickly accumulated many responsibilities. First Ângelo questioned this, and then Daniel."

Aretuza and Daniel met on the Copacabana beach. They hugged and cried. Then they talked at length about the fact that Ângelo had been badly tortured. The meeting served to console two very lonely people, who were separated from beloved revolutionaries. Daniel and Aretuza met several other times in Rio, and she will never forget her eighteenth birthday: "He asked to arrange a meeting with me. I knew I was supposed to meet someone, but I didn't know who it was. And when I got there, he gave me some roses as a present."

All available evidence indicates that Daniel found numerous ways to retain a modicum of normalcy while operating underground, which no doubt aided him in the difficult tasks at hand. COLINA had been virtually annihilated in Belo Horizonte. More than a dozen were in prison. The police were seeking many more. João Lucas Alves had been tortured to death by the political police in March 1969. Nevertheless, a sense of optimism revived the organization, as prospects for unification with other revolutionary groups emerged.

7

Unity and Disunity

(1969)

> Daniel was capable of eloquently creating an extraordinary theory about anything in five minutes and proving it.
>
> — ALFREDO SIRKIS

A process was taking place in 1969 that Daniel and his colleagues did not notice or recognize as a threat to their movement: the country was becoming more prosperous. In the early years of the dictatorship, high rates of inflation continued, undercutting one of the justifications for the coup, namely, that a stable military government would fix a floundering economy. At first it appeared that the generals couldn't fulfill that promise, but in 1968, the economy began to take off. It soared to an average 11 percent annual growth rate between 1969 and 1973, which the regime called an "economic miracle."[1] Student mobilizations, especially after the death of Edson Luís in March 1968, had won popular backing during the first half of that year. However, improving economic conditions combined with antileftist rhetoric slowly eroded public support for opposition forces. Only belatedly would Daniel and other former guerrillas understand that economic growth, which increased consumer possibilities and mostly favored the middle classes (while working-class wages remained stagnant), contradicted their optimistic predictions that capitalism was in crisis and the regime was teetering.

At the same time, government crackdowns increased. Early in 1968, Alex Polari, Alfredo Sirkis, and other high school students had spent endless hours debating politics, sexuality, music, and culture. However, after December 1968, authoritarian edicts placed a damper on ebullient social and cultural transformations. Censorship augmented, and music idols, such as Caetano Veloso, Gilberto Gil, and Chico Buarque de Holanda, went into exile. The broad-based student movement that had involved hundreds of thousands collapsed.[2] The dictatorship purged left-wing professors from the major universities and issued edict 477, which prohibited student activism on campus.[3] Due to these and many other factors, the majority of students involved in politics withdrew from participation in direct antiregime protests.

At the same time a radicalization took place among hard-core activists. Small study groups met to debate Marxist ideology. Discussions became more polarized among those who insisted that the time was ripe to join the armed struggle and those who were not quite convinced. Alex Polari recalled the choice: "The alternatives were limited. Go all the way in the armed battle against the regime or embark on a trip toward self-awareness through cultural marginality, drugs, and the experience of communal living."[4] Throughout 1968, Sirkis, like Polari, struggled between a desire to participate in cultural changes taking place around him (labeled as petty bourgeois by his political peers) and a commitment to the revolutionary cause.[5] Daniel had faced a similar quandary: should he openly embrace his homosexuality, arguably associated with the new cultural changes, or abandon his most basic instincts to pursue his political ideals? All three opted for the armed struggle.

In spite of the dilemmas that Alfredo, Alex, Daniel, and others pondered, the consolidation of small revolutionary nuclei continued, even in the wake of measures that had eliminated democratic protections and an economy that dampened any popular support. The 1968 unification of the O. in Belo Horizonte with former members of POLOP in Rio attracted two small radical student clusters that had split off from larger dissident left-wing organizations. One of the two break-offs, the Marxist-Leninist Group, formerly had been linked to the Maoist-leaning Ação Popular. Among the leadership of the group was Carlos Minc, a student activist who had ties to Maria do

Carmo and Juares. The Marxist-Leninist Group had influence over fifty or so radical high school students, who had formed the High School Students' Command (COSEC) and were attempting to sustain the student movement in 1969 even though its power and influence were ebbing. The other group was composed of students who disagreed with the politics of the Dissidence, a group that had broken with the PCB and criticized its moderate response to the 1964 coup. Calling itself the Dissidence of the Dissidence (DDD), its dozen or so adherents also operated within COSEC.[6]

At the same time that COLINA was attracting the Marxist-Leninist Group and the DDD into its fold, the leadership also reached out to a group in Rio Grande de Sul led by Carlos Franklin Paixão de Araújo. The son of a labor lawyer linked to the PCB, Carlos also practiced labor law and had a following of thirty or so workers.[7] The group published two small mimeographed journals and attempted to recruit the proletariat through political education and by addressing labor concerns. In November 1968, Breno met with the group, and subsequently Maria do Carmo invited them to a meeting with the leadership of COLINA to discuss possible unification. The final outcome was an agreement to meet within sixty days to map out the details of an amalgamation.

In late April the leaderships of the two groups met for several days in a rented house in Teresópolis, a mountainside town near Rio, to carry out a merger and elect a new leadership. It was composed of Breno, Juares, Maria do Carmo, Daniel, and Dilma from COLINA, and Carlos and another comrade from his group.[8] Rather than adopt a new name, they chose to sign their documents "ex-COLINA." Their reasoning was that they favored unification with the People's Revolutionary Vanguard (VPR), a São Paulo–based guerrilla group, and they didn't want to assume a new name that they might then soon have to cast aside when they merged with the VPR.[9]

Like COLINA, the VPR was founded in part by POLOP dissidents from São Paulo who had broken with that organization in late 1967. In January 1968, they merged with the National Revolutionary Movement (MNR), a group of ex-members of the armed forces. The MNR largely comprised former soldiers and sailors who had supported Goulart's reforms and had become further radicalized while being purged from the military. The merger with former POLOP militants gave the unified organization a corps of people with actual military experience. The VPR also recruited workers, some of them, like Antonio Espinosa, who were also students, and a few union leaders. Among these were José Ibrahim, the president of the Osasco Metalworkers' Union, and Roque Aparecido da Silva, a rank-and-file union activist. They and others from the industrial belt near São Paulo had led the wildcat strike in Osasco in July 1968, which, along with a labor upsurge in Contagem, had challenged the regime's labor and wage policy.[10]

Over the course of 1968 and early 1969, the VPR operated essentially in São Paulo. In addition to supporting the Osasco labor action and participating in the student movement, its militants engaged in arms expropriations and bank robberies to fund its operations. The VPR also carried out the political assassination of Charles Chandler, a U.S. army officer studying in São Paulo, who was accused of being a member of the CIA.[11]

In late 1968, Captain Carlos Lamarca of the Fourth Infantry Regiment stationed at the Quitaúna army barracks in Osasco on the outskirts of São Paulo secretly joined the VPR.[12] From a humble family in Rio, while still a teenager in the early 1950s, he had participated in demonstrations in favor of the nationalization of oil. Lamarca had entered a preparatory school for cadets at age nineteen and studied at the Agulhas Negras Military Academy. He had also been part of a Brazilian contingent of UN peacekeeping forces in the Sinai in 1962–63. Promoted to captain in 1967, he made contacts with sergeant Darcy Rodrigues, who had been expelled from the military in 1964 but was later reinstated.[13] Rodrigues, a veteran political organizer, exposed Lamarca to Marxist ideas, and they attracted two other members of the regiment to their cause. Lamarca was an excellent marksman, and the army recommended him to train Bradesco Bank tellers in using arms against bank robberies, which gave him visibility in the press.[14]

In December 1968, Lamarca came into contact with Onofre Pinto, who had been expelled from the army in 1964 and was a VPR leader. Impatient to join the armed struggle against the regime and imbued with a belief that the political and economic situation favored revolutionary action, Lamarca presented a plan that involved a dramatic public exit from his barracks with a significant number of arms, ammunition, and explosives that would supply the VPR with sufficient firepower to mount a rural guerrilla offensive. The VPR considered coordinating his action with attacks on strategic army sites and radio communications in the city. Three days before the planned event, however, the army discovered preparations, forcing the VPR to abort their original idea and help Lamarca and Darcy Rodrigues evacuate the Quitaúna barracks along with Corporal José Mariani and Private Roberto Zariato. They absconded with sixty-three rifles, three light machine guns, and ammunition, but managed to take much less than they had originally planned. As a precautionary measure, Lamarca and Rodrigues had previously arranged to have their wives and children sent to Cuba for their safety. Lamarca then spent the following months moving from *aparelho* to *aparelho* to avoid arrest. He quickly became a symbolic figure representing the

FIGURE 7.1 Captain Carlos Lamarca giving arms training to bank employees.
COURTESY OF THE ACERVO ICONOGRÁFICO.

possibility of dissension within the armed forces that might be sympathetic to the guerrilla strategy.¹⁵

Although VPR militants considered Lamarca's recruitment a sign of their political success and the growing strength of the revolutionary movement, it is important to keep in mind that there were probably no more than five thousand militants and several thousand additional close supporters in the dozen or so groups engaged in armed struggle that operated in Brazil in the 1960s and early 1970s.¹⁶ One of the largest at the time was National Liberating Action (ALN). In 1967, Carlos Marighella, a historic PCB leader, left that organization and secretly traveled to Cuba to attend a meeting of the Organization of Latin American Solidarity. He then clandestinely returned to Brazil to found the ALN.¹⁷ Marighella recruited other PCB militants, especially from the state of São Paulo, along with students and intellectuals who had been energized by the Cuban Revolution and had criticized what they considered to be the cautious policies of the PCB toward the military regime.

On numerous occasions these different groups engaged in joint actions and collaboration that seemed to suggest the possibility of greater unity, if not mergers, but that was not easy. When Lamarca fled his regiment, for example, the VPR didn't have the capacity to store the arms and ammunition that he had taken with him and asked for the ALN's help. After Lamarca was successfully hidden, the VPR requested that the material be returned. The ALN countered that it would return only a portion of the arms, and a dispute between the two organizations resulted in the suspension of any close cooperation for over a year. At the same time that relations soured between the two largest revolutionary organizations in São Paulo, the VPR was reeling from a wave of arrests. These two factors pushed its leadership to accelerate the proposed merger with ex-COLINA. Similarly, Daniel and the other ex-COLINA leaders were sorely aware of their weaknesses and therefore were eager to negotiate with the VPR. Unification seemed the perfect strategy to draw both groups out of their crises.

In April 1969, VPR organized a Congress in a rented house on the coast of the state of São Paulo in which the organization set up three armed tactical units and voted to deepen its conversations with ex-COLINA about unification. Less than two months later, representatives of VPR and ex-COLINA met again along the Paulista coast and issued a "joint report" that described the "perfect political agreement of the two groups" and called for another meeting at the end of the month to formalize a fusion that would subsequently be ratified in a Congress. The follow-up meeting, known as the Fusion Conference, was held in two subsequent gatherings, at the end of June and in early July, but only the key cadre of the two organizations attended, making the meeting in reality a summit of the two leadership bodies.[18]

The merger agreement included adopting a new name. Several proposals were considered: VPR; Revolutionary Armed Vanguard—Palmares; Revolutionary Socialist Organization; and Revolutionary Armed Vanguard—Inconfidentes.[19] The latter, proposed by Daniel, referred to the *Inconfidência Mineira*, the 1789 conspiracy organized against excessive taxation and colonial rule in the gold-mining region of Minas Gerais.[20] The group ended up choosing the name Revolutionary Armed Vanguard—Palmares (VAR-Palmares). This designation declared the new organization's overt commitment to the armed struggle and its confident affirmation that it had constituted itself as a leading guerrilla organization. According to Daniel, the Uruguayan urban guerrilla group, the National Liberation Movement, popularly known as the Tupamaros, inspired the name Palmares.[21] The Tupamaros had selected that designation to draw on traditions and myths surrounding the historical figure José Gabriel Condorcanqui, known as Tupac Amaru, an eighteenth-century Peruvian who led a rebellion against Spanish colonial authorities. VAR's secondary name, Palmares, was an allusion to a Brazilian example of popular resistance. Palmares was a seventeenth-century runaway slave community (*quilombo*) located in the backlands of the northeastern state of Alagoas that survived for almost a century.²² Palmares had become a symbol of the fight against slavery, and the name signaled a commitment to the poor and oppressed of Brazil, although the new organization never specifically addressed race or the legacies of slavery in its political propaganda.

The new VAR-Palmares governing body was composed of three former leaders of VPR: Carlos Lamarca, Antonio Espinosa, and Cláudio de Souza Ribeiro, who had been a member of the radical sailors' movement prior to the coup. Juares, Maria do Carmo, and Carlos joined the leadership from ex-COLINA. The new organization probably had three hundred or so active militants operating underground and an additional hundred or more sympathizers living legally and offering logistical support.²³

In the process of unifying the two groups into a new organization, Lamarca was assigned the responsibility for the Main Struggle Sector with the immediate task of setting up a guerrilla column in the countryside. Carlos Franklin and Antonio Espinosa took charge of the Complementary Struggles Sector that would offer logistical support in urban areas and coordinate the different groups in São Paulo, Rio de Janeiro, Rio Grande do Sul, Brasília, Minas Gerais, and Bahia. The two also headed the preparations for a unification conference of the organizations later that year.²⁴

To achieve that end, militants were dispatched to other cities to facilitate unification. Among them was Iara Iavelberg, who was sent to Rio from São Paulo. Iara had been a member of POLOP and then VPR. She had majored in psychology at the University of São Paulo after leaving an unsuccessful early marriage. Attractive and free-spirited, she was among the women within the Left who had broken with conservative taboos that restricted female sexuality and comportment. Iara had a series of affairs with student activists from different left-wing currents, and her indifference to commitments, which seemed to mirror leftist men's behavior, was considered somewhat scandalous at the time. It also marked her as a person in the forefront of the shift toward freer sexual relations among middle-class youth in the mid-1960s.²⁵

As a militant of POLOP, Iara had attended the 1967 conference that spawned the faction supporting the guerrilla movement. During the gathering she had a brief affair with Breno, who was representing the POLOP dissidents from Belo Horizonte.²⁶ For a short time, she paired up with Antonio Espinosa. She also had a fling with Ladislau Dowbor.²⁷ "Iara made comrades insecure," Espinosa recalled. "Because she was very beautiful and sought after and because she was a person who was much freer than the type of women we were used to."²⁸ Dilma Rousseff remembered her with affection: "I think she was the first feminist that I knew . . . [with] a boldness that by

FIGURE 7.2 Iara Iavelberg. COURTESY OF SAMUEL IAVELBERG.

our standards today would be somewhat timid. But at the time, it was very daring."²⁹

In the comings and goings of underground operations, Iara's path crossed Lamarca's on numerous occasions, and she soon found herself attracted to the lean and austere revolutionary captain. Lamarca held back from becoming involved because of guilt about his wife and children. For a time Iara vacillated about her feelings toward Lamarca, and on assignment in Rio she rekindled her attachment with Breno, sharing an *aparelho* with him for a month or so. However, living together didn't seem to work out. After Iara returned to São Paulo, she and Lamarca became involved. When Darcy Rodrigues found out about the relationship, he tried to convince Lamarca that it was a mistake, arguing that it would soil Lamarca's impeccable moral image and weaken his support and legitimacy among the former military men within the organization. (Many years later, Rodrigues said that he was wrong about his opposition to Lamarca's involvement with Iara.)³⁰ Lamarca ignored his warnings, and the couple remained together until their deaths in 1971.

Now that the new organization was growing in size and focusing on the rural guerrilla movement, funding became a more urgent problem. Bank robberies were both dangerous for the organization's security and logistically complicated to carry out. Moreover, they sometimes netted little money. But there seemed to be few other options. Then, a fortuitous opportunity arose. Gustavo Buarque Schiller, a supporter of ex-COLINA and an activist in the high school students' movement, informed the leadership that his aunt, Ana Benchimol Capriglione, had millions of dollars stashed away in several safes in Rio. Capriglione had been the mistress of Ademar de Barros, recently deceased, who had been governor of São Paulo from 1947 to 1951, and then again from 1963 to 1966. A phrase attributed to him—"I steal but I get things done"—captured a generalized impression that political power had greatly increased his personal wealth. According to Gustavo, his aunt kept several million dollars in a safe on the second floor of a mansion that she and Gustavo's family shared in the elegant hillside neighborhood of Santa Teresa.[31]

It took some insistence on Gustavo's part to assure the leadership of the veracity of his claim. When convinced, Juares organized an operation that mobilized fifteen militants from Rio and São Paulo. They carefully cased the house, entered during the light of day, locked up the servants in a pantry, and absconded with a safe that weighed almost half a ton. They took it to a warehouse on the outskirts of Rio, where a mechanic bored holes through the thick walls, poured in water to cool down the interior so the contents wouldn't be incinerated, and used a blowtorch to cut through the door. To their delight, the safe contained more than US$2,600,000, which would amount to approximately US$18,000,000 today. The organization now had sufficient cash to support its operations for several years.

Daniel played no direct logistical role in the operation. Removed from the action, he hid Gustavo after the robbery. Suspected of being an accomplice, the rebellious nephew had to disappear. "I brought him food, newspapers and political discussion to the *aparelho* where he spent his first days underground," Daniel recounted in his memoir.[32] The resources from the robbery greatly alleviated the financial pressures that the underground militants had been experiencing. There was now no excuse to put off the long-awaited rural guerrilla strategy.

The euphoria from the successful acquisition of so much money and the unity forged in the midyear leadership summit, however, didn't last long. As the VAR-Palmares prepared for the upcoming Congress to vote on a new program and ratify the unification, fissures began to appear. Lamarca, many of the former VPR members from the military, and a core of the leading cadre of the ex-COLINA insisted on immediately preparing rural guerrilla actions, while other former members of COLINA from Belo Horizonte, militants from São Paulo, and comrades from Porto Alegre supported a strategy that combined the armed struggle with work among the masses through an approach they called Workers' Unity.[33]

The internal debate revolved around a document prepared by Ladislau Dowbor, using the pen name Jamil. In 1968, Dowbor returned from having studied abroad in Switzerland. He had made connections with the VPR in Europe, and he had become a leader in the organization before the merger. The document that he prepared for the Congress, "The Path of the Vanguard," made several key arguments. First, it sustained the idea that Brazil was ripe for a socialist revolution. Second, the Brazilian working class was relatively small and weak in relationship to large sectors of the population that had not been fully integrated into the workforce. These marginalized people would be sympathetic to revolutionary violence against the state. Third, focusing exclusively on political organizing among the working class was secondary to emphasizing the establishment of mobile tactical units with the ability to move easily from one area to another in efforts to attack, defeat, and demoralize the military. At some point, the guerrillas' actions would win peasants' sympathy, and they would join in a generalized uprising against the regime.[34] In retrospect, it was a rather vague and optimistic blueprint for how to overthrow the dictatorship.

While no one in the organization questioned the plan to carry out an armed struggle in the countryside, disputes immediately arose about the relationship of the guerrilla movement to organizing among the urban working class. Breno, Helvício, Dilma, and others who had originally belonged to POLOP and then COLINA had attempted to organize workers in Belo Horizonte. They retained the Marxist notion that privileged grassroots work among the proletariat. Similarly Carlos Franklin, a labor lawyer, had built a small area of influence among workers in Rio Grande do Sul before going underground. Antonio Espinosa had been actively involved in the VPR's intervention in the Osasco strike in 1968 and still felt close ties with the working class of greater São Paulo. On the other hand, most of the former military in the VPR, including Lamarca and Rodrigues, shunned lengthy political discussions and were anxious for the organization to commit itself once and for all to implement the guerrilla strategy. Daniel, Maria do Carmo, Juares, and Inês from COLINA, along with former student activists such as Chuzuo Osawa (known as Mário Japa) and Iara Iavelberg, among many others from VPR, were also impatient to implement the rural guerrilla effort.

The unification conference took place in September 1969 in a large isolated house in Teresópolis, near Rio. Espinosa recalled that "the Congress lasted 26 days—it was supposed to last a week—because there was distrust in the air."[35] Twenty-seven delegates and ten people involved in support and logistics spent the month together, as tensions mounted during lengthy meetings that extended into the night.[36]

Early in the proceedings, the gathering received word that two other revolutionary organizations, ALN and MR-8 (October 8th Revolutionary Movement), had abducted Charles Burke Elbrick, the U.S. ambassador to Brazil. The MR-8, largely based in Rio and named after the date that Che Guevara had been killed in Bolivia in 1967, initiated the idea. In exchange for freeing the ambassador, the two groups demanded the release of fifteen political prisoners, including two who had been important members of the VPR: José Ibrahim, the president of the Osasco Metallurgical Union during the 1968 wildcat strike, and Onofre Pinto, formerly of MNR and who had been a leader of VPR.

The abduction caught the Brazilian government by surprise. By coincidence, the second dictatorial president, General Artur Costa e Silva, suffered a debilitating stroke on the eve of the action. With the president incapacitated, a three-man junta of the armed forces opposed allowing Vice President Pedro Aleixo, a civilian from the ruling ARENA party, to take office because he had opposed AI-5 the year before. With the executive in flux and the Nixon administration demanding that the Brazilian government secure the ambassador's release unharmed, the three-man junta ceded to the organizations' demands, and the fifteen revolutionaries were flown to freedom in Mexico.

Needless to say, those gathered in Teresópolis were ecstatic that two of their leading members had been released through the actions of other revolutionaries. It no doubt reinforced the idea that their overall revolutionary strategy was on the right track. According to Sirkis, who was not at the clandestine Congress, the reaction among young leftists to the announcement of the dictatorship's capitulation to the revolutionaries' demands was as jubilant as if Brazil had won a soccer championship.[37] Still, it is hard to gauge the actual popular support that the revolutionaries from the ALN and the MR-8 garnered for such an audacious action although it seems possible that some ordinary citizens were amazed that the ambassador from the apparently all-powerful U.S. government could be so easily taken by a band of young people with claims to idealism.

Whereas the release of fifteen political prisoners might have received some ephemeral rooting for the rebels, in Teresópolis it soon became clear that an unresolvable polarization existed within VAR-Palmares. On one side were former members of the armed forces—Carlos Lamarca, Cláudio de

Souza Ribeiro, Darcy Rodrigues, José Raimundo da Costa, and José Araújo de Nóbrega—who were joined by other historic militants from ex-VPR, such as Chuzuo Osawa and a student activist named Celso Lungaretti. They were eager to initiate rural guerrilla activities immediately. Others wanted to combine the armed struggle with labor organizing. Antonio Espinosa, who agreed with this orientation, recalled that Mário Japa (Chuzuo Osawa) had said, "If they want to do all of this with the labor movement, there won't be any militants left over to organize a guerrilla column."[38] Rodrigues reconstructed Lamarca's words: "Everyone believes in the armed struggle. Let VAR do mass movement work, and I doubt they will be able to. We're going to carry out the guerrilla struggle."[39] To consolidate support for their position, Lamarca and the others formed what was called the Group of Seven. On the other side of the schism, now in full motion, were some other important historic leaders and militants of COLINA, such as Breno and Dilma, who were joined by Carlos Franklin and Antonio Espinosa in defending the importance of ongoing political activities within the working class, although they did not deny the importance of the armed struggle.[40]

After tense discussions almost degenerated into violence, the Group of Seven broke with the majority of delegates and left the Congress. Maria do Carmo, Juares, Daniel, and Wellington Moreira Diniz, also a former militant of COLINA, tried to find a middle ground between the two groups, but after leaving the site, they held conversations with Rodrigues and decided to join the Group of Seven, along with Liszt Vieira, a militant from Rio working underground in Porto Alegre.[41] Apolo Lisboa and his wife, Carmem, disagreed with both factions about the nature of the guerrilla strategy and ended up forming the VAR (Palmares) Dissidence, or DVP.[42] What had started as such a promising effort to forge unity in the revolutionary Left ended as a dismal failure with dire consequences.

Soon after the Congress, the two major sides in the split held a meeting in Rio to negotiate the division of money and arms between VAR-Palmares and the Group of Seven plus Five. Unable to come to an agreement, the two factions went their separate ways, each keeping the resources they controlled at the moment. Dilma remembered Daniel's last words as he left Teresópolis: "Don't do it. You're going to end up a political professional. Stay with us."[43] She ignored his plea, and each went on to rebuild their separate organizations. As soon as the Congress was over, the battle to gain the allegiance of the rank-and-file militants began.

For rank-and-file militants, the decision about whether to continue in the VAR-Palmares or instead to join those who had broken with the organization was not easy. Sônia LaFoz had participated in the PCB while a student at the University of São Paulo and had then joined VPR in 1968. The daughter of a French World War II resistance fighter, she was trained in firearms and was soon recruited to the armed actions group, despite initial resistance from Rodrigues, who objected to the participation of women in these special units. When approached by both sides within VAR-Palmares, she was living in Rio. She remembered how hard it was to understand the nature of the rupture and why it had happened. She finally decided to join the reconstituted VPR.[44] Vieira chose to leave with Maria do Carmo, largely for personal reasons: "My friends were all there, and I wasn't going to be on the other side. . . . Moreover, at the time we didn't have the slightest chance to organize the working class in the cities."[45]

If the issue was difficult for seasoned revolutionaries, it seemed even more complicated for younger student supporters who had less political experience. Soon after the Congress concluded, Minc was arrested. He had been responsible for carrying out political discussions with the radicalized student core close to the VAR-Palmares in Rio de Janeiro. His detention was traumatic news for the young militants who were considering their political options and knew that his arrest inevitably meant that he would be tortured.[46] After Minc's arrest, Dowbor was assigned to meet with the group of high school students to convince them to choose the splinter group. Sirkis recalls that Minc's detention and subsequent torture and the discussions with Dowbor made it very clear that joining the VAR was serious business.[47] Polari was eager to participate in one of the armed tactical groups, as the small squads of revolutionaries involved in bank robberies were now called. Sirkis, however, had serious reservations. "I tended to agree more with the people [who stayed in the VAR]. . . . The problem was that our icons were in the other group. I was fascinated by the idea of being in Lamarca's organization, which we thought was prepared to carry out big actions. We ended up being more closely aligned with Lamarca's group because we thought it was more serious about the armed struggle, whereas the tendency of the VAR was to retreat and become reformist at some point."[48] Paulo Brandi opted to become an active supporter of the new organization. As far as he was concerned, "It was the group most willing to engage in confrontation, to fight."[49] However, most of the student activists involved in the restricted protest movements of 1969 declined to join the armed struggle. The news that an ALN leader, Carlos Marighella, had been killed in a police ambush in São Paulo on November 4, 1969, no doubt shook the morale of militants and supporters alike.[50]

By mid-November, the battle for the loyalty of the rank and file had ended, as people had chosen sides, and the group, which assumed the name

VPR, had managed to gather around it approximately one hundred or so militants plus several dozen additional supporters. With a cascading string of arrests and the additional loss of a number of demoralized members who left the organization, the VAR-Palmares probably had a similar number in its ranks.

Soon after the Teresópolis conference, Lamarca began training with several militants on rural property that the organization had purchased in August in the state of São Paulo. He therefore was not present in Rio in early November when the group held a congress and officially reconstituted the VPR. The body chose Lamarca to be one of three members of a new national command, along with Maria do Carmo and Ladislau Dowbor. Recounting those moments, Maria do Carmo stated that she very reluctantly assumed leadership in the organization. Dowbor argued that her organizational skills made her invaluable and that she could rely on Juares and others for logistical support.[51] She recalled that she had tremendous doubts about continuing the guerrilla struggle and shared her reservations with Daniel, as well as with Iara. But leaving the organization meant separating from her husband and her closest friends, so she decided to remain.[52] (Given the fortunes of the armed Left, it is perhaps surprising that there were not more of this type of crisis of faith.) Whether Daniel himself shared her misgivings about continuing in the guerrilla movement or merely listened empathetically to Maria do Carmo's confession of profound ambivalence is unclear. His self-critical memoir about his revolutionary experiences doesn't indicate that he experienced those doubts in 1969 or 1970.

As they had insisted in the Congress of Teresópolis, the new leadership of the reconstituted VPR prioritized immediate measures to implement their guerrilla strategy. Mário Japa secretly went abroad to explore possibilities of guerrilla training in Algeria, and Maria do Carmo was charged with searching for appropriate areas for a mobile tactical unit of guerrilla fighters somewhere in the southern part of Brazil.[53] The organization set up a rural command under Lamarca's guidance, while the VPR continued to operate in the cities with an Intelligence Sector and units in charge of expropriations and other armed actions. Dowbor was assigned to lead VPR's work in São Paulo, and therefore Daniel took over his responsibilities among their young student recruits and supporters in Rio.

The last time that Brandi saw Daniel during this period was sometime in late December 1969 or early January 1970. It was a farewell conversation filled with emotion and excitement. Daniel had informed him: "I'm going to do something very serious, which we have all dreamed about: the struggle in the countryside." Paulo recalled the scene: "We knew that he was going to the countryside. . . . Daniel told us that he had ordered a pair of glasses that would stand up in war. This I remember. He appeared with different glasses." Perhaps in a slightly boastful tone, Daniel also commented to Paulo about a backpack that he was carrying. "It might not look like it, but I have an amount of money, a large amount," Daniel is said to have commented. Paulo continued reconstructing the moment: "I don't remember the amount, but it was a lot. And he walked around calmly with that backpack and the money that he had to transport."[54]

Sirkis was more precise in pinpointing the date of his last meeting with Daniel. He had met Sirkis and Polari on New Year's Eve. Daniel informed the starry-eyed young revolutionaries that he had been assigned to go to the countryside for guerrilla training under the leadership of none other than Lamarca. Sirkis remembers that Daniel's face was aglow as he purportedly said, "I know that the average life of a rural guerrilla is less than a year, in addition to the fact that I am not the most able person for this kind of thing. But I'm not worried. I don't feel the least bit afraid."[55] (As the literary reconstruction of a conversation that had occurred years earlier, Sirkis's recounting of the dialogue is unlikely to be entirely accurate. The tone of the retelling is excessively heroic, but it probably captures the sentiment that Daniel felt at the moment.)

As might be expected, Polari has different recollections of that New Year's Eve departure. Daniel was hidden in the maid's room in the apartment of a supporter because he had no other place to live. When the end-of-the-year festivities began, security rules were broken, and Daniel was invited to join the party. As Polari describes the scene, Daniel, clad only in red Zorba underwear, eyes sparkling, toasted the group with a glass of champagne and predicted a glorious revolutionary future.[56]

8

To the Countryside!

(1970)

> He was very intelligent, but discreet in personal relations. He was talkative, but in meeting he preferred to remain in the rearguard.
>
> — DARCY RODRIGUES

Why Daniel was among those selected to join the guerrilla-training camp in the Vale do Ribeira (Ribeira Valley) in early 1970 still remains a mystery. It certainly wasn't because of his physical prowess. Darcy Rodrigues, one of the subcommanders of the operation, considered that Daniel's pedagogical skills and his mastery of Marxist theory earned him the job, for the operation was designed to offer both political and military training. His medical knowledge also may have been a consideration.[1] Daniel was immensely proud and honored for having been among the eighteen people that joined Comandante Carlos Lamarca in the first contingent of rural guerrilla trainees.

All of the different left-wing organizations to which Daniel belonged had tried to implement the rural guerrilla strategy. Throughout 1968, Breno traveled to distant parts seeking the ideal place for a guerrilla base.[2] While police were dismantling COLINA, he was investigating a site near the Araguaia River, where, unbeknownst to him, the pro-Chinese Communist Party of Brazil was establishing its rural guerrilla activities.[3] A VPR leader named Onofre Pinto had, in part, seduced Lamarca into abandoning military service with optimistic projections of Amazonian possibilities.[4] Ladislau Dowbor also traveled to central and northeast Brazil seeking sites to launch a guerrilla initiative, with little luck in finding a suitable area.[5] Soon after the split with VAR-Palmares, Maria do Carmo took on the assignment, hiring a plane to take aerial photographs of the region along the Argentine border to look for areas that could potentially protect guerrilla fighters.[6] Although today it might seem to have been a failed strategy from the start, given the revolutionary Left's relative weakness and the military's strength, the Cuban Revolution and the ongoing resistance of the Vietnamese to U.S. intervention in Southeast Asia seemed to validate the potential of rural guerrilla warfare to topple the dictatorship.

Thus, establishing a training camp in southern São Paulo near the coast and the border of the state of Paraná was considered an important step in putting the strategy into practice after so many delays. The site was close enough to São Paulo to receive logistical support. The thick vegetation and relative isolation in the state's poorest region theoretically protected trainees from government detection.[7] With a population of two hundred thousand, the area was sparsely inhabited, and the poor local residents were accustomed to seeing hunters comb the hilly backlands. Had a guerrilla-training unit been spotted trekking through the forest, the region's inhabitants might easily have mistaken it for São Paulo vacationers on a weekend hunting trip. Alternatively, the country folk might presume that a cluster of young men was looking for food for their families.

The training camp was conceived of as a place to prepare the first cadre that would then train dozens, and then hundreds, to form the core of a revolutionary army.[8] The operation was also understood as an opportunity for future leaders to engage in political education, as the underground nature of the organization made it difficult to carry out systematic ongoing group discussions in the cities.

Prior to the split in VAR-Palmares, members of the former VPR had already taken steps to establish some sort of military base there. Using a false name, Celso Lungaretti, a young militant from São Paulo, purchased 240 acres.[9] After the VPR was reconstituted in late 1969, Lamarca, Lungaretti, and three others explored the area and began military training.[10] In fact, Lamarca insisted on being there rather than in Rio during the November VPR Congress.[11] Maria do Carmo and Ladislau then traveled to Ribeira to convince him to become part of the leadership. They spent Christmas 1969 inspecting the area and deciding who would be among the first contingent to participate in the training.[12]

After exploring more closely the land that they had purchased, Lamarca deemed that it was too close to Route 116, which cut through the valley, and decided to seek a better location. He surveyed the region and chose another plot of land twice the size. It was more remote and inaccessible and therefore more secure. It also happened to be owned by the same person who had sold Lungaretti the first property. Without considering the potential security risk related to the fact that the two plots were linked through their former owner, another militant bought the land. Lamarca moved some of the first trainees to the second location, leading militants to assume that the first area had been entirely dismantled.

Because the operation sought to prepare future fighters rather than politicize the region's inhabitants, discretion was a priority.[13] Tercina Dias de Oliveira, the mother of a militant, agreed to occupy a small shack-like house at the property's entrance and lived there with an adopted child and three grandchildren. The simple dwelling served as the communication center and the supply base for two encampments that Lamarca set up deep within the property. Tercina also sewed clothes for the trainees that could withstand the wear and tear of hiking through the thick undergrowth. From a humble background, she easily blended into their surroundings as yet another poor person trying to eke out an existence on the land. Lamarca also arranged for José Lavecchia, a former PCB militant in his early fifties, to live in a small hut nearby and serve as a liaison with two base camps. A radio transmitter provided ongoing communication.[14]

As the New Year began, the trainees started to arrive in groups of two. First volunteers from São Paulo, then Rio de Grande do Sul, and finally Daniel, Darcy Rodrigues, and others from Rio, who showed up in late February.[15] Roberto Menkes remembered his instructions: "They gave us a detailed list of essential purchases: two thick, dark-colored, long-sleeved shirts, blue jeans, high leather boots, a cap, a canteen, and other utensils."[16]

Reaching the region was complicated, as the VPR imposed strict security procedures so that no one would actually know the location. Participants were told to meet at an assigned place in São Paulo. Daniel described what happened next: "I was placed in a jeep, lying down and blindfolded, as we traveled for several hours."[17] The trainees were not allowed to see regional maps, as the site was for ongoing secret training of successive teams of revolutionaries. It was essential that people could not identify the location, should they at some point be arrested and tortured.

Lamarca, acting as overall commander, named the entire training operation Carlos Marighella, in honor of the ALN leader who had been killed by police in November 1969. The gesture suggested the unity of the revolutionary Left. The eighteen volunteers were then divided into two units that settled into base camps two hundred yards from each other. Forest completely separated the two locations.

The first encampment was named for Eremias Delizoikov, a São Paulo high school student, who had been killed by the police the previous month.[18] This unit, led by Yoshitame Fujimore, an electrical technician who joined the VPR in early 1968, included Ariston de Oliveira Lucena, at age seventeen the youngest member of the training camp; Edmauro Gopfert, who had been a member of the original VPR; Carmen Monteiro Jacomoni, who joined the VPR in São Paulo; her partner, Roberto Menkes, who had been arrested in the clandestine National Student Union congress in October 1968; Diógenes Sobrosa de Souza from Rio Grande do Sul; José Araújo Nóbrega, a former army sergeant who had adhered to the VPR along with Lamarca; and Ubiratan de Souza, previously a student activist.[19]

The second base was named to remember Carlos Roberto Zanirato, who left the army to join VPR along with Lamarca in January 1969 and had been assassinated while under arrest several months later.[20] Headed by Rodrigues, Lamarca's closest ally in the army, Daniel was assigned to this unit, along with Iara Iavelberg. It also included Antenor Machado dos Santos and Delci Fensterseifer who had been a part of Carlos Franklin's group in Rio Grande do Sul; Gilberto Faria Lima; José Lavecchia; Mário Bejar Revollo, a Bolivian and the only non-Brazilian member of the training force; and Valneri Neves Antunes, a former soldier. In order to symbolize the unity of the revolutionary Left, two of the trainees were invited from other organizations: Revollo, who had lived in Rio for five years and had been a supporter of VAR-Palmares before joining the dissident group led by Apolo Lisboa, and Gilberto Faria Lima, from Democratic Resistance (REDE), a group that had split from VPR in 1970 when it decided to merge with ex-COLINA to form VAR-Palmares.

As indicated, two women were among the eighteen: Iara Iavelberg and Carmen Jacomoni. Iara had insisted on joining Lamarca in the training camp. Although there were reservations about her fitness for guerrilla activities, Lamarca defended her participation. Carmen, who had been an accomplished actress, joined VPR in 1969 and participated in at least one armed action before being selected for more training. Both Iara and Carmen received cursory first-aid instruction, which seemed to justify their participation and silenced those who didn't think that women were fit for rigorous guerrilla activities, even though there were at least two other precedents in the VPR for allowing women into guerrilla-training units. Maria José Nahas had participated in COLINA's expropriations unit, and Sônia LaFoz, a member of VPR and an excellent sharpshooter, was active in armed actions in São Paulo.[21]

Veterans of the training remembered that the landscape was majestic and the experience unique. Rodrigues described the region: "It was a different situation, living in the midst of beautiful scenery of forests and rivers, prodigiously gifted by nature, with a river with many waterfalls and another higher river that gave the landscape a special color."[22] Carmen Jacomoni named the area Patropi, a contraction of the words *país* (country) and tropical. Those idyllic portraits, however, obscure the harsher aspects of living in this rugged terrain. Mosquitos infested the area and left everyone's faces swollen with bite marks. It was cold and humid; sanitary facilities were minimal; and most didn't bathe enough. They wore the same clothes day and night.[23] Meals were monotonous and many times tasteless.[24]

Yet it was still a special place for Daniel. After three years of reading about Debray's theories of revolution, abandoning his medical career, and living precariously underground, he had finally fulfilled a dream. A decade later he reminisced: "Ribeira: there I was happy, completely. The world was green and the future was good. After much waiting, the revolution started to take form for me, in the density of that forest where I arrived with so much enthusiasm, willing to confront all of my hesitations, and embrace what the struggle had to offer."[25]

Daniel and the others quickly settled into the camp, although Iara, who had arrived a few days before Daniel, commented to him on how difficult it was for her to adjust to the noisy night sounds of insects, birds, and other animals.[26] For both, this foray into nature was the first time they had lived in the wilderness.

As part of equipping the training site, Rodrigues had obtained specialized nylon hammocks with mosquito nettings.[27] Rodrigues's hammock was hung close to the entrance of the encampment, near those of Lamarca, Iara, and Daniel. The rest slept further back in the forest, away from the river and more protected from any possible assault. This also gave Iara and Lamarca a bit of privacy, although Rodrigues insists that they were very discreet and never showed any affection publicly.[28]

The volunteers took turns doing guard duty at night and preparing meals. For the morning repast this meant making a fire in a dugout lined with stones while it was still dark. Small pieces of bamboo fashioned into tiny chimneys mixed the rising smoke with the natural mist that emanated from the forest floor as the sun rose. The dissipation of smoke prevented anyone from noticing their presence.[29] When it was their turn, Iara and Daniel were a cooking team. Daniel lit the morning fire, and Iara did the cooking, as Daniel readily admitted that he had no vocation for preparing food.[30] The morning meal usually consisted of rice and beans mixed with game hunted in the region, and heart of palm. It was meant to be hearty fare to sustain the trainees during rigorous daily activities.[31]

Then the entire group of eighteen gathered for basic military training led by Lamarca and Rodrigues. This included assembling and disassembling arms, receiving instruction in the theories of guerrilla warfare, and learning combat techniques. A light lunch of instant coffee, cooked manioc, or fruit was followed by afternoon activity: marching through the backlands, learning how to find their way in the Atlantic rain forest, and perfecting their shooting skills. They enjoyed another heavy meal at dusk, when smoke couldn't be detected, and then usually relaxed around a campfire.

The group conducted an evening session of criticism and self-criticism at least once a week. They also enjoyed playing charades, engaging in playful teasing, and recounting past exploits.[32] Daniel also perfected his literary skills by firelight as he composed letters to friends that he could not send and jotted down secret reflections. He then burned his writings in the fire.[33] On the weekends, when hunters meandered through the area, the trainees stayed close to the camp, with guards posted to look out for unwelcome visitors. During the day they carried out political discussions based on books and documents, including some Marxist standards. Daniel and Iara usually conducted those classes.

For personal reading, Daniel kept a copy of João Guimarães Rosa's masterpiece *Grande sertão veredas* in his backpack. The acclaimed novel, set in the dry backlands of northern Minas Gerais in the early twentieth century, probably comforted him in his intimate loneliness. The title refers to *veredas*, small pathways that crisscross the semiarid and immense *sertão* (dry backlands). Within the complex story about rural bandits and their henchmen, Riobaldo, the narrator, tells an anonymous listener from the city about his life as a former mercenary bandit (*jagunço*). In one subplot, young Riobaldo becomes close to Diadorim, another *jagunço*, who is ambiguously gendered and "who doesn't fornicate with women." Over time, Riobaldo develops a passionate relationship with Diadorim. "But I loved him, day by day I loved him more. Perhaps you will say it is a kind of spell. That's it. It was like a spell. Let him be near me and I lacked for nothing. Let him frown or look bad, and I would lose my peace of mind. Let him be far from me, and I thought only of him."[34] (Even though in the novel Diadorim ends up being a woman dressed as a man, the "queerness" of the novel must have intrigued Daniel.) Among the writings that he burned in the campfire were letters written to characters in the book, who had become his imaginary friends. Perhaps the homoerotic subtext of the plot inspired him to daydream about falling in love with a fictitious *jagunço* or writing to a fantasy epistolary confidant.

While Daniel managed to repress his desires, or at least not act on them, it was certainly hard for other members of the group to deal with their sexual needs. Carmen Jacomoni and Roberto Menkes were a recognized couple, and no one seemed to comment on their being together in the training camp although they refrained from any overt expressions of affection and managed only one furtive sexual liaison while in Ribeira.[35] Lamarca and Iara, for their part, also avoided any public appearances of intimacy, but even so the couple's relationship provoked dissatisfaction among members of the group.[36] As Rodrigues reconstructed the situation, Delci Fensterseifer complained to him about Iara's presence: "'There's privilege here. Why did Lamarca bring Iara?' And I went to talk to Lamarca, 'Look, there's discontent about the presence of Iara, and I agree with it because this is not the place to maintain couples, is it?'" However, as commander of the operation, Lamarca overruled his objection.

Fensterseifer's dissatisfaction about Iara implied a larger criticism about favoritism within the revolutionary hierarchy, which allowed the commander to have a companion while others could not. Frustrations about sex arose in another context as well. At some point during the two months Daniel was in the encampment, several members prepared a document articulating political disagreements and a desire to break with the VPR. It must have been an unnerving moment for Daniel, who was so convinced about the mission. As he later described the scene, the group gathered to discuss the document. Finally Daniel asked to speak, and proceeded to dismantle the critics' arguments one by one. He suggested the real problem of those wanting to split was personal. After his intervention, he reported that the discussion's tone changed. A lengthy give and take ensued, and the crisis dissipated. After the meeting ended, one of the document's proponents asked to speak with Daniel privately. He confessed that he, indeed, was having personal problems in the guerrilla training, because he missed being with a woman.[37]

In reflecting on the event, Daniel wrote that he himself had *not* experienced a personal crisis while in Ribeira, because he understood his celibacy was part and parcel of his revolutionary commitment. "I felt as we all should have felt, that the lack of sex was a necessity of the struggle, as were the discomforts that we experienced, the scarcity of food, for example. For me the repression existed in the cities, because the lack of sexual relations wasn't a condition of the struggle. It was a silence. An exile. . . . I wasn't a homosexual militant. I was an exiled homosexual."[38]

Yet even in this exile, Daniel had difficulty in entirely repressing some manifestations of his homosexuality. When I asked Rodrigues whether he suspected that Daniel was gay when they were in Ribeira, he said he had assumed so because of Daniel's somewhat effeminate mannerisms and a specific joke Daniel once told him. "There was a guy—at the time you didn't say homosexual or *bicha*; it was *viado*. A *viado* was under a bridge with Jorge. I remember it vaguely. When a policeman arrives and says, 'What are you doing there?' Jorge answers, 'Is this your bridge? Is this asshole yours? Then what business is it of yours?'"[39] Alfredo Sirkis remembers Daniel telling the same joke about Jorge and the *viado* a year later when they were holed up together during the abduction of the Swiss ambassador. Reflecting back on those times, Sirkis understood it as a pejorative joke about gays.[40] Daniel offered a much more colorful and detailed rendition of the same joke with extensive commentary in his book *Jacarés e lobisomens*, which came out in 1983.[41] It was obviously something that Daniel considered humorous and enjoyed repeating. Sirkis thought that the joke was a way for Daniel to deflect any insinuation about his own homosexuality. By telling risqué faggot jokes, and Sirkis remembered Daniel told many, he seemed to be affirming his heterosexuality. Darcy interpreted the telling of the humorous tale as a sign that Daniel was gay—a *viado* telling a joke about a *viado*.[42] One could also understand Daniel's jokes as a subconscious wish to reveal his most closely held secret or, contradictorily, to affirm that Jorge's and his own sexual desires and/or practices were nobody's business.

While Daniel and others coped with everyday sacrifices associated with the training program, the VPR faced a serious crisis. In late February 1970, less than a week after the last trainee arrived, Shizuo Osawa (Mário Japa) was in a car accident. He had recently arrived from an assignment seeking support for guerrilla training abroad. Returning from a late-night meeting, he fell asleep at the wheel and crashed his car. A policeman who came to his assistance found revolutionary literature and arms. He was immediately taken to the political police headquarters (DEOPS) in downtown São Paulo, where Sérgio Fleury, notorious for his treatment of political prisoners, interrogated him. Osawa underwent two days of torture. However, those in charge of Operação Bandeirantes (OBAN), a new state entity designed to more effectively extract information from antigovernment activists, learned of his arrest, and a dispute between the two agencies ensued. Under threats to invade the DEOPS headquarters, Fleury ceded to OBAN's demands and turned Osawa over. He was tortured for two more days and then held at the military hospital.[43]

When the VPR leadership heard about Osawa's arrest, they panicked, because he had been at the Ribeira training site. Fearful that he might reveal information that would lead authorities to the encampment, the organization decided to abduct a prominent person in order to obtain Osawa's release. After discarding the notions of capturing a military leader or a U.S. businessman, they settled on the Japanese consul in São Paulo.[44] Lacking sufficient firepower and the backup to carry out the operation alone, they recruited two other small revolutionary organizations—REDE and Tiradentes Revolutionary Movement (MRT) to help carry out the abduction, which took place on March 11, 1970.

Picked up on the way home from the consulate, Nobuo Okushi was taken to an *aparelho*. The VPR then insisted on the release of five political prisoners, including Mário Japa. (They had to refer to him by his code name because no one knew his real one.) Within twenty-four hours five political prisoners, along with the three children of one prisoner, were flown to Mexico in exchange for the safe return of the Japanese consul.[45]

As soon as Osawa and the other released prisoners had safely arrived in Mexico, the organization sent an envoy there to find out whether he had revealed information about the VPR's activities in Ribeira. He had not, so Lamarca continued training operations. In mid-April, Iara, who had become seriously ill, was evacuated from the region to an *aparelho* located in the nearby coastal town of Peruíbe. Joining her was Tercina Dias de Oliveira, who was to serve as the public cover for the house.[46] Several days later, Lamarca held a meeting there with the VPR's leading cadre to discuss, among other issues, the future of the training operations. In recent days other militants had been arrested, and the leadership was concerned about the ongoing security of the location. They decided that, after the first group's training ended at midyear, they would abandon the site and find another location.[47]

The day after Juares and Maria do Carmo returned to Rio de Janeiro from the meeting in Peruíbe, Celso Lungaretti and several other members of the organization were arrested in Rio. Under torture, Lungaretti revealed information about the first training camp on the property that he had purchased for the organization. He assumed that because the encampment had been dismantled, the information he provided would temporarily free him from electric-shock torture while the police verified his statement. He didn't realize that the leadership had decided to buy another plot of land through the same owner.⁴⁸ The Army Intelligence Center immediately transmitted the information to the Second Army in São Paulo, which dispatched teams from the Second Battalion Army Police to the Ribeira Valley. There they arrested the man involved in the land sale. During interrogation, the authorities learned that there had been a second land transaction, and so the Second Army dispatched another group to confirm the existence of a guerrilla operation. By chance, Lamarca was in a small town near their training site when he saw the intense movement of troops in the region. The following day, Lamarca ordered the camp dismantled.⁴⁹

While the military police were verifying information about the first training site, Juares and Maria do Carmo were trying to salvage the organization in Rio. The two drove to a *ponto* with Wellington Moreira Diniz, although they suspected that the militant might already have been detained. Realizing that the police had brought Wellington to the *ponto* to ambush them, Juares and Maria do Carmo attempted to rescue their comrade. Their effort failed, and the police closed in. Having made a suicide pact with Maria do Carmo, Juares shot himself in the head. Maria do Carmo was unable to follow through with the agreement and was arrested. Under torture, she confirmed Lungaretti's statements about the first land purchase.⁵⁰ A cascade of arrests followed, touching dozens of members, including Dowbor, Vieira, and other key VPR members.

Meanwhile, in Ribeira, Daniel accompanied Lamarca on a reconnaissance mission to see to what extent the army had penetrated the region. Suddenly helicopters hovered overhead, and Lamarca instructed Daniel to prepare to shoot at their gas tanks to bring them down. Not noticing the two on the ground, the helicopter pilots moved on. Lamarca realized that the army would soon be upon them and instructed eight members of the group to leave immediately. They departed on April 20, two-by-two in ten-minute intervals, still wearing their rough and odorous country clothes. Daniel and Revollo, the Bolivian volunteer, left in the first group, followed by Roberto Menkes and Carmen Jacomoni. The other four slipped off quickly thereafter.⁵¹

As Daniel described the incident in his memoir, the exit from the region was much simpler than they had imagined. "We chose the easiest way out. Peacefully, like all other inhabitants of the nearby towns, we hailed the interstate bus and left. The driver gave no sign that what we did was unusual. At the time, our faces, marked with insect bites, had lost their urban look. After months of hiking, our clothes were tattered and smelled bad. We looked like peasants visiting the big city."⁵² On route, numerous military vehicles filled with soldiers passed by the bus without bothering to stop it.

Had they done so, Daniel wrote, they would have met resistance since the fleeing guerrillas were armed. "The army believed that the guerrillas were implanted in the area and would fight them. That's why they weren't worried about people traveling around them," he wrote.

While the first eight members of the training group managed to get out safely, the remaining eight comrades followed Lamarca into the forest with the intention of remaining in the region to outmaneuver and outlast the army occupation.[53] That same day, the Second Army located the encampments. In the abandoned palm frond–covered huts they found provisions—canned milk, chocolate bars, oil, rice, and beans—that Lamarca and his followers had not carried off in backpacks as they quickly left.

As it turned out, the region had indeed been a good site for the training camp. According to a report prepared by the Second Army after a relatively unsuccessful search-and-destroy mission against the guerrillas' endeavor, "observation from land and air is extremely difficult, which facilitates hiding in the forest."[54] The report noted that the abundance of banana and palmito plants offered sustenance to the guerrillas, and the rugged terrain crisscrossed with streams hampered army maneuvers to track them down.

The government attempted to control news of the army's occupation of the region, which they called Operation Registro. However, the *Jornal do Brasil* managed to issue one story, which reported that the Brazilian army had dropped significant amounts of napalm in a massive drive against leftwing guerrillas, a fact that was doubted at the time but confirmed forty-four years later when a declassified army report told about the use of incendiary bombs on civilian populations.[55] How the reporters at *Jornal do Brasil* received their information is not clear, but it seems that someone leaked information obtained by captured and tortured VPR members.

Operation Registro was the largest counterinsurgency mobilization in the Second Army's history. The campaign used 2,954 men, including the Army Intelligence Center staff, infantry and Special Forces paratroopers, military police, highway officers, and the political police in their dragnet to capture the nine men remaining in the region.[56] On April 27, Rodrigues and José Lavecchia, who had become separated from the others, were picked up while trying to catch a ride on the highway. They were detained in the area for twenty days and, as was to be expected, horrendously tortured.[57] Two others, José Araújo Nobrega and Edmauro Gopfert, lost contact with the unit at night and the army also arrested them.[58]

On May 8, Lamarca and the four remaining men came into contact with a squad of soldiers. After a short battle, Lieutenant Alberto Mendes, the commanding officer, agreed to surrender under the condition that the

FIGURE 8.1 José Lavecchia (left) and Darcy Rodrigues (right), detained by the army in the Vale do Ribeira.

guerrillas not execute any of them. Lamarca promised to get immediate medical help for the wounded. In exchange, they took some of their arms and made an agreement that Mendes would help them get through an army barricade in the next town. When they got to the blockade, the guerrillas realized that they had been ambushed. Managing to escape, Lamarca took Mendes and his group as hostages. Two days later, Lamarca ordered the lieutenant's execution for having violated their agreement. He was killed with a blow to his head and buried in a shallow grave. Lamarca later justified his decision in an open letter.[59]

By now the army occupation of the region made it impossible to get any help from local peasants, and several residents informed the authorities when they saw the tattered band moving through the backlands. On May 30, Lamarca dispatched one of the group to attempt to break through the military blockade in order to get assistance from comrades in São Paulo. He hailed a bus and escaped the region. The next day, Lamarca and his three men captured an army vehicle, took the soldiers' uniforms, tied them up in the back of the truck, and then drove out of the area unharmed.[60]

Immediately after Lamarca returned to the routine of urban underground life, he gave an interview to the European press that spoke about the Ribeira experience in optimistic terms.⁶¹ He readily acknowledged that the operation was merely a training endeavor, and not the beginning of a guerrilla war. He affirmed that the VPR had set up the camp in Brazil because it didn't want to rely on foreign assistance or training, a claim not entirely accurate, given Mário Japa's recent mission to seek support in Algeria and Cuba. (It appears that Lamarca's claim was designed to undercut any nationalist criticism that the VPR's effort wasn't 100 percent Brazilian.) Lamarca estimated that the armed forces had mobilized twenty thousand soldiers in their attempt to crush the guerrilla encampment. The extremely poor training of the government troops, inadequate supplies, and disorganized communications among the forces sent to capture the guerrillas also contributed to what Lamarca deemed a success.

Lamarca made this assessment less than a month after having escaped encirclement, and it is unlikely that he had accurate information about the actual number of troops sent to capture him. An inflated estimate of his enemy's numbers strengthened the idea that the guerrillas were superior to the state. The implied David and Goliath comparison—a handful pitted against a multitude—reinforced the idea that the guerrilla project was still viable. Moreover, as Lamarca pointed out, the fact that a few members from other organizations had participated in the training camp gave credence to the promise that their effort was "a step toward diminishing the sectarianism and the differences that can be overcome through moving forward together."⁶² Lamarca also saw the experience as a vindication of the split in late September 1969 that had divided VAR-Palmares and left the reconstituted organization with fewer than two hundred militants and supporters. "Carrying out this pioneering experience in our country mainly represents the victory of a political position. And it is the practical demonstration of an awareness of the necessity of going forward with guerrilla warfare." Lamarca considered the effort a "qualitative advance" in the Left's activities, showing that there were militants capable of learning how to fight in the countryside, not as reflected in their combat successes but instead in their ability to "engage the masses in the process." Given the fact that several of the peasants that they had encountered in their exit from the region had collaborated with the occupying armed forces in turning them in, Lamarca's assessment of their successes with the local population seems overdrawn. Nevertheless, the nearly three months of training had toughened up the mostly urban recruits and allowed them to slip out of the region with few casualties and few imprisoned.

In response to a journalist's query about whether the conditions were ripe for rural guerrilla activities in Brazil, Lamarca optimistically claimed:

"Not only in Brazil but in all of Latin America." The countryside, he explained, was "where capitalist exploitation was most inhuman, where one finds the system's weakest link, where the repression is greatest against all struggles that are waged."

In spite of Lamarca's positive view of the Ribeira experience, Daniel later wrote that the VPR leadership had concluded that setting up another training area within Brazil had become a "utopian" dream. The only alternative was choosing an area to actually conduct guerrilla warfare, a place where conditions favored combat and where the revolutionary troops also could engage in political work among the populace.[63]

For their part, the government's armed forces realized that their ineptitude could not be repeated and prepared a more effective counterinsurgency plan to put down any future rural guerrilla effort. Neither the VPR nor the military knew that the pro-Chinese Communist Party of Brazil was already establishing a rural guerrilla force and was quietly transferring militants to the Araguaia region in the Amazon to do political work with the local people and train for combat against the dictatorship. When discovered in 1972, it took two years and four repressive campaigns to annihilate this guerrilla operation.[64]

When Daniel reached São Paulo in late April 1970, the first thing he did was to pick up a newspaper in the bustling downtown bus station. He still didn't fully understand the extent of the damage done to the organization.[65] Lamarca had given him a mission to perform for the VPR. He was to inform the urban leadership of the situation in Ribeira and prepare for the reception of those who had remained with Lamarca. When he managed to contact scattered members in Rio and gauge the group's strength, Daniel realized that he had two more major tasks ahead. He had to find a way to prevent VPR's total destruction and at the same time secure the release of the growing number of members who had been imprisoned and were facing torture.

9

40 + 70 = 110

(1970–1971)

Daniel was brilliant, and he knew that anything that he did, he would do well. For that reason, he was a bit arrogant, in the good sense arrogant, because he understood his intelligence.

— ZENAIDE MACHADO DE OLIVEIRA

The VPR was in shambles in late April 1970. When Daniel arrived in Rio, he had no place to stay. Juares de Brito was dead. Of the national command, both Maria do Carmo Brito and Ladislau Dowbor were in prison, and Carlos Lamarca was trying to outmaneuver the Second Army and slip through encirclement. With little money in his pocket and his face on a "Terrorists Wanted" poster, Daniel's only option was to hope he would run into a contact. Quite by chance, he encountered someone he knew.

Paulo Brandi was changing money in preparation for a trip abroad when the two met. After Juares died, Paulo told his father about his VPR connections. Extremely worried about their son's safety, his parents arranged for him to join them on a trip to Europe. Paulo was at the Copacabana Palace

Hotel changing money when he accidentally met up with Daniel. "He was lost without contacts. It was really a coincidence."[1]

Alex Polari and Alfredo Sirkis had continued to be in touch with Paulo after they went underground, calling him regularly. With the wave of VPR arrests, the two novice guerrilla fighters lost communication with other militants and thought that the organization had simply dissolved. The next time Alfredo contacted Paulo, he was shocked to learn that Daniel had escaped. Alfredo recalled: "Daniel showed up. . . . The guy had returned from the other side. We met with him in a bar; the other high school students were there . . . and he said, 'I'm letting you know that I am officially assuming the VPR command.'"[2]

What led Daniel to anoint himself the comandante of the VPR, if only provisionally? While he had been part of COLINA's leadership when it merged with the groups in Rio de Janeiro and Rio Grande do Sul in early 1969, he played a secondary role in the united organization. He had served as an emissary in the unification discussions with the original VPR, but was not a member of the leadership of VAR-Palmares prior to the September 1969 Congress, again acting in an ancillary capacity. Although a delegate to the Teresópolis Congress, both Darcy Rodrigues and Antonio Espinosa remembered that Daniel hadn't stood out in the daily debates about politics and strategies. In the first two months of the VPR's reconstitution, he had responsibility for the high school students, among other duties, and attended the new VPR's founding Congress, but he was not among the triumvirate that took the organization's helm.

Daniel's decision to confidently take on this new role as interim VPR leader was due to a combination of factors. First, he had played an important political role in Ribeira in the Marxist study sessions and the day-to-day political conversations with Lamarca.[3] Prior to being at the rural training camp, Daniel had had only cursory contact with the revolutionary captain. In the Atlantic rain forest, Daniel's admiration for Lamarca had grown. For his part, Lamarca was impressed with Daniel's intellectual prowess.[4] Since Daniel's adolescence, he had close personal relationships with a small circle of people who valued his sharp, cultured mind and acerbic humor. It is unlikely that Daniel developed that same level of friendship with Lamarca, but while training together, they became close. Later that year, Lamarca even told Daniel he considered him a son. This actually surprised Daniel, because he had not felt this paternal element in their relationship.[5] Still, when Comandante Lamarca assigned him the task of rebuilding the organization, their emotional bond and his political commitment inspired Daniel to do so with determination. The task of piecing together the organization was daunting, and more urgently he needed to get imprisoned VPR comrades released from jail.

In early 1970, the VPR had planned a highly visible abduction to obtain the freedom of a large number of political prisoners. Given the VPR's organizational strength in Rio, where many foreign embassies were located, they focused on the diplomatic corps located there. The leadership considered several targets and decided on the German ambassador. Juares had meticulously planned the action.[6] When Shizuo Ozawa unexpectedly crashed his car, the organization suspended that plan and instead abducted the Japanese consul in São Paulo, a less complicated and speedier operation. The success of the action bought time for the VPR leadership to decide the fate of the guerrilla-training camp and whether they should continue plans to kidnap other foreign diplomats. During the meeting in Peruíbe, the leadership endorsed the proposal to proceed with the abduction of the German ambassador.[7] However, after Maria do Carmo's arrest, the police invaded her apartment and found Juares's detailed blueprints for the action.[8]

The idea to go on with the action, when the authorities knew about the operation, was a bold move. Zenaide Machado de Oliveira, a key VPR operative in Rio, attributes the strategy to Daniel.[9] Zenaide's mother had been close to the PCB. When Zenaide started studying at the Fluminense Federal University in the mid-1960s, she participated in Marxist study groups, eventually joining the dissident PCB youth that supported the armed struggle. Managing to avoid arrest when her organization collapsed, Zenaide sought out Maria do Carmo, whom she knew from the student movement. She joined the VPR, in large part because it seemed politically sophisticated.[10] In May 1970, she was one of the people that Daniel tracked down to rebuild the organization.

"Daniel was a very determined person," she reminisced. "He brought people together and gave them a direction. It was his idea to kidnap the German ambassador. There was no other way to free our imprisoned comrades. They were crucial, and there was the question of lifting the spirits of those who wanted to free them. The kidnapping was the solution, and he managed to get everyone behind this idea." According to Zenaide, getting their comrades out of prison was an essential element of their moral code. "Daniel assigned us tasks. He had a tremendous capacity. He became the comandante, and he was such a small guy."[11]

It was not a particularly propitious time for the revolutionary Left. After the abduction of the U.S. ambassador in September 1969, the military's repressive forces escalated their efforts to track down and dismantle the guerrilla groups.[12] As previously noted, economic growth was becoming palpable for significant sectors of the middle classes, as well as many skilled workers, which reinforced allegiance to the regime.[13] Nationalistic propaganda campaigns created a climate overtly hostile to the revolutionary Left, and President Médici showed no intentions of revoking AI-5.[14] Moreover, Brazil was gearing up for the World Cup, which was to take place in Mexico in June 1970. Soccer fans were focused on a potential championship for the Brazilian team.

In spite of this unfavorable political climate, Daniel was determined to free his jailed comrades. As a first step, he gathered together the scattered members in Rio, now the core of the entire organization. Inês Etienne Romeu played a key role in helping him. After the split in VAR-Palmares, she was a member of the VPR regional leadership in Rio when dozens of its members were arrested in April. Just as she had done in January 1969 when COLINA was crumbling, she stepped forward to help save the organization.[15]

Lamarca arrived in São Paulo on May 31. Soon thereafter, Daniel met with him and told him of the plan to go forward with the abduction of the German ambassador. He immediately agreed. Acknowledging the VPR's logistical weaknesses, Lamarca convoked a meeting with the heads of the ALN and the MRT. The three leaders settled on a joint action and established a list of forty political prisoners. The ALN and MRT committed arms, money, and people, but the bulk of the militants involved in the kidnapping came from the VPR.[16]

On June 11, 1970, German Ambassador Ehrenfried Von Holleben left his embassy in a black Mercedes Benz with an armed bodyguard, followed by a car staffed with Federal Police security agents. Traffic was light because people were watching the World Cup soccer match between England and Czechoslovakia. As the limousine was approaching his residency, José Gradel, a former high school activist, rammed a jeep into the Mercedes Benz, while another militant sprayed the security car with bullets, wounding two Federal Police agents.[17] Simultaneously, Eduardo Leite, who led the operation, killed Irlando de Souza Régis, the police agent accompanying the ambassador. Daniel, armed with a .45 pistol, ordered the ambassador out of the limousine and into a getaway car. En route to the hideaway, the group changed vehicles and placed the ambassador in a large box to move him into the *aparelho* without alerting neighbors. He was then whisked away to a northern district of Rio. The entire action involved nine militants and took four minutes, leaving one Federal Police agent dead and two others seriously wounded.

Most memoirs written by participants in the armed struggle make little mention of the hundred or so police, soldiers, bank guards, or bystanders who were killed during these actions. "War is war" is usually the justification that former revolutionaries offer when one raises the issue of the death of government agents or innocent bystanders during operations carried out by the armed Left. They usually point to the illegality of the 1964 coup and the brutality of the military regime, including the torture of political prisoners. It is likely that Daniel saw the death of Irlando de Souza Régis as merely an unfortunate by-product of a battle between an illegitimate regime and warriors for a better and more just Brazil. Although he would later criticize many of the actions he and others committed during their involvement in the armed struggle, he never discussed these deaths explicitly.[18] This is particularly surprising, given the fact that his father and brother were part of the military police.

Rather, it seems he had one thought in mind—the action would free imprisoned comrades. News of the torture of political prisoners had circulated in Brazil since 1964.[19] It became increasingly clear that authorities systematically used it to extract information to dismantle methodically oppositional organizations. News about the practice also created a climate of terror that discouraged sympathizers from assisting underground organizations for fear of similar treatment.

With the escalation of repression in 1968 and 1969, reports of the torture of political prisoners increased within Brazil and abroad, and an international campaign developed against the Brazilian government's gross violation of human rights.[20] The fifteen political prisoners flown to Mexico after the release of the U.S. ambassador denounced their treatment in Brazilian jails. Moreover, Ângelo Pezzuti and the other political prisoners from COLINA, who had been arrested in early 1969, wrote detailed descriptions in the "Letter from Linhares," which was smuggled out of prison and distributed widely.[21] The document incontestably confirmed the veracity of allegations, which the regime insisted was merely communist propaganda, and offered sufficient evidence for Amnesty International to condemn the Brazilian government.[22]

Daniel and other members were well aware they would receive similar treatment if captured, and the thought haunted Daniel.[23] The vivid description of the treatment of Ângelo Pezzuti and other close friends was unquestionably a powerful motivation behind the action. The abduction served another equally important purpose. Releasing political prisoners and sending them abroad meant enabling the most important leaders to organize their covert return to Brazil to continue the fight. As Daniel later explained, "We considered that among them were the best, and freed they could begin to do political work abroad to improve our situation—and above all return after being well prepared."[24]

FIGURE 9.1 Political prisoners released in exchange for the freedom of the German ambassador, June 1970. COURTESY OF THE ARQUIVO NACIONAL.

The overall operation went smoothly. Two militants, Gerson Theodoro de Oliveira and Tereza Ângelo, had rented a house in a distant suburb and had developed cordial relations with neighbors, who had no idea that the German ambassador was being hidden next door. During day-to-day interactions with Von Holleben, his captors remained hooded so as not to reveal their identities. Alfredo Sirkis acted as interpreter, and Eduardo Leite wrote the communications to the government that were deposited in different places around the city. The government transmitted its responses to the revolutionaries' demands on Radio Nacional. After five days, the ambassador was released unharmed, and news agencies published a picture of the forty freed political prisoners and four children in preparation for being placed on a plane destined for Algeria.

Among the forty released prisoners were people very important to Daniel. Ângelo Pezzuti; his brother, Murilo da Silva; Maria José and Jorge Nahas; Marco Antonio Azevedo Mayer; and Mauricio Vieira Paiva all had been members of COLINA and had been arrested after the January 1969 bank robbery in which Daniel participated. Maria do Carmo Brito and Ladislau Dowbor had been members of the VPR's National Command. Five—Darcy Rodrigues, Edmauro Gopfert, José Araújo Nobrega, José Lavecchia, and Tercina Dias de Oliveira, plus Tercina's three grandchildren and an adopted child—had been in Ribeira with Daniel. All in all, twenty-seven of the forty political prisoners had been members of the O., COLINA, the original VPR, or the reconstituted VPR after the split with VAR-Palmares. The remaining thirteen belonged to five other organizations.[25] Although the VPR selected these people as a gesture of revolutionary unity, the release of its own militants was by far the main focus of the action. As in the case of the revolutionaries flown to Mexico in September 1969, the forty were stripped of their citizenship and banned from returning to Brazil.

Daniel was very proud of his role in the abduction. He once recounted to Sirkis his feelings when he ordered the German ambassador out of his car: "At that moment I felt tall, strong and handsome," he is said to have commented.[26] Writing in the third person, Daniel relayed his exhilaration when the operation was over: "Our character, leaving the action and running to his room to await news on the radio, still wasn't sure if things had gone well. When the newspapers published the photo of the forty, it would be one of the happiest days of his life."[27] Soon after the successful action, Lamarca chose Daniel and Inês Etienne to replace Maria do Carmo and Ladislau Dowbor as members of the National Command, no doubt in recognition of their efficacious rebuilding of the organization, in addition to Daniel's political talents and writing skills and Inês's organizational abilities.[28]

It is interesting to point out that unlike other revolutionary organizations, the reconstituted VPR during its short duration consistently maintained a woman among its top leadership, whether by accident or design. It is impossible to measure how this affected its internal dynamics, but one can suppose that it undercut, at least partially, the excessive emphasis on revolutionary masculinity that was pervasive throughout the radical Left. At the same time, while the VPR appeared to the world to be a strong and efficient revolutionary organization capable of obtaining the liberty of almost three times the number of political prisoners that had been exchanged for the U.S. ambassador, in fact it was headed for a deep crisis.[29]

Soon after the release of the forty political prisoners, several key participants in the Juares Guimarães Brito Combat Unit, including Sônia Lafoz, its commander, began to demand better infrastructural support. Frustrated with the leadership's inability to respond to their requests, they negotiated their transfer to MR-8, imagining that organization to be more equipped to carry out armed activities. Sônia LaFoz, José Gradel, Jesus Paredes Soto, Manoel Henrique Ferreira, and Roberto das Chagas e Silva had all been directly involved in the plot regarding the German ambassador. Roberto Menkes and Carmen Jacomoni had participated in the Ribeira training. Losing these experienced urban guerrillas was a serious blow to the organization.

Yet the new leadership seemed to weather this storm. Lamarca remained hidden in São Paulo until October and then moved with Iara Iavelberg to a secluded, primitive dwelling in Rio D'Ouro, set in a mountainous region on the road to Teresópolis. It was a secure meeting place for the National Command and allowed Iara and Lamarca to spend an extended period of time together. This location also created an opportunity that the new leadership needed to consolidate a collective praxis, which would turn out to be more difficult than they imagined. They also did not realize that a police agent had infiltrated the organization.

José Anselmo dos Santos, known as Cabo (Corporal) Anselmo, had been a leader of the sailors' movement during the Goulart government. After the 1964 coup, the new regime expelled him from the navy, stripped him of his political rights, and later jailed him. In 1966, he escaped from prison and fled to Uruguay and then traveled to Cuba where he participated, along with Carlos Marighella, in the Solidarity Organization of Latin America that promoted the armed struggle throughout the continent. While in Cuba, he joined the VPR and took part in guerrilla training. Cabo Anselmo secretly returned to Brazil in September 1970 and made contacts with the VPR in São Paulo.[30]

Those are the facts that most people who have studied this controversial figure agree upon. The rest of his biography remains clouded in ambiguities and contradictions, many of which he himself has created. Some argue, based largely on circumstantial evidence, that Cabo Anselmo had been a government informant and possibly a CIA agent *before* the 1964 military takeover.[31] The sailors' rebellion and Goulart's inability or unwillingness to contain it fueled anxieties among the top brass in the armed forces and helped precipitate the military takeover. This interpretation presents him as an agent provocateur.

Others place the date when he became a double agent some time later. After his return to Brazil in September 1970, Anselmo arranged a meeting

FIGURE 9.2 Cabo Anselmo during the sailors' revolt in March 1964. COURTESY OF THE ARQUIVO PÚBLICO DO ESTADO DE SÃO PAULO.

with Lamarca at Rio D'Ouro. Inês escorted him to and from the encounter, following the usual procedure of blindfolding "Jonathan," as he was known. During his visit Iara recognized "Jonathan" as the famed sailors' movement leader and revealed that fact to Inês.[32] Had he already been collaborating with the police, some argue, this would have been the ideal time for authorities to capture Lamarca.[33] The fact that Lamarca remained untouched is proof, they argue, that Cabo Anselmo had not yet "gone to the other side." Still, a string of unexplained arrests of VPR and ALN members in São Paulo led others to speculate that Cabo Anselmo began passing on information about his covert meetings to the police in late 1970, if not earlier, possibly contributing to the death of Yoshitane Fujimore, a São Paulo VPR leader who had participated in the Ribeira training, among many others.[34] On different occasions Cabo Anselmo has offered distinctly different versions of when and why he became a police informant.[35] His most recent account is that he was arrested in late May 1971 and then began collaborating with the police. He makes no apologies about being responsible for the detention of dozens of leftists, including the VPR leader José Raimundo da Costa, who died while in police custody in August 1971.[36] Even though it is still difficult to pinpoint when Cabo Anselmo began working for the repressive apparatus, he was slowly penetrating and ultimately destroying what was left of the VPR in São Paulo.

Even though the VPR was in a critical situation, the leadership was still optimistic about what it might accomplish.[37] This involved, among other activities, building a united front of the revolutionary Left, which they called the Action Front. In the second half of 1970, the VPR sought out closer collaborations with the ALN, MRT, and MR-8. One plan entailed simultaneously abducting three ambassadors in order to demand the release of two hundred political prisoners and mark the anniversary of Carlos Marighella's death.[38] In late September the four groups also agreed to implement an "armed propaganda campaign" that would call on citizens to spoil their ballots in the upcoming congressional elections. In the "Manifesto to the Brazilian People against the Electoral Farce," distributed in October, the Front argued that the elections were "an attempt to give the illusion that the people could elect their representatives" when both the pro-government ARENA and opposition MDB "openly defend the regime."[39] This characterization of the MDB derived from the fact that the military regime had abolished political parties in 1965 and then artificially created the two new parties to offer a semblance of democracy, while using its arbitrary powers to curb dissension by canceling the political rights of those congressional representatives too critical of the regime. According to the Front's analysis, the eviscerated opposition party collaborated too much with the dictatorship. Given that voting was obligatory for literate people, the Front considered the campaign a way to register popular protest against the dictatorship.

During the weeks before the elections, armed squads distributed pamphlets in Rio, São Paulo, and a scattering of other cities and also painted slogans on walls, at times having run-ins with the police.[40] When valid votes were counted, ARENA enjoyed a landslide victory over the MDB, although a full 30 percent of the ballots were blank and invalidated, compared with just 21 percent in 1966.[41] While many observers interpreted the results as a clear legitimization of the regime, in many ways the blank and spoiled ballots were early indicators of the tremendous victory that the MDB would achieve four years later. Nonetheless, the campaign didn't give the revolutionary Left the visibility or win the popular support that it had expected.

The members of the Front faced other challenges. On October 23 the arrest and death under torture of Joaquim Câmara Ferreira, an ALN leader, had weakened his organization. Disputes between the VPR and the MRT, ALN, and MR-8 about the proportion of political prisoners from each group to be freed in the planned abductions created a fissure within the Front. Soon after the elections, Daniel and Yoshitane Fujimori, representing the VPR, met with the other leaders of the Front in São Paulo to try to come to an agreement. The MR-8 proposed suspending the multiple operations, and the majority concurred. The VPR National Command then decided to go it alone. The target would be the Swiss ambassador.⁴²

In early December, when the abduction took place, the VPR had been reduced to several dozen members nationwide. As a result, the leadership had to mobilize almost all of its experienced militants to carry out the action. Gerson Theodoro de Oliveira and Tereza Ângelo once again rented a house in which to hide the ambassador. The couple had joined the VPR in São Paulo, after moving to the left of the PCB. In mid-1969, they fled to Rio to avoid arrest. Gerson was Afro-descendant and Tereza was of a mixed racial background and peasant origins. Unlike many of the white and middle-class youth in the organization who had been recruited from the student movement, they easily blended into the multiracial poor and working-class neighborhoods of Rio where the VPR decided to hide both ambassadors. Tereza stuck very close to security procedures and knew how to fit into her surroundings. She explained how she managed to maintain three houses—the place where she and Gerson lived, the *aparelho* for the ambassador, and a getaway hideout—without being detected: "I knew how to relate to people, watch soap operas, bake a cake, give it to a neighbor, . . . hang clothes on the clothesline that weren't even dirty, bring back a shopping bag of vegetables from the market and give some to the neighbor."⁴³ Daniel moved in with Tereza and Gerson in late 1970. They created the cover that Daniel was Tereza's half-brother from a different father. Daniel's mixed racial background made the story plausible.⁴⁴ With a new combat unit in place under the leadership of Lamarca and Gerson, the itinerary of the ambassador carefully noted, and a secure place to hold the diplomat, everything was set.

Given the recent wave of attempted and actual abductions of foreign envoys, the Brazilian government had recommended heightened security measures. Yet Ambassador Giovanni Bucher, a gregarious and fun-loving fifty-seven-year-old bachelor, refused to have an additional security car.⁴⁵ With the precision of a Swiss watch, Bucher maintained his normal daily route, which allowed the action to proceed as clockwork. The eleven directly involved in the operation followed what had become a standard procedure: blocking the car, disarming police agents, removing the ambassador, and quickly driving off. When the Federal Police officer, Hélio Carvalho de Araújo, assigned to protect the ambassador, began to pull out his revolver, Lamarca fired, fatally wounding him. Even so, the whole action took less than a minute. Blockades set up around the city caused major traffic jams, but they were put in place too late to prevent the getaway car from easily reaching its destination in a northern working-class suburb. Rather than hiding the captured diplomat in a box to get him into the house, this time he was dressed in work overalls and a beret. Ângelo had already planted her cover story among her neighbors, telling them that she needed to call in someone to do some painting.[46] Bucher was unobtrusively escorted into the house in broad daylight. Daniel, who participated in the action and was dropped off soon after the cars sped away, took hours to reach the hideaway because of the roadblocks set up throughout the city. When he finally arrived, Lamarca, Ângelo, Gerson, and Alfredo, who was to serve as the translator, were anxiously awaiting him. Bucher had been safely placed in a small windowless room at the back of the house. Authorities didn't have a clue about where the ambassador was being hidden. Negotiations began.

The first communiqué made three major demands: (1) the publication of the "Manifesto to the Brazilian People," which explained the reasons for the kidnapping; (2) the suspension of train fares on the two main working-class commuter trains; and (3) the release of seventy political prisoners, who were to be flown to Chile, Algeria, or Mexico. Copies of the communiqué were placed in small envelopes along with a letter by Bucher in his own hand. Tereza Ângelo took them to a rendezvous with Zenaide Machado, who then dropped them in different locations and called the media, who presumably would pass them on to the government.

There was complete silence. Two days later authorities responded that they were concerned about the ambassador but demanded proof that he was alive through a letter in his own handwriting. It also requested the names of the seventy political prisoners the VPR wanted freed. Something was wrong. The VPR had already provided proof that it held the ambassador. Instead of immediately complying with their demands, the military seemed to be stalling. Three more communiqués drafted over the next week insisted that the government needed to publish the VPR manifesto and provide free public transportation before they would supply the names. Finally on December 17, the government acceded to the VPR's demands that they release the political prisoners but refused to comply with the other requests. The next day, Lamarca and Daniel sent a fifth communiqué with the names of the seventy political prisoners. Three days later, the government replied, agreeing to release fifty-one, but refusing to free nineteen others. Referring to those nineteen political prisoners by their numbers on the list and not by their names, they argued that six had been involved in kidnappings, four had been sentenced to lifetime imprisonment or long sentences, three had committed homicides, one was unidentifiable, one didn't want to be released, and four were not detained. The minister of justice issued the same note to the press but otherwise remained silent about negotiations.[47]

The Médici government had clearly changed its bargaining strategy. While in June it had consented to freeing militants of the MR-8 who had been involved in the abduction of the U.S. ambassador, authorities had now established new criteria for who could be freed. With the media censored, the organization faced a serious dilemma about how to proceed. Daniel suggested negotiating a ransom payment from a Swiss multinational corporation for the release of the ambassador, but the idea was vetoed because the main purpose of the operation was not gaining funds but releasing political prisoners.[48] Seeing no other solution, the leadership faced two options: agree to the government's terms or remain intransigent and not only threaten to execute the ambassador but actually do it. Lamarca insisted on polling the core members of the organization. An intense internal debate ensued. The final vote was fifteen to three in favor of a "revolutionary execution." Of those holed up with the ambassador, Daniel, Gerson, and Ângelo were in favor, while Sirkis opposed the idea. After careful consideration, Lamarca, arguing that he had ultimate power to decide as the VPR commander, vetoed the plan.[49]

Daniel was then responsible for communicating Lamarca's decision to the membership. Years later, he described what took place. "It wasn't easy to convince people. People pulled their hair out; they got angry in the middle of the street because of the decision, but everyone ended up accepting it. Deep down people felt that it wasn't that simple."[50] VPR submitted an additional nineteen names. After another delay, the government once again vetoed most of the new names and informed the VPR that several more people had refused to be freed. While the names of the other prisoners on the list were not revealed to the media, the government allowed the press to publish the identity of those who had turned down the possibility of being released. At least one pledged loyalty to the regime and declared that he'd rather stay in jail than lose his citizenship.[51]

Additional names were sent, and the back and forth continued into the New Year until the two sides had finally agreed on seventy prisoners. This time a slim majority were militants of COLINA or VPR, eleven were from MR-8, and the rest represented an array of revolutionary organizations.[52] One prominent figure was Jean Marc Van der Weid, a Swiss-Brazilian citizen, the underground president of the National Union of Students, and a militant of Ação Popular. Another was Maria Auxiliadora Lara Barcellos (Dodora), who had been in medical school with Daniel but had remained in VAR-Palmares. Gathered together in Rio at midnight on January 13, 1971, the government flew the seventy to Chile, where Dr. Salvador Allende of the Socialist Party had assumed the presidency as the head of the Popular

FIGURE 9.3 Seventy released political prisoners immediately prior to flying to Chile.
COURTESY OF THE ARQUIVO PÚBLICO DO ESTADO DE SÃO PAULO.

Unity electoral coalition. The ambassador was released two days later. He had been held for forty days.

The ordeal had been extremely difficult for the entire organization, to say nothing of how Bucher must have experienced it, since at one point he risked being executed. He had cooperated with his captors from the beginning. For example, he agreed to answer questions submitted by a journalist from *Stern* magazine, the popular German weekly, who had obtained an exclusive interview. Bucher posed for pictures showing him reading and calmly playing solitaire with a nearly empty bottle of whiskey by his side.[53] His cooperation, no doubt, resulted from a desire to protect his life.

For five and a half weeks during a hot Rio summer, Bucher was held in his cramped room. He was allowed minimum exercise and regular exposure to the sun. Over time, some of his captors, especially Sirkis, stopped following proper security measures. Tereza Ângelo remembers how Sirkis created larger and larger holes in his hood until Bucher could easily identify him, a fact that Sirkis himself later acknowledged.[54] According to Daniel, at one point, the ambassador had viewed Lamarca unhooded and then had let him know that he would forget that he had seen his face.[55] While his promise could have been a strategy for self-preservation, in police interrogations after his release Bucher did not reveal much about their operations and failed to identify any of his assailants, insisting they had been hooded during his entire captivity. Tereza Ângelo remembers Bucher warmly kissing her when he left, whether it was out of gratitude that his life was saved or from some sort of real affection is not clear.[56] Nonetheless, the authorities never discovered where the VPR had hidden the ambassador.

However successful this operation turned out to be, the prolonged negotiations created a certain paralysis in the organization. A heated internal debate had already begun with a flurry of documents exchanged among militants. These discussions continued after Bucher was released. Years later, Daniel described the kidnapping experience as "forty days of hell" because he lived in "the fear of some kind of error, of revealing some clue" that might aid the police. "But then it all worked out," he recalled.[57] Although they managed to free seventy comrades from prison, the organization was headed for a total collapse.

10

Falling Apart

(1971)

> Daniel was a very charismatic and captivating person, a person passionate about life.
>
> — PAULO BRANDI DE BARROS CACHAPUZ

Daniel had not been feeling well for some time. Whether it was from the constant tension he experienced during the abduction of the Swiss ambassador or for some other reason, he needed to see a doctor. He finally did so in February 1971. After a medical examination, he was told to return with a relative to hear the diagnosis. Daniel recruited Inês Etienne to pose as next of kin, and the two heard the news: leukemia.[1]

Both were shocked, and Inês broke into tears.[2] It turned out to be a false diagnosis, but Daniel had considered it a death sentence.[3] Years later, he speculated that his real health problem probably had been parasites, which he had gotten while in Ribeira, or even anemia, given his poor diet during guerrilla training.[4] However, it might have been a psychosomatic reaction to the organization's slow-motion disintegration and a subconscious desire to withdraw from the fray in some way. Whatever the cause of his ill health or its possible psychological connections, Daniel requested a leave of absence from the National Command. Lamarca and Inês then co-opted José Raimundo da Costa into the leadership body. Zé Raimundo had been expelled from the navy in 1964 and had joined the VPR in São Paulo. A participant in the abduction of the Japanese consul, he had been developing work among contacts in the northeast when chosen for this new responsibility. Daniel's exit from the leadership body was yet another early sign that the organization was in crisis.

After the plot involving Bucher, those in the *aparelho* holding the diplomat had split up. Daniel, Gerson, and Tereza moved to a far northern suburb into another house that Tereza had rented as their escape refuge. Acquired far in advance of the abduction, no one suspected that they were possible "terrorists." Lamarca and Iara stayed with a couple and their two small children. Sirkis returned to his rented hideaway. With no more than two dozen militants and a scattering of reliable sympathizers, the VPR needed to decide what to do next.[5]

That discussion actually began in late December 1970 while holding the Swiss ambassador. Sirkis wrote a document titled "The Armed Propaganda Path" that argued for the confiscation and distribution of foodstuffs among the poor so that "we are no longer, for the masses, the 'guys that rob banks' but 'the guys who take hold of a milk truck and distribute milk.'" He argued that the organization needed to combine these actions with leafleting, painting slogans on walls, and holding short, fast rallies among the people.[6] After having so adamantly rejected the proposals of their ideological opponents in the VAR-Palmares who had defended organizing workers, suddenly VPR militants were advocating activities that involved interacting with the "masses." Alex Polari responded almost immediately in favor of continuing the tactic of abducting ambassadors.[7] Lamarca then joined the discussion, supporting Sirkis and arguing that the VPR needed to engage in "linked armed propaganda" as a way of breaking its isolation.[8] It was a futile attempt to reorient the organization. Since the massive wave of arrests that began in April 1970 and the demobilization of the training camp, the prospects of the rural guerrilla strategy had dimmed. Alternative sites had become unavailable, and the organization had few resources to mount a mobile tactical column as they had planned when the VPR was reconstituted in November 1969. The VPR's surviving militants seemed to be grasping at straws.

With no other clear options available, the combat unit went into action with the tactic of armed propaganda, even while the leadership was still negotiating with the Brazilian government over the fate of the Swiss ambassador. Mobilizing almost the entire organization, a dozen revolutionaries appropriated some cars and a truck. Then, on January 26, they entered the Mundial Armazéns supermarket, robbed the safe, and loaded a truck with provisions, which they distributed among the residents of the Rato Molhado (wet rat), a poor community in an outlying neighborhood of Rio.[9] While this Robin Hood–esque action may have created a momentary boost in the VPR's popularity among the residents of this destitute district, it was a measure that seemed to have no apparent long-term purpose. The lightning-speed nature of the action made it impossible to recruit anyone to the organization, and it's not clear if the recipients of this aid fully understood the revolutionaries' intentions. Soon thereafter, Sirkis requested his separation from the organization. Since his real identity was still undetected by the police, he was able to apply for a passport and leave the country for exile in Chile.[10]

By March, the organization had reached an impasse. Reflecting on the political crisis within the VPR a decade later, Daniel wrote, "At that moment, the masses retreated and the repressive phase prevented any advance. The armed struggle—as it presented itself at the time—didn't have a solution other than the rebellion of the masses, rising up in arms. It's important to remember that the main argument that justified the guerrilla movement was that the objective conditions were given, that the masses were prepared for an insurrection. That incorrect evaluation was the actual basis for its defeat."[11]

Daniel had founded his assessment on simple observations. During his daily missions coming to and from the *aparelho* where the Swiss ambassador was being held, he sensed public opinion, as people reacted to police blockades that paralyzed traffic while the authorities carried out systematic but futile attempts to discover the ambassador's whereabouts. Daniel realized that ordinary citizens had become passive spectators in the battle between the government and the guerrillas. He later wrote, "The struggle was among *them*, two armed detachments [fighting] while the public watched. People's only option was to root [for one side or the other] on television."[12]

With this realization in mind, Daniel began elaborating a new perspective for the organization. The VPR had entered a vicious cycle, "the dynamics of survival," as he called it, in which its actions were designed merely to guarantee its ongoing existence and nothing more.[13] It had lost sight of its political motivations and had become caught up in the day-to-day actions not connected to its strategic goals.[14] Daniel began to argue that the VPR needed to retreat and get Lamarca and Iara safely out of the country, so that the comandante could play an important leadership role among the organization's exiled members. He also proposed that the VPR organize a congress abroad in order to rethink its future. Daniel, who by this time was sharing an apartment with Inês, won her over to the same point of view and later convinced Zenaide as well.[15]

Lamarca himself was experiencing his own doubts about the organization. Cognizant of the VPR's logistical and numerical weaknesses, he had begun considering the possibility of joining the MR-8 and asked Sirkis to make contact with its leadership.[16] At the same time, he appeared to go along with the proposal advanced by Daniel and Inês that he leave the country. Zenaide started the laborious task of obtaining false passports and other documents through revolutionary intermediaries in Brazil and abroad.[17] But in early March, Lamarca did an about-face and became suspicious that other comrades were actually trying to undermine his role as a leader and get him out of the way. Iara also backtracked on the idea of leaving the country, and the two began to plan their exit from the VPR. Two decades later Daniel speculated that Iara had realized that her destiny was to remain with Lamarca in Brazil. Moreover, he ventured, Iara would have been the "other woman" abroad, given the fact that Lamarca's wife and two children were in Cuba.[18]

Harsh words between Lamarca and Inês in a leadership meeting held in mid-March merely exacerbated the situation. The political altercation took place in the small house shared by Alex Polari and his partner, Lúcia Velloso. The place was also used for leadership meetings that sometimes lasted several days. Lúcia described the scene. "Zé Raimundo even had problems with his heart; he started to have palpitations. . . . Inês spent hours lying on the couch crying. Lamarca and Iara were closed up in their room, and they stayed there. It was a horrible situation. I remember that I made a bread pudding for dessert, which had infinite psychological interpretations, because the only thing sweet in that house was the bread pudding."[19] Inês ended up turning in her resignation to Lamarca and Zé Raimundo, but, like Daniel, she agreed to continue to help support the organization's daily operations.[20]

On March 22, in broad daylight, police gunned down Gerson, who headed the combat unit, and Mauricio Guilherme da Silveria, a twenty-year-old high school student.[21] Both had helped to abduct the Swiss ambassador. Lúcia remembers the impact Mauricio's death had on her when she heard the news, since she identified with him: "Mauricio was a kid. . . . He didn't have the slightest [notion] of the dimensions of what he was doing."[22] It shook her to the core.

Lamarca was equally upset by Gerson's death, but by this time he had become convinced that it was no longer viable for him to remain in the VPR.[23] The MR-8 leadership assured him that he would be transferred to a rural area to begin working among peasants. At the end of the month, Lamarca produced a document explaining that, in spite of the fact that he was commander in chief of the VPR, he disagreed with the political line of the organization, its sectarianism, and the ideological deformations of many of its leaders.[24] On March 27, Alex Polari assisted Lamarca and Iara in their transfer to the MR-8.[25]

To this day, Lamarca's decision to leave the VPR elicits different interpretations among former members. Ubiratan de Souza, who trained with him in the Ribeira, believes that if he had left the country, the military regime would have labeled him a double deserter—first for abandoning his barracks and then for abandoning Brazil.[26] Lúcia still has tremendous respect for Lamarca, but she reflected that his decision was much more personal than political. "For a person of Lamarca's stature to leave the organization without causing a split is completely strange. It wasn't a political decision because no one left with him."[27] As Daniel later wrote, "It would be the first time that a Commander separated himself from his army without disbanding it."[28]

Zé Raimundo cobbled together a new provisional leadership composed of Zenaide Machado, Alex Polari, and Ivan Mota Dias, who had been recruited to the organization from the Fluminense Federal University. As promised, Inês and Daniel continued to help sustain VPR's operations, at the same time trying to convince the others that the only solution for survival was a planned retreat. However, the police were closing in, and the efforts of Cabo Anselmo, if he had in fact turned police informant by this time, were apparently producing results in São Paulo. On May 5, Inês reluctantly went to São Paulo for an appointment with a peasant contact, who had already been arrested and had informed the police of the meeting. Captured and immediately tortured, Inês made up a story about a supposed appointment that she had in Rio the next day along a busy street. Under close surveillance, the police released her to meet with her alleged contact. Inês immediately threw herself under the wheels of a passing bus. Miraculously she survived, but she fell into a coma.[29]

When Inês didn't return to Rio the night of May 5, Daniel failed to follow the security procedures and immediately evacuate the apartment. "I simply wouldn't allow myself to believe that you might have been arrested," Daniel is said to have told Inês, the first time they met again many years later.[30] The next day, however, he realized the gravity of the situation, and he asked

Tereza to help him clear out their apartment.[31] That same week, the police captured two other key VPR members. José Roberto Gonçalves de Resende had participated in the abduction of the Swiss ambassador and was one of three militants that had voted against his execution. Aluísio Palhano Pedreira Ferreira, operating in São Paulo, had trained with Cabo Anselmo in Cuba and had just secretly returned to Brazil. He died in custody after being mercilessly tortured.[32] The organization was rapidly unraveling.

On May 12, the police captured Alex Polari, once again depriving the organization of an essential member of what was becoming a highly unstable provisional leadership.[33] Daniel had moved in with Alex and Lúcia the week after Inês's arrest. This time, when Alex failed to return home at the agreed-upon time, Daniel and Lúcia immediately evacuated the small house. In addition to making their home available as a meeting place for the leadership, Lúcia had been in charge of typing and reproducing political documents. The space also stored arms and material to produce false identity cards and other items. Daniel hurried into the street to hail a cab while Lúcia scrambled to tear up as many pieces of paper as possible. It was a futile effort, as they were able to destroy only some of the documents stored in the house. When the taxi arrived, they wouldn't let the driver help them place a large, heavy bag in the trunk because it was laden with guns. At the last minute, Daniel rushed back into the house to get his playing cards. While living underground he had learned that a game of solitaire could be his best company during trying times.[34]

The two asked the driver to drop them off near Paulo Brandi's parents' apartment. In the middle of the night they knocked on the door, requested that he store the bag, without offering any explanations, and then disappeared into the dark. With nowhere to go, that night Daniel and Lúcia stayed in a hotel in Copacabana. They then went their separate ways, each seeking housing. Two days later they heard news that Ivan Mota Dias, who had only recently become a member of the leadership, had been arrested. He too would die under custody.[35]

For a time Lúcia, Tereza, and Zenaide, posing as students, rented a large room from a couple, but the owners became suspicious, so they quickly abandoned that locale.[36] By this time, all of the organization's militants were only one step ahead of the police.

June, July, and early August were months of bare survival. Daily *pontos* maintained contact among the remaining half-dozen militants. Daniel rented rooms in unsuspecting people's homes. During these trying three months, Daniel and Lúcia spent as much time together as was reasonably safe, and she became Daniel's new confidante. Perhaps because he was no longer able to contain his most intimate secrets, Daniel shared with her the fact that he was sexually attracted to men. In turn, she discussed her relationship with Alex, which had gone through rough times. Lúcia was heartbroken about Alex's arrest, and Daniel gave her significant support.[37]

The two arranged meetings with Paulo Brandi as well. While never joining the VPR, Paulo had remained a loyal ally. After the release of the seventy political prisoners in January 1971, Paulo continued to see Daniel regularly. "I think that I was really important in Daniel's life at that moment. First, because I think he did, indeed, fall in love with me, and because I reciprocated through our friendship. . . . We met almost daily."[38] At one point, Daniel wrote a very personal and tender letter to Paulo. "The letter was a declaration of love, but I didn't read it as such at the time. I saw it as a statement of our deep friendship." Paulo's mother found the letter and understood it quite differently. "She said that she didn't like anything in the letter and wanted to know what was happening. But I changed the subject." Still, the two remained incredibly close, and Paulo openly confided to Daniel his personal insecurities about women, sex, and relating to others.[39]

One day in July 1971, amid the VPR's total disintegration, Daniel set up an appointment to meet Paulo. Today Paulo can't remember exactly how it happened, but one of the two came up with the idea of getting tickets to see the latest show of Maria Betânia, the dramatic songstress and diva. That month she had opened the show "Rosa dos Ventos: O Show Encantado" (Rose compass: The enchanted show) in the Teatro da Praia. With a strong and theatrical voice, Betânia, the younger sister of the singer/composer Caetano Veloso, had charmed Rio in 1965, when she took over a leading role in the protest musical *Show de Opinião* at the Arena Theater, delivering with power and passion the famed song "Carcará" about poverty in the northeast. She soon rose to national fame because of her formidable personality, rich vocal delivery, and majestic performances. It was also rumored that she had affairs with women, which added an aura of exoticism to her personality. Her performance that July included an eclectic repertoire of musical selections, combined with dramatic readings of Portuguese and Brazilian poets Fernando Pessoa, Clarice Lispector, and Vinícius de Moraes. Critics consider it one of the best concerts of her career.[40]

Daniel had never been a part of Rio's middle-class student and cultural milieu, so he didn't have to worry about being recognized by former classmates or friends as he waited in line to enter the show or when he mingled with the crowd during intermission. Still, being so exposed in public represented a risk, one that he was willing to take for the privilege of seeing

Betânia in a live performance. Paulo fondly recalled, "In such difficult times, the show was a moment of joy."[41]

By early August, the VPR had virtually ceased to exist. On August 4, José Raimundo da Costa of the Provisional National Command was picked up in Rio and was killed under torture, although authorities claimed he died while resisting arrest.[42] Even though Daniel had resigned from the leadership, he was probably the VPR member most sought by the police. Lúcia recalls the situation was so dangerous for him that he had to stay hidden in an apartment, and they could no longer meet in person. However, they exchanged letters through a courier. With nothing to do, Daniel wrote long, personal missives to her. In one of these letters, twenty pages or more in length, he wrote about his ardent admiration for Lamarca and his passionate love for Paulo.[43] It was as if he could no longer contain the emotions he had repressed since opting for the revolution.

In the midst of the organization's dismal political situation, Daniel also felt a tremendous responsibility to save those who had not been arrested or killed, and he continued to communicate with Zenaide about what they should do. Because he had resigned from the National Command, he and Zenaide agreed that she, as a member of the provisional leadership, should be the person who officially informed their supporters abroad that the end was near. Zenaide was hiding in the house of friends, and she remembered typing the declaration demobilizing the organization on an old typewriter on a kitchen table using onionskin paper to be able to fold and insert it into the belt of an Indian dress that she planned to send to Chile with a supporter.[44]

She wrote three communiqués on August 7. The first explained that the documents were issued by the new Command that had been established following the organization's normal procedures and requested that the remaining militants "obey centralism and maintain a cool head in this chaotic situation." The second presented immediate measures couched in language clearly penned by Daniel: "The evolution of the situation that apparently has developed as a 'political crisis' running parallel to a 'security crisis' is in reality the dynamic of the Armed Organizations of Brazil, [namely] the 'dynamic of survival,' which has led to the organization's extinction." The document furthermore declared that the leaders had demobilized the organization and called for a second national congress. The third communiqué, addressed to "comrades abroad," painted a sober picture of the state of the organization, describing the wave of arrests and elimination of the leadership. It ended bluntly. "In short, the O. is today dead in Brazil."[45]

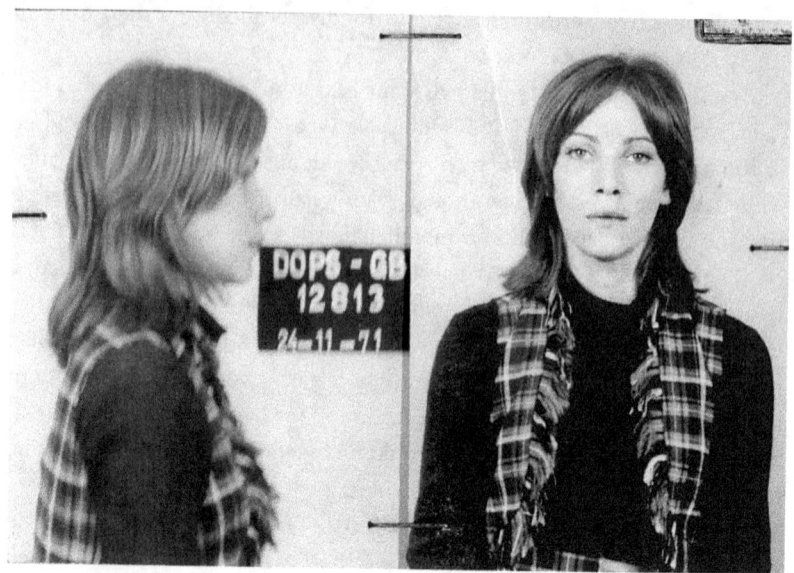

FIGURE 10.1 Mug shot of Lúcia Velloso. COURTESY OF LÚCIA VELLOSO MAURÍCIO.

Two weeks later, Zenaide and another comrade were arrested. The next day Lúcia was picked up. Zenaide believes that the police followed her and others, in spite of their careful efforts to avoid being trailed, determined to find each and every remaining member of the organization.[46] Zenaide and Lúcia were among the first political prisoners to be submitted to a new form of torture, developed by the British in Northern Ireland, which had just been exported to Rio.[47] The *geladeira* (freezer), as it was known, was a large box in which prisoners were placed. Constant light, unbearably loud music, and freezing temperatures left its victims dazed, numbed, and vulnerable to revealing information. It also left no marks.[48]

After Lúcia's arrest on August 31, 1971, there were only three people left in the VPR. In a letter from Daniel to Lúcia written four years later, recounting those desperate moments after her arrest, he explained his situation: "I was completely lost. I vaguely had the idea that it was possible to reactivate communication with people outside the country, with whom I had absolutely baseless but boundless faith." When Daniel finally established contact with Tereza Ângelo and Adair Gonçalves, the two other surviving VPR militants, they informed him, as he later wrote, that they were going to "continue the struggle." Tereza and Adair, who remained underground in Brazil until 1981, told him that they planned to join the ALN.[49] They did not part ways amicably to say the least.[50]

Daniel had no money, nowhere to go, and was on the police's most wanted list. His attempt to "make the revolution," a decision he had made in 1967, had run into a dead end.

Nor could he turn to Paulo Brandi for help. In late August, Paulo had been picked up for questioning. After he was released, he cut his contacts with Daniel. "My major fear . . . was that they would use me as bait or as a means to get to Daniel." Paulo was brisk over the phone. Daniel must have understood the message, as he didn't contact Paulo again.

Now Daniel was entirely isolated. On Sunday, September 19, 1971, only three weeks after Lúcia and Zenaide were arrested, he was living in the home of people who knew nothing about his political activities. That morning, he glanced at the newspaper and saw a front-page article that described how Lamarca had been killed in the backlands of Bahia. Military police gunned down the guerrilla leader, who had been fleeing authorities and was resting under a tree with another revolutionary. The same newspaper account also revealed that Iara had allegedly committed suicide in Salvador in August rather than allow herself to be captured.[51] "I saw his dead face in the newspaper. . . . It was breakfast, and I had to put on a show with the other people. Later I went into the bathroom and cried. I couldn't cry in front of others. It was horrible." With no secure place to stay, he didn't know what to do.

Then, by chance, Leonardo Valentini, known to his friends as Leo, came to his aid. Leo had previously been involved in the high school students' movement and Marxist study groups and had circulated widely among left-wing youth in the city in 1968 and 1969.[52] At one point Leo had been a member of the DVP, the dissident group of the VAR-Palmares led by Apolo Lisboa, who had known Daniel since their university days. After leaving the DVP, Leo created his own underground political organization, the Movement of Popular Resistance (MRP), which Daniel later described as being made up of a total of two people and was based on an incomprehensible seventy-page "basic document," which was a hodgepodge of Marxist-Leninist quotations and confusing formulations.[53] Nevertheless, Leo was willing to take the risk of hiding Daniel.

How this serendipitous connection happened we may never know. At any rate, sometime in late September 1971, Leo led Daniel to an apartment in Niterói, across the bay from Rio. Daniel arrived in his new hiding place wearing a ragged t-shirt, Bermuda shorts (once used by Lamarca), and shoes riddled with holes.[54] But he was alive.

Leo had lived there with his girlfriend, but they had recently broken up and the apartment was empty. It was a perfect place to hide someone wanted by the police. Daniel lost all notions of time, as he remained hidden in a darkened apartment, out of harm's way. Lethargic days slid into weeks, and then drifted into what seemed like months. Although Daniel was safe, he was trapped in a box. He didn't dare appear on the street. Blanket-covered windows blocked out much of the sunlight and prevented any curious eyes from peeking into what was assumed by neighbors to be an empty residency, which meant that Daniel could only read by the natural daylight that seeped into his gloomy quarters. Any unexpected noise or sudden motion had to be suppressed, because it might arouse the neighbors' suspicions. He couldn't move about in the kitchen or even run tap water. Leonardo appeared irregularly, every three days or so, with meager provisions. Only then could Daniel flush the toilet. The rest of the time he lived in the silence of a presumably empty apartment, subsisting mostly on instant coffee or cocoa mixed with milk and sliced white bread.[55]

With nothing to do but read during the daylight hours, he devoured everything in the eclectic collection of books in the apartment's library. "What interested me wasn't exactly the quality or the subject. I was interested in passing the time. Waiting."[56] And wait he did for weeks on end.

Then on Sunday, November 28, 1971, Cláudio Alves de Mesquita Filho walked into his life.

11

Cláudio

(1972–1974)

> Daniel was tremendously charismatic. He had an enormous influence over others.
>
> — MARIA ELISALVA OLIVEIRA JOUÉ

Cláudio Alves de Mesquita Filho was born in Poço de Caldas in southwestern Minas Gerais, but he grew up in Rio. His father earned a modest living as a taxi driver and was active in his union, rising to the presidency in the early 1950s. Cláudio studied in the prestigious federal public high school, Pedro II, and lived a rather ordinary childhood.[1] When he was fifteen or so, he had his first sexual experience with a woman. As he recalled several decades later, the rumor had been circulating that he was a faggot (*bicha*), because he had effeminate mannerisms, stayed quietly at home, liked to draw, and was very polite. Concerned about the gossip, Cláudio's father arranged for a cousin to set up a rendezvous with a young women. Cláudio lost his virginity, reassuring his father about his son's masculinity. But the experience left doubts in Cláudio's mind. A brief sexual encounter with an effeminate gay man provoked a crisis. "It was a surprise, a shock, and I panicked." Suddenly it was as if the whole world knew. "I had the idea that God's eye could see the whole situation and that it wouldn't do any good to hide, because God was watching."[2]

When his father suddenly died of a heart attack in 1966, Cláudio's mother took in sewing and sold embroidery to make ends meet. Although the family budget was tight, Cláudio was encouraged to continue schooling. In 1967, when preparing for his college entrance exams, he became friends with Diana Goulart, and they started dating. Many years later, Cláudio described her: "She was very much like me, very quiet, introverted; she loved music, design, and languages."[3] Five months later they were married in a civil ceremony, but the union lasted only a year or so. His sister Magaly speculated that Cláudio married as a way of trying to escape his homosexual desires in order to live a "normal" life.[4]

Soon thereafter, Cláudio moved into a cousin's apartment in the hillside neighborhood of Santa Teresa with José Carlos de Medeiros Gondim, who directed a theater group at the Fluminense Federal University, where Cláudio was studying. Gondim was left-wing and against the dictatorship. He and Cláudio ended up having an affair.[5] Cláudio recalled, "It was the first time that I had a relationship between equals, that is, going to bed without feeling that someone was pushing you; no one was forcing you."[6] Magaly, Cláudio's younger sister, shared the apartment, and she found Gondim attractive. It was then that she learned about her brother's sexual involvement with men. "He told me to stay out of his territory," Magaly remembered. Nonetheless, Cláudio remained tormented about his sexuality, and the relationship was short-lived.[7]

While still struggling with his sexual identity, like so many students of his generation, Cláudio was moving toward the left. "On a trip I made between Rio and São Paulo, I bought a copy of the *Communist Manifesto* by Karl Marx and read it on the way. I thought everything he said was fantastic, and I agreed with all of it." His newly found ideology, however, led Cláudio to repress his sexual attraction for other men. "At a given moment, I placed a political discourse over another discourse that I was hearing and developing within my head, which said that being a faggot was not good."[8] In the midst of all of this internal turmoil about his sexuality, he became closer to Maria Elisalva Oliveira, a friend he had known at the university since 1968, when he was doing theater while studying literature.[9] They remained in touch after Cláudio's separation from his wife, and eventually he and Elisalva moved in together.

FIGURE 11.1 Cláudio and Elisalva at their wedding in 1971. COURTESY OF MIGUEL MESQUITA.

Elisalva had worked hard to get to the university, study literature, and become a French teacher. She fell in love with Cláudio because he was extremely handsome, creative, warm, and loving. She cited an example about their wedding that reflects one of many of his qualities. Her parents were very strict Catholics and insisted on a religious ceremony. Cláudio had a flair for colorful clothes and decided to design matching purple outfits for their wedding ensemble that his mother then sewed. Both wore long flowing hair, making them look almost identical when they appeared before the altar in the local church.[10]

Sometime in 1970 or early 1971, Cláudio joined DVP through his cousin, Leo Valentini. Cláudio soon convinced Elisalva to participate in its underground activities. Elisalva remembers they made stickers that said "Down with the Dictatorship" and "Long live Lamarca," and they discreetly placed them on the backs of bus seats and in public spaces.

After splitting from the DVP in late 1971, Leo joined João Belisário de Sousa, known as Jonjoca, to form the Movement of Popular Resistance (MRP) to offer logistical support to the revolutionary Left. Leo knew Jonjoca from the high school students' movement. When the two learned about Daniel's dire situation, they immediately wanted to help.[11]

Leo and Jonjoca decided to ask Cláudio and Elisalva to assist them in this effort. Leo explained to the couple that he was hiding an important revolutionary leader who was wanted by the police and had been involved in Ribeira guerrilla training.[12] Although he didn't say so at the time, Leo was planning to travel to Chile to make contact with the VPR on Daniel's behalf and needed someone to take care of Daniel while he was abroad.[13] Elisalva and Cláudio agreed to look after the fugitive for a month and moved into the apartment Leo maintained in Niterói where Daniel had been staying. They created a cover story to tell the neighbors that the newly married couple had rented the apartment along with "Marcelo," Elisalva's supposed brother. As Elisalva explained, "Daniel and I were both mestizos, so it made sense."[14] Daniel credited Marcel Proust as the inspiration for his newly adopted underground name. The title of Proust's masterpiece, *In Search of Time Lost*, also expressed Daniel's anguish over having been hidden away in a closed-up apartment for so long.[15]

In his second book of reflections about his revolutionary life, Daniel described the moment when he met Cláudio and Elisalva. "Real live people, of flesh and bone, with their own opinions and voices that talked back. They were a recently formed couple in many ways. As neophytes of the enchanted world of the Left, they really enjoyed hiding a 'prize' . . . who told stories and theorized about everything. Damn, I needed to talk so much. And I did. God, how I talked."[16] Cláudio and Elisalva so relished Daniel's company that they agreed to continue living with him, and the three ended up creating an extended family when Cláudio's mother, Mercedes, and his sister Magaly moved in as well.

Many of the quotidian details of those days in late 1971 and throughout 1972 remain hidden. Elisalva, one of the only living witnesses to this year, passed away as this book was being finished. Daniel refers to some of his conversations with Cláudio obliquely in his memoir, in his letters to Lúcia Velloso written in exile, and in a second volume that combines creative fiction with glimpses of Cláudio's and Daniel's first encounters. These accounts are like tiny scraps of paper torn from a larger volume that is never fully revealed. From what we know, however, it seems that Cláudio spent many hours listening to Daniel's long expositions on the history of the Brazilian Left, its divisions, and its dissidents.[17] To his surprise, Daniel discovered that Cláudio found nothing exciting in the endless reams of discussion documents produced by clandestine organizations. He had politely received them from his cousin Leo and then stored them away in a drawer or closet, unread. Cláudio, an artist at heart, complained about their boring content and unattractive graphic layout.[18]

Although political discussions didn't particularly interest Cláudio, the two still found plenty to talk about. Their time together was a series of informal interactive therapy sessions in which both worked out their repressed homosexual desires and began to create new political frameworks that adjusted to the country's changing situation. At some point they started talking about their "intimate personal lives, desires, and sexuality."[19] In his second seminovel, Daniel describes these interactions with Cláudio, re-creating a conversation between them: "I don't know. . . . I think that homosexuality is a kind of . . . moral weakness," Cláudio reportedly confessed. "I don't let it dominate me. I don't accept it. We have to work harder when the tendency is great."[20]

At first these discussions seemed to be monologues about each man's own sexual repression, which might explain why Elisalva is excluded from Daniel's literary re-creation of their time together. When Cláudio and Daniel first met, neither seemed clear about how to deal with his homosexuality. Daniel had chosen not to act on his sexual desire for other men, so he relied on masturbation as an erotic outlet.[21] In early 1972, Cláudio still seemed uncomfortable about his homosexual tendencies.[22] In reading Daniel's condensed accounts of those times, one might come to the conclusion that the two had become romantically and sexually involved, but that was not the case. Nonetheless, their dialogues about sexuality, monogamy, and promiscuity were constant and continuous. Daniel was easing out of his reclusive emotional shell, and Cláudio was engaged in conversations with an erudite revolutionary capable of endlessly theorizing about almost anything. The differences between Daniel, the political intellectual, and Cláudio, the sensitive artist, seemed to complement each other and bind the two together. They forged an intimate friendship that lasted two decades.

Ever since Daniel's discreet cruising in the parks of Belo Horizonte, he had felt awkward about his homosexuality, especially among his revolutionary peers. On numerous occasions he attempted to hide his feelings by creating the fiction that he was sexually attracted to women but suffered endlessly because his affections were never reciprocated. Zezé Nahas claims that Daniel proposed marriage to Laís Pereira during an end-of-the-year gathering in 1968, only weeks before he went underground.[23] Laís doesn't recall the incident, which may indicate that it was either a playful joke or an insignificant event for her. It might have been a gesture that Daniel made to reassure himself about his potential heterosexuality or to share later with others to confirm his heteromasculinity.[24] Daniel had revealed his "impossible" adoration of Marilyn Monroe to Maria do Carmo, which led her to become suspicious of his heterosexuality.[25] Alfredo Sirkis remembers that while living underground, Daniel told him about his frustrating relations with women that never seemed to work out. It led Sirkis to conclude that Daniel was heterosexual.[26] Lúcia recalls that when she, Alex, and Daniel shared the same *aparelho* for a brief time, the two young men engaged in a typically sexist habit of analyzing the buttocks of women they saw on the streets. Lúcia thought that Daniel's comments were delivered in a tone that would lead one to believe he found women sexually attractive, although she later discovered that this was not the case.[27] Given the climate of compulsory heteronormativity and revolutionary masculinity embedded in the gendered practices of left-wing militants, it is comprehensible that he engaged in these performances of masculinity to affirm his heterosexuality and avoid being marginalized by other comrades.

Cláudio, on the other hand, had been in the much more permissive world of the theater in 1968 and had lived with a man in 1969. He experienced the cultural changes that were taking place in Brazil and was transformed by them.[28] In the midst of the political turmoil of 1967 and 1968 and repressive responses by the military dictatorship thereafter, rigid gender norms were beginning to soften slightly among certain sectors of the middle class. Simultaneously, the international countercultural movement was taking hold in Brazil among a sliver of the population. Cláudio seemed to embrace all of these changes that offered him more social and cultural space to openly express his bisexuality.

Cláudio was shaped by his experiences as an artist and a theater enthusiast but also considered himself a leftist. Daniel, emerging out of isolated years living underground, was still confused about his homosexuality and its relation to his revolutionary commitment. Now the two were slowing converging in the process of elaborating a different way to think about politics, the body, sexuality, and personal behavior. These shifts in understanding their own sexuality reflected changes taking place in Brazil at large, as well as globally, which apparently had an effect on Daniel's and Cláudio's personal transformations as they started accepting their sexual and romantic desires.

Daniel describes the time in Niterói as a moment in which it was impossible to carry out political activities, calling the period a lamentable "exile," to use the metaphor that is a major theme throughout his first book.[29] "Exile, as distancing, is a form of silence," he wrote. "As if we had awoken from a dream: we found ourselves living a strange life; and if one talked about the dictatorship, it was as if it were a distant phenomenon that was far away from small day-to-day annoyances. We talked a lot among ourselves, and we were silent with others." Daniel acknowledged that although he would end up in exile abroad in 1974, two years earlier he considered himself to be banished within Brazil as he was separated from the Left, his family, and political work.

Yet despite this version of that year as a moment in which Daniel did nothing politically, a scattering of documents and personal accounts indicate that he had actually attempted to rejuvenate his political life in the midst of an extremely repressive climate. Daniel had just lived through the VPR's traumatic disintegration. Yet, less than a half year later, he decided to create another organization to coalesce and give direction to the circle of people already working with Leo and Jonjoca. That effort, no doubt, was a combination of the idealistic enthusiasm and sacrifice of a small group of sympathizers with the revolutionary Left who wanted to offer their support to underground militants and Daniel's ability to inspire people to take risks for a noble cause. (His silence about this activity in his books might have been due to its ultimate failure.) With Daniel's experience, charisma, and rhetorical talents, he transformed the MRP into a reincarnation of the VPR. He even gave this new revolutionary operation a second name, in homage to Gerson Theodoro de Oliveira, his former roommate who had been slain by police in March 1971.[30] As he later wrote to Lúcia Velloso, "The fact that I was not living in the old kind of clandestine life, that is, within the framework of the O., began to force me to think about things differently, to make an analysis (if I can call it that) of what I was, what I could be, and what I should be."[31]

Throughout 1972, Daniel built up a simple cell structure among a dozen or so people connected to this new political initiative. They published documents and produced three or four issues of a small clandestine journal. Leo made connections with new supporters and arranged meetings with Daniel to recruit them to the organization.[32] It was a tribute to Daniel's tenacity that he started all over again after the successive defeats of the previous year. This time, however, his approach was different. In order to avoid what Daniel had called the dynamics of survival, which was part of the political justification for VPR's demobilization, there would be no "expropriations" or abductions. Instead they would support themselves through legal means as they tried to figure out how to proceed politically.

"Opening up," or *abrindo*, as they described it, enabled Daniel to escape from the tension he had experienced living underground for three years, and it helped him regain a "normal life." An ad agency was the medium. Founded by Magaly, in late 1971, Public Publicity occupied rented space amid the hustle and bustle of Rio's commercial center. Magaly had just picked up two new clients, when one of her graphic designers moved on to another job. Magaly's mother convinced her to hire Cláudio and Daniel to replace the employee she had just lost. Over the course of 1972, they developed a diverse portfolio. Cláudio contributed his artistic talents by doing graphic design. Daniel employed his gifts for writing by producing creative copy. Elisalva put in start-up funds from her earnings as a French teacher. She also translated texts of French clients into Portuguese. Magaly oversaw the operations. When the French-owned Danone Yogurt Company entered the Brazilian market, Elisalva came up with the idea of an ad in which a person eating the fruit-flavored yogurt spoke with a French accent. Cláudio packaged the idea, and they got the contract. Public Publicity also won the bid for the ad campaign of another French company that was selling automatic door openers for garages.[33] The Mexican and Chilean consulates hired them to produce promotional material in Portuguese about the two countries.[34] Ironically, Public Publicity took advantage of the spectacular expansion of the Brazilian economy, which had been one of many factors that had made it so difficult for the guerrilla organizations to win popular support.

Cláudio also persuaded Daniel to do a physical makeover, convincing him to stop straightening his hair and let it grow longer; exchange his heavy, dark-framed glasses for contact lenses; and modify his wardrobe to appear more like a freewheeling hippie with bellbottom jeans and colorful shirts. Looking nothing like the media's projected stereotype of a "terrorist," Daniel was able to move unperceived on the commuter ferryboat from Niterói across the bay to their office in downtown Rio.

Elisalva remembered that Daniel would point to his wanted poster attached to the walls of public buildings and tease her about the double life they were living. At the time she thought that the image very much resembled Daniel, even though contact lenses and a new hairstyle had changed his appearance somewhat. In his memoir, Daniel wrote that the picture on these posters didn't really look like him, and it turns out that he was right.[35] At some point (probably in 1970), someone in the Belo Horizonte police department or among federal government security forces accidentally or purposefully mixed up Daniel's photograph with that of Irani Campos, another militant from COLINA, who served a year in prison and then was released in the exchange following the abduction of the Swiss ambassador. It was actually Irani Campos's headshot and not that of Herbert Eustáquio de Carvalho that appeared on the wanted poster throughout Brazil along with two of his code names—Olympia and Daniel.[36] In reality, these posters served more to intimidate revolutionaries and the general public than to function as a means of identifying and capturing anyone. Daniel had learned simply to ignore them.

While previously Daniel had always tried to blend in by acting like a high school student, an office boy, or a run-of-the-mill youth, in 1972 he took another approach. He explained, "We became people living in a fantasy. We completely forgot the police. We got work as two perfectly legal citizens. . . . Our documents were as false as the optimistic statistics of the [economy], but they (in fact like those statistics) were good at deceiving."[37] It was as if he had lowered a magic protective shield around himself and those around him. And it worked for a while.

While apparently safeguarded from the police, Daniel attempted to break the isolation from his comrades living in exile. In May 1971, Maria do Carmo had received a letter from Inês Etienne, just before she was arrested, describing the plan for Daniel and her to obtain passports and leave the country.[38] That effort was foiled both by arrests in the following months and by Daniel's inability to make connections with people or other underground organizations that could obtain usable passports. Then Daniel reestablished contact with Ângelo Pezzutti and Maria do Carmo Brito, who had resettled in Chile after being flown to Algeria. For a time, the two were a couple, and Maria do Carmo got pregnant. Underground communications between Santiago and Rio were such that Daniel and others in Brazil even participated in helping them select a name for the child: would it be Juarez Carlos or Carlos Juarez?[39] Maria do Carmo and Ângelo finally decided on naming their newborn son Juarez Carlos after Juares Guimarães de Brito, Maria do Carmo's revolutionary partner. Ângelo and Maria do Carmo's relationship, however, suffered from the many stresses of living in exile, and they ended up separating, although they continued to collaborate politically for a time. Ângelo returned to school to get training as a psychiatrist, and Maria do Carmo eventually established a relationship with Shizuo Ozawa (Mário Japa), who had coordinated VPR's activities in Cuba and then moved to Chile in late 1972.[40]

During this period, from afar, Daniel attempted to follow the internal struggles that were happening in Algeria, Chile, and Cuba among those exiles who had once been a part of the string of organizations that he had joined. Constant infighting, distrust, demoralization, police infiltrations, and the realization that the political situation in Brazil had changed radically caused these scattered revolutionary forces to slowly disintegrate. Onofre Pinto, the former sergeant who was among the fifteen political prisoners freed in exchange for the release of the U.S. ambassador, had assumed leadership of the VPR abroad and circulated easily through Cuba, Algeria, Europe, and Chile with money that remained from the Ademar de Barros safe heist. Yet some VPR exiles had lost confidence in his leadership abilities. In addition to the tensions that this created, a controversy ripped through the exile community in Chile about how to deal with rumors that Cabo Anselmo had been arrested, had become a double agent, and had infiltrated what was left of the organization.[41]

The original source of this information was Inês Etienne. After her arrest in May 1971 and her attempted suicide to avoid revealing information under torture, she was then taken to a residency in Petrópolis, known as the House of Death, where she was kept for several months. There she was raped and tortured during incessant interrogation sessions.[42] At one point while imprisoned there, she overheard the voice of Cabo Anselmo. She immediately recognized it as that of "Jonathan," whom she had escorted to and from the meeting with Lamarca and whom Iara Iavelberg had recognized as Cabo Anselmo.[43] Later that year, when she was serving several lifetime sentences in jail, she heard through the revolutionary grapevine inside the prison that Cabo Anselmo was making contacts with members of the Left. She urgently sent word to comrades abroad that Cabo Anselmo was a police agent. While she was desperately trying to communicate with her comrades outside prison, Anselmo visited Chile and met with Onofre Pinto, who still considered the former corporal a loyal revolutionary.[44]

When multiple sources confirmed Inês's suspicions, Ângelo and Maria do Carmo confronted Onofre and insisted that the rumors be investigated. Ângelo was already locked in a larger political battle within the organization, and so his accusations against Anselmo, whom Onofre continued to trust, were seen as merely part of an internal factional battle to unseat the leadership.[45] Left free to inform the police on the activities of the revolutionary Left in Brazil and abroad, Anselmo continued to turn in people he was in contact with underground, while at the same time serving as an advisor in police interrogations.[46] He also infiltrated an operation that the VPR had set up in Cuba involving the dispatch of five Brazilian revolutionaries and one Paraguayan revolutionary, Soledad Barret Videma, to Recife in late 1972 with the goal of rebuilding the VPR in the northeast. Through Onofre he communicated with the group and even began a relationship with

Soledad, who became pregnant by him, while remaining in constant contact with his police handlers in São Paulo.[47] In early January 1973, members of the group became suspicious of Anselmo, but before they could act, he called in the police. On January 8, 1973, state agents captured and killed all six revolutionaries in what is known as the Massacre of the São Bento Chacara.[48] Authorities successfully eliminated the remnants of the VPR in Cuba through this ambush in Brazil. Although Anselmo had managed to infiltrate the remnants of the VPR structure in Rio in 1971, the wholesale collapse of the organization that year left the police agent without direct means to find Daniel, which probably saved his life. In fact, it seems that Daniel first learned about the decimation of the VPR group in Recife through a newspaper account. Almost immediately thereafter, but due to other circumstances, things began to fall apart for Daniel's new group as well.

At least twice in 1972, Daniel sent Leo and another militant to Chile to make contact with Ângelo and Maria do Carmo and to receive money and logistical support. He even requested a passport so that he could leave the country, but one was not easily forthcoming.[49] The connection between Rio and Santiago was strengthened when Jonjoca moved to Chile that year and served as an intermediary for VPR members and the envoys Daniel had dispatched from Brazil. The several thousands of dollars that they sent back to Rio allowed Daniel to obtain a mimeograph machine he used to run off copies of the organization's modest political publication and other material.[50] Elisalva traveled to Chile in February 1973 to obtain additional funds to keep Public Publicity solvent and to finance their operations in Niterói.

When she returned to Rio, Elisalva criticized Daniel for not taking appropriate security precautions. These lax practices allowed her to learn the identity of potential recruits to the organization who had met in the house where they lived. In response to her criticisms, Daniel agreed to set up a secret safehouse with funds that she brought back from Chile. Daniel moved to this new *aparelho* around the time that some students from Minas Gerais, who had been hiding in Rio, were arrested by the police. The group was linked to the DVP, and Leo had agreed to help hide them. Under torture, one of the detainees stated that he had met Daniel in a house in Niterói. He also identified Elisalva, who had come home from teaching to find the meeting still in progress and saw the fugitive face-to-face.[51]

When they heard about the arrests, Elisalva, Cláudio, and Daniel took the precaution of hiding. A few days passed and everything seemed fine. Carnival was approaching, and it was a perfect time to disperse. The group, however, didn't realize that the young revolutionary who had run into Elisalva after a meeting with Daniel had revealed the location of their apartment.

On returning home, the police were waiting for Magaly.[52] Elisalva stopped by a little bit later and was also captured. Wasting no time, the police began interrogating her, using the apartment's electrical outlets to inflict shocks on her body. Leo and others in the group were arrested soon thereafter.[53]

When Cláudio and Daniel heard that Elisalva and Magaly had been detained, they panicked. Daniel later related the incident in a letter to Lúcia: "It happened during Carnival. It was so strange to be in the middle of crowds that were celebrating, completely defeated, absolutely isolated."[54] Daniel and Cláudio had run out of options with no place to go. Cláudio wanted to do something to save Elisalva, but when he contacted her family, they told him that he should disappear instead.[55] Daniel described living through a nightmarish evening trying to come up with an "objective" solution. "I concluded that I should commit suicide, since my arrest was inevitable."[56] He preferred death in this way to torture. Cláudio, he thought, could either turn himself in or wait to be arrested since he wasn't very involved. After considering the plan for a while, they realized how ridiculous it was. They later jokingly called the incident, which took place on a Friday, as the "night of the chicken," a playful reference to St. Peter's denial of Christ at the rooster's crow, and a reference to the fact that the only instrument that Daniel had at hand to kill himself was the type of a razor blade used to slaughter chickens in Afro-Brazilian religious ceremonies.[57]

Desperate to escape arrest, the two came up with another solution: contacting Daniel's family. They managed to get word to Dona Geny and Geraldo, who drove from Belo Horizonte to Rio during Carnival, picked them up on a street corner, and spent the day watching the city's raucous street celebrations. Daniel's parents drove them to Belo Horizonte where they hid in Hamilton's house for a few days, and then they took the pair to Barbacena to stay with Dona Geny's sister.[58] Hiding in an obvious place turned out, once more, to be a good strategy. Authorities never bothered to look for the fugitives among Daniel's relatives. Like Edgar Allan Poe's purloined letter, Daniel and Cláudio had been hidden so obviously out in the open that the police never thought to look for them there.

Barbacena is a bucolic city set high in the mountains of southern Minas Gerais that enjoys a tropical climate with humid summer days and refreshingly cool nights. Cláudio and Daniel were a new attraction that spiced up the humdrum daily life of the backwater town.[59] While Daniel recounted that he and Cláudio seemed to blend in as just two more members of the family, it still remains odd that neighbors never commented about Daniel's presence. Daniel's cousin, Cleide Brunelli Caldas, postulated that since her family did not share the last name of the Carvalhos, people didn't associate the notorious "terrorist" with them.⁶⁰ It is hard to imagine, however, that people didn't at some point gossip about Geny Brunelli's revolutionary son, especially since the two families visited each other frequently. Perhaps the famed *mineiro* reserve about outsiders predominated, or Daniel and Cláudio simply seemed so unlike anyone remotely dangerous that they remained undetected.

Almost immediately, the pair found everyday life in a small city in the hinterlands to be excessively tedious. With only two movie houses in town and a limited number of places to eat, Barbacena's major entertainment for its youth was hanging out at the Andradas Square and flirting with the opposite sex.⁶¹ Engaging in political activities was out of the question, so the two had little to do to occupy their time. Daniel read incessantly, and Cláudio painted a bit, but in general they were extremely bored.⁶²

Then they came up with the idea of opening up a discotheque. They called the club Dinosaurus. Daniel's aunt loved the idea. Recently widowed and free-spirited, she let them use an unoccupied family property downtown. Cláudio painted murals on the walls with Stone Age motifs and decorated the ceiling with stalactites. Heavy stone tables were scattered throughout.⁶³ They served drinks and light fare. Daniel was the disc jockey, and Cláudio managed the kitchen and the money. Among their varied clientele were the young cadets from the Brazil Air Force Preparatory School for Air Cadets.

Daniel's cousin Cleide became a constant fixture at the place. She fondly recalls how the nightclub's dark corners were perfect places to spend time with a boyfriend. Considered a wild and rebellious child, she found it exhilarating to work with Cláudio, who was called Lauro, and Daniel, who had taken the name Roberto. The club opened at seven in the evening and closed at five in the morning, and Cleide came there after school every day to help out. Although not overtly a gay bar, no doubt it also gave Cláudio and Daniel the opportunity to flirt with young men who frequented the establishment, and for a sleepy town it was a new and different place to spend time.⁶⁴

Unfortunately, Dinosaurus made no money. Dona Geny lamented this fact many years later as she complained about the recklessness of the venture.⁶⁵ Having accumulated a debt with beer suppliers and other businesses, Daniel and Cláudio were forced to close the place after six months or so of operations. Several months later, when Cleide discovered that she was pregnant, Daniel and Cláudio helped smooth over the family drama of having a single mother in the house. To avoid small-town gossip, Cleide's mother decided to relocate the family to a working-class neighborhood in Rio, and Daniel went along, serving as an important support to Cleide during her pregnancy and delivery.⁶⁶ Cláudio moved to Belo Horizonte to live with

FIGURE 11.2 Herbert Daniel (right) and Cláudio Mesquita in Argentina, September 1974. COURTESY OF GENY BRUNELLI DE CARVALHO.

Dona Geny and Geraldo, posing as a nephew.[67] While in Rio, it is likely that Daniel also made discreet inquiries to find out what had happened to his comrades who had been in Chile when the military, under the leadership of General Augusto Pinochet, took power on September 11, 1973.

Thousands of Brazilian revolutionaries had moved there during the government of Salvador Allende. Many had had warrants out for their arrests, while others fled Brazil, fearing possible persecution. Almost immediately after the military took power, the new government issued a call for "patriots" to turn in all foreign "subversives." While many Brazilian exiles attempted to make contacts with the Chilean Left to resist the coup, they soon realized that their foreign accents and tenuous legal status gravely endangered them. There was a rush to get into foreign embassies and request political asylum. Jean Marc Von der Weid, released from prison in exchange for the freedom of the Swiss ambassador, played a key role in saving the lives of dozens of revolutionaries that he ferried to different embassies, using his Swiss passport as a protective shield against arrest.[68] Maria do Carmo, Mário Japa, Maria Carmo's son Juarez and her mother, Angelina, along with Ângelo Pezzutti and his new Chilean partner, Maria Elena Advisa, all managed to get into the Panamanian embassy, a three-room apartment that soon was occupied by 250 asylum seekers. Eventually they were allowed to leave the country. Maria do Carmo, Mário Japa, and Juarez received asylum in Belgium, while Ângelo and Maria Helena ended up in Paris. Once they had settled, they started making inquiries to see if anyone knew the whereabouts of Daniel and Cláudio. They were especially worried about his safety after they received news of the killings of VPR militants in Recife. No one had a clue.[69]

After Ângelo Pezzuti, Maria do Carmo Brito, and Mário Japa settled in Europe, they sent a message to Jonjoca, who had escaped from Chile to Argentina, and asked him to come to Europe to carry out a mission. They gave him money and instructions to get two modified passports, discreetly enter Brazil, find Daniel, and convince him to leave the country. Ângelo gave Jonjoca his aunt's address and instructed him to contact her for help.[70] Ângela Pezzutti was shocked when an unknown person knocked on her door and wanted to talk with her. When he gave her a note from her nephew identifying him as a trustworthy envoy, she immediately agreed to help out.[71] In interviews for this book, Ângela and Jonjoca gave detailed but differing accounts about how money and false passports ended up in Daniel's hands. However, the essential specifics remained the same. Jonjoca had obtained two passports from Argentine revolutionary contacts and passed them on to Daniel with the message that his comrades insisted that he leave the country. It took some time for the documents to be appropriately modified. Meanwhile, Daniel moved to Belo Horizonte to be with Cláudio and arrange their departure, while still operating under the assumption that he was invulnerable to detection and arrest. Lenice Leandro de Carvalho, Hamilton's wife, tells the story that Daniel and Cláudio gathered a group of students together at the university to rehearse a play written by the pair, while they were waiting for the altered documents to be ready. She vaguely remembers the story line of the theater piece to have been a critique of the military regime set in a circus.[72] It was never performed, but the very fact that the two had even considered putting on a play in Belo Horizonte was both an indication of their boldness and the ongoing decision—in retrospect both naïve and amazingly clever—to simply ignore the dangers around them.

On September 7, 1974, Brazilian Independence Day, Daniel and Cláudio crossed over the border into Argentina with modified passports from a Central American nation in hand. Daniel feigned laryngitis to avoid talking to strangers, but Cláudio, loquacious and friendly, chatted in a strange mixture of Spanish and Portuguese that amused fellow passengers but failed to raise the suspicions of the authorities.[73] After almost six years living underground, Daniel moved from an internal and domestic exile to a new dislocation in Europe.

12

Red Carnations

(1974–1975)

> Exile is a negated certainty, an affirmative absence, a faraway place, another world.
>
> — HERBERT DANIEL

There were good reasons for Daniel to leave Brazil when he did. He had been accused of multiple violations of the National Security Act and faced several lifetimes in prison.[1] Under Institutional Act No. 14 (1969), he risked the death sentence. Moreover, government authorities were killing an increasing number of revolutionaries while under custody, claiming they had resisted arrest.[2]

When Cláudio and Daniel slipped across the border, Brazil's political future was by no means certain. On March 15, 1974, Ernesto Geisel became the fourth four-star general to assume the presidency. He pledged to shepherd in political liberalization soon after assuming office, but Presidents Castelo Branco and Costa e Silva had made these same assurances when they took power and had not fulfilled their promises. Médici hadn't even bothered to offer that hope. Given this track record, there were certainly no guarantees that promised "slow, secure, and gradual" changes would take place. Although Geisel lifted restrictions on censorship and opened up the election process somewhat, it was reasonable to be cautious, if not cynical, about an imminent liberalization.[3]

International oil prices soared in early 1974. Brazil was still highly dependent on large-scale petroleum imports to sustain its expanding economy. Faced with substantial energy shortages, the government had to borrow large sums to increase supplies, leading to inflation and economic deceleration. These measures contributed to undercutting support the regime had received from the middle classes and some sectors of the working classes during the "economic miracle." The military dictatorship started showing signs of weakness.[4]

The economic crisis was also a factor in a shift in partisan allegiances. A comparison of 1966 congressional election results to those of 1970 reveals that blank and spoiled ballots increased sharply, possibly representing a dispersed dissatisfaction with the regime, although political scientists have suggested socioeconomic factors as a cause.[5] Still, ARENA remained firmly in control of the national and most state administrations and legislatures. Four years later, the political climate had changed. Discontent with the status quo was now channeled through support for the MDB, which aggressively campaigned against the economic marginalization of the poor and working classes and criticized the lack of democracy. Only two months after Daniel and Cláudio left the country, the military faced surprising election results. In Senate races, the MDB received 14.5 million votes, or 59 percent of the total, and won sixteen of the twenty-two contested seats. While ARENA retained a majority in the lower house, the opposition expanded its representation, especially in urban areas. These outcomes indicated that the regime was quickly losing its political appeal, especially in Brazil's major metropolises.[6]

This process did not automatically lead to a decrease in torture or political repression. While armed-struggle organizations were decimated by 1974, the political police operated unabated against other left-wing groups. In 1975, Vladimir Herzog, a prominent São Paulo journalist linked to the PCB, died while being interrogated.[7] The next year, the army violently attacked a meeting of the Communist Party of Brazil's Central Committee, killing three leaders.[8] These actions revealed that Geisel had not reigned in hardline military forces that wanted to continue annihilating all left-wing opposition. Daniel was much safer abroad.

Daniel and Cláudio's arrival in Paris was a cause for tremendous celebration. Finally, after almost six years of separation, Ângelo Pezzuti and

Daniel were reunited. Although Daniel was incredibly excited about seeing Ângelo and other exiles, leaving Brazil had not been easy. He later wrote he had only agreed to abandon his homeland because the modified passport he had used could allow him to return in the near future to continue the struggle.⁹ After much discussion, Ângelo, Maria do Carmo, and others convinced Daniel that if he were to sneak back into the country and get arrested, the military would once again torture other imprisoned comrades in order to extract new information based on anything he might reveal. Moreover, the killings in Recife strongly suggested that government authorities might simply assassinate Daniel if he were caught. Slowly the idea of secretly returning faded. He gradually adjusted to the idea of living abroad.¹⁰

While in Paris, Daniel met Maria Helena Tejo, who had joined VAR-Palmares in Rio Grande do Sul in 1969 and then escaped to the northeast when police arrests forced militants to scatter to avoid capture. She finally managed to leave Brazil and arrived in Paris at the end of 1973. The two became instant friends. She recalled: "After Daniel arrived, we must have stayed a month or two [in Paris], and then Maria do Carmo . . . arranged a way for us to go to Portugal. . . . Because of the Carnation Revolution, we had the chance to find jobs there."¹¹

By late 1974, Portugal was an attractive destination for many Brazilian exiles who had fled Chile. The revolutionary upheaval taking place there offered an optimistic counterpoint to the recent defeat of Chile's "peaceful road to socialism." Moreover, although Brazil had long before achieved independence from Portugal, a shared language and historical and cultural ties still bound the two countries and their peoples together.¹²

The Portuguese Carnation Revolution, as it was called, began on April 25, 1974, when a group of captains and other soldiers, who had secretly formed the Movement of the Armed Forces (MFA), seized control of key locations in Lisbon.¹³ They announced an end to the *estado novo* (new state), the fascist regime in power since 1933, and outlined a far-reaching program. It included ending Portugal's ongoing war against the independence movements in its African colonies and in East Timor. Almost immediately, the rebels began dismantling the repressive apparatus. The MFA called for the establishment of a democratic regime that would foster sweeping economic and social reforms. Initially influenced by the outlawed Portuguese Communist Party and other left-wing groups, which now were able to operate legally, the April 25 rebellion ignited popular sentiment in favor of radical change.

On the day of the revolt, as tanks rolled into the city center, the MFA broadcast radio messages calling on the population to stay indoors. People ignored the request, and thousands flooded into the streets. Soldiers and civilians gathered up red carnations (which were in season) at the flower market and on corner stands and placed them in the muzzles of rifles and on the uniforms of soldiers to symbolize a peaceful (and revolutionary) defeat of the fascist regime. The MFA's program of democratization, decolonization, and development unleashed a two-year clash between the Left and the Right that came to be called the "ongoing revolutionary process," as different political forces fought to influence the political outcomes of the 1974 uprising. Daniel and Cláudio arrived in Portugal later that year, when this pitched battle was in full force.

The decision to leave for Portugal happened rather quickly. Neither Maria Helena nor Daniel and Cláudio had found any immediate way to support themselves in Paris. None of them spoke French, and Portugal became an enticing option. Maria Helena recalled, "Daniel stopped by my house in a taxi.... I was depressed with all of the moving around, not knowing where I was going to live, and Daniel said to me: 'Things are not always as we would like them to be.'" A veteran revolutionary nomad, Daniel had had endless experiences adapting to new places and precarious situations, so he probably saw the plan to resettle in Portugal as just another stop on a long journey that had begun, when he gathered up a few clothes, including the brown sweater his mother had knit for him, and abandoned Belo Horizonte. After a string of defeats in Brazil, this was an opportunity to experience the revolution he had dreamed about since 1967. He had spent the past year and a half enduring a rather tedious and uneventful time in Barbacena and Belo Horizonte. He was up for another adventure. Maria Helena remembered: "So we got on a train—Maria do Carmo, Jonjoca, Daniel, Cláudio and I, and we went to live in Lisbon."

After staying with former VPR members for a short time and then living in temporary housing provided to political refugees, the group found a large apartment across the Tagus River from Lisbon. Daniel and Maria Helena shared a room, while Cláudio, Jonjoca, and Maria do Carmo settled in other quarters. The apartment was near the beach, and it quickly became a gathering point for Brazilian exiles.[14]

Seen in retrospect, Maria Helena judged that the living arrangement didn't work out: "Daniel and Cláudio made friends with the gay community, so it became [a] gay [place]. If you got home at a given time, there wasn't even a place to sleep. It was too much for Maria do Carmo and Mário Japa, who later joined her, along with Juarez, Maria do Carmo's son." Reflecting on the experience, Maria do Carmo explained, "I was the only person who was working. When I got home, I washed everyone's clothes, made food for everyone and then went to work. When I returned, the dishes were in the sink. I had to wash everything to make dinner. That's the difference between a group and a family. . . . It didn't work. . . . We didn't fight. Before quarreling, we moved to another house."[15]

While idealized communist principles about equal sharing of duties and tasks between the sexes might have circulated among Brazilian exiles, putting them into practice was another matter. Few male revolutionaries had embraced feminist ideas in 1974, and so the burden of housework remained on women's shoulders and was seen as a natural division of labor. Maria do Carmo, Mário Japa, and Juarez moved out to form a nuclear family. Daniel, Cláudio, Maria Helena, and Jonjoca remained in the apartment living a more communal existence. Over subsequent months they received visits from dozens of other Brazilian exiles that had scattered all over Europe but took advantage of the roomy and strategically located apartment near the beach to see their friends in Portugal.

Daniel experienced new energy and creative excitement during the ebullient first year or so of the Carnation Revolution. "Portugal, a curbside without prohibitions, where I could feel and write little verses," he penned.[16] For those used to a repressive situation, where frank and open political conversations were impossible, Portugal was a unique experience. "It was a party. . . . Everyone discussing things everywhere. In public plazas, day and night we gathered in small groups talking about the revolution." He also noted: "After so many years, I was able to rest quietly in a café, on a public bench, even on the sidewalk, if I wanted to. The day that I was at that curbside, on an avenue, which happened to have the name Liberdade [Liberty], the world felt different. This reinvented calmness gave me a big push. Oh, how things can be fantastic seen from the surprising perspective of the edge of a walkway."

Daniel wrote many letters from his Portuguese exile. Few have survived. Fortunately, Lúcia Velloso saved all of their correspondence. The exchange of letters began soon after she was released from prison in 1975. In Lúcia's first communication, hand delivered by Alfredo Sirkis, she began simply but with remarkable intuition, considering that they had not been in touch for almost four years: "My dear. What do I now call you? I was going to write Dan, but I stopped. I remembered that you liked your name Herbert. But you also liked Daniel. And now what do you prefer? Maybe a new name, a new relationship, new perspectives; even Portugal has renewed itself."[17]

Lúcia was right. Daniel had changed, and since he liked both his given name and the name he assumed underground, it was slowly sticking as his permanent composite moniker. They both had gone through many transformations since their intimate conversations in mid-1971. In her first lengthy epistle, Lúcia related her experiences while in jail and after she was freed. She described the ups and downs of her marriage to Alex, who was serving a life sentence, and her personal search for a new identity as she readjusted to life outside of prison.

Daniel wrote an exuberant and equally long response that confirmed her speculations: "I've changed so much that it is hard at times to remember who I was. I can't even explain in what ways and how I have changed." He went on to state: "For the first time in my life, without exaggeration, having found a sure path, I am happy."[18] These self-descriptions were incisive reflections on his personality. "I'm older; less of a dreamer. That is, I dream a lot, but the dreams are smaller. I'm still problematic and a megalomaniac, but a bit more ironic and mistrustful." Daniel had also changed physically. Losing weight helped him begin to feel good about his body for the first time.

After recapping what had happened following Lúcia's arrest, he came to what seems to have been the point of the letter: Cláudio. He described Cláudio affectionately to Lúcia. "He is absolutely sensational. . . . For the last three years, we formed a friendship that was for me a rebirth." Daniel recounted the journeys they had shared: "It so happens that Lauro [Cláudio] and I have been together for three years, running around the world, in good times and bad times, connected, glued together, dependent. But we were friends. We shared everything except our bed. Exactly two weeks ago things changed. We ended up doing the most natural thing in the world: we love each other. It was an incredible experience. It continues to be. It's not that we have changed the actual basis of our relationship. It's just that we have accepted it."

Although Daniel and Cláudio only consummated their relationship in 1975, many people who interacted with them on a day-to-day basis assumed they had been sexually involved long before that date, especially those who knew or speculated about Daniel's homosexuality. Maria Helena, Daniel's closest friend in Portugal, knew intimate details of her roommates' personal life, but others had created false assumptions about their relationship. In recalling interactions with the two during their first six months in Europe, Alfredo Sirkis, Liszt Vieira, Maria do Carmo, and Mário Japa told me that Daniel and Cláudio had arrived in Paris as a gay couple, shared the same room, and presumably the same bed.[19] Carlos Minc, who had been a member of VAR-Palmares, but hadn't known Daniel in Brazil, met him in Portugal and assumed that he and Cláudio were together.[20] Daniel's cousin Cleide insisted the two had been sexually intimate in Barbacena.[21] As far as those surrounding the pair were concerned, their personal closeness meant sexual involvement.

In Daniel's second book, he gives the reader a peek into how the romance started. Cláudio had been cool and detached during the previous few days. They spent Saturday at the beach. Unexpectedly, Cláudio gave Daniel a letter: "If we say that we love each other, why don't we take our love to its ultimate consequences?" he wrote. Daniel wasn't sure if he wanted to go ahead, but he did. "It wasn't the best sex that I had had in my life," he later admitted. "But in fact it gave me exclusively unexpected and unexplainable pleasures."[22]

Maria Helena remembered the initial psychological drama surrounding their love affair: "Cláudio was more certain that he wanted it, and Daniel was rather confused because they were such good friends. . . . This is just my interpretation because he never told me this, but I think that Daniel had difficulties entering into things [relationships] that would work, and Cláudio was something that would work. . . . He [Daniel] had gone through many traumas, for example Ribeira was really hard for him. He didn't have sex, and no one knew that he was a homosexual." In fact, in his memoir Daniel insisted his experience in guerrilla training had been positive because he had given up sex for a cause, but it is clear that his repressed sexuality tormented him.

Maria Helena also reflected on deeper anxieties that Daniel faced. "I think that he created a persona that didn't include opening up this part of his life. For the first time he had found a viable partner in Cláudio. Because he was in exile and wasn't a member of any organization, and the people around him didn't have any problems with it, suddenly he realized: 'I can do it here.' I think this scared him a bit." Since Daniel had decided to repress his sexuality in order to join the O., he had had a string of infatuations with heterosexual men that had no chance of leading anywhere. Far from Brazil, he slowly realized Cláudio was a person who could potentially be his partner, and perhaps, as Maria Helena speculated, it disrupted a pattern of falling in love with people who couldn't reciprocate his passion. These one-sided crushes were actually emotionally safe, because they prevented him from having to act on his feelings. Repeatedly developing "impossible" infatuations and being constantly rebuffed, whether overtly or indirectly, also seems to have reinforced Daniel's natural timidity and insecurity in these personal matters, making it hard to imagine a romantic relationship with Cláudio, who was potentially available. That Cláudio was so handsome made it even harder, since Daniel considered himself to be unattractive.

Maria Helena offered a vivid portrait of Cláudio: "Cláudio was flamboyant; he wore dresses; he used makeup. He was very calm about his homosexuality. He even called himself Maria da Glória because he was the one who did the shopping for the house. He would say, 'Maria da Glória is going to the market,' and then he'd bring home fruits and vegetables." According to Maria Helena, Daniel was so secretive about his homosexuality that she thought he hadn't even come out directly to Maria do Carmo, an observation confirmed while researching this book.[23] Having a love affair with Cláudio inevitably would lead to full disclosure. It is also possible that Daniel's reluctance to become involved with Cláudio meant acknowledging the end of a period in his life when remaining unattached symbolized on both conscious and unconscious levels that he was an independent individual wedded to the revolutionary cause. Starting a relationship with Cláudio marked a new phase in his life; it also meant leaving behind practices that had restrained his emotional and sexual options but had become familiar and therefore comfortable ways to interact with others.

Even though Daniel dearly missed Brazil, he had finally found a freer space in Portugal to become more creative, which included being more open about his feelings and gaining the confidence to confront the norm of compulsory heterosexual behavior embedded in leftist ideology that had constrained him in Brazil. For many exiles, being forced to live outside one's country and culture can feel like being suspended in time and space, as if the normal flow of life has been put on hold. One goes through the motions of living without fully connecting to other people and one's surroundings. In many ways, this had been Daniel's situation since February 1969, when he fled to Rio, although that exile was actually an internal, psychological one. Daniel had been hiding his homosexuality from people around him since the mid-1960s; going underground merely intensified his inward emotional alienation. In that shadowy world, he had to deal with the dissonance between necessary actions and his true feelings and desires. Furthermore, he faced a stressful situation in which, as a revolutionary, many people with whom he interacted couldn't know that he was involved in subversive political activities. This meant projecting the persona of a committed guerrilla to his comrades that was layered on top of intimate secrets about his sexual identity, and then creating fake personalities for those he met so that he could operate underground.

In his memoir he recounted how he invented characters and cover stories, when, for example, he chatted with the person next to him on a bus traveling between cities on a revolutionary mission. He admitted there was a creative excitement in weaving together entire life histories that seemed logical, consistent, and without internal contradictions, which might create suspicion. Apparently, he was quite good at it.[24] Because he had already accumulated experience hiding his homosexuality to become a revolutionary, it must have made the process of constantly making up new identities even easier. Still, at the same time, it created a deep estrangement from the world around him.

Living in Portugal during the Carnation Revolution without any real fear of arrest was a liberating experience. Talking openly about being gay to his circle of friends and publicly admitting he was in a relationship with Cláudio forced him to come out of a tightly woven protective cocoon. It also meant leaving behind ties of dependency on others for survival that had been essential while living underground. In Portugal, for the first time since Daniel entered medical school, he was again free to choose his friends, the nature of his interactions with others, and when and how he wanted to divulge personal details. He could do all this without having to worry about his safety or the dangers related to intimate revelations. He also no longer needed to depend on the willingness of supporters and strangers to hide and protect him.

The political transformations he experienced since the months of lonely self-reflection in a closed-up apartment also contributed to a reevaluation of his relationships with friends and associates. While living in Lisbon, Daniel realized he had little in common with many former comrades, though he once had been willing to risk his life to free them from prison. "I can't have a pleasant conversation with people who continue to get excited about (*curtir*) the Brazilian revolution," he confessed to Lúcia in a second missive. "Moreover, I'm a bit embarrassed about being 'retired.'" He also faced another disappointing reality: "I think that in general the Brazilians don't accept the fact that I have calmly come out about my homosexuality."[25]

Daniel mentioned his "retired" status several times to Lúcia and readily admitted the lingering guilt he felt for having given up on the revolutionary promise for Brazil. But he added, "What's more, I live with a guy, I don't smoke grass, and I don't hang out at other Brazilians' houses." Many of his fellow exiles living through the Carnation Revolution saw their political activities in Portugal as linked to their previous militancy, and they retained traditional left-wing prejudices about homosexuality as a "petty-bourgeois deviation" or as a "product of bourgeois decadence."[26] Being open about one's homosexuality within a left-wing milieu was still a novelty, and as Daniel noted, many comrades did not easily embrace the news. Other Brazilians living abroad had chosen a new, less politically committed life and enjoyed smoking pot now and then, a practice also disdained by many on the Left. Daniel didn't feel comfortable in either subgroup of Brazilian exiles, so he and Cláudio withdrew from the social networks of Brazilian exiles and lived a relatively quiet life with a few close friends.[27] They moved across the Tejo River to a charming old apartment with their friends Maria Helena and Liszt Vieira, who had become a couple.[28] As Daniel explained, "My former house was very big and constantly invaded. Literally invaded, as we never had less than 10 people in the house. Because I needed a little bit of solitude, we moved."[29]

Although Daniel never finished a course in medicine during his European exile, he did enroll in medical school. He also found work writing articles for *Modas e Bordados* (Fashion and embroidery) a traditional weekly magazine "for women," which was a supplement of the newspaper *O Século*. Maria Antónia Palla, a well-known left-wing journalist, had started changing the magazine's content a month or so before the Carnation Revolution to include feminist ideas, especially those focusing on family planning and abortion.[30] "What better end could there be in the life of a retired terrorist than to become a writer for *Modas e Bordados*, nostalgically looking at the women on the editorial staff while crocheting endlessly?" Daniel jested in a letter to Lúcia. "Don't worry," he assured her. "The magazine is very serious. It was an attempt to take a basically reactionary magazine and offer something new to the female readership (the magazine is almost one hundred years old). We're not trying to turn the readers into 'revolutionaries,'" he explained. "Rather [we're trying] at least to neutralize a sector of the petty bourgeoisie."[31]

As in many other situations when Brazilian exiles sought employment or other assistance, Daniel landed the job through personal contacts. Maria António Fiadeiro, a left-wing activist who had lived in exile in Brazil from 1968 to 1974, had known Maria do Carmo in Rio and was an editor of the magazine.[32] Daniel inquired about possible work. Fiadeiro asked for a writing sample, liked it, and hired him as a freelancer. He later became a member of the editorial staff. The experience was politically transformative.

The main concerns of the organizations to which Daniel had belonged focused on carrying out a revolutionary guerrilla strategy. The Marxist backdrop for these ideas privileged the working class, although in practice after 1968 this sector of the revolutionary Left did little actual work among the proletariat. Issues such as the unequal treatment of women in the Left and in society more generally or questions about racism were considered problems that would be resolved after seizing power and building a new socialist society.

HERBERT EUSTÁQUIO DE CARVALHO

1. Filho de GERALDO FELICIANO DE CARVALHO e de GENY BRUNELLI DE CARVA_
LHO, ambos brasileiros, nascido a 14FEV46 em BOM-DESPACHO/MINAS GERAIS/BRASIL, não é
portador de qualquer documento de identificação; residiu na Av. 25 de Abril nº9-18º
andar Dtº em ALMADA.

2. Declarou que abandonou o Brasil por motivos políticos, depois de ter
tomado parte em manifestações públicas, reuniões e crítica directa através dos jornais
contra o actual regime brasileiro. Estes actos motivaram-lhe perseguições, por parte
da polícia política, que o obrigou a andar refugiado por diversas partes do territótio
do seu país. Depois de lhe terem sido imputadas acusações, sem provas, foi-lhe orga_
nizado o respectivo processo que com consequente julgamento, à revelia teve como deci_
são, a sentença de prisão perpétua. Verificando então, que era impossível permanecer
no Brasil nem, mais tarde ou mais cedo, ser preso, para cumprimento da pena que lhe
tinha sido imposta, resolveu vir para a Europa, mormente para Portugal, em virtude
da mudança política operada no 25 de Abril de 1974. Para isso, serviu-se dum passa_
porte dum amigo seu, ao qual apenas mudou a fotografia, embarcando num avião que
tomou no Rio de Janeiro com destino a Paris, seguindo dali para Lisboa por caminho
de ferro; entrou em Portugal a 21OUT74 por Vilar Formoso. Em seguida remeteu ao seu

FIGURE 12.1 Portuguese political police file on Herbert Eustáquio de Carvalho.
SOURCE: MINISTÉRIO DOS ASSUNTOS INTERNOS.

In Europe, Daniel discovered new revolutionary ideas (among them feminism). During his first months in Portugal he seems to have ignored the fact that many women, like Maria do Carmo, are oftentimes burdened with double duties of work inside and outside the home without much male support, but over the next year his views about the way rigid gender roles are constructed slowly changed. Daniel still held an anti-imperialist and anticapitalist worldview and considered himself aligned with revolutionary movements throughout the world, but his work at Modas e Bordados put him in touch with female leftists who discussed discrimination against and oppression of women that pushed him to rethink or expand beyond the traditional parameters of Marxist ideology. Daniel's recent acceptance of his homosexuality and the process of revealing his sexual and romantic feelings to his closest comrades dovetailed with this new contact with feminist ideas. It offered him a new framework for understanding politics.

In order to work for the newspaper, Daniel had to try to legalize his situation, which required creating a narrative about his former political activities in Brazil that would allow him to obtain papers with his real name. According to the files compiled by the Ministry of Internal Affairs, he had "abandoned Brazil for political reasons, after having taken part in public demonstrations and meetings directly criticizing the regime. These acts resulted in persecution by the political police, forcing him to flee to different parts of his country."[33] While this explanation for why he had gone into exile described his political activities in general terms, it glossed over most of the details about his revolutionary life. This was to be expected, as exiles had been advised to stick to the story that they were merely student activists being unjustly persecuted, so that they could obtain legal residency in Europe.[34] The report went on to state that "after pressing charges against him without proof, a trial was held in absentia, and he was condemned to a lifetime in prison. Realizing that it was impossible to remain in Brazil, without sooner or later being arrested and having to serve out his term, he decided to come to Europe, namely Portugal, given the political changes that had taken place since April 25, 1974." Again, while the overall story is quite accurate, the report (and presumably the story Daniel gave to authorities) leaves out the real reasons why he had been sentenced to such a long prison term. In order to explain why he didn't have any documents, Daniel told government agents that someone in Brazil had lent him a passport. He changed the picture and flew from Rio to Paris. He then traveled by train to Portugal, after which he returned the passport to the person who had lent it to him. It is not clear from these records whether or not the Portuguese police believed his story, but, in any case, he never managed to legalize his situation.[35]

Even without legal papers, for the first time in six years, Daniel could use his real name again, and he signed the articles he wrote for *Modas e Bordados* H. de Carvalho. Using the initial "H." rather than his given first name was probably designed to hide his gender and make his columns more acceptable to the magazine's mostly female readership. From April to October 1975, Daniel wrote over a dozen articles on a range of topics. The language of his texts still relied in part on Marxist ideas and terminology, as was befitting someone with his political past living in the turbulent revolutionary upheavals of Portugal. However, now he addressed many new subjects that had never been mentioned in the reams of documents he and others had written about tactics, strategies, and the socialist revolution.

Daniel's background in medicine also came in handy. He was able to write comfortably about health, especially about reproductive issues, which may have been one of the reasons he was hired. For example, in one of his first articles, "The Time I Spent in my Mother's Uterus," Daniel invented an "intimate diary of a fetus," which creatively describes the gestational process as a means of educating the reader about the complexities of pregnancy.[36] One article adamantly defends a woman's right to a safe abortion.[37] Another discusses the government's new policy of providing universal health care.[38] Other columns analyze women's role in the workplace, the importance of leisure time, and the positive effects of sports in improving one's health. Still another article describes racism as a social disease and racists as mentally ill.[39]

The United Nations had declared 1975 to be International Women's Year, and Daniel penned a series of columns entitled "Thirty Days of Women around the World" that included coverage of the international conference held in Mexico City. One item written by Daniel evaluates the event critically.[40] Daniel points out the weaknesses of the Portuguese delegation, which he argues had done virtually nothing to create visibility in the Mexican gathering. In another article, still wedded to a Marxist logic in which class trumped gender oppression, Daniel criticizes the speech of a Portuguese delegate because she discussed development without linking it to the means and relationships of production and promoted the idea of the international solidarity among women as if they could be defined as a unified group unto themselves without any class differentiations.[41]

In general, Daniel remained on the side of socialist feminists in the political debates within the women's movement. However, he wrote an interesting article about Marilyn Monroe, his "idealized love," as Maria do Carmo had described the Hollywood star that Daniel talked about so much while underground. The essay offers a complex analysis of the role of the media in producing sex symbols while simultaneously reinforcing conservative ideas about sex. It begins forcefully: "A woman is a woman. In certain conditions, created by society, she turns into a man's slave, housewife, prostitute, object, and semi-goddess. Marilyn was a woman. . . . She turned into a thing, merchandise. Myth. Why? She continues to be presented as a symbol. Her story endures as a fable telling how a human, and specifically a 'FEMALE' human, becomes an object of fantasies. Why?"[42] The article stands strangely out of place in comparison to other columns he penned, in part because he focuses on a woman largely disdained by the international feminist movement for seeming to reproduce and reinforce traditional gender roles.

At the same time, Daniel displays a fascination with the blond "sex goddess" not unlike one shared by many gay men of his generation who identified with Monroe's frailty, vulnerability, and tragic ending, because they themselves experienced being social outcasts with complicated and emotionally difficult lives.[43] The article came out two months after Daniel and Cláudio began their love affair, and this insightful essay on a gay icon might have been a way for Daniel to suggest publicly that he was gay.

Daniel's analysis is quite sophisticated. Implicitly, capitalism produces and promotes "an idealization of feminine sexuality through physical beauty," as well as "sexual freedom ardently desired and equally feared." Monroe's infantile simplicity and her animal-like sexuality, he argues, promote the myth of "free, natural sex without repression." At the same time, her sexuality borders on the scandalous, and her tragic ending is a morality tale that marks the limits of transgression and the dreadful consequences of sexual freedom. Daniel continues: "An enormous mechanism of ideological information (and deformation) portrays Marilyn as the epitome of 'sex,' while at the same time insisting on the fact that it is 'immoral' and 'infamous' and will lead to unhappiness and disgrace." Daniel's reflections on mass media, culture, sex, women, morality, and the role of publicity in creating and reinforcing myths mark his journey away from reductionist Marxist formulations about class to analyses that are as erudite as the best feminist writings of the time, even though there is no indication that he had any knowledge of these works.[44]

While Daniel honed his literary skills and expanded his political perspectives as a writer for a women's magazine, Cláudio managed to find a job with the MFA preparing and illustrating pamphlets and other educational material. The revolutionary government had decided to focus attention on the poor regions of northern Portugal by organizing adult literacy brigades that went to villages and used the Brazilian educator Paulo Freire's approach to educate peasants. Inspired by that work, Daniel reported to

FIGURE 12.2 Article on Marilyn Monroe that appeared in *Modas e Bordados*, July 30, 1975.

Lúcia he was working on a book with Cláudio about new ideas regarding education, influenced by Freire's writings. He told her the book (which was never published) was going to be entitled "The School Is Dead! Long Live the School," was a critique of the bourgeois educational system, and proposed a "dialectic method of teaching."[45]

In addition to working in the MFA's literacy campaigns, Cláudio joined Daniel as a collaborator at *Modas e Bordados* by producing illustrations for several articles about health and the body. It is interesting to note that although Daniel was slowly revealing his homosexuality to his Brazilian friends, he remained discreet about his personal life and his political past while working for the magazine. Maria Antónia and Daniel never talked about his time as a Brazilian revolutionary, nor did he ever openly reveal his relationship with Cláudio to her. She assumed that they were merely close friends.[46]

That was to be expected. After having guarded the secret of his sexual identity so carefully in Brazil, Daniel was gifted in carefully measuring whom he could trust or in whom he wished to confide. As he wrote to Lúcia, it was also quite new to openly embrace his homosexuality. Some of his Brazilian friends seemed nonplussed about his relationship with Cláudio. Long-term bonds of friendship had been forged through excessively dangerous times, and no doubt due to solidarity with and respect for Daniel, their comradeship was stronger than pervasive conservative attitudes of the international Left about homosexuality. Perhaps in a measure of self-preservation, he simply remained on guard at work, just as he distanced himself from those former comrades whom he sensed had not changed with the times.

In addition to working for the magazine, Daniel began two other projects in 1975. Like enrolling in medical school and writing the book on new forms of pedagogy, they were never finished. At the end of the year, he wrote Lúcia that he had published a volume of poetry, although no one who lived with him in Portugal remembers this, leading one to believe that it was more an intention than an actuality.[47] He also shared his excitement about preparing a manuscript on the Portuguese Revolution, which didn't come to fruition, even though he wrote that he had secured a publisher.[48] Though these ventures were never realized, the enthusiastic way Daniel described them, as well as his creativity in thinking about women's issues, reveals that he had become excited about his opportunities to write passionately about new topics far afield of the Marxist language and ideology that had constrained the content of the many political documents he had written while underground. "I've achieved a certain intellectual maturity," he confessed to Lúcia, "which is truthful, rather pernicious, and misanthropic, but regardless, which is more secure and 'professional.'"[49]

There may be, however, another explanation for Daniel's failure to complete his multiple literary plans. On September 11, 1975, the second anniversary of the Chilean coup, Ângelo died in a motorcycle accident in Paris. The news devastated Daniel, who commented two months later to Lúcia that its "absurdity" was what most marked that year.[50] Although Daniel had just found the love of his life, the loss of Ângelo superseded the joy he felt about his new relationship when he looked back over the year.

Daniel felt emotionally unable to go to Paris for the funeral, and so Maria Helena, who had become a good friend of Ângelo's partner, Maria Luisa Advisa, represented him and Cláudio. According to Maria do Carmo, Maria Elena Advisa preferred that she not come, so Mário Japa went in her stead.[51]

By all accounts, the graveside ceremony was an exceedingly emotional event, and Carmela Pezzuti, who had followed her son into revolutionary politics, had a tremendously difficult time accepting his death.[52] Half a decade later, Daniel wrote in his memoir, "Ângelo escaped prison in Brazil; he escaped the coup in Chile; but he couldn't escape his uneasiness about living life to the fullest. He also didn't live to see any results."[53] Maria Helena considered that Daniel entered a mild depression after Ângelo's death, which was exacerbated by the political situation unfolding in Portugal.

By late 1975 the radical left-leaning forces had lost out to sectors in the military and those in the general population that wanted to slow down the revolution's pace. On November 25, 1975, more conservative groups gained control of the government. In the aftermath, soldiers invaded the apartment shared by Daniel, Cláudio, and Maria Helena, allegedly seeking arms that might have been stored there.[54] Although none were found, the raid shook all three of them profoundly, and they began plans to leave Portugal. Maria do Carmo and Mário Japa were invited to Angola to support the newly independent country.[55] For a while Cláudio suggested that they go to Africa as well.[56] In the end they opted to move to Paris. In part it was a way for Daniel to defy Ângelo's "stupid" death, as he called it. He also didn't want to witness the red carnations of the Portuguese revolution wither away as had his hopes for a similar revolution against the Brazilian military regime.[57] Daniel had just turned twenty-nine; he needed a rest from revolutionary politics.

13

Marginalia

(1976–1981)

> He wasn't someone with fixed, preconceived ideas. He was someone who permanently questioned things . . . and he had a fantastic sense of irony.
>
> —JEAN MARC VON DER WEID

In January 1976, Daniel, Cláudio, and Maria Helena settled into a one-bedroom apartment in Paris. After ten intense years of "making the revolution," Daniel's mind and body were weary of political fervor, and he wanted to get his papers (and perhaps, symbolically, his whole life) in order. Fortunately, Liszt Vieira, who had also moved back to France but had separated from Maria Helena, managed to penetrate the complexities of the UN refugee system's application procedures and came to their assistance, serving as guide and translator. Daniel and Cláudio repeated the same stories they had told the Portuguese police. To their benefit, the flood of Chilean refugees to Europe had created a credible narrative about systematic political persecution in Latin America, which allowed the pair to get political asylum without alerting the authorities to the extent of Daniel's subversive past. Finally, they received UN travel documents that legalized their stay in France.[1]

Soon after arriving in Paris, Daniel contracted syphilis, as he recorded in his first published memoir. Going to a public health clinic enabled him to get treated.[2] Daniel doesn't indicate whether Cláudio infected him or if he acquired the disease through someone else. Whichever scenario is correct, the couple had an "open relationship." Cláudio had never hidden his promiscuity. Maria Helena remembered: "Cláudio would go out to buy a Coca-Cola and disappear. He would come back three hours later. 'Where were you?' 'I met a guy and went with him.' . . . After they were together for awhile, they each had sex with other people; the kind of thing that was open."[3] In spite of their agreement, Daniel was jealous of Cláudio's escapades, and it would lead to spats.

In the years between joining the O. and settling in Paris, Daniel had developed a series of close attachments. Each person in succession took on a special and unique role in his life. All of them became intimate friends and confidants, and Daniel demanded their attention and loyalty. His single-minded commitment to the revolutionary cause, the precarious nature of his underground activities, the instabilities of exile, and later new adaptations upon returning to Brazil: all disrupted these friendships at some point. Only Cláudio was a constant for the last two decades of Daniel's life. However, while the two remained inseparable partners, their mutual sexual attraction waned over time.[4]

It took Daniel and Cláudio almost nine months to fully settle into their newly adopted country and find work. Cláudio got a steady job as a graphic designer for the Communist Party–led General Labor Federation. He worked long hours producing material that promoted the activities and ideology of the French Communist Party, an organization Cláudio found abominable.[5] Daniel landed work in the cloakroom of the Continental, a Parisian gay club located near the Opera. The Continental had both a swimming pool where men swam nude and an elegant restaurant with waiters and crisp white tablecloths. Additional facilities consisted of a television room, a steam bath, three hot saunas, a gym, and a few cubicles where men could have sex. It served an upscale clientele of closeted married men, international tourists, and middle-class French men interested in anonymous sex.[6]

In his first memoir, Daniel wrote that a prominent Brazilian actor walked into the club one night and tried to pick him up, even offering him one hundred francs to have sex. Although Daniel turned down his advances, he admitted he had enjoyed "the silent satisfaction of being desired, intensely

FIGURE 13.1 Herbert Daniel in Paris. A heavy smoker, Daniel never gave up his predilection for cigarettes. COURTESY OF GENY BRUNELLI DE CARVALHO.

desired, so much so that he was worth money."[7] Daniel had gained confidence in his looks in Portugal; working in the sauna, exercising regularly, and eating properly transformed his body. In a gay world where a handsome face, a beautiful body, and sexual allure were premium commodities, the realization that he was actually attractive strengthened his self-esteem.

Daniel described his new employment: "I earned very little and worked harder than I had ever worked in my life. I wasn't forced to do it because I was starving or because of being in exile. It was a rupture."[8] Indeed, there probably wasn't any job he could have taken that was more distinct from his previous profession as a revolutionary. Daniel observed that many exiles lived in a nebulous never-land, waiting for a mythical return to Brazil to continue the struggle. "I refused to survive in closed smoke-filled rooms and useless solemnities, where you discuss everything and decide nothing." Daniel had experienced an insular life, carrying out political work that was cut off from the reality surrounding him. Now in exile, he abhorred the incessant infighting, backroom dealings, and endless debates. "Life abroad didn't change the main problems of the groups. Rather, it accentuated dogmatism and crystalized sectarianism," he observed.[9]

His new job also allowed him to affirm his erotic desires. It gave him opportunities to explore a hidden world he wanted to understand. However, he entered into this second clandestine life of same-sex sociability and unrestrained sexuality with ambivalence and ended up rejecting it. "If I escaped from a sect, it wasn't to join a ghetto," he later wrote.[10]

MARGINALIA   173

Describing specific spaces of same-sex erotic sociability—bars, clubs, restaurants, saunas, or sections of public parks—as a "ghetto" was not unusual terminology in early 1970s radical gay French circles. In the aftermath of the May 1968 revolts, a variety of new movements exploded onto the political scene, including militant feminism that challenged the Left's sexism. In early 1971, lesbians and gay men formed the Homosexual Front for Revolutionary Action (FHAR). Eclectic in political composition and loose-knit in organizational structure, it tended toward anarcho-libertarian criticisms of the orthodox Left, traditional politics, and the state. Because many of FHAR's active members had previously been on the Left, they saw it as a privileged target and mounted flamboyant protest actions against its conservative positions.[11] The "ghetto"—the commercial world of bars, nightclubs, and saunas—was another subject of their criticism. One FHAR manifesto stated, "A nightclub is a kingdom of cash. You dance there with other men: you size up each other as commodities: heterocop [heterosexual] society exploits us there. Fear persists. Regular raids by the cops, legal roundups."[12]

Calling gay spaces "ghettos" suggests their insularity, but as scholars have argued, they have also been locations appropriated or occupied to provide a "free zone" where people can interact with less social repression or stigmatization.[13] Entrepreneurs soon realized that there was a profitable market in providing these locations as places of same-sex sociability and sexuality. At the same time that Daniel was criticizing the Parisian gay ghetto, LGBT activists in the United States were celebrating the relative freedom afforded them in San Francisco's Castro District or New York City's Greenwich Village, where a concentration of gay and lesbian residents patronized LGBT-friendly establishments and created a visible presence in those neighborhoods. Tens of thousands of people chose to live there because these spaces provided a sense of independence and openness. French society had few such exposed sites for sociability. While many bars and other places identified with homosexuals existed, there were no comparable urban areas that had gained a distinct character or a population that asserted its unique gay identity. Thus, in France, the term "ghetto" was used to describe being cut off and isolated in a specific establishment, in this case a bathhouse. Perhaps Daniel also disdained the "ghetto" because it reminded him too much of his former clandestine life. Ironically, while Daniel rejected the notion of the ghetto intellectually, it was a site where he labored in thirteen-hour shifts.[14]

After a few months at the Continental, Daniel found work at Tilt, a less upscale sauna located on Rue Sainte-Anne, a commercial street during the day and the site of gay bars and clubs at night. Although the FHAR had dissolved by 1974, successor militant gay organizations, such as the Homosexual Liberation Group (GLH) decried this street as the commercialization of the ghetto.[15] Tilt, which opened in 1974, was the first distinctly French sauna that catered to a specifically gay crowd without the pretense of being a "club," where homosexual escapades just happened to take place. It contained a dry Finnish sauna, the first place in France to show gay porn on television, and a dark backroom for anonymous sex.[16] Daniel worked in the thick of it all, while he simultaneously criticized its alienating qualities.

While employed there, Daniel began composing his first book. When not busy with his duties as a bathhouse attendant, he scribbled the text for one of the most original accounts of the Brazilian revolutionary movement and the most piercing criticisms of the armed struggle's errors and failures among similar works penned by contemporaries. The manuscript also takes the reader on a graphic tour of a gay bathhouse in which he provides a thick anthropological description of the orgiastic escapades of sauna customers, combined with a sophisticated analysis of the construction of homosexual identities and the nature of the gay ghetto, as he understood it. When it was published in Brazil in 1982, this must have been shocking, especially for those who had bought *Passagem* to read about the adventures of a rebel who had abducted ambassadors and trained as a guerrilla fighter.

Although Daniel doesn't cite any sources that might have influenced his ruminations about homosexuality, it is likely that he was aware of the ideas of Guy Hocquenghem, a writer and leading FHAR militant. According to one historian, Hocquenghem's article, "The Revolution of Homosexuals," published in January 1972, "set the tone for the homosexual movement in France." In that piece, Hocquenghem details his adolescent sexual adventures and his militancy in the French Left as "an unstable mixture of guilt and revolt."[17] The same year Hocquenghem published a short book, *Homosexual Desire*, that presents a theoretical criticism of homosexual identities that is not unlike Daniel's own thoughts on the subject, especially Hocquenghem's critique that "the establishment of homosexuality as a separate category goes hand in hand with its repression."[18] Daniel develops this idea in his manuscript and argues that any political organization of homosexuals fighting against "sexual repression" merely reinforces their relationship to the ghetto *and* their separation from society.[19] *Homosexual Desire* circulated widely in France, and it is hard to imagine that Daniel did not read it.

Other publications, such as *Gai Pied*, produced at the time may have influenced Daniel's ideas as well. This monthly periodical featured a wide variety of articles about gay life in France. Michel Foucault published an essay in the first issue, and it is almost certain that Daniel at least paged through the magazine while at work. Even though neither Hocquenghem nor Foucault, or any other international gay writers for that matter, is cited by name in his texts, their ideas were indubitably in the air for Daniel to appropriate.

Daniel's observations reflect sharp criticisms of the commercialization of homosexuality that French gay militants and theoreticians also articulated. "Sodomy is a city," Daniel wrote. "Capitalist. That is to say, in short, a market. . . . The homosexual ghetto today in the developed countries is a body of businesses: bars, cinemas, restaurants . . . [offering] all possible consumer attractions."[20] Working in the midst of a small but vibrant commercial center for gay sociability, Daniel clearly saw the capacity of capitalism to respond to this market niche. He illustrates this by offering the reader a tour of the sauna as seen through the eyes of a man from the provinces. This anonymous fictional figure has come to Paris in search of sex, and the establishment where Daniel worked provides him that opportunity "in many flavors" for only fifty francs, the price of admission.

Daniel abhorred the ways in which "extremely profitable" gay establishments catered to a homosexual clientele, "from a bookstore to parrot shops," as he describes them.[21] Yet his criticisms ignore the contradictory flip side of the coin, namely, that these spaces, while commercialized, were also locations of relative freedom in a hostile society, much as the club Dinosaurus might have been for isolated young men in Barbacena. He fails to point out that his fictitious provincial homosexual seeking a night of unfettered pleasure in Paris had few if any options in a small town, other than the chance meeting of a like-minded soul or a furtive encounter in a public toilet or park. While a Parisian sauna provided the same opportunity for anonymous sex that, theoretically, a person from the provinces could find in a public park back home, the price of admission afforded the eager client a range of sexual possibilities, as well as protection from police arrest. A gay bookstore, in turn, provided access to literary works not found in provincial shops or local libraries. Similarly, restaurants frequented by gay men and lesbians were spaces where friends could gather to laugh, camp it up if they so chose, and even show affection to a friend, without fear their actions would cause a scandal. Daniel's invective against the ghetto, while a justified critique of consumer capitalism, ignores the ways these spaces provided safe places for people to affirm their homosexuality while living in a society inimical to that sexual orientation.

There is a familiar thread of Marxism in Daniel's criticism of the ghetto that attributes a "false consciousness" to those who patronize these establishments. "The struggle against 'sexual repression' and the organization of homosexuals as a defined social interest is supported by those social forces that are interested in a fully functioning ghetto. The ghetto demands the freedom to exist. A strange freedom to be tied to a specific market that is linked to a society that apparently rejects this ghetto."[22] Daniel considered this to be a paradoxical situation attributable to the ability of capitalism to create contradictory and absurd ways of making profits.

Strangely, Daniel never wrote about the gay rights movement that had developed in France in the 1970s. While the FHAR had dissolved two years before he moved to Paris, the GLH retained the radical and critical tone of the early movement, as well as much of the internal wrangling among its members. One split-off group, GLH—Politics and Daily Life (GLH—P&Q) carried out militant actions in Paris, including protests when, on January 27, 1978, the Ministry of Culture shut down the screening of a movie during a gay film festival.[23] Jean Le Bitoux, a leader of the GLH—P&Q, published an ad in the left-wing daily *Libération* calling for a protest demonstration on Rue Sainte-Anne, where Daniel's sauna was located. Many years later, Bitoux admitted that his group was hoping for a "French Christopher Street," that is, a revolt of gay men similar to the New York City Stonewall Rebellion of June 1969. When a hundred or so people blocked traffic and started to build a barricade from cobblestones, the police came, tore down their banner, and began making arrests. Security staffs at the gay bars and bathhouses blocked fleeing protesters from entering their establishments. The protest failed to provoke a major reaction from people in the "ghetto."[24]

In *Passagem*, Daniel presents a mini-chronology of his life in the third-person singular. Some years have long entries; others are short. In the first year of Parisian exile, he describes the intricacies and frustrations of trying to use appropriate French expressions. The year 1977 is left blank, and the following year has two simple sentences. "1978—Paris is certainly the most beautiful city in the world and offers all imaginable advantages. There he would live calmly."[25]

Why, then, is there no mention of Parisian militant gay groups? Perhaps Daniel wasn't working the night when activists tried to raise the consciousness of those who patronized the gay "ghetto," but he surely would have heard the news during his next shift. Perhaps he was tired of participating in any political activities and saw the internal fighting of left-leaning gay and lesbian groups as a reproduction of the incessant ideological battles he had lived through in Brazil and avoided while in exile. Perhaps Daniel considered these radical gay groups as yet another manifestation of the ghetto's power to separate and isolate people from society and preferred instead to enjoy a quiet life with Cláudio, in which he could peacefully work, read, and write.[26]

FIGURE 13.2 Cláudio Mesquita in Paris, c. 1978. COURTESY OF MIGUEL MESQUITA.

Whatever the explanation, while Daniel wrote his memoir, far across the Atlantic Ocean new political movements were stirring in his homeland. Ernesto Geisel's promised liberalization was actually taking place, albeit unevenly. In 1975, Terezinha Zerbini founded the Feminine Committee for Amnesty in São Paulo, which called for the release of political prisoners and the right of political exiles to return. Over the next four years, a national movement emerged demanding a "broad, general, and unrestricted amnesty."[27] Taking advantage of this new political conjuncture, left-wing activists began publishing "alternative" newspapers that battled the censors while criticizing the dictatorship.[28] Students reorganized banned university entities and participated in campus protests against the regime. In 1977, tens of thousands took to the streets of São Paulo and stood down the police, revealing its defensive posture. The following year, São Paulo metalworkers went on strike, demanding wage increases and placing in check the government's regressive wage policies and its bans on work stoppages.[29] Between 1975 and 1978, feminist and black consciousness movements also emerged.[30]

Then in early 1978, a group of gay intellectuals from Rio and São Paulo founded a monthly newspaper, *Lampião da Esquina*. Its first editorial optimistically stated, "Brazil, March of 1978. Favorable winds are blowing in the direction of some sort of liberalization of the national landscape. In an election year, the press broadcasts promises of a less rigid Executive Power, speaks of creating new political parties and of amnesty. An investigation into the proposed alternatives allows one to discern an 'opening' of Brazilian discourse. But a homosexual newspaper, why?"[31] Aguinaldo Silva, the newspaper's de facto editor-in-chief, agreed with Daniel's political critique of urban gay life: "It is necessary to say 'no' to the ghetto and, consequently, to leave it. What interests us is destroying the stereotypical image of the homosexual that portrays him as a being who lives in the shadows, who prefers the night, who faces his sexual preference as a kind of curse, who is given to exaggerations, and who always stops short of any attempt at becoming a thoroughly self-actualized human being because of this primary factor: his sexuality is not what he would wish for." The tabloid newspaper's first editorial continued by declaring that it would become "a voice to all groups that are unjustly discriminated against—blacks, Indians, women."[32]

Quickly reaching a monthly circulation of ten thousand copies, *Lampião* inspired the founding of the country's first gay and lesbian activist group, which eventually took the name Somos: Grupo de Afirmação Homossexual (We Are: Group of Homosexual Affirmation).[33] In February 1979, the left-wing/libertarian student association of the University of São Paulo's social science department invited representatives of Somos to participate in a weeklong debate on "minorities," conceptualized as women, blacks, indigenous people, and homosexuals. The evening on homosexuality provoked a heated discussion among the hundred or so that attended the event, held in a large university classroom.

Eduardo Dantas, who covered the evening for *Lampião*, commented that February 8, 1979, was a historical date: "After all, one can't remember such an open and polemical debate about a topic that the police and a larger segment of Brazilian society still considers to be taboo."[34] During the discussion, audience members, who were representatives of different semi-underground left-wing organizations, argued that gays and lesbians were engaged in a "secondary struggle" that divided the movement against the dictatorship. Somos members countered that the Left was homophobic and hostile to its demands. Dantas finished his article by pointing out that, "in spite of contradictions raised during the debate[,] . . . the general conclusion was that there is a single march toward social, racial and sexual freedom. Each minority group should unite, organize its members to fight

FIGURE 13.3 Article in *Lampião da Esquina* about the debate on homosexuality at the University of São Paulo.

for real democracy in Brazil. Only then will broad and unrestricted happiness be achieved for all."[35] Dantas's last phrase, borrowed from the main slogan of the Brazilian amnesty movement, reflected the ethos of the moment, when the excitement surrounding these emergent groups created a sense that the country was finally on the road to an inclusive democracy.

Three months later, a similar debate about homosexuality took place within the Brazilian exile community in Paris. Even the idea of holding a discussion about the topic was so controversial that it almost caused a permanent split in the Brazilian Amnesty Committee (CBA), the Parisian affiliate of the Brazilian amnesty movement.

Paris had the largest concentration of Brazilian expatriates in Europe, an estimated 370 or so official exiles. Others, who found the political situation in Brazil intolerable, had moved to Paris and circulated among the émigrés. The CBA tried to form a united front for all the Brazilian left-wing groups with members in France. In spite of their political differences, they agreed on the call for a blanket amnesty for all exiles and political prisoners and held events to mobilize support among the French for their cause.[36]

Parallel to this unified activity of Brazilian political émigrés, a number of exiled women founded the Brazilian Women's Circle in 1976.[37] Influenced by European feminists, they began to reflect on the sexist behavior of the revolutionary groups' male members and established an autonomous space to discuss these issues. As the historian Denise Rollemberg observes, the arrival of Brazilian exiles in Europe "took place within the context of the defeat of a political and individual project that had offered these women a specific identity."[38] For many, the process of rethinking their relationship to the revolutionary movement had already begun in Chile. A former militant, Glória Ferreira, recalled, "Europe created the possibility of an intellectual and emotional opening up. We weren't going to return in a few months or a year. We had to open up."[39] Maria Helena joined the Brazilian Women's Circle, which was founded soon after she arrived in Paris with Daniel and Cláudio. "We decided to do this work for two reasons. One was for women to know ourselves more, regarding affection, sexuality. We discussed abortion, sexuality, everything. It was an on-going discussion. We also decided to show the male comrades how things should be."

The introduction of feminist ideas in small consciousness-raising groups; the elaboration of documents, pamphlets and manifestos; and participation in political activities with French feminism ended up having a ripple effect throughout the Brazilian exile community. The traditional arguments that the oppression of women would only be eliminated after a socialist revolution or that feminist ideas divided the revolutionary movement by pitting comrade against comrade lost ground to discussions about power dynamics in relationships, unequal treatment of men and women in politics, and the sexist behavior of many male comrades. These debates exposed many Brazilian revolutionaries to new ways of thinking about the body, sexuality, reproduction, childrearing, and relationships. It also provided more fertile ground for a serious discussion about homosexuality.

One day at work, Daniel was surprised when he received a telephone call from the CBA Cultural Group asking him to participate in a public discussion about homosexuality. The Cultural Group organized events about theater, art, and literature with Brazilians passing through Paris. Its other mission, according to the CBA president, Jean Marc Von der Weid, was to build links with French artists and intellectuals who might support the amnesty campaign. It was an eclectic collective, some of whom, like Glória Ferreira and Vera Sílvia Magalhães, had been freed from prison in exchange for the release of the German and Swiss ambassadors. When the Cultural Group proposed a special event with the theater director and left-wing militant Augusto Boal the previous year, several CBA leaders, including Von der Weid, opposed the idea, arguing that the Cultural Committee's mission was to reach out to French society around the single issue of amnesty and not hold events in Portuguese catering to a limited audience.[40] Vera Sílvia, who had participated in abducting the U.S. ambassador, strongly disagreed and argued that the type of activity that the Cultural Group proposed was designed to encourage debate and discussion among Brazilian émigrés. The dispute was taken to a CBA general meeting, which voted to endorse the event.[41]

Several months later the Cultural Committee proposed holding the debate about homosexuality. There was immediate opposition among sectors of the CBA leadership, who insisted that the theme had nothing to do with its goals and should not be held under its auspices. Others argued that the issue was important and merited a discussion. Having established the precedent of sponsoring cultural events that were not directly related to the amnesty campaign, the majority of participants, in a fiercely contested CBA general meeting, voted to hold the debate, with Von der Weid throwing in his support with the majority.

Daniel and Cláudio had been only intermittently involved in the array of activities that the CBA organized, occasionally attending events but generally staying out of the political fray. Now they were in the eye of the storm. Despite the democratic decision to hold the debate, it continued to provoke discord among CBA members. "Truthfully, we innocently thought that overt and medieval prejudice didn't exist in that milieu at that time," Daniel wrote in his memoir. "Rarely does prejudice against homosexuality (in general and sexuality in particular) show itself within the Left with such open aggression."[42] The dispute about whether or not to hold the debate became so intense that Von der Weid invited Daniel and members of the Cultural Group to a meeting to see how to overcome the impasse. Everyone finally agreed to organize the event without the official CBA sponsorship.[43]

In his letter to Lúcia, Daniel explained that the original proposal was for a panel that would include a psychoanalyst. "I was immediately against it. . . . The subject is a political one and should be discussed in that way. My proposal: a political debate about homosexuality without hiding anything."[44] Daniel explained his approach: "It's not about introducing a homosexual discourse into the Left. It already has one. . . . The question is to criticize this discourse inherited from exotic ideologies." Daniel prepared the document "Homosexual: Defense of Interests?" for the debate, and it was later published in a small exile journal entitled *Notas Marginais* (Marginal notes).[45] In his letter to Lúcia, Daniel confessed he was nervous about the event. "It's going to be really difficult (*barra pesada*) as it's been very hard to explain what I think in trying to offer a political vision of a topic that until now only receives snickers or empty ideological discourses about poor oppressed people."[46]

The debate "Homosexuality and Politics" took place on May 29, 1979, at the Casa do Brasil, a residency and cultural space located at the Cité Université. Ferreira recalled they had prepared *caipirinhas*, which they served as people arrived. It immediately put everyone in a lighthearted mood. Ferreira projected slides onto a wall with images of people of the same gender interacting: "Not necessarily homosexual, but soccer players and [other] situations and familiar photos." She also played the song "Ilegal, imoral ou engorda" by the pop singer Erasmus Carlos with the refrain "Is everything that I like illegal, immoral, or fattening?"[47]

Cláudio designed a provocative invitation with a drawing of a public toilet with graffiti on the walls and the invocation "*Se você É, vem que tem*," which roughly translates as "If you Are, come, there's something you'll like."[48] He also decorated the small auditorium with panels on which were attached pages from gay porn magazines. The phrase "We are all in the same bathroom," a play on the expression "We're all in the same boat," also decorated one wall.[49]

According to Von der Weid, the room was packed with two hundred or more people. With members of the Cultural Group sitting up front, Daniel presented his ideas. Time has erased or distorted the details of that night in the eyewitnesses' memories. Ferreira remembered that Daniel kicked off the debate by asking members of the Cultural Group why they were heterosexual. She recalled that Helinho, one of the Cultural Group members, replied, "I'm black, poor, and a leftist. If I were also a homosexual, it would be a disaster." Von der Weid recounted that Daniel made an "extremely intellectualized presentation," addressing the subject with complex theory. "When he finished, the public was silent, not knowing whether they should applaud."

Then the debate began. Ferreira reminisced, "It was incredible. The most hard-nosed people (those who were against the event) started to talk about themselves, their problems, their prejudices. The subject was still a taboo within the Left. It was really a happening."⁵⁰ In his memoir, Daniel retells how he spoke about his own experiences in repressing his sexuality while an activist of the Left: "Silence is the discursive form of a certain sector of the Left about homosexuality. It is a way to exile homosexuals. The most subtle means of censorship is the imposition of self-censorship."⁵¹

In interviews for this book conducted thirty-five years after the event, all recalled one incident that Daniel also described in his memoir. Valneri Neves Antunes, known as Átila, his underground name, had participated in guerrilla training with Daniel in Ribeira and was totally against holding the debate. Nevertheless, he showed up to express his position: "I don't have anything against you. I'm against homosexuality, and I want to discuss that," Daniel quotes him as saying.⁵² Because the debate was not recorded, and the memory of the participants in that night's event is admittedly faulty, one can assume that the details of the exchange have been embellished. Von der Weid recalls Átila as saying, "'Daniel, you talked, talked, talked, and I didn't understand anything that you said. I want to know the following: Are you a *viado* or not?' And Daniel replied, 'Look, Átila, if you want it in those terms, yes, I'm a faggot.' And he said, 'Fuck, you never would have said that in the Vale do Ribeira.' And Daniel replied, 'Of course Átila, I know you and the others, so I would never have told you there.' And everyone laughed." After the debate ended, the gathering turned into a party with everyone dancing. Míriam Grossi, who was visiting Paris at the time, remembered women dancing with women.⁵³ According to Von der Weid, at one moment Átila even danced with Daniel.

We can assume that Daniel's contribution to the debate that night was similar to the document "Homosexual: Defense of Interests?" that he had written and distributed days before the evening at the Casa do Brasil.⁵⁴ He described the reaction: "The document that I wrote circulated a lot, but much of it wasn't understood. They said that it was too theoretical. I more or less agree. But since I wanted to offer solid arguments, I had no choice."⁵⁵

While the essay is an original contribution to the discussion about homosexuality, it is dense, abstract, and hard to understand. Daniel embraces the idea that homosexuality is a category that was invented over the last two centuries and serves to reinforce "normalcy" by establishing a deviant "other." He criticizes the way one's sexuality becomes associated with one's entire being and attributes this process to capitalism. "In 'accepting' the status of a minority that fights for its rights, what one is doing in the form of protest and rebellion is linking capitalist discourse to the repression that one wants to fight."⁵⁶ Daniel rejects the notion that there is a single homosexual prototype. But above all, he criticizes the ghetto. "The interest of homosexuals is precisely not to be closed up in a group with common interests, in a kind of homosexual ghetto, as a homosexual 'social minority.'"[57] In short, he writes, "For this reason, homosexuals should not build movements or organizations, but as *homosexuals*, as people, or, better said, as *political militants*, 'individually' fight against *all* attempts to build a homosexual ghetto, all attempts to reduce the homosexual to a sexual totem."[58]

Although it is not explicitly stated, Daniel seems set on not being marginalized in the role of a homosexual. This was one of the reasons he decided to repress his sexuality in order to join the revolutionary movement. In the late 1960s it was clear to him that the Left, on the whole, wouldn't accept his homosexuality. When he finally had the courage to confront the Left's prejudices, he refused to consider that his sexuality represented his entire being. Rather than seeing the potential of the "ghetto," or gay and lesbian forms of sociability, as constitutive forces that could engender a political movement capable of tearing down the walls of prejudice that make gay enclaves so attractive and desirable, he blames the ghetto for producing and reproducing that prejudice. This early rejection of identity politics at a time when a Brazilian movement barely existed and the kinds of debates about homophobia in the Left and society in general were in their incipient stages can be read as a desire to belong and feel included rather than isolated and set apart. Daniel's thinking, however, was at odds with Brazilian activists trying to forge a new political movement that would challenge homophobia and reshape traditional stereotypes about homosexuals. As we shall see, his position would slowly change over time.

Whereas the debate in Paris ended as a festive mixer, in 1979 the Brazilian Left, in exile and at home, remained largely hostile toward homosexuality.[59] Lúcia's answer to Daniel's letter captures some of the reaction in Rio: "I had already heard about the debate on homosexuality. However, obviously, what we hear is vilification (*pixação*). I get extremely angry. I want to throttle the people that talk to me about you with distrust because you have taken the stand that you have taken. I imagine that you have suffered and still suffer a lot about this. I think, since '71 when we started talking about your homosexuality, I have always wanted you to find the best way not to be frustrated and to suffer the least."[60] Lúcia expressed how proud she was Daniel had participated in the debate and urged him to continue the fight.

While reports on the controversial debate circulated throughout the exile community and among left-wing activists in Brazil, another political event quickly refocused people's attention. Faced with this growing pressure on the government to pass an amnesty law, a little over a month after the event at the Casa do Brasil, Brazil's fifth military president, João Batista

Figueiredo (1979–85), introduced a bill in Congress. Among its provisions was a blanket amnesty for those in prison, in hiding, or abroad who had committed "political crimes." An item in the draft bill included granting amnesty to state agents involved in torture and killing under a vague provision regarding "related crimes," a term meant to protect them from future prosecution. At the same time, it excluded those who had been convicted of the crimes of "terrorism, robberies, kidnapping."[61] It was not the broad, general, and unrestricted amnesty that the CBA had fought for. Members of the congressional opposition denounced the inclusion of torturers in the bill as beneficiaries of the amnesty. At the same time, they insisted that those who had fought against the military regime using violent tactics should be released from jail or not prosecuted for actions they had committed.[62]

The new law meant that most exiles could return to Brazil, and many began the trek back almost immediately after it was passed in Congress. Daniel, however, fell into the category of those excluded from the 1979 Amnesty Bill. While all of his friends were leaving, he was stuck in Paris.

14

Returning to Rio

(1981–1982)

> At the moment I want to say little, listen a lot, and learn more.
>
> — HERBERT DANIEL

As news of the anticipated amnesty law circulated in Paris, Daniel and Cláudio excitedly prepared their return. After the law was enacted, however, it became clear that Daniel would not be covered because he had been involved in actions in which people had died. In 1972, Daniel had been sentenced in absentia to a lengthy prison term for his participation in the ambassadorial abductions. Although an appeal reduced his prison time, he still faced the possibility of incarceration for a decade or more.[1] Ironically, most of the 110 political prisoners he had helped release from Brazilian jails and who had been permanently banned from the country were allowed to return without threat of incarceration. Daniel had no such guarantees.

He immediately turned his personal situation into a political campaign to show how the exclusion of some revolutionaries from the amnesty law was a means of delaying the consolidation of Brazilian democracy. In an open letter he emphasized how the generals still remained in control. "It's important [to point out] that there are those who were not amnestied. Not because of us, as we are of little significance, but as an example and a warning to the real democratic forces: exile, political prisoners, and the arbitrary rule of law still exist."² Earlier that month Daniel had gone to the Brazilian embassy to request a passport, but his petition was turned down. "They refused my citizenship rights, which is an abuse characteristic of a police state where the denial of basic rights is a way of carrying out the law."

Daniel also rejected the idea that those who had defied the military regime needed to request forgiveness. "We were never wrong in challenging the dictatorial government, and the amnesty simply shows that if there was any criminal wrongdoing, it wasn't carried out by the opposition." Daniel argued that he didn't need to justify why he had participated in the armed struggle. Even though he admitted that it had been an ineffective political choice, he refused to disparage his past revolutionary activities. Instead he pointed to the future: "Amnesty should not come as the last act of a political error, but as the first moment of a renewal, where self-criticism is not merely a declaration of intentions but a commemoration of the advances of Democracy."

As was mentioned in this book's introduction, Daniel's open letter wasn't read at a Brazilian Amnesty Committee national meeting. According to a *Lampião* editor, Aguinaldo Silva, opposition to the appeal revolved around some activists who dismissed Daniel's call for support because he was a *bicha*.³ Daniel learned of these alleged comments secondhand by reading *Lampião*.⁴ Whether or not that version of events is actually accurate, Daniel insisted that the national CBA as a whole shouldn't be blamed for some of its members' attitudes.⁵

Yet as he admitted in correspondence with Ana Maria Muller, a Brazilian lawyer whom he hoped to retain, his open letter had received "little coverage in the Brazilian press."⁶ Friends had recommended Muller, a progressive lawyer involved in the amnesty movement, and Daniel clarified his situation to her in a handwritten letter: "I returned to the [Brazilian] consulate in February, and the Consul, Roberto Peres Coutinho, told me that 'a conviction against me was still in effect,' although he didn't tell me which one it was."⁷ The Brazilian official instructed Daniel to send a formal letter to the consulate, and at the same time he denied a second passport application. Daniel explained to Muller that he sought her legal assistance to challenge in court the limits of the amnesty law. Muller agreed to represent him, and the legal process began.

Now, each time another friend departed to Brazil, Daniel became more disheartened. In his account of that period in *Passagem para o próximo sonho*, he wrote a brief entry: "1980—Nothing new. Most Brazilians have returned. Exile is the same. Loneliness is what seems to be new."[8] His wait would end up lasting almost another two years.

In late March 1980, Daniel shared his frustrations in another short message to Lúcia: "Hi, I'm here. Still. It's hard, very hard to put up with these snowy spring times, this wait for a summer that has never been more impossible. . . . And I wanted to return in August. I made plans. Now I know that I won't be able to. . . . Now and then Cláudio and I talk about things that we'd love to see in Brazil. Among them, of course, you."[9]

Daniel remained dispirited and began gaining the weight he had lost.[10] In April 1981, he answered a letter from his family explaining why his correspondences were infrequent. "I have nothing to write about. I'm not in the right place. I have no patience. My head's screwed up. It's hard putting up with exile. It was always difficult, but now it's worse. I'd rather not write so that I don't send you my anguish. If I write to you that I am bad off, what are you going to be able to do? . . . I have always tried to write upbeat letters, saying that everything is all right. But in exile, *nothing ever* goes well. Everything is sad. Everything is difficult. Everything is horrible."[11] He went on to lament that he thought he would be the last person to return. "Everyone seems to have 'forgotten' me, as if I stayed here these last two years for pleasure, as if I were on vacation." Daniel was desperate to be in Brazil: "I'm not enjoying myself or traveling. I'm in exile. I can't be amnestied. I can't do anything but wait. It's another abuse of the dictatorship. But no one says anything, as if they are waiting for the dictatorship to solve my problem by granting me a 'pardon.'"

Then in May 1981, his legal appeal finally succeeded. His sentences were reduced to three and a half years, and then were annulled because of the statute of limitations. But he still couldn't get a passport. A burst of publicity, however, turned the tide in his favor. In July 1981, *Veja*, Brazil's most widely read weekly magazine, published a full-page article about him. A picture of Daniel with scruffy, curly hair and slightly overweight captures him gazing out onto a Parisian street. With the banner "Exiles" and the title "He gets by on odd jobs," the article announced that *Veja* had found a real-life version of Sebá, a fictional character created by Jô Soares, a leading comedian and television personality. Sebá, short for Sebastian, was a maladapted political outcast living in Paris. A picture of Soares doing his routine—talking on the telephone with a cap covering his head and a scarf around his neck to symbolize cold Parisian winters—suggests the similarity between the two figures, one real and one invented. According to the article, Daniel was the incarnation of Soares's popular comedy character. The subtitle announces: "Sebá exists and is a doorman in a sauna in Paris."[12]

FIGURE 14.1 *Veja* article describing Daniel's exile in Paris.
SOURCE: CALVACANTI, "ELE VIVE DE BICOS."

In regular skits broadcast on Globo, Brazil's largest television network, Soares's comic character spoke French with a thick Portuguese accent. He called Brazil from malfunctioning public telephones that allowed illicit long-distance communication. Sebá was hopelessly behind the times about changes taking place in his native country. What's more, his girlfriend, Madelena, whom he had left behind, constantly postponed purchasing a return ticket for him, arguing that the exchange rate for the dollar was perpetually increasing. This left Sebá abandoned in Europe as the supposed last exile and led him to suspect that Madelena had replaced him with someone else.[13] The *Veja* article seemed to confirm the veracity of Soares's humorous late-night television sketches, and the combination of the two ended up branding Daniel with the status of being Brazil's "last exile."

Daniel, unlike Sebá, did not anticipate returning to Brazil to fall into the arms of a girlfriend. In a tone reflecting a modest shift in media coverage, the article revealed Daniel's homosexuality in a respectful and positive way. Daniel described his relationship with Cláudio as "one of the most solid marriages around." This affirmative use of terminology about a same-sex relationship had been virtually nonexistent in the media, despite the emergence of a Brazilian gay and lesbian rights movement in 1978. In this regard, Daniel was one of few individuals willing to go public about his homosexuality, and the *Veja* reporter presented his relationship with Cláudio in a positive light, without any ironic or deprecating undertones. The article made Daniel somewhat of a national celebrity, a former revolutionary with an unusual twist to his story.

As in most later journalistic accounts of Daniel's political career, his past was succinctly summarized: medical student in 1968, a member of the People's Revolutionary Vanguard, and guerrilla trainee under Carlos Lamarca's command. The article described Daniel as lowering his voice when he talked about his revolutionary past and made a reference to the debate in Paris about homosexuality. "The relationship that links him to Cláudio Mesquita, his apartment mate, forced Carvalho to respond to a long interrogation by the Brazil-Amnesty committee," the *Veja* report explained. "He was annoyed by the incident, but now is upbeat about the information that the Brazilian Left is less intolerant of the sexual practices of its allies." The reporter wrote that Daniel commented: "It's about time for this to happen."

Daniel was not very pleased with the article, and he wrote an open letter to *Veja*'s editors that criticized its content. Although the magazine never published his reproaches, the left-wing political cartoonist Henrique de Souza Filho, commonly known as Henfil, reprinted Daniel's complaints about the article in a column that appeared in *O Pasquim*, the popular alternative Rio weekly, under the headline "The Last Exile."[14] Now both *Veja* and *O Pasquim* had awarded him that title, and it seemed to stick.

In his letter to *Veja*, Daniel had three criticisms of the reporting about his life in Paris. First, he had never lowered his voice when talking about his participation in the Left. Rather, he wrote, "I'm used to raising my voice, because one needs to shout in order not to forget a period about which our people have so little information. I don't want to 'erase' any past. On the contrary, I want to clarify one of the worst moments in the country's history. I'm not the one who wants to forget; it's the torturers [who want to forget]." Daniel also censured the magazine for not writing about the plight of those who remained in exile since the passage of an amnesty law that he characterized as an arbitrary imposition. Finally, he criticized the article for referring to a supposed "interrogation" by the "Brazil-Amnesty Committee" (CBA) about his private life. "There was, indeed, a debate about homosexuality in which people presented different opinions. I was never interrogated nor did I experience personal attacks from the CBA as an organization. The invention of this posture by *Veja* is simply defamatory and offends thousands of Brazilians who sincerely have been dedicated to the struggle for Amnesty and Democracy." This final comment indicated how Daniel continued to operate within the parameters of the Brazilian Left.

When Daniel and Cláudio received news in late May that all charges against Daniel had been dropped, they precipitously dispatched some of their belongings to Brazil. In the subsequent months, the Brazilian government offered no sign that a passport was forthcoming. Therefore, in early August, Cláudio was forced to travel to Brazil to get their possessions out of customs.[15] Cláudio's departure left Daniel desperately alone. In a letter written to his mother in August commemorating her fiftieth birthday, he relayed his frustrations: "My solitude has deranged me, but I try to remain calm. Patience. Because I am very patient. That's not the way that they are going to break me. I'm resisting, although I feel entirely deprived of comrades and friends."[16] He later recalled Cláudio's absence: "It was the first time that we had been separated for so long. And we didn't know if it would be for two months or two years. I wrote him every day. We talked on the telephone two or three times a week. We were very sad."[17]

In July, Daniel once again requested a passport. Again the consul stalled. Then the Parisian CBA stepped in and appealed to "all Brazilian and international democratic forces to carry out a campaign" to force the government to issue the passport. They also sent a delegation to the Brazilian consulate with representatives from five French human rights and political organizations. This combination of efforts in Brazil and abroad finally forced authorities to provide Daniel with official documents to depart for Brazil.[18]

On October 8, 1981, Daniel boarded a Swissair flight with a ticket provided by the UN High Commission for Refugees. He arrived at Rio's Galeão International Airport early the next morning. Anticipating possible problems with authorities, two opposition congressmen and human rights lawyers—Raimundo de Oliveira and Antônio Modesto da Silveira—were on hand, along with Daniel's lawyer, Ana Maria Muller. When Daniel got off the plane, the federal police detained him for an hour because his name appeared on a list of "undesirables." After the team of lawyers straightened out the situation, Daniel was allowed to enter the waiting area. News cameras filmed his arrival. He and his father remained locked in a tearful embrace for several minutes. Someone began to sing. Daniel recalled that it had seemed like a surrealistic dream that included people from all of the phases of his life, "except those who had died."[19] For his part, Cláudio couldn't contain himself and wept incessantly. Dona Geny was notably absent. She had decided not to come to Rio, because she couldn't deal with the emotional excitement of meeting her son after so many years of separation.[20]

Although the moniker "the last exile" continued to be associated with Herbert Daniel, increasingly a different public persona defined him as a former revolutionary who had declared his homosexuality to the world. As we shall see, Daniel offered a series of criticisms of the pervasive notions regarding same-sex sexuality that reproduced medico-legal discourses and reinforced the idea that the "homosexual" was a specific pathologized personality. Daniel also had reservations about the nature of the emergent Brazilian gay rights movement. Nonetheless, the fact that he unabashedly talked about his relationship with Cláudio and referred to himself as a homosexual in the press provoked a voyeuristic curiosity about this former guerrilla leader.

Government propaganda campaigns against the armed Left had invented the idea that radical opponents of the dictatorship were virile, reckless, and dangerous individuals who resorted to senseless, unrestrained violence to achieve their goals. Moreover, the culture within most underground organizations promoted an ethos of masculinity that supposedly was embodied in the revolution itself. Armed opposition demanded discipline and extreme sacrifice for the cause and the advent of (in the words of Cuban revolutionary leaders) an *hombre nuevo*, a "new man," who, motivated by socialist morality, was willing to carry out dangerous tasks in order to overthrow the dictatorship and solve the country's socioeconomic problems.[21] These two images—one produced by the military regime and the other promoted within the Left—together had forged a prototypical revolutionary figure that simply didn't match Daniel's persona.

While the ubiquitous figure of a male revolutionary guerrilla fighter was that of a hypermasculine heterosexual, Daniel was timid, soft-spoken, and gay. He certainly didn't exude the bravado, self-confidence, and aggressiveness associated with the stereotype promoted by the regime's radical opponents. Daniel was fascinating in part because he was illegible to a public that remained tied to traditional typecasting and a simple binary that posited two distinct figures representing opposing lifestyles: the manly revolutionary and the passive and effeminate homosexual.

In the two years since the amnesty law had been enacted, an incipient gay and lesbian movement had begun to challenge pervasive stereotypes about homosexuality. Sympathetic journalists and editors had started to publish articles that were less imbued with traditionally pejorative representations, and in this context Daniel was an intriguing figure for multiple reasons. First, he simply didn't fit into the category of the superficial, effeminate, limp-wristed man, interested in fashion and gossip. Fashion designers and Carnival luxury contest winners, such as Dener, Clodovil, and Clóvis Bornay, were prototypical homosexuals. Daniel was just the opposite. Moreover, he offered an articulate and reasoned critique of the armed struggle without denying that it had been a legitimate means of opposing the dictatorship. He destabilized all of the assumed understandings about who the people involved in the revolutionary opposition had been. He conformed neither to the traditional representation of a homosexual nor to the formulaic vision of a masculine revolutionary hero. In short, Herbert Daniel did not match any of the standard representatives of male homosexuals or the images constructed by the regime to depersonalize, and therefore dehumanize, members of the revolutionary Left. What's more, Daniel insisted on talking about politics. His ideas were innovative, carefully thought out, and avant-garde. They were certainly not the kinds of pronouncements that many might have expected from a former guerrilla turned gay bathhouse attendant.

Daniel was not the first former guerrilla to offer a systematic critique of his revolutionary past and the homophobia and sexism that were still pervasive within the Left. Fernando Gabeira, who had helped to abduct the American ambassador, returned to Rio in 1979 to much fanfare. The bestselling account of his revolutionary escapades, *O que é isso, companheiro?*, made him an instant literary celebrity. Yet he was not immune to criticism by some on the Left. His support of feminism and the gay and lesbian movement, especially an interview that appeared in *Lampião* and his controversial use of a skimpy, crocheted, lilac-colored swimsuit on Ipanema Beach, fueled speculations that he was gay. As Gabeira explained, "After that interview, the rumors [about my sexuality] increased. Some old friends congratulated me for my sincerity and even thought that my deposition could help them in a reevaluation of their own trajectory as machos. Others didn't keep up with my rhythm. They accepted me as a terrorist, but not as a homosexual."[22] In reality Gabeira was not gay, but that didn't seem to matter to some.

Gabeira had returned to Brazil two years before Daniel, and he captured the mood of the country as it experienced a cultural renaissance linked to the promises of political liberalization. By the time Daniel's family and friends greeted him in Rio, the ideas that Gabeira had preached in late 1979 about the environment, feminism, gender equality, and tolerance of homosexuality were no longer novelties. As Daniel commented in his second book, "Curiously, many have told me that I came back late. The talk about 'returning exiles' is out of fashion."[23] Yet Daniel's openness about his homosexuality was something quite new, especially for someone with his background.

After a brief stay in Rio, Daniel traveled to Belo Horizonte for another equally emotional reunion with his mother, brothers, other relatives, and hometown friends. Prior to leaving Paris, Daniel had gone on a strict diet and worked out regularly.[24] He looked good. He enjoyed seeing his mother and his younger brother, Hélder, whom he really didn't know, but after an intense visit, Daniel quickly returned to Rio. There, he and Cláudio set up a small apartment in the neighborhood of Laranjeiras, eight blocks or so from Flamengo Beach, and began organizing their lives together.[25]

One of Daniel's first orders of business was getting his manuscript published. He had completed *Passagem* in May 1981, and he was anxious to get it into print. Gabeira's book about his revolutionary activities, issued by the Codecri publishing house, had been an unexpected blockbuster. It was the logical place to seek out an interested editor. His friendship with its cofounder, Henfil, opened the door to the press, which immediately agreed to a contract. Henfil wrote a laudatory and playful blurb on the book flaps, and Cláudio designed the cover. *Passagem* was launched in March 1982.

Unlike Gabeira's hit memoir, or Alfredo Sirkis's best-selling account of his adventures in the VPR, *Passagem* had a short shelf life.[26] Although there was media coverage when it was published, after it sold out, there was no second edition. Daniel's literary production is virtually unknown to the current generation of Brazilian LGBT and HIV/AIDS activists. On the other hand, scholars working on the military regime frequently cite the book, because his analysis of the armed struggle is poignant and perceptive. Nevertheless, it is a difficult book. The subtitle, translated as "a possible self-critical novel," expresses its ambiguous nature: it is neither a classic autobiography nor a work of fiction. Daniel's complex and nimble use of the Portuguese language, while pleasing to sophisticated readers, remains somewhat impenetrable for an average audience.

Passagem is divided into four sections with symbolic titles—SÓ (alone), S.O.S. (help), SOL (sun), and SOLO (soil). The narrative proceeds in erratic chronological order, weaving back and forth in time, as the author describes his life trajectory: from his inner struggles with his homosexuality before, during, and after his participation in the revolutionary Left, through his complete isolation underground, to exile and the promise of return home.

Unlike Gabeira's and Sirkis's adventurous and linear tales written in an entertaining cops-and-robbers style, Daniel's text contemplates the complexities

FIGURE 14.2 Cover of *Passagem para o próximo sonho* (1982).

and uncertainties of those who took up arms and then found themselves underground and isolated from the population they had hoped to reach. Here, Daniel introduces the idea of an internal exile, which is not personal, but collective: "Wouldn't it be better to state clearly that this period is the real beginning of exile? Isn't it there, in political 'isolation,' in the inability to establish a *real* dialogue that the armed Left would live its first exile?"[27] According to Daniel, while the radical opposition was unable to carry out a "conversation" with the Brazilian masses, and therefore was "alone," the dictatorship engaged in a successful "monologue" with the population.

The title of the second section makes a reference to the Morse code signal for assistance. Here Daniel writes about his political activities and explains the decision to repress his homosexuality. Peppered throughout are piercing observations about the ways in which the guerrilla movement was out of sync with reality. Implicit is an argument that the revolutionary Left needed assistance, which never arrived, to get out of its dilemma. Similarly, Daniel needed help to resolve the predicament of having felt the need to repress his homosexuality in order to join and remain in the revolutionary movement. His account of meeting Cláudio signals that he has found an exit from this contradiction. Dispersed throughout this and other sections are short fables and other tales that represent Daniel's first foray into fictional writing.

Much of his life story contained in the third section operates, presumably, in the light of day. The author, now in exile, no longer lives in the shadows of the underground. Most of this section relates experiences working in the Parisian gay saunas (as has been discussed in the previous chapter), without noting the irony that he worked at night in a dark and steamy place.

The final section references his longing to repatriate to his native soil. He describes the debate about homosexuality at the Casa do Brasil in Paris and recounts his frustration with not mastering French, which leads to a constant estrangement from his surroundings. Daniel ends the work with a phase that explains the volume's title: "I'm not returning. I'm going. Who knows if we might find ourselves in our Brazil on the curve toward the next dream."[28] In spite of his seemingly pessimistic evaluation of the past, the book's title and tone are optimistic, mirroring the author's own persistently upbeat outlook on life.

Among the newspaper reports about the book's launching is a lengthy interview that offers several insights into how Daniel understood his own literary production. He describes the book as a "novel about the darkened decade of the 70s, where the coincidences are intentional similarities. It's the itinerary of a person, me, in the midst of other people, us, and a self-critical view of my life." Daniel goes on to comment: "I tried to photograph myself without creating a portrait. I don't want to ask for forgiveness, but rather to share my experiences." When questioned about why he combined an analysis of the armed struggle with a discussion of sexuality, Daniel articulates a version of the 1970s feminist notion that "the personal is political": "I'm not the one who put the two together. Life does that. There is no such thing as politics where sexuality is not present, and there are no sexual relations where political options are absent. It's a big mistake to separate major political questions and issues of an intimate nature."[29] When asked what he was now seeking, he answers, "To learn, to dialogue, to listen. Contribute in the way that I can. I'm looking for solidarity, more noble ways to love. But that's an endless search, which is constantly being renewed. You know, I am embarked on the way to the next dreams."

Daniel seemed to enjoy this flurry of publicity, which even garnered him a note in the "People" section of *Veja*.[30] The item stated that Daniel intended to enroll at the UFMG medical school to finish the course and get his diploma, while harboring no plans to join a political party. Daniel, however, never completed his medical degree and had actually already joined the left-wing Workers' Party (PT).[31]

FIGURE 14.3 Photo of Daniel in *Veja* magazine, March 1982, announcing the publication of his book. REPRINTED BY PERMISSION OF ABRIL COMUNICAÇÕES.

In spite of this spotlight on a promising new author, adapting to Rio de Janeiro was not as easy as Daniel and Cláudio had expected. Daniel put on weight again, and the couple began to fight. Then Daniel met a young man named Paulo, and the two had an affair. Daniel later wrote that the problems that he and Cláudio were having were a result of the shock of their return.[32] Throughout their relationship in Europe, Cláudio had been much more promiscuous and now Daniel had chosen to experience a more open relationship. Perhaps the fact that someone found Daniel sexually attractive, even when he was gaining weight, played a role in his decision to be with Paulo. The affair lasted only a year or so, and throughout that period Daniel still remained emotionally committed to Cláudio.

Soon after launching *Passagem*, Daniel landed a job with Codecri, the publishing house that produced his book. Gustavo Barbosa hired Daniel as an internal editor. Since Daniel loved to read, the job was perfect. All he had to do was sift through a closet full of manuscripts that authors had sent the publishing house and write two-page summaries, either recommending publication or rejection. He was responsible for fiction, politics, and literature and sat on a small committee that made the final editorial decisions.[33] Barbosa remembers how good he was at his job. "It was more than his tremendous intelligence and wisdom. It was his knowledge about literature and political thought that was extremely deep and was linked to his ability to articulate ideas with great agility." Daniel would come into the office, pick up work, and take it home, where he wrote his critical reviews.

While reading piles of manuscripts, Daniel came across a thick text pieced together with adhesive tape in an accordion-like fashion. The author, Eliane Maciel, was sixteen and had just given birth to a baby boy. The year before, she had fought with her family in Rio and then escaped to a city in the hinterlands where she lived in near poverty, scraping together enough money to survive while trying to avoid being picked up by the police and forced to return to her parents' home. Daniel loved the raw testimonial account of a rebellious youth trying to live her own life while confronting the conservative mores of her military father and her homemaker mother. He recommended that Codecri publish the work, and the editors agreed.

Maciel remembers her first encounter with Daniel as having been magical. "It was one of the most unforgettable scenes in my life; that short, chubby person with his hand on his shoulder bag—he had this habit of walking around with his hand on the bag—always looking down, with round-framed glasses. Quietly he sat down on a bench, looked at me, and smiled."[34] They talked for five or six hours that day. It was the kind of conversation that Daniel had had while operating underground, when he extended rapid meetings into hour-long discussions about art, film, and literature. "He didn't criticize anything [about the book]; he didn't give any advice about the original version. He only said: 'Look, it needs to be shortened. And you need to tell me what I need to do to cut it—because I don't know what to tell you, as your story is your story—it is not soap that can be broken in two.'"

In many ways, Maciel's book portrays the children of the dictatorship, who were raised under an authoritarian regime and had to live with its conservative cultural and social norms.[35] In conveying her personal tale about confronting her parents and living on her own, Maciel captures the rage and frustrations of youth who were attempting to break out of the rigid confines that were side effects of the dictatorship. The book became an overnight success, selling over a million and a half copies. In the process she and Daniel become close friends. "Herbert Daniel was a person who was absolutely fundamental for who I am," she recalls fondly and emotionally. "He was a person who was a part of my human development, my ability to see the world from a larger perspective, to become more inclusive." Since both were insomniacs, over the coming years they would wander late at night along the beach and talk about anything and everything. "We discussed our anguishes, our other lives, our fears, and those things we didn't quite yet understand." Once again, Daniel had found a female friend and confidante with whom he could share his most intimate thoughts. Eliane Maciel attributed the relationship to his feminine side, the part of him that showed compassion and understanding for others.

While Daniel's work at Codecri offered him the opportunity to discover new literary talents, and at least on one occasion a new best friend, the job also gave him the flexibility and financial security to pursue another long-term interest: politics. The 1979 Amnesty Law had been part of a general strategy of the dictatorship to slowly relinquish power to civilian rule in a carefully coordinated fashion. The stunning 1974 MDB electoral victory had alarmed the generals. In anticipation of the 1978 elections, the military temporarily closed Congress to amend the constitution without political resistance. The April Package, as it was known, created "bionic," or government-appointed, senators, who automatically gained seats in the Congress, ensuring that Geisel retained control of this legislative body. The package also reduced from two-thirds to a simple majority the number of votes required to amend the Constitution, thus guaranteeing that ARENA could continue to manipulate the rules of the game to stay in power. In the 1978 elections, there were twenty-three bionic politicians appointed to the Senate and twenty-two seats elected by direct vote. Through this maneuver, ARENA retained a majority in the upper house, but the MDB candidates received five million more votes nationwide, evidence that the opposition continued to grow in strength, especially in the urbanized southeast. As a result, the military adopted a new "divide-and-rule" tactic, allowing former political leaders to return from abroad in the 1979 amnesty and approving new legislation that disbanded ARENA and MDB and permitted the formation of new political parties. The goal was to splinter the opposition.

At the same time, a 1978–79 wave of strikes by industrial workers in the greater São Paulo region, led by the metallurgical union president Luiz Inácio Lula da Silva, challenged the government's regressive wage policies and its strike ban. This renewed labor militancy led to the founding of the PT, one of the new opposition parties that were established after the military dissolved the MDB. In its formative years, the PT coalesced large sectors of the union movement, grassroots organizations led by progressive forces within (and outside of) the Catholic Church, a new generation of left-wing activists, and former revolutionary militants who had returned from exile.[36]

All of these political changes had a direct impact on Daniel. Two months after he landed in Rio, Liszt Vieira visited him. In a manner both serious and

FIGURE 14.4 Liszt Vieira's electoral campaign material for the state legislature of Rio de Janeiro, 1982.

ironic, Vieira informed Daniel that he planned to run for state legislature on the Workers' Party ticket. Daniel, who had just recently become a registered member of the PT, was excited about the idea and immediately volunteered to help with the campaign.

The 1982 election was the first time that the population was able to choose governors by direct vote since 1965. An array of new political parties also disputed congressional and state legislative offices. In June 1982, in the midst of the campaign, Daniel noted that the people working with Vieira were "strangely incredible." Rather than spending time in endless meetings, as had been the custom when he began his political career in the mid-1960s, "they come together to get things done." Even though there were few gay men and lesbians in the campaign committee, Daniel wrote, "They drew up a platform that integrated the 'questions of our time,' mainly ecology and sexuality, within a concept of democracy that emphasizes alternative lifestyles."[37]

The electoral material produced for the campaign was original and unique. "We're against all forms of violence and discrimination," it said. "We fight for everyone's right to land, work and freedom. We want an ecological, democratic, libertarian, and socialist society, where there are no exploiters and the dignity of each person and the environment is respected." The program pushed a traditional socialist agenda but also addressed discrimination and ecological issues, ideas reluctantly adopted by minority sectors within the Left. Vieira recalls the tension between left-wing developmentalism and concerns about the environment. "When we returned from exile, the Left in Brazil, even in the PT, said: 'In Brazil there is no ecological question, only the social question.'"[38]

The campaign tried to contradict this notion in creative ways. Cláudio, for example, designed a long mural that wrapped around the Largo de Machado Square near downtown Rio, and volunteers then executed the painting. The images portrayed the kind of urban environment and social services that they were fighting for. Fernando Nogueira da Costa, a young radical economist who met Daniel during the 1982 campaign, recalled that the mural portrayed a "cidade feliz" or a happy city, a play on the words *feliz* (happy), *cidade* (city), and *felicidade* (happiness), suggesting a connection between these words' roots. The colorful mural became a trademark of the campaign and contrasted markedly with the usual ubiquitous use of red in propaganda.[39]

Daniel also launched a new political slogan "*Qualquer maneira de amor vale a pena*" (All forms of love are worthwhile), which was taken from the lyrics of a 1975 song by Milton Nascimento and Caetano Veloso. The text of the campaign flyer accompanying the slogan merits being quoted at length: "We want to win our rights to love and live better. What's more, homosexuals are not second-class citizens. Today, in our country, prejudice makes people think that homosexuality is officially a sexual deviance, but sexual deviants are those who don't understand that sexuality is always good and beautiful and that one should love with joy. Without fear. Prejudices only create violence and oppression. Homosexuals, women, blacks, and all those who are exploited and oppressed, let's build, along with the PT, a new socialist, democratic, libertarian and ecologically-aware society. Don't be ashamed. Don't vote in the closet. Vote for yourself. Vote for the PT. If you don't do it, no one will do it for you. We are the PT. Down with prejudices."[40]

Although the electoral material was produced on a shoestring budget, the content was quite revolutionary. People like Vieira and Daniel, who

FIGURE 14.5 Herbert Daniel (left), volunteer (center), and Cláudio Mesquita (right) painting a public mural for Lizst Vieira's 1982 electoral campaign. COURTESY OF FERNANDO NOGUEIRA.

FIGURE 14.6 Lizst Vieira campaign mural, designed by Cláudio Mesquita, at the Largo de Machado. COURTESY OF FERNANDO NOGUEIRA.

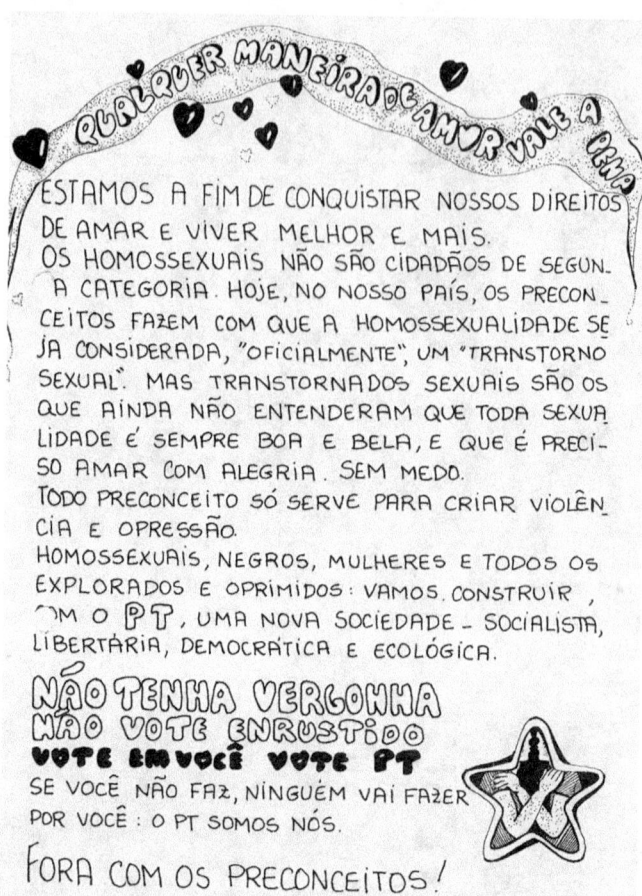

FIGURE 14.7 Campaign material for the 1982 election.

had been steeped in a traditional Marxist ideology that emphasized class exploitation, had developed what scholars today call transversality, namely, an analysis that presents the connections among economic, social, and cultural conditions that marginalize certain sectors of society, using justifications that rely on deep-seated and pervasive ideologies.[41] In 1982, only a handful of activists in a half-dozen electoral campaigns mentioned in passing the oppression of homosexuality, linking it to issues facing other sectors of society. However, in Vieira's campaign, rather than being a secondary issue, it was a central theme.

Not unexpectedly, militants both within the PT and in the Left more generally made fun of Vieira's campaign for its support of environmental questions and rights for homosexuals. They teasingly called Vieira the *viado verde* (green faggot). (The pejorative expression *viado*, derives from the word deer [*veado*], but is pronounced with an "i" rather than an "e," and is a very derogatory epithet.) Rather than denouncing the term as a slur, the campaign decided to embrace the name proudly and to refer to Vieira as the *viado verde*, even though he wasn't gay. The attempt to demoralize the campaign backfired and actually helped increase Vieira's name recognition among voters.[42]

As Election Day approached, campaign activities picked up momentum, and Daniel divided his time between creating clever electoral copy during the day and writing manuscript evaluations for Codecri at night. Cláudio continued designing posters and other literature that they distributed. At the same time, Daniel, who had once again put on weight, went on another strict diet. It was a battle with his body and his self-image that he would wage incessantly over the next decade.

In 1982, the Workers' Party was relatively weak in Rio. Leonel Brizola, the former governor from Rio Grande do Sul and then a congressman from Rio in the years before the 1964 coup, remained a popular leader. He had returned from exile in Portugal and established the Democratic Labor Party (PDT), which made a significant dent in the support that the reorganized MDB had in Rio. Since the election of federal representatives and state legislators was based on proportional representation, gubernatorial and senatorial candidates who headed a party's ticket were important for pulling in votes for the entire slate. Lysâneas Maciel, the PT's candidate for governor, had been an intransigent MDB politician and human rights activist who lost his mandate for Congress in 1976 because of his opposition to the dictatorship. Vladimir Palmeira, the candidate for senator, had been a popular student leader in 1968. Despite their recognized histories of combativeness against the dictatorship, these two heads of the ticket didn't win as much support as had been expected. Instead, Brizola won the gubernatorial election. However, to everyone's surprise Vieira received 10,301 votes and was elected to one of the seventy seats in the state legislature, along with another PT candidate, Lúcia Arruda, who ran on a feminist platform.

Daniel, needless to say, was jubilant. The ballot box, it seemed, had replaced the barrel of the gun as the means for attempting to change Brazil.

15

Words, Words, Words

(1983–1985)

> Daniel was frank, transparent, friendly, affectionate, . . . with a delicious sense of humor come rain or come shine, even if the worst things were happening.
>
> — CRISTINA MONTENEGRO

The 1982 elections marked a turning point in the controlled liberalization with the victory of nine gubernatorial candidates from the PMDB, the reconstituted main opposition party. These wins, along with Leonel Brizola's electoral success in Rio, registered the growing weakness of the regime's popular support. The three main opposition parties—the PMDB, PDT, and PT—won 52.3 percent of congressional votes in the lower house and a majority of ballots cast for senatorial candidates.[1] The dictatorship was on the defensive.

Daniel was optimistic about the new political situation.[2] When Liszt Vieira invited him to join his legislative staff as a political advisor, he enthusiastically agreed. Throughout the mid-1980s, Daniel's daytime job was merely one of many activities he took up as he combined his long-term interest in politics with his talents as an author.

In 1967, Daniel had abandoned a budding career as a playwright and movie critic to dedicate himself to the revolutionary cause. Eight years later, while living in exile in Portugal, he began perfecting those nascent literary skills. Abandoning Marxist terminology, Daniel sought a new style to address a wide range of subjects.[3] The fruits of that transition, *Passagem*, gained him the reputation as a gifted, although somewhat baroque memoirist and a self-reflective left-wing critic. The campaign copy for Liszt Vieira's electoral bid revealed his aptitude for elaborating an innovative political vision for Brazil's unfolding democracy. In the essays, books, novels, and a play published over the following years, Daniel expressed his thoughts about feminism, his body, (homo)sexuality, AIDS, and alternative ways of thinking about politics. His experiments with different literary genres established him as a multifaceted, though not always successful, author.

Daniel's second book, *A fêmea sintética* (The synthetic female), appeared in early 1983, and it offered a criticism of a male-dominated society.[4] It was Daniel's first lengthy experiment in writing science fiction, a literary genre that he, Dilma, and Maria do Carmo had relied on to distract themselves from the tensions of living underground.[5] As was the case for *Passagem*, Cláudio designed the cover. The dedication contains the names of 132 women, beginning with Dona Geny, who had been important throughout his life, from childhood to his return to Rio. The list of women—young, old, neighbors, relatives, comrades, and confidantes—indicates how important female friendships were to him.

The story's plot, too complex to summarize fully, revolves around the exploits of Eduardo Soares de Guerra, known as Duda, a sexually frustrated, politically conservative medical student and heir to a great fortune. While living in a solitary room in a boarding house, Duda falls in love with a beautiful young woman named Edna, and he finally gets the courage to approach her one night on the street. Their interactions lead to a misunderstanding, an altercation, and later an accusation of sexual assault, forcing Duda to hide at his family's ranch until his mother can whisk him off to Europe, where he completes his medical training. When Duda returns to Brazil as Dr. Guerra, he allies himself with Hans, a friend of his father's, who had fled Germany after World War II because he had been involved in Nazi death-camp medical experiments. Dr. Guerra establishes a company called Genetic Project to generate human beings in its laboratories. Subplots of revolutionary exiles and a military coup draw on Daniel's own history and mingle somewhat awkwardly with the main story. Finally, Dr. Guerra creates an ideal synthetic woman, whom he christens Edna. She is beautiful and totally dedicated to him. Her unconditional love, however, finally bores the crazed doctor, and so he arranges for her to develop leukemia and die. He then buries her in a luxurious tomb within view from his bedroom window, so that he can morosely mourn her death. His youthful and idealized fixation continues to haunt him into his old age.

Daniel weaves ideas into the story that are familiar themes in his other writings.[6] However, the main thrust of this tale about genetic engineering is a criticism of idolizing and degrading women, which causes them to become mere appendages of men, without any independence or autonomy. It is feminist science fiction that criticizes traditional gender norms, although most of the main figures are men, and the female characters are not strong, sovereign beings. Leila Míccolis, who collaborated with Daniel on his next book project, didn't really like the work: "He wrote fiction that I think was too cold and wasn't his style. I don't see him in the book."[7] Whether her evaluation is accurate or not, *A fêmea sintética* did not receive an enthusiastic response in the media, nor did it merit a second edition.

Daniel's third book, published later that year, was a slim volume written with Leila Míccolis, an emerging poet in Rio's literary circles.[8] The title, *Jacarés e lobisomens: Dois ensaios sobre a homosexualidade* (Alligators and werewolves: Two essays about homosexuality), refers to the pejorative saying "A woman with another woman produces an alligator; a man with another man produces a werewolf." The first of Daniel's two essays in the volume, about the social construction of homosexuality, is an innovative reflection that anticipates queer theory, criticizes fixed sexual identities, rejects the commercialization of gay enclaves, and opposes hypermasculinity among male homosexuals that, according to Daniel, reinforces rigid bipolar notions of gender and sexuality. His second essay about how to respond to AIDS is remarkably prescient.

Míccolis met Daniel shortly after he had returned from exile. She originally considered interviewing him for *Lampião*, where she worked as its only female journalist. Although the interview never took place, they became friends. Both criticized the ways they thought the organized homosexual movement reinforced gender roles and restricted people's natural polymorphous sexual desires. "It was a passionate friendship at first sight, because he shared many of my ideas. He was against the ghetto, against coming out for its own sake, and against a series of positions very common at the time."

With so few books about homosexuality written for a Brazilian audience, their concise tome offered a set of ideas that had neither circulated in the pages of *Lampião* (which had stopped publication in 1981) nor had been discussed among the activists within the nascent homosexual movement. "We are talking about a new sex—or better yet, 'new sexes'—without rules," they wrote in the introduction.[9] "*New* because it's the sexuality each person renews every day. The plural refers to the diversity not only of attitudes but of tastes, choices, and especially personal histories." These views directly contradicted the dominant discourse among activists. Moreover, the concepts insist that sexuality and gender are fluid and not fixed: "The multiplicity of sexes that we are trying to reveal by writing about them disrupts the fable of a sexual bipolarity that confuses sexuality and genitalia."

Daniel's first essay begins with his observations of a drag queen performing a raucous version of Marilyn Monroe during Carnival. Noting her skill at entertaining her audience with verbal jabs and ironic comments, Daniel uses this vignette to emphasize the socially constructed nature of gendered behavior, prejudices against effeminate men, and the misogynistic ways in which many males who dress as women produce an exaggerated, stereotypical idealization of femininity.

He then returns to the joke that he had told on numerous occasions while underground about the two men (a *bicha* and Jorge) having sex under a bridge. What had seemed to comrades in the VPR to be an off-color, somewhat humorous anecdote Daniel endlessly repeated either to deflect suspicion about his own homosexuality or to insist that it was nobody's business becomes the centerpiece of a seventeen-page meditation about social attitudes toward gender roles and sexuality. Daniel meticulously deconstructs the different elements in the joke and ends with the conclusion that "sex is the continuation of politics by other means."[10] After having fixated on the story over the years, he now uses it as a means to criticize social prejudices about formulaic caricatures of effeminate men and the cultural context that makes the joke seem funny.

Daniel then offers a brief overview of the history of homosexuality, drawn from many of the ideas that Michel Foucault produced at the time, but without citing him or other authors. The arguments are familiar today to anyone who has studied the history of sexuality, but in the early 1980s they were radical and innovative. Homosexuality, he argues, is a category invented in the late nineteenth century to control and contain sexuality. "The creation of a group or a ghetto doesn't derive from the preexisting differences in individuals, but from the power that regulates and controls them. In the case of homosexuals, it is the very creation of difference that is the sphere in which power operates."[11] Daniel also questions the notion that there should be a gay movement fighting for its rights, because this effort isolates people from society as a whole.

The call for an end to discrimination against homosexuals, which had been an innovative plank of Vieira's 1982 electoral platform, takes second place in this essay to a dense and at times hard-to-understand censure of what has come to be known as identity politics. Both *Lampião* and the dozen groups that made up the Homosexual Movement built their organizations around a call for men and women to affirm their same-sex sexual desires and to challenge society's prejudicial attitudes and moral condemnation.[12] Daniel's essay questions the value of organizing separately as homosexuals, because, in his opinion, this construction and affirmation of a homosexual identity reinforces rigid notions of what it is to be a homosexual. His ideas also stand apart from the disputes within movement, when some leftists called for strategic alliances with sectors of the Left while others argued firmly in favor of an "autonomous" movement.[13] Although Daniel did not embrace the movement, he still leveled criticisms against the Left because of its traditional attitudes about homosexuality. His comments came from someone who aimed sharply at those on the political spectrum with whom he had common ground and are reminiscent of his writings from Paris: "Speaking about sexuality as a homosexual, I am not attempting to introduce a homosexual discourse in the Left, but instead offer a *criticism of the homosexual discourse that the Left has*."[14] According to Míccolis, the book did not receive favorable reviews or popular acclaim. "The homosexuals threw stones at it because we didn't come out as homosexuals, and, at the same time, the heterosexuals thought that we were posturing. It was horrible."

Yet a twelve-page annex to the volume entitled "The Syndrome of Prejudice" is the first in-depth critical analysis about AIDS produced in Brazil. Daniel decided to include the brief essay as an afterthought. His medical-school training gave him the technical background to understand the nature of the disease. The ideas that young medical students had developed at the UFMG to replace outdated medical practices offered him a framework for his assessment of the social response to AIDS, when the media began transmitting misinformation about what it originally called the "gay cancer."[15] Daniel's essay notes the alarmist nature of news coverage, the immediate and direct linkage of AIDS to homosexuality, the panic provoked by the lack of clear information about the disease, and the failure of members of the "ghetto" to respond politically to this health threat.

His essay also contains two revolutionary ideas mentioned in passing but which would later become the core concepts behind his own AIDS activism. The first precept is that the best way to combat the exclusive focus on the medical aspects of the disease is to create a solidarity network to support people living with AIDS. His second concept calls for homosexuals and others infected with the disease to participate actively with medical professionals and government officials in finding ways to prevent new infections and discover a cure. He argued, "Of course, this implies a more democratic attitude on the part of the medical profession in carrying out relations with other *bodies* over which it considers it has the qualifications to manipulate, without allowing for reciprocal participation."[16] In the early 1980s, there was no notion of patients' rights, nor emphasis on involving those living with an illness in learning about and advocating for ways to treat and cure a given disease. The essay plants the seeds for a political response to AIDS that would revolutionize the relationship between patients and doctors.

A month or so before *Jacarés e lobisomens* was published, the weekly magazine *Isto É* featured Daniel in a three-page interview that, in part, was to promote the book.[17] Daniel outlines some of its core themes: homosexuality only exists in the plural; it is erroneous to say that gay men prefer anonymous sex over intimate relationships; and traditional gender roles reinforce forms of oppression.[18] When asked about the Homosexual Movement, Daniel responds emphatically, "I prefer to think of a liberation movement that fights for a new idea about the body. In it would be homosexuals, women, children, blacks, all of those who in one way or another feel the need to re-examine the discrimination of the body."[19] Perhaps because of his evaluation of the mistakes that the revolutionary Left had made in the previous decade, Daniel also criticizes the Homosexual Movement's vanguard nature "in which a few good people, who consider themselves enlightened about sex will lead the broad masses to consciousness about their bodies."[20]

Daniel's evaluation is perplexing. Both he and the reporter seemed to think that suddenly the Brazilian Left accepted same-sex desire and different gendered behavior as normal and matter of fact. That was far from the case. In response to the journalist's comment that "today there isn't a party that does not have a homosexual faction," Daniel states, rather forcefully, "The Left today glorifies the Homosexual Movement. But being a homosexual doesn't transform someone into a prophet for a better world."[21] Although the Socialist Convergence had formed a gay and lesbian caucus in 1979, and Workers' Party militants in São Paulo had made unsuccessful attempts to organize internally during the 1982 election campaign, the rest of the Left was still quite hostile (or indifferent) to the Homosexual Movement.[22] This is, in part, why Liszt Vieira's election campaign had been so groundbreaking: it stood out as a distinct new way of talking about discrimination. Why Daniel and the *Isto É* reporter had the impression that

FIGURE 15.1 Cover of *O Pasquim* with articles on Cabo Anselmo.
COURTESY OF THE ARQUIVO GERAL DA CIDADE DO RIO DE JANEIRO.

somehow there had been a sea change in the Left's attitudes about homosexuality is unclear. For Daniel, perhaps it was a way to dismiss the movement as merely a fashionable trend without serious content. He could position himself to its left with a radical outlook that rejected identity politics, as well as the supposed "messianic ideas that the Left tried to impose on homosexuals at all costs."[23]

Daniel addressed the issue of homosexuality once again in early 1984 when he wrote a two-part article for *O Pasquim* about the controversy surrounding the reappearance of José Anselmo dos Santos (Cabo Anselmo). As mentioned earlier, the former sailor had led a rebellion immediately prior to the 1964 coup. He then lived in exile in Cuba from 1966 until 1970 and then secretly returned to Brazil to join forces with the VPR. After becoming a police informant, he turned in dozens of revolutionaries who were captured and assassinated. Government authorities later gave him protection and support to undergo plastic surgery and change his identity. Living incognito for a decade, in March 1984, he gave a lengthy interview to the investigative journalist Octávio Ribeiro, which appeared in *Istó É* and later that year in a book.[24] In his deposition Cabo Anselmo details his role as a government infiltrator.[25]

This extensive coverage about betrayal within the Left came out precisely at the moment in which the country was going through a major political upheaval. In late 1983, a movement began demanding a constitutional amendment to allow direct presidential elections.[26] In mobilizations throughout the country, known as the *Direitas Já* (Direct elections now) movement, prominent opposition politicians stood side by side with entertainment celebrities calling for a return to democratic rule. On April 10, a million people protested in front of the Candelária Church in Rio, and 1.5 million flooded into downtown São Paulo a week later. On April 25, the Dantas de Oliveira Law, the constitutional amendment to allow direct presidential elections, was voted on in Congress with 298 in favor, 65 against, and 112 abstentions. The bill, however, lacked a quorum and failed. For the sixth time in twenty years, the Congress chose the president through an indirect electoral procedure. It was within this context—the fight for democracy after the defeat of the revolutionary opposition—that Daniel published an interview with Cabo Anselmo. Daniel wanted to intervene in the debates about the extent to which the revolutionary Left's defeat was due to "betrayal from within.".[27]

In October 1974, only a month after he had fled Brazil for safety in Europe, Daniel interviewed Ângelo Pezzuti in Paris to record his version of the events surrounding Anselmo's visit to Chile in late 1971 and Pezzuti's suspicions that he was a government infiltrator. Daniel decided to publish the interview a decade later as a counterpoint to Anselmo's *Isto É* deposition, in which the turncoat defends his actions. The interview with Pezzuti offers details about Anselmo from the Left's perspective and includes information about the internal politics of VPR members operating in Chilean exile between 1971 and 1973. Pezzuti relates his understanding about when Anselmo decided to collaborate with the police and how Onofre Pinto, the leader of the VPR in Chile, had dismissed his and Maria do Carmo Brito's serious doubts about Anselmo's trustworthiness. He also states rather unequivocally that Anselmo was a homosexual who had been caught several times attempting to seduce male members of the Left. Moreover, Pezzuti adds that the VPR leader Onofre Pinto was also a homosexual, which supposedly explains why he had refused to acknowledge reports that Anselmo had "gone to the other side."[28]

It's hard to pinpoint exactly when the allegations that Cabo Anselmo was a homosexual began to circulate widely within the Left, but likely it was soon after the news broke in January 1973 that the police had assassinated six VPR members in Recife with Anselmo's collaboration. Pezzuti alleges that one of Anselmo's fellow sailors told him that Anselmo had engaged in homosexual activities while in the Navy, which resulted in "problems."[29] Pezzuti also states that Anselmo had made a sexual pass at one of the six militants (who later joined him in Recife) and was obliged to offer a self-criticism in front of his comrades in Cuba.[30] Moreover, Pezzuti insists that Onofre Pinto, who had authorized the decision to send militants from Cuba to Recife and had rejected any accusations that Anselmo was a police informant, was also a "typical" homosexual, which colored Onofre Pinto's ideas about Anselmo.

Unlike in some other writings, when Daniel is elusive about his sexual identity, in this article he affirms it as a means of making a point: "Personally, as a homosexual I was shocked by the first comments that I heard 'explaining' the case when I went into exile in 1974. People insisted *way too much* that Anselmo was a 'homosexual.'"[31] For leftists, Daniel maintains, it is too easy an explanation for his traitorous actions, and it draws too simplistically on stereotypes about homosexuals. Daniel argues there is no such thing as a prototypical homosexual, and that heterosexuality or homosexuality does not predispose people to certain actions. He also criticizes what today is known as homophobia: "Prejudice against the 'homosexual' incites shocking reactions. Either it provokes disgust, as if it were a kind of deformity, or it makes people laugh for reasons that are often the same. Prejudices are bad in both cases."[32]

Rather than pointing out that the Left's assertions about Anselmo's sexual proclivities could have been an easy way to discredit the police informant, Daniel accepts Pezzuti's supposition as a fact. At the same time, Daniel refuses to deem Anselmo a "faggot" for other reasons. Anselmo, he argues, denied his own sexuality, and this internalized repression, imposed by a macho society, was one reason for his traitorous acts. "I don't consider him a homosexual but rather a person in an intense conflict with his sexuality," he posits.[33] In other words, a homophobic society and an equally prejudiced Left are the ultimate explanations for Anselmo's betrayals, not his sexuality. A side comment by Pezzuti in the 1974 interview indicates that Daniel had thought about writing a book on Anselmo.[34] He didn't, and to date, in some left-wing circles, rumors about Anselmo's homosexuality linger as the explanation for his treachery.

Daniel continues to discuss the tensions between homosexuality and the Left as one of the themes in his next book, *Meu corpo daria um romance: Narrativa desarmada* (My body could become a novel: Disarmed narrative), published in August 1984. The four-hundred-page volume combines more semiautobiographical information about his revolutionary past, his relationship with Cláudio, and his time in exile interspersed with ruminations about homosexuality and his body. It also contains an interesting story within the story about an episode that today would be called gay bashing.

The narrative begins with the description of an eleven-minute incident, related eleven times throughout the work, each time told slightly differently. A character, presumably Daniel, kisses a male "friend" goodbye on the lips at a bus stop and then enters a bus. The other passengers immediately gaze on him with hostility. Even two young men wearing political tee-shirts—one with the Workers' Party's five-pointed red star and the other with the banner of the Polish workers' movement Solidarnosc—are antagonistic toward the protagonist because he is apparently gay. "Vi . . . a . . . do . . . ," someone drones, just to provoke the main character. Daniel's point is clear. The passengers' indifference about this aggression reveals a lack of authentic commitment to social justice. Left-wing militants can support abstract workers in Poland and identify with the labor movement in São Paulo, but they are incapable of defending someone on the bus under attack. In fact, they are part of the problem rather than the solution.

In the eleven distinctive versions of this incident, the details shift, as if Daniel had experimented multiple times in his attempt to tell the story just right, or as if he had wanted to offer eleven alternative perspectives on a single moment. The different iterations allow Daniel to present varied imagined responses that the aggrieved person considers while sitting uncomfortably on the bus. The story's retelling also emphasizes the nature of the day-to-day violence that homosexuals experience when they manifest behavior different from heterosexual norms of masculinity.

The other main theme, Daniel's ambivalent relationship with his body and his sexuality, is woven throughout the book. In vignettes he describes in some detail his first same-sex adventures, his passionate love for Erwin Duarte, his struggles to repress his homosexuality while underground, his newly found freedom in exile, and the open relationship with Cláudio in Rio. Daniel explains how he had dealt with his homosexuality "in silence."[35] He also discusses his torment over the self-perception that he is ugly, wondering if he would have become a guerrilla if he had been born handsome. "I would have been 'another' kind of homosexual. Even an obnoxious faggot."[36] This admission may offer an insight into why Daniel despised the "ghetto." It wasn't simply because he didn't care about the latest fashions and never felt comfortable dancing, which were two interests closely associated with gay urban social life in Paris and Rio in the 1970s and 1980s. He knew that beauty and signs of affluence were highly valued commodities in places where homosexuals gathered. With painfully self-flagellant reasoning, Daniel wonders whether hiding his homosexuality for so long and feeling guilty about his sexual desires made him even uglier.[37] Cláudio's and Daniel's love for each other ends up helping him overcome his negative feelings about his body and his looks. "We discovered that we live together not because we have to, but because we have a vocation for it. . . . We opted for a life together, because we always have a lot to say to each other, and there have never been silences between us."[38] This mutual devotion explains why the book is dedicated to his lifetime partner.

Like *Passagem*, the volume doesn't follow a strict chronology or a simple narrative style. Leila Míccolis considers that Daniel extrapolates a lot in *Meu corpo*. "He jumps over linear chronology, that which is certain. . . . And he says, 'I don't want to know any more if it is fiction or reality. That is who I am. It is I; that which I want to live or could live. My real past, the past that I could have lived, and my future that I will perhaps live.'" If this assessment is accurate, using the book as a historical source becomes tricky. This is especially the case since Míccolis believes Daniel began to merge his biography with fiction: "Many times you don't know where the fiction ends and reality begins. And this was a little like him. He was a bit delirious. He liked this mixture. It was the same in his life. Many times he would say: 'Is this really happening or is it fiction?' Then he would laugh and say: 'I don't know any more.'"

Yet when one examines the stories about his life underground with Cláudio and his interludes in Portugal and Paris sprinkled throughout the volume, these accounts coincide with facts in contemporaneous letters and memories offered by friends. Some names are changed to protect the identity of people from Daniel's past. Erwin Duarte, for example, becomes Renzo. One can also assume some poetic license in retelling the story of his time cloistered in a darkened Niterói apartment and in recounting the day when Cláudio writes a note proposing a romantic sexual relationship. Still, his biographical narrative seems closer to fact than fiction.

Nevertheless, he leaves at least one story only partially told. When describing his life as a sexually repressed revolutionary, Daniel recounts an incident about an important member of the organization, whom he calls Alencar, and who, like Daniel, felt he had to hide his homosexuality. According to Daniel, Alencar had considerable responsibilities within

COLINA, and at one point had made a sexual pass at Ângelo, who rebuffed him "because he didn't like to be forced."[39] Alencar and Daniel, it seems, never got along. "He thought that I was ugly, since he kiddingly told me so two or three times, but I knew he was [actually] serious. I realized looking into his eyes that he was [gay], as much as I knew that he knew I was. He also, I am certain, abstained from his homosexuality; he was as totally secretive as I was."[40]

Daniel then tells a story that is shrouded in just enough ambiguity—perhaps to hide the identity of Alencar—that it is somewhat difficult to determine precisely when the incident took place. At some point, presumably in 1969, VAR-Palmares held a meeting in a house in the middle of a forest, and it was Daniel's turn to be a night lookout. While patrolling the area, he heard a noise coming from a small shack next to the house. With flashlight and pistol in hand, he nervously approached and opened the door. His light beamed onto two men, their pants down at their ankles, with Alencar being penetrated by the other. Daniel writes, "After a moment of shock, they pulled up their pants, like two young boys caught in the act, and the next day they acted as if I didn't exist, and they didn't look at me. There became this strange thing between us, as if I had done something really bad to them, until the day that we departed, and Alencar looked at me in a way that made me believe that if I said anything about it, he would kill me."[41]

Less important than figuring out Alencar's identity is what the story says about the homophobic climate that affected anyone within the revolutionary Left who experienced same-sex desires. Daniel felt he had to repress his sexuality and be abstinent for almost five years while Alencar's concern that Daniel might reveal his (or their) secret seemed to engender terror. The revolutionary Left certainly had no monopoly on its homophobic attitudes, and it merely reflected pervasive social attitudes. Still, while risking their lives to overthrow the dictatorship and build a new socialist society, the revolutionary Left remained remarkably "unrevolutionary" when it came to rethinking traditional sexual and social mores.

Meu corpo was less successful than *Passagem*, perhaps because the fad of reading revolutionary memoirs had long passed or because the book's postmodernist structure seemed difficult to follow for those used to more conventional narratives. Still, Daniel was producing works at breakneck speed. After his acclaimed performance as the director of the Show Medicina in 1967, its founder, Jota Dângelo, wrote him a congratulatory note praising his creative use of words. Seventeen years later, Daniel finally returned to the theater with equal verve. In November 1984, he published his first play and began organizing its production on a Rio stage.

As três moças do sabonete: Um apologia sobre os anos Médici is a complicated title to translate.[42] Its first part is a direct reference to a 1931 poem by the modernist writer Manuel Bandeira entitled "The Ballad of the Three Young Women of the Araxá Soap [Bar Poster]." In Bandeira's original verses, he sees a poster ad of three beautiful women and asks, "Are they prostitutes, reciters of poetry, or acrobats? Are they the three Marias?" Daniel uses this as the signature line for his play. The ambiguity in the possible life stories that Bandeira sees in these three commercial models is reformulated into a dramatic tale drawn from Daniel's own history. The subtitle, "An apology of the Médici years," places the piece in the early 1970s at the height of political repression.

The protagonist Tiago is a handsome revolutionary whose organization has collapsed. He has fled to a small town in Minas Gerais to seek help from João, his best friend from university days and a former revolutionary sympathizer. João has lost his job at the university for political reasons and has returned to his hometown with his wife and small children. Tiago soon confesses to João that he is a homosexual, and later in the play that he, in fact, was in love with João while at the university. Much like Duarte's reaction when Daniel declared his love, João accepts his friend's confession with a degree of compassion, although he still doesn't quite understand homosexuality.

Dovetailing with the developments of this story is another narrative about Lulu, a gay beauty salon owner, and his young cousin Tina, whose real name is Fausto and who dreams of going to Rio for a sex change. The two are from a prominent family, and, although ridiculed for being *bichas*, they still enjoy a certain protection from social ostracism. Zé Barbosa, their effeminate Afro-Brazilian shop assistant, however, is not so lucky. Poor, nonwhite, and unmasculine, he is mistreated by Lulu and Tina and suffers social marginalization for being dark-skinned and a *viado*. Along with Direne, a brassy and foul-mouthed woman of questionable virtue who is Lula's friend, the four exchange aggressive and campy banter, using crass slang that was common to gay circles and must have both amused and shocked many theatergoers. The four also express a disdain for each other and themselves that is reminiscent of the 1970 Broadway hit *Boys in the Band*, which appeared on the Brazilian stage a year after its U.S. debut: it dramatizes a group of self-hating homosexuals who snap at each other during an evening get-together.[43]

In a strange and somewhat improbable twist, the dashing young Tiago, who has been celibate throughout his underground years and yearns for human contact, falls in love with Zé Barbosa, who is neither intelligent nor attractive. In the end, the police surround the town, hunt down Tiago, and kill him. In the final scene, the lights come up, and the actors introduce themselves, give their real names, and tell the fate of their characters. Lulu's business goes bankrupt, but his mother sets him up in a successful women's clothing store. He hires Direne to work with him. Tina moves to Rio but doesn't have a sex change. Zé Barbosa later shows up in Bom Despacho (where Daniel was born), but no one knows much about his fate. Tiago has been on the list of the disappeared since 1973. João, for reasons that are not specified, commits suicide in 1976, but before his death, he names his newborn son Tiago.

Almir Martins, who starred as Tiago, fondly remembers Daniel. He recalls the first time that he ever encountered Cláudio and Daniel in Rio, sometime in 1982 or early 1983, on the way to the neighborhood street market. "I saw two men dressed in tight shirts and even tighter shorts, wearing clogs, carrying a shopping bag, and walking together to the market. I had never seen anyone like them so I followed them, and listened to their conversation."[44] For Martins, who had fled to Rio from the conservative small-town atmosphere of São Carlos in order to become an actor, the pair was something new and fascinating. They were living their daily lives as if they did not care what others thought. Martins was later invited to lunch at the house of his neighbors Gustavo Barbosa and Vanja Freitas, where he met Daniel. Barbosa had worked with Daniel at Codecri, and Freitas, an actress, had become a close friend.[45] After a conversation with Almir Martins at lunch, Daniel announced that he had found the person to play Tiago.

Given the inclusion of Daniel's own experiences as a revolutionary and fugitive in the plot, one would assume that he had modeled the main character after himself, but he made him an attractive young revolutionary, perhaps to push back against his own negative self-image. Yet Martins clearly remembers that Daniel insisted he didn't consider himself to be Tiago but instead the poor, black/mulatto, and somewhat ugly Zé Barbosa. "Had a person who looked like Daniel declared his love for João, it would have seemed pathetic," Martins reasoned. Assuming that Daniel wasn't being facetious when explaining his literary intentions, his identification with Zé Barbosa must have reflected his ongoing negative feelings about his effeminacy, his body, and his looks. It also gave him the opportunity, through the character of Zé Barbosa, to portray the story of a dashing revolutionary falling in love with an unattractive person. Significantly, Daniel identified himself as a person of color, indicating that his racial background was slowly becoming an integrated part of his identity, although it was something he rarely wrote or talked about explicitly.

The play was booked at the Delfim Theater for a two-month run and had good ticket sales, but a devastating review published in *O Globo*, Rio's most important newspaper, totally shattered Daniel. Martins remembers that one of the problems with the production was its director, Milton Gonçalves, a prominent actor who agreed to direct the play. "He simply wasn't sensitive about the subject. He was the wrong choice."[46] Severino J. Albuquerque, a scholar of Brazilian theater, points out two reasons why the play was unsuccessful: "the disfavor that befell politically engaged plays . . . at a time when the theatergoing public had shifted their interests from social issues to the individual," and a rejection of the types of plays of the 1970s and early 1980s that offered stereotyped images of homosexuals as "weak, effeminate men," as personified by Lulu, Tina, and Zé Barbosa.[47] When the contract with the theater expired, the play shut down. It has never been performed again.

This did not discourage Daniel, however, from continuing to work in the theater. Almost immediately, he began directing a children's play about sex entitled *Cegonha . . . Que cegonha?* (Stork . . . what stork?). It was a success and ran in Rio theaters for two years. Daniel adapted the play from Marilu Alvarez's successful São Paulo production, *Cegonha boa de bico* (Stork, a good talker). Cristina Montenegro, who, along with Almir Martins, was a member of the theater group that mounted the production, recalls that Daniel charmed the playwright into allowing him to rework the piece, which included eliminating the adult characters and making gender roles more fluid and egalitarian. He also insisted that at least one black actor participate in the production, revealing sensitivity to institutional racism that was still a controversial topic to raise in the mid-1980s.[48] Cláudio designed the costumes and stage sets, continuing his creative partnership with Daniel.

The piece reflected Daniel's new approach to politics. In a theater review that appeared in *O Globo*, Daniel explained, "It is a play about sexual education that doesn't teach or offer answers but merely shows an approach."[49] Rather than preaching a received truth to a misinformed public that needed its consciousness raised, Daniel presented possibilities, alternative ways of thinking, and new slants on a subject. Since initiating an active literary career, he had experimented with various ways to reach out to others with new ideas. The quickly changing political and cultural climate in the country offered him a new opportunity to do just that.

After the 1984 defeat of the constitutional amendment to allow direct presidential elections, opposition political parties chose Tancredo Neves as a unity candidate to oppose the military's choice. Neves, who had briefly been the prime minister in 1961–62, was elected the governor of Minas Gerais two decades later. At first it seemed as if his candidacy was a symbolic

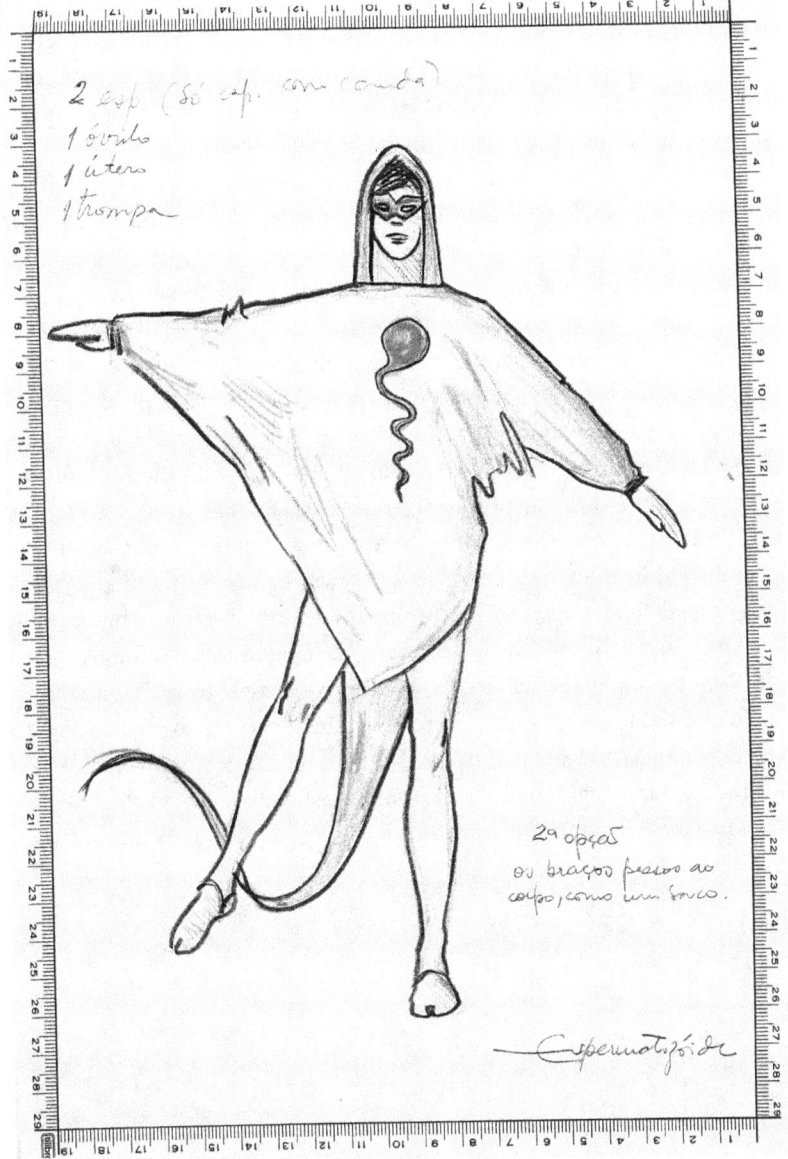

FIGURE 15.2 Cláudio's design of the costume for the spermazoid in the play *Cegonha? . . . Que cegonha?* COURTESY OF CRISTINA MONTENEGRO.

gesture. The right-wing pro-military Social Democratic Party (PDS) had a majority in Congress, virtually ensuring the election of its candidate. However, an unexpected split among the PDS ranks and the defection of Senator José Sarney altered the odds. Sarney had been the president of ARENA in 1979 and became the head of the newly created PDS the following year. Dissatisfied with the candidate that the PDS was likely to choose, he left the party to form an alliance with Neves's electoral coalition. Sarney, a loyal defender of the dictatorship, became the opposition's vice presidential candidate and brought enough votes with him for Neves to be chosen as the first civilian president in twenty-one years.[50]

Then, on the eve of his inauguration, Neves was hospitalized with an intestinal infection. Sarney was quickly sworn in as vice president and assumed the role of acting president. For thirty-seven days the country remained fixated on Neves's daily medical reports. He finally died on April 21, 1985, and Sarney became president. After a decade-long struggle to restore democratic rule and the apparent victory of the opposition, the reins of power were in the hands of a politician who had been the dictatorship's long-term defender. For Daniel, the outcome must have been a bitter irony.

With the military no longer in charge, the upcoming 1986 congressional elections became the vehicle to choose representatives to a Constituent Assembly to write a new constitution. Liszt Vieira decided to seek a congressional seat to participate in the process. He asked Daniel to run on his ticket for the Rio state legislature. Daniel enthusiastically accepted the offer. He now had a new platform upon which to discuss his ideas about transforming Brazil.

16

The Politics of Pleasure

(1986–1988)

> There is no democracy if it stops at the factory gate or at the edge of the bed.
>
> — HERBERT DANIEL

Liszt Vieira's 1982 election to the state legislature was the beginning of a new phase in Daniel's political life. At the same time that he was creating a reputation as an up-and-coming writer, he produced speeches, elaborated political proposals, and attended meetings to develop legislative strategies.[1] His monthly salary stabilized Daniel and Claúdio's economic situation, and they moved to an apartment in the hillside neighborhood of Santa Teresa. Daniel's job as political advisor helped consolidate his criticisms of the conservative tendencies within the traditional Left. Later, his role as a candidate in 1986 offered him a unique opportunity to develop and refine an alternative political agenda.

One of Vieira's electoral promises was to disseminate the radical program that Daniel and the election committee had developed. Soon after

Vieira took office, he gave a series of speeches on the floor of the state legislature. One, delivered on August 25, "Soldiers' Day," honored Carlos Lamarca's memory as a patriot and a revolutionary. One might expect it to have caused a scandal among legislators or in the media. However, Sérgio Pinho, a former VAR-Palmares militant who was on Vieira's staff, claimed that other legislators, the mainstream press, and the public paid little attention to these speeches.[2] Still, this declaration and many others were ways of rearticulating issues discussed in Vieira's electoral campaign literature.

Some of these ideas, however, were not very popular with leading PT activists and among other Left sectors. In the early 1980s mounting inflation and a recession reinforced left-wing ideas that emphasized economic issues. Vieira remembered the political climate within the PT: "There were three major currents: the trade unionists that divided the world between the bosses and the employees; the ideological Left that divided the world between the bourgeoisie and the proletariat; and a grassroots sector of the Catholic Church that divided the world between the oppressors and the oppressed. . . . There was no other discourse. Then suddenly I talked about minorities, ecology."[3] Rio's PT leaders and many of its supporters were still immersed in a worldview that emphasized one-dimensional dichotomies. "They thought that ecological questions had been imported from Europe and had nothing to do with Brazil, where socio-economic issues were more important." Alfredo Sirkis also recalls the difficulties of introducing ecological questions into political debates: "In the 80s we were the 'enemy of developmentalism,' and 'romantics' in the eyes of businessmen, the media, and traditional politicians. The Left was ferocious: 'Environment is the thing of rich countries. We have to solve hunger and poverty first to later deal with these superfluous issues.'"[4] Indeed, many of the ideas that Vieira, Sirkis, and others presented about the environment were new to the country's political debates, although there were a few groups in Rio and São Paulo working on these issues.

Several processes, however, helped widened political debates. The Direct Elections Now movement incorporated a new generation of activists into the country's political life, among them thousands concerned about the environment.[5] Water and air pollution, the lack of adequate urban green areas, and the dangers of the Angra I nuclear power plant in the state of Rio de Janeiro all emerged as pressing issues.[6] In this regard, Vieira's campaign was incredibly forward thinking and gained the support of many who were focusing on problems that the Left had heretofore largely ignored.

In Rio's 1985 mayoral elections, the PT supported Wilson Farias, a trade union leader who received less than 1 percent of the vote. His devastating

FIGURE 16.1 Event founding the Green Party in Rio de Janeiro. Left to right: Fernando Gabeira, Lucélia Santos, Alfredo Sirkis, John Nesching, Luís Alberto Py, Carlos Minc, Herbert Daniel, and Guido Gelli. COURTESY OF THE PARTIDO VERDE.

defeat motivated some to propose a new approach to the 1986 elections. Disillusioned with the single-minded emphasis on traditional Marxist ideas that relegated other issues to the sidelines, a collection of activists began discussing political alternatives. The German Green Party and the strong European antinuclear movement served as two examples of successful new progressive coalitions. Over the course of 1985, diverse individuals and groups came together to consider founding a new political party. For some it was a question of leaving the PT, which they thought was too sectarian and politically narrow. For others it was the first time that they had actively engaged in partisan politics. Herbert Daniel was intimately involved in these discussions.[7]

In January 1986, the Green Party (PV) was officially launched at Rio's Carla Nunes Theater. A panel of prominent intellectuals and public figures presented their reasons for its founding. Four had been involved in the armed struggle and had lived in exile: Fernando Gabeira, formerly of the MR-8, and Carlos Minc, Alfredo Sirkis, and Herbert Daniel, who had all been in the VPR. Others who participated were Lucélia Santos, a popular television actress; John Nesching, an orchestra and operatic conductor, at the time married to Santos; Luís Alberto Py, a psychoanalyst; and Guido Gelli, an environmentalist. According to Gabeira, "A large number in the group had worked in other leftwing parties, such as the PT and the PDT, and they presented criticisms about the limitations of raising green issues in these spaces."[8]

Unfortunately, no one filmed the event, nor are there transcripts of the speeches. Daniel left no record of his talk. However, Vieira's electoral program of 1982 had contained items addressing environmental issues, and the notion of an alternative lifestyle (*uma vida alternativa*) spoke to a sentiment against excessive consumption that fit neatly with Daniel's longtime practices. Never a person concerned about material possessions, Daniel paid little attention to what he wore and didn't spend money on nonessential items. In this regard, he followed his parents, who had lived a frugal life. Eliane Maciel remembers that "Daniel was extremely self-contained, simple, and critical of the consumer society. He got irritated when Cláudio wanted to buy a car. He said: 'Why buy a car? People can take a bus.'"[9] One can suppose that the combination of his ongoing reservations about the sectarian and rigid nature of sectors of the Left and his affinity with many of the values embedded in the Green movement were among the reasons that he decided to join forces with others to found this new party.

At the same time that PV advocates began the legalization process, complex maneuvering within the PT ensured that Gabeira was nominated as the gubernatorial candidate on a joint PT-PV ticket. Gabeira had become a media celebrity, and diverse political forces thought that he could strengthen the Left's electoral showing.[10] Liszt Vieira opted to run for Congress on the PT-PV ticket, and Daniel agreed to run for the state legislature on the same slate.

Unlike a system based on the selection of state and federal representatives by district, the Brazilian electoral code provides for proportional representation. Members of state and federal legislatures are chosen based on two criteria: the sum total of votes received by the party coalition and the actual number of votes individual candidates for the legislature win in relationship to others running for the same office in that party coalition. Thus, building a constituency across the state, rather than in a specific geographical area in Rio, was essential for Daniel's victory. The fact that he planned to run as an openly gay candidate fueled hopes that he would gather enough votes among gay men to meet the threshold to be elected.

Although a dynamic surge of gay and lesbian activism had occurred after 1978, the movement stagnated and then went into decline in the early 1980s. A severe economic recession forced many activists to focus on solving day-to-day problems and employment issues.[11] The initial news about AIDS caused confusion within the movement, as groups struggled to respond to an onslaught of homophobic and contradictory reporting that created panic in the general population and anxiety among gay men. Some activists began concentrating entirely on the disease and how to respond to an increasing rate of infection among gay men.[12] Others retreated from activism altogether. Divisions within the movement also stunted its growth.[13] In 1986, only two groups—Gay Group of Bahia (GGB), headquartered in the state capital of Salvador, and Triângulo Rosa (Pink Triangle) of Rio—had an official, registered legal status, while a scattering of small groups aggregated no more than a dozen or so active members each.[14]

Could, then, Daniel gain the support of gay men and lesbians for his electoral bid? For decades Rio had been a magnet for those who had discovered their same-sex desires and found it oppressive to live under family scrutiny in hostile social environments in their hometowns.[15] There are no statistics available from the 1980s to measure the number of gays and lesbians among Rio's nine million residents, but there were certainly tens of thousands, if not more. That would have been a sufficient number to supply the votes Daniel needed to be elected. However, few were open about their homosexuality beyond their circle of friends, and there was no guarantee that gay people would vote for gay candidates.[16]

Nevertheless, Daniel sought out Triângulo Rosa for political support. João Antônio Mascarenhas, who created the group in 1985, had been a member of *Lampião*'s editorial board.[17] Fluent in English, he maintained an intense correspondence with the half-dozen other Brazilian gay groups, as well as international organizations.[18] He also owned a comfortable apartment in Ipanema that served as a meeting place.[19] Daniel was a founding member of the organization, and Cláudio was the vice president. In a meeting held in October 1985, the group unanimously decided to endorse Daniel's electoral bid.[20]

In spite of the movement's small size, Daniel's candidacy engendered enthusiastic support. The GGB president, Luiz Mott, sent the campaign a wholehearted endorsement signed by the organization's members stating that "in the history of the movements in defense of human rights in Brazil, we consider of crucial importance the courage and determination of Herbert Daniel, the first candidate to publicly declare that he will defend the interests and civil rights of homosexual citizens."[21] Fernando Gabeira also issued a statement six weeks before Election Day proclaiming that "we consider unacceptable each and every act that discriminates against citizens based on sexual orientation, an expression that defines questions related to homosexuality, heterosexuality, and bisexuality, without trying to classify medically any 'pattern' of sexual behavior, and seek instead to guarantee the autonomy of citizens in their right to make use of their own bodies for their own sexual enjoyment." The letter goes on to state quite emphatically, "We are thinking of broad governmental action that will reach, in this case, education, information, health, justice, and politics. It is important to guarantee the rights and stimulate the free organization of homosexual movements and punish any discriminatory violence." The statement concludes with a promise to support an item in the new constitution barring discrimination based on sexual orientation.[22]

It was a remarkable declaration for Gabeira to make, as it incorporated all of the major demands of the gay and lesbian movement: the use of the term "sexual orientation" as a way of countering conservative religious, medical, and psychological ideas about homosexuality; the recognition of multiple normal sexual desires; the condemnation of discrimination and violence; and support for the movement. Still, Gabeira and the PT-PV coalition only represented a small segment of the population, and there were many leftists who didn't share his views about homosexuality. Nonetheless, the gubernatorial candidate's declaration reveals the growing influence of the movement's ideas on at least some progressive forces.

Building on the success of Vieira's 1982 electoral victory, Daniel's campaign developed a similarly broad program. In an interview published in *OKzinho*, a newsletter produced by Turma OK, a gay social and cultural group, Daniel declares, "It is only possible to fight prejudice when we are willing to participate in the transformation of society by creating an alternative life[style].We need to establish collectively a libertarian and ecological democracy."[23] As this statement implies, Daniel had moved away from Marxist formulations that focused exclusively on class conflict and had embraced values that stressed freedom. At the same time, he believed in integrating ecological questions into a holistic understanding of social change, one that promoted individual quotidian commitments to transforming thought and behavior. In other words, he wasn't a single-issue candidate and saw that political action and social transformations were a result of concrete interaction of people with the world around them.

The effort to forge links between specific problems facing gay men and lesbians and other social questions was tantamount to achieving gay rights in Daniel's opinion: "We homosexuals have to be visible in political life. Acting as homosexuals, we are not only defending our rights, but also are intervening in society as a whole. We are radically demonstrating our choice in favor of freedom and our willingness to reorganize our daily lives so that we engage in solidarity with others." Whereas a decade previously Daniel would have argued that social change could only occur with radical socioeconomic structural transformations through the overthrow of capitalism and the establishment of a revolutionary government, he now saw these transformations linked to individuals' actions, including empathy and the support of others. Moreover, even though he rejected unilateral notions of "the homosexual," he used the term as a collective identity of people with a shared political agenda. This political approach would become even more evident in the late 1980s, when he developed new language to argue about the most effective ways to fight AIDS.

In his campaign literature, Daniel outlined a series of measures that he pledged to carry out if elected, which included presenting legislation to outlaw discrimination based on sexual orientation. He also recognized that legal provisions alone were insufficient to change entrenched intolerance. "Even though homosexuality is not considered a crime or an illness in Brazil, there are many prejudices whose origins are deeply embedded in Brazilian culture. So, in addition to legislation, one must engage in another arena, using the legislative assembly as a megaphone to speak out against prejudices and abuses."[24] Finally, he offered his unconditional support to the gay and lesbian movement and his willingness to present their ideas and proposals in the legislature.

It is possible to consider this shift in his attitudes toward the Homosexual Movement as an electoral campaign ploy, given an apparent resistance to organized groups in his previous writings. However, it seems to have reflected the accumulated experience of comprehending political changes taking place, now that he had fully immersed himself in Brazilian society again after years of living underground and then in exile. When he returned to Rio in 1981, the country had changed dramatically, and the enthusiastic response to Vieira's 1982 electoral campaign revealed the fact that new political ideas and social movements were taking hold. The growth and strength of these perspectives encouraged Daniel to rethink some of the harsh criticisms he had made of the Homosexual Movement a few years previously. At the same time, he continued to challenge the notion of fixed sexual identities and the belief that there was an "essential homosexual."[25]

Daniel's election material was lively and colorful. In addition to reusing the 1982 campaign slogan "Any form of loving is worth it," he coined a phrase that is the epigraph cited at the chapter's opening: "There is no democracy if it stops at the factory gate or at the edge of the bed." It encapsulates his attempts to integrate discussions about democracy, class politics, and sexuality. It suggests that working-class people also can have same-sex sexual desires. That sentiment had been captured a half-decade earlier by a group of activists in São Paulo linked to Somos, who joined the massive 1980

May Day demonstration in the midst of a general strike with a huge banner reading "Down with the discrimination against homosexual workers."[26] Both messages confronted a preconceived idea, which many leftists and union leaders still clung to, that insisted there were no homosexuals within the working class. And, *if* they existed, they represented sick, perverted, or immoral behavior that needed to be ignored or eliminated. Although Luiz Inácio Lula da Silva had declared that homosexuals were welcome within the PT at its 1981 founding convention, the party's leadership did little, in practice, to make that affirmation a reality.[27] Daniel's message challenged the political inertia within the Left.

Working under the assumption that gays and lesbians would vote for a gay candidate, a good portion of Daniel's campaign literature was directed specifically to that public and was distributed in nightclubs throughout the city. A small handbill using the slogan "Any kind of love is worth it" contains a bold text: "They have called me many names because I am a man who loves other men. But the person who curses me only shows that he is a stupid *machista*. I am a homosexual, yes, but this doesn't make me any better or worse than anyone else. . . . We need to affirm who we are, how we are, and what we want. We are many. Let's affirm our desire for freedom. We are many. Let's prove that we have strength."[28] The text also links the appeal to gay people to other issues: "Our struggle is the same one that unites all those who are exploited and repressed to create a democracy where there are no longer any second-class citizens." The political supposition was clear: in order to fight discrimination against homosexuals, one needed to build alliances with other sectors of society.

Another campaign flyer proclaims "we are a majority," and then lists a string of issues related to Daniel's program, ranging from the defense of the right to an abortion, which was (and still is) illegal in Brazil, to the protection of indigenous people's land rights. Each item begins with "We are the ones who," followed by a creatively worded political position that articulates a platform plank. It was an ingenious way to map out the campaign's principles that emphasized inclusion. "We are a majority" also countered a formula elaborated in some left-wing circles that considered women, blacks, gay and lesbians, and indigenous people as separate "minorities." In this regard, the campaign sought to build a collective majority rather than speaking to atomized and splintered sets of people competing for recognition and rights. Yet the material was not always easy to understand and contained prose similar to that found in *Passagem* and *Meu corpo*. It was dense, poetic, and probably inaccessible to the average reader.

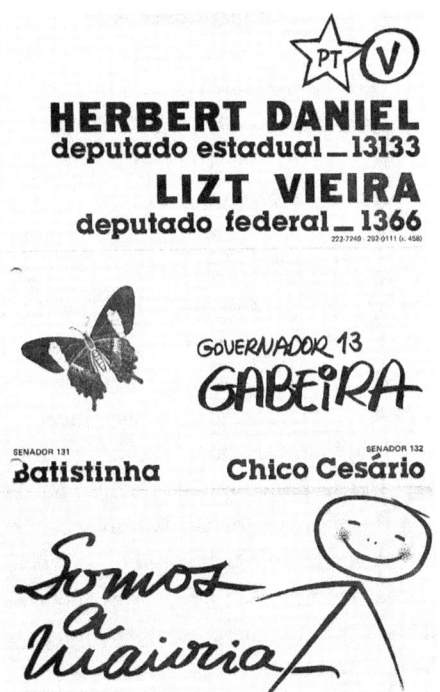

FIGURE 16.2 Electoral handbill stating "we are a majority," which includes the campaign's platform on the reverse side.

Volunteers were the campaign's backbone, and participants have fond memories of their involvement. Sílvia Ramos recalled that "it was really fun, almost irresponsible. It afforded a tremendous amount of pleasure."[29] André Campos, a young professor, volunteered for the campaign because Daniel linked the issue of homosexuality to left-wing causes.[30] Others joined the effort because they were already Daniel's close friends and wanted to support him. The writer Eliane Maciel, the actress Cristina Montenegro, and the poet Leila Míccolis all nostalgically remember the energy and excitement that the campaign generated.[31]

Lula Ramires recognizes the lasting impact of the campaign on his life. Originally, he had been drawn to the PT in São Paulo through his experiences in the left wing of the Catholic Church. He moved to Rio in 1985. There he finally accepted his homosexuality and spent a lot of free time socializing in gay locales. Participating in Daniel's electoral campaign was exhilarating, and he enthusiastically volunteered to distribute handbills to reach gay voters.[32] Still, Ramires found the experience frustrating at times. The many nights spent leafleting at gay clubs earned him only a mixed reaction from the public. "The PT was still a new party with an image of being radical and subversive," he remembers, pointing out that many of the middle-class people he talked to were very conservative.³³ Ramires recalls how he shared his frustrations with Daniel in a meeting of the campaign committee. Daniel listened to him patiently and then reassured him by recounting his own experiences with conservative gay men in Portugal who had wanted a return to the Salazar regime after the Carnation Revolution of 1974.³⁴

This conversation took place in one of the regular campaign committee meetings held in a public school near downtown Rio. These gatherings were the mainstay of the electoral campaign and were coordinated by Sheila Gomes Gliochi, who had met Daniel in Paris and immediately became a close friend. She later worked with Daniel on Vieira's campaign and then joined his staff after Vieira's 1982 electoral victory.³⁵ The weekly meetings functioned as a special forum where volunteers agreed on Daniel's political program, planned diverse activities, and sustained the energy of the campaign. Daniel participated in these gatherings as an equal, warmly receiving volunteers when they arrived, and sharing his thoughts and experiences. Ramires remembers how much he learned from Daniel's stories about his past and how carefully the candidate listened to others' opinions so that the group could reach consensus on how to proceed.³⁶

One serious challenge revolved around financial resources. Short of money to produce campaign literature, Daniel's supporters organized a series of inventive and entertaining monthly fundraising parties in clubs and discotheques throughout Rio and across the Guanabara Bay in Niterói. Cláudio, as usual, provided artistic support. One poster features an iconic image of Marilyn Monroe, Daniel's beloved sex goddess. Another references the popular gay-themed novel, *The Kiss of the Spider Woman*, and announces the participation of some of Rio's leading artists, actors, and intellectuals. These posters not only used symbols and images that might attract a gay public, but also signaled to their intended audiences that Daniel's campaign was on the cutting edge of Brazilian (and gay) culture. It was an attempt to reach beyond the gay ghetto that Daniel had disdained, while ironically employing its language.

André Campos helped out by organizing events at his apartment in Santa Teresa and invited friends to hear Daniel talk about his campaign. He also remembers driving Daniel to a working-class lesbian bar in the distant region of the Baixada Fluminense for him to talk to potential voters.³⁷ To attract support for Daniel's candidacy, Leila Míccolis put together several poetry readings entitled "Love Is Not a Personal Matter," which featured twenty-two emerging or established poets. In addition, the campaign organized a major political forum on sexuality in late June that coincided with

FIGURE 16.3 Poster for an electoral campaign fundraiser.

international commemorations of New York City's 1969 Stonewall Rebellion. The campaign event headlined Marilena Chauí, a philosophy professor from the University of São Paulo, and Lorna Washington, one of Rio's most famous drag queens. Co-sponsored by Triângulo Rosa, the event took place in a crowded university auditorium. Ramires remembers that Chauí delineated how the Left conceptualized minorities and then deconstructed the idea to reveal how much it served to diminish the rights of marginalized social sectors. Washington's campy humor gave a festive tone to the forum discussion and demonstrated the respect that Daniel had gained from one of the most popular performers within Rio's gay world.[38]

Ramires also fondly recalls the final fundraising event at the end of the campaign held in the upscale beachfront neighborhood of Leblon in a large space that, he estimates, held 1,500 people. The singers and songwriters Caetano Veloso and Gilberto Gil were present and endorsed Daniel's campaign, as did the vocalist Marina Lima, who, after performing a song, ended by saying, "I'm proud to be gay."[39] In short, the entire electoral effort was dynamic and energetic. In Ramires's opinion, Daniel was certain to be victorious.

The PT-PV campaign organized two major mobilizations to garner media attention for Fernando Gabeira's gubernatorial candidacy and help the entire ticket. The first, "Speak, Woman," gathered eighty thousand people, who paraded through downtown Rio to raise issues related to domestic violence, the right to abortion, and equal treatment of women. The second event brought together an estimated one hundred thousand people, who joined hands to surround the Rodrigo de Freitas Lagoon in the affluent southern region of Rio to protest water pollution.[40] Both mobilizations attracted large numbers of middle-class supporters who formed the electoral base of Gabeira's campaign.

When the ballots were finally cast for governor, Gabeira received 529,603 votes, or just 7.8 percent of the total. Moreira Franco, the moderate candidate of the PMDB, won the contest. The PT elected Valdimir Palmeira, a former student activist and revolutionary, and Benedita da Silva, an Afro-Brazilian activist from humble beginnings, to congressional seats. Carlos Minc, the former VPR militant, who had joined the PV along with Daniel and ran on the joint PT-PV ticket, amassed a sizable vote and won a seat in the state legislature. As a university professor and union member, a visible leader in the environmental movement, and a prominent supporter of land reform, he had built multiple constituencies to support his candidacy.[41] Liszt Vieira, however, didn't get enough votes to make the cut-off to be elected to Congress. Daniel also lost his race, collecting only 5,485 votes. It was 2,643 votes less than the number he needed to be elected.

The results were devastating for Lula Ramires, who had put so much energy into the campaign. He was still downhearted when, a couple of weeks after the defeat, he went to a meeting where the results of the race were evaluated. Daniel was the person who cheered him up. According to Ramires's reconstruction of the conversation, Daniel stated, "'Lula, that's the way it is. We're still inside a ghetto. We still need to speak to society as a whole. We still haven't been able to do it. We have to keep trying.'" Daniel's response totally surprised him. "I felt the defeat, but he was the candidate, and had the right to feel defeated, and he told me, 'No, comrade, the struggle is just beginning,' as if to say that the struggle didn't begin today and wouldn't end tomorrow."

Like Ramires, the Triângulo Rosa president, João Antônio Mascarenhas, was also deeply disappointed with Daniel's loss. Still he had hope for the possibility of getting enough votes from the members of the Constituent Assembly to include a provision in the new Constitution barring discrimination based on sexual orientation.[42] For the next year and a half he led a tireless effort that managed to garner the support of 25 percent of the delegates to the Assembly and all of the representatives from each of the left-wing parties. Even though he waged this campaign diligently through endless correspondence with representatives from various political parties, the effort failed. Still, in his mind, it was one more step on a long road toward equality.[43]

Gabeira recalls how disillusioned many Green Party activists were with Daniel's defeat. "One of the things that we regretted in the campaign was precisely the fact that he wasn't elected, because honestly compared to the quality of all of the elected candidates, he could have offered an enormous contributon to politics in Rio and even Brazil." Gabeira noted, however, that Daniel was a shy person and that this may have been one of the factors that restained his success as a candidate.[44]

From all accounts, it appears that Daniel, unlike many of his supporters, was not overly disheartened with the electoral results. But then he had been used to operating at the margins for causes that seemed impossible to win. Even though he had not amassed as many votes as he had hoped, the campaign reached thousands. It was a dialogue with "the people" that had not taken place as a guerrilla fighter cut off from "the masses." Though he recognized that his avant-garde ideas reached and convinced only a few, Daniel remained optimistic. At the same time, he had to face more immediate and practical considerations. He was now unemployed, with campaign debts to cover. He needed to find a job.

Cláudio had been contributing to the household income through work in freelance graphic design. Throughout 1987 Daniel sought writing jobs to cover their expenses, which were fortunately modest. At the end of the year, Sílvia Ramos invited him to join a recently founded AIDS organization: Brazilian Interdisciplinary AIDS Association (ABIA). One of his first jobs was editing ABIA's newsletter. The first issue came out in January 1988. Once again, Daniel had the opportunity to use his creativity and literary talents to reach people about an important cause.

At some point in early 1983, Vieira, Ramos, and Daniel had spent a week together in the countryside while Daniel was finishing *Jacarés e lobisomens*, with its pioneering essays on AIDS. Ramos recalls discussing the disease with Daniel. "At the time I was reading a lot of Foucault and thought that

AIDS was part of a process of disciplining bodies. I vividly remember Daniel, who was a libertarian, saying, 'Hold on. The virus is coming, and it is very strong. It's no game.'"[45] Up until then, Ramos hadn't thought much about homosexuality or AIDS, and Daniel's emphatic response left a strong impression on her. Over time they became good friends. She helped with his campaign and admired the boldness of its message. When positions opened up at ABIA, she immediately thought of hiring Daniel.[46]

The first HIV infections in Brazil likely occurred in the mid-1970s, if not earlier. In 1981, the Brazilian press starting publishing articles about a strange new disease. In 1983, accounts about the initial cases of AIDS in Brazil appeared in the media, with gay men and hemophiliacs reported as most at risk. Inaccurate and sensationalist coverage caused panic and confusion among those who thought they were vulnerable to being infected. It also produced prejudice and acts of discrimination against people whom the media had associated with this new illness. With no clear and reliable information about the nature of the disease, former members of the group Somos approached the São Paulo State Health Secretary, calling on the government to respond to the growing epidemic.[47] Almost immediately, a working group under the direction of Dr. Paulo Teixeira developed the first Brazilian public health strategy to tackle AIDS.[48] In November 1984, a meeting of gay activists, public health officials, and others interested in responding to the disease led to the founding of the Support Group for AIDS Prevention (GAPA). The organization sought to educate the public about AIDS, offer legal assistance to those facing discrimination, and refer people to charities and social services.[49] Many of the activists in these first efforts eventually became national leaders in the fight against AIDS.

The reaction to the disease was somewhat slower in Rio. With the closure of *Lampião* in 1981 and the dissolution of the two main political groups, Somos-Rio and Auê, by the end of 1983, there was no real aggregation of activists that might respond effectively to this new crisis. When Mascarenhas founded Triângulo Rosa in 1985, he steered the organization away from AIDS activism because he believed the press associated the disease too closely with homosexuality, further contributing to homosexuals' stigmatization. Not everyone, however, agreed with Mascarenhas. Paulo Fatal, a member of Triângulo Rosa, began working with the Secretary of Health on AIDS prevention campaigns. His efforts led to the formation of GAPA-Rio, which followed the same approach to prevention, education, and antidiscrimination actions, and also offered the practical responses that GAPA-São Paulo had pioneered.[50]

ABIA, however, ended up having a different mission. The nongovernmental organization grew out of the same desire to find an effective response to AIDS. Like other groups, it was also a convergence of many different interests and people. ABIA elaborated policy, conducted research, and disseminated information about the disease. Two main forces behind the new organization were Herbert de Souza and Walter Almeida.

In the early 1960s, Herbert de Souza, commonly known as Betinho, had been a founding leader of Ação Popular. Forced underground in 1964, he went into Chilean exile in 1971. After the military takeover, Betinho sought political asylum in Canada and later moved to Mexico. Returning to Brazil with the 1979 Amnesty Law, he and others set up the Brazilian Institute of Economic and Social Analysis (IBASE), a think tank and progressive consulting firm that worked on issues ranging from land reform and the environment to race and gender.[51] Throughout his long, political activist career, he had to deal with the fact that he was a hemophiliac, and in 1985, he found out that he had been infected with HIV through a blood transfusion. Both of Betinho's brothers—Chico Mário de Souza, a musician, and Henfil, a political cartoonist who wrote the dust jacket blurb for *Passagem*—also contracted the virus through the blood supply. Chico Mário died in 1987, and Henfil passed away the following year.[52]

Walter Almeida, Betinho's physician, was also crucial in establishing ABIA. During a 1985 visit to the United States, he learned about the International Interdisciplinary AIDS Foundation and thought of establishing a Brazilian affiliate as a clearinghouse for information and research, as the disease seemed to be spreading exponentially. He and Betinho worked tirelessly to bring together important public figures, politicians, social scientists, public health specialists, and leaders of social movements to discuss how to respond to AIDS. The result was ABIA, which was officially established in early 1987. Betinho offered Sílvia Ramos a contract to establish the association that made her salary contingent upon raising funds. Two government grants allowed Ramos to set up an office in a rented space in front of IBASE and install telephones and computers. A Ford Foundation grant gave her the resources to hire a staff. Betinho became the president of ABIA and Ramos the executive director.[53]

Initially Betinho had reservations about hiring Daniel when Ramos suggested his name. Betinho feared that Daniel might be too radical or be the wrong fit for an association that was both seeking resources from international foundations, government entities, and private enterprises and also developing ways to convince the state to adopt a proactive policy to combat AIDS. Ramos, however, sensed that Daniel was perfect for the job. Betinho's public profile as a longtime social activist with impeccable moral and progressive credentials enabled him to bring the problem of the contamination of Brazil's blood supply to the fore. However, the virus was also having a devastating effect on gay men, and in Rio, Daniel was a talented writer and a "public" homosexual. Ramos was convinced that his presence would guarantee that the association could reach one of the groups most affected by the virus. When Sílvia insisted, Betinho conceded. She still wasn't sure, however, if Daniel would accept an ordinary staff position, given his image as a "personality." When she asked, he immediately responded: "Sílvia, I need money. I'll accept any work at ABIA doing anything. We just finished the campaign. We have an enormous amount of debt. Any money is welcome."[54]

Daniel's lyrical command of the Portuguese language permeates the texts in *Boletim ABIA*, the association's newsletter. Unlike some of his earlier works, his writing is clear and direct, but at the same time gracefully sophisticated. It's perhaps his best prose. The final phrases of the first editorial are an example. A translation cannot adequately capture the underlying cultural references that impart many layers of emotional meaning to Brazilian readers when Daniel cites lyrics from a popular song to make a poetic point. "To live is to create life. It can, it is true, be lived any old way. But it's not worth living that way. Life has to be lived in the best way possible. With tenderness, indeed, but also with outrage against evil and lies. With poetry and humor."[55] These words carry a message that Daniel would refine and develop over the next four years. They synthesize his life history as a person who endeavored to experience each unfolding chapter with intensity and passion, combined with an awareness of social injustices and the desire to combat them. With no cure for AIDS in sight, the question became: How do people live with the disease? How do they cope? How do they survive psychologically, especially when the media and society in general believe an announcement that a person has HIV is a death sentence?

If celebrating life is the core message of ABIA's first newsletter, the second issue offers a political strategy for dealing with HIV/AIDS. Rejecting bellicose language to combat the disease, Daniel writes, "It's not about a war that demands the presence of heroes and victims. It's an effort that requires the participation of brothers and sisters. Solidarity is the basic tool in the task of eliminating the epidemic by valuing life."[56] The appeal to solidarity means gaining sympathy and support from broad sectors of society for those living with the disease. It requires addressing irrational fears about the supposed casual transmission of the virus through normal social contact. It also signifies confronting discrimination. It is a call for a different approach to engaging with AIDS and those affected by it.

At the same time, the newsletter entered into a polemic that had already polarized activists regarding how to educate the public. Daniel and others strongly criticized the government for alarmist educational campaigns intended to shock people into changing their sexual behavior. Some, such as Luiz Mott, the GGB president, thought differently. He wrote a letter to ABIA on behalf of GGB questioning an article in the Boletim's second edition that outlined eleven major criticisms of the government's AIDS campaigns. In that piece, Daniel had argued that officials had presented inaccurate information about the disease and had offered inadequate and ineffective measures to deal with the virus. Daniel had insisted that "those who sow panic will reap an epidemic." Mott, opposing this approach, wrote that it was a shame that the government campaign had not been "more aggressive and dramatic" in its portrayal of the effects of AIDS on people.[57]

Rather than responding directly to Mott's disapproval of ABIA's political perspective, Daniel points out in an editorial in a subsequent issue of ABIA's newsletter that the government "continues to insist on fear, shock, arrogance. International experience has shown, and not only for the case of AIDS, that public health campaigns don't work when they are based on promoting fear."[58] Daniel goes on to contend that, "regarding AIDS, one of the most prejudicial information policies is associating the disease directly and immediately with death. . . . In all government campaigns, as well as in all official initiatives in Brazil about AIDS, the person most forgotten is the one who is infected by HIV or who is sick because of AIDS." He concludes the editorial with a biting comment: "Officially, they are already *dead*, since the formula that guides all government policy about AIDS coincides with the equation that being infected with HIV means Death."[59]

Throughout 1988, many of Daniel's criticisms of official AIDS public health policy focused on the indecisiveness of the Sarney administration (1985–89). Daniel blasted its passivity and inaction in much the same way that U.S. AIDS activists insisted that similar indifference by the Reagan administration (1981–1989) meant death for those infected. In 1987, radical New York AIDS activists translated this idea into the "Silence = Death" slogan. Soon thereafter they developed a more positive mantra: "Action = Life." Daniel was aware of these international articulations when he penned the Boletim's editorials that shaped ABIA's approach to AIDS. One could already find the core elements in his strategic thinking in his 1983 essay "The Syndrome of Prejudice," outlined in chapter 15. By 1988, many of his ideas had matured, and similar perspectives on how to deal with AIDS had been elaborated in the United States and Europe, circulating rapidly among activists across continents. Yet Daniel's ideas are notably original. His background experiences as a medical student, underground activist, guerrilla fighter, political exile, and left-wing candidate, as well as his intensely loving personal interactions, all seem to have converged to create a fresh and innovative strategic approach to tackling the disease.

Meanwhile, ABIA achieved a victory in 1988 by working in a broad coalition to convince a majority of the Constituent Assembly to include a provision in the new Constitution that regulated the Brazilian blood supply by prohibiting the commercialization of blood products and by increasing controls against contamination.[60] At the same time, ABIA reached out to private enterprises, trade unions, and government agencies to convince them to engage in educational campaigns about HIV/AIDS.[61]

It was a productive year for Daniel. He was channeling his literary and political creativity and seeing positive results. Nonetheless, since late December, he had been feeling ill. He thought it might be pneumonia. A fever lingered though sleepless nights, so he and Cláudio scheduled an appointment in early January 1989 with a doctor recommended by a friend.

17

Forty Seconds

(1989–1992)

"That's all the time it took. Forty seconds."

— HERBERT DANIEL

Daniel's medical appointment, scheduled for January 9, 1989, followed standard procedures. The physician took a sputum sample and left Daniel and Cláudio in the waiting room. When he finally called Daniel into the consulting room, he quickly gave his diagnosis: "*Pneumocystis carinii* (pneumonia). A sure sign of an immune deficiency." The doctor scribbled a prescription for Daniel and stated that he would order a test for "the other disease." The bill was 40,000 *cruzados* or about US$80. The consultation was over in less than a minute.[1]

When Daniel met Cláudio in the waiting room, he was in a state of shock. The doctor's diagnosis signaled that he had AIDS. He had not expected to hear this news, let alone have it delivered in such an abrupt way. In a few short seconds, Daniel had already convinced himself that he would die within a couple of years. When he told Cláudio his prognosis, Cláudio replied, "Come on, let's get into the elevator." Daniel replied, "I just told you I have two years to live, and you want me to get into the elevator?" Cláudio retorted, "Okay, but you don't want to wait the next two years here in the doctor's hall, do you? Let's go home."[2]

Daniel quickly changed his mind about how to assess his projected life span. He later found out that, in fact, he had contracted glandular tuberculosis and not pneumonia, as the doctor had diagnosed. Still, the information about Daniel's health turned his world upside down, and it didn't take him long to realize that he had a new mission: to affirm that he was still alive and to politicize the fact that he was living with AIDS. Decades of a passionate engagement in politics gave him the fortitude and persistence to take up this new struggle with vigor and clarity. At ABIA he had already begun elaborating a complex series of criticisms of the government's AIDS policy and was offering alternative strategies for dealing with the disease. The news that he was infected with the virus gave new immediacy to the issues he had been writing about since working there in late 1987.[3]

Within a month after receiving the startling news, Daniel reported his momentous visit to the doctor in ABIA's newsletter. "Forty Seconds of AIDS" became the first of many biting indictments of the medical profession for its cold indifference to patients with HIV/AIDS. As Daniel wrote, "Forty seconds. That was the amount of time that he gave me to absorb the news. It was sufficient time, above all, to give me the horror of seeing, in that clinical indifference, perhaps a certain amount of cruelty: could he be taking 'vengeance' on me because I was a homosexual and deserved to be punished?"[4] The article ends: "I left that office deeply troubled. Forty seconds of AIDS! I had escaped. Cláudio, my companion, was waiting for me outside. My friends were waiting for me. Life was waiting for me. I freed myself from the frightful disease that had killed me for forty seconds. I escaped—with the conviction that it is necessary to free other sick people from this trap. Real AIDS is something far too serious to be treated by 'doctors,' by that brand of medicine that AIDS has demonstrated is a failure. What's left is life. Forty seconds at a time. Intensely."[5] These words, and their underlying meaning, became his message to the world for the next three years.

Soon after sharing the news with his friends and workmates, Daniel decided to go public. His chose the *Jornal do Brasil*, a leading Rio newspaper, for a feature essay entitled "News from Another Life." A brief biographical sketch noted that the forty-two-year-old writer had already fought in many trenches: as a guerrilla fighter, in exile, and as a candidate for public office. Now he was "the first Brazilian homosexual intellectual to talk publicly about his illness."[6] The lead header, a quote by Daniel, affirmed: "When I got sick with an infection typically associated with AIDS, I realized that the questions to be answered were whether there is life, and what kind, before death." In inverting the age-old query about the nature of the afterlife, Daniel turned people's focus to the present, and in doing so dismissed the death sentence associated with a diagnosis of the disease.

Daniel had already pointed out the year before in ABIA's publications that there continued to be a morose notion in Brazil that becoming infected with HIV was a provisional death certificate. Now he was experiencing that sentiment firsthand. In the *Jornal do Brasil* article, Daniel developed all of the points that would become the discursive themes for the subsequent interviews he would give and the articles he would write: "From one moment to the next, the simple fact of saying 'I am alive' becomes a political act. Affirming my condition as a citizen *perfectly* alive is an act of civil disobedience. For this reason, since I found out that I have AIDS, I constantly repeat that I am alive and a citizen. I don't have a deficiency that immunizes me against having civil rights in spite of the worn-out propaganda to the contrary."[7]

Several interwoven themes stand out in this comprehensive essay. He blasted the use of the word *aidético*, patterned after the Portuguese term for a diabetic that had come to be widely used in Brazil. The term had acquired implied meanings: inescapable connections between a person living with HIV/AIDS and the disease itself, as if the two had merged. In addition, media associations between a person with HIV/AIDS and death had become pervasive. Daniel sought to uncouple the idea of inevitable death from HIV/AIDS by rejecting the negative images identified with the expression.[8] Moreover, he argued, discrimination against those with HIV/AIDS was more deadly than the disease itself. Prejudice and marginalization condemned him and others to what Daniel called a "civil death" (*morte civil*), or the loss of all rights to exist, to be, to be alive.

It was precisely this direct challenge to the ways in which the Brazilian media and public opinion treated people living with HIV/AIDS that made his message so potent. Instead of becoming victims of the disease, people should be active agents, insisting they have the same civil and human rights as any other person. Daniel offered a mobilizing slogan that affirmed life over death. He went on the offensive against those who wished to deny him and others their right to live, even when AIDS seemed to mean eventual death. His words, simple as they may have been, offered hope, dignity, and a positive approach to confronting the disease. For Brazil, his ideas were revolutionary.

Daniel packed so many activities into 1989 that it is hard to imagine how he managed to sleep that year. In late May, he founded Pela VIDDA, a nongovernment organization (NGO) for people living with HIV/AIDS. In early June, he traveled to Montreal for the Fifth International Conference on AIDS, where he drew attention with his passionate participation in the proceedings. While taking part in endless meetings related to the Brazilian AIDS movement, he also found time to finish *Life before Death*, a short bilingual Portuguese-English volume published by ABIA, which synthesized his thinking about AIDS and the effects of the disease on Brazilian society.[9] In July, he was invited to a meeting in Geneva sponsored by the Global Program on AIDS of the World Health Organization and the UN Commission on Human Rights. Back in Brazil, Daniel enthusiastically participated in the preparations for two national meetings of AIDS NGOs, one in July and another in October, and he was involved in controversies with other activists about the movement's direction and program. For two months, a television crew followed Cláudio and Daniel in their daily routines as it filmed a documentary that featured the couple's intimate, ongoing, and loving relationship. In addition, Daniel was nominated to be the candidate of the Green Party in the first democratic presidential election to be held since 1960. Throughout the year, he continued to publish articles for ABIA's newsletter, as well as others that appeared in the mainstream press. By all accounts, the intensity of his activities equaled, if not surpassed, his undertakings between 1968 and 1971, when he was involved in the guerrilla movement. By the end of the year, he was exhausted, and the virus had taken a heavy toll on his body.

The founding of Grupo Pela VIDDA (Group for the Valuing, Integration, and Dignity of Those Sick with AIDS) became that year's core activity. It required much of Daniel's endless energy and helped him deal with the news that he had AIDS.[10] The acronym for the group's name, which means "for life," became the slogan that Daniel promoted as a response to ongoing negative representations of AIDS. Because of his important role within ABIA, a close partnership developed between the two organizations. ABIA allowed Pela VIDDA to operate out of a small converted garage in the back of its spacious headquarters, and the new organization mobilized people to become involved in public protests and other activities.

Pela VIDDA drew on the experiences of Brazil's first gay and lesbian rights organizations, feminist consciousness-raising circles, and the participatory group dynamics used in social movements that proliferated in the late 1970s and 1980s during the democratization process. As devised by Daniel, a weekly discussion group, known as Tribuna Livre (Free tribunal), offered people the opportunity to inquire about the latest news of the disease. It was also a support group.[11] From the beginning, Daniel's personality

FIGURE 17.1 Pela VIDDA demonstration in downtown Rio. Left to right: unknown activist, Carlos Minc, Herbert de Souza (Betinho), and Herbert Daniel. REPRINTED WITH PERMISSION OF THE ASSOCIAÇÃO BRASILEIRA INTERDISPLINAR DE AIDS.

dominated. Veriano Terto, who in the early 1980s had been a member of Somos-Rio, remembers the key role that Daniel played in consolidating the group. "Daniel led the meetings . . . sometimes talking for an hour or two at a time. There would be fifteen people or so. We listened. Sometimes in the beginning of the meeting, people would talk about themselves . . . their lives, what was happening to them." When asked if Daniel's prominence evoked a negative reaction, Terto explained: "No, because he spoke in such a brilliant way that people listened to him. . . . I think that it didn't inhibit growth. Just the opposite, he helped the group grow."[12] Julio Gaspar, who became a Pela VIDDA activist when the group expanded to São Paulo in 1990, reflected on the nature of the organization. "Pela VIDDA started from a different place, less service oriented, in which AIDS was a problem for everyone, whether HIV positive or not. It was very powerful, very beautiful to develop love of oneself among those who were sick and thought they were at the end of their lives."[13]

In 1989, five thousand Brazilians were diagnosed with AIDS. Of these, 4,419 were men and 581 were women. In 79 percent of the documented cases, transmission occurred through sexual relations with other men.[14] While the mass media no longer used the initial language associated with the disease, which had referred to it as the "gay plague," Daniel still recognized that terminology's effects on gay men.[15]

For years Daniel had shunned the gay ghetto and downplayed the Homosexual Movement. His engagement with AIDS, especially after the 1986 electoral campaign and his involvement with ABIA, changed those perspectives. While he had previously rejected the unilateral embrace of homosexuality as an identity, he now faced a situation in which age-old prejudices about homosexuality had a profound effect on those living with the disease.[16] Embracing his AIDS status in a manner not unlike that of gay and lesbian activists who chose to affirm their sexuality served to counter widely held negative attitudes. Panic and misinformation had obfuscated any serious discussion about the impact of AIDS on homosexual men. "The imposition of silence about the sexual life of those who are sick is . . . a prejudicial element in efforts to prevent the epidemic," he wrote. "When homosexuals are more conscious about the importance of the epidemic, the community as a whole reacts to the disease. For this reason, an open discussion about sexuality (which is obviously basic when dealing with a sexually transmitted disease) is a key element in the policy for AIDS prevention. This has been systematically lacking in Brazil."[17]

Daniel also criticized government inaction: "Until now the official response of the Brazilian government has been, to say the least, irrelevant and timid. Erroneous declarations about the characteristics of the epidemic, in addition to prejudicial opinions demanding abstention, lead us to conclude that the government still has not seriously confronted the epidemic."[18] Daniel's reaction to this potential "disaster" was to call on the mobilization of civil society and the creation of alternative means of pressuring the government. "If we don't confront it NOW, there soon will be no solution," he insisted.[19]

Pela VIDDA's program, as devised by Daniel, articulated an action-oriented agenda. The organization's objectives were plainly stated: "battling against the isolation, concealment, and discrimination that people live with who are HIV-positive or sick with AIDS; critically following government policies related to controlling and combating the AIDS epidemic; providing specific information for people who are sick or HIV-positive, as well as helping them with the options that they have given their situation; incessantly fighting to guarantee complete citizenship and the full enjoyment of civil rights for those who are HIV-positive or sick; and guaranteeing all forms of full social participation for people who are HIV-positive or sick."[20] Pela VIDDA was run by volunteers, and in spite of the tendency for Daniel to dominate discussions, the open-ended meetings offered people the opportunity to exchange ideas, information, and experiences.

In addition to Pela VIDDA gatherings that focused on living with HIV/AIDS, Daniel also initiated a weekly summit that was called a political-administrative meeting to deal with the everyday practical issues related to the organization. These could be long, drawn-out meetings in which everyone had the right to offer their opinion about a political question or an administrative decision. These assemblies were democratic opportunities for full participation and became an important part of Pela VIDDA's institutional culture. Márcio José Villard, a longtime Pela VIDDA leader, attributes its participatory and inclusive nature to Daniel's commitment to an egalitarian decision-making process that offered all those people who joined the group a real stake in determining its direction and activities.[21]

In part, Pela VIDDA's immediate success was due to the fact that Daniel had been slowly elaborating an appropriate response to AIDS since 1983. "Solidarity will counter being alone. This seems to be the simplest prescription for the only medicine capable of curing AIDS," he wrote soon after its founding.[22] Although this proposition might seem to be an ingenuous response for those infected with the virus, embedded in the statement is a complex notion of what was necessary to deal with all of the social, political, and medical components of the disease. Daniel recognized that even though scientists did not know how to destroy HIV, it was still possible to evade infection. It was also possible, he argued, to fight against social prejudice as a way to improve the lives of those living with HIV/AIDS. It required disseminating accurate information about the disease and how to avoid it. It also meant criticizing false, bad-intentioned, and alarmist material about AIDS.[23]

Daniel worked as the staff writer for ABIA during the day, while he spent the evenings in Pela VIDDA meetings, nurturing a group that grew to a hundred members in less than a year.[24] He also took advantage of ABIA's international connections to seek new perspectives on how to fight the epidemic. Because of ABIA's growing prominence, a representative was invited to participate in the Organizing Committee of the International Gathering of Non-governmental Organizations in Montreal. That committee was tasked with preparing a preconference meeting entitled "Opportunities for Solidarity" immediately prior to the Fifth International AIDS Conference, whose official theme was "The Scientific and Social Challenge." The back-to-back gatherings represented the first international assembly of AIDS experts that included social activists and allowed NGO members to present their research, ideas, and experiences. ABIA managed to raise funds to send a large Brazilian delegation representing different AIDS organizations.[25] Daniel presented a paper entitled "The Social Impact of AIDS in Brazil."[26] He also enthusiastically participated in the preconference gathering of three hundred AIDS organizations.[27]

The Montreal conference marked a turning point for international AIDS activism. The lack of an effective U.S. government response to the epidemic had led to the formation in 1987 of ACT UP, a radical direct-action group. ACT UP and its Canadian counterparts prepared an intervention at the Montreal event that shook up the AIDS research establishment. Activists argued that people with HIV/AIDS should be closely involved in discussions about research priorities. To make their point, three hundred people stormed the stage during the opening ceremony, carrying posters that read, among other slogans, "Silence = Death." Tim McCaskel, a person with AIDS, took over the microphone and announced that the conference was being inaugurated "on behalf of people with AIDS from Canada and around the world."[28] Conference organizers managed to negotiate an agreement that allowed activists to participate in all of the proceedings, which set the precedent for the involvement of people with AIDS and their allies in future conferences.[29]

Members of the Brazilian delegation vividly remember Daniel's presence. Gabriela Leite, the Brazilian Prostitutes Network founder, cited the impact of Daniel's speech on her own commitment to activism. "Daniel went up to the front and said: 'I was a guerrilla, an out [*assumido*] guerrilla, and today I'm out about something else. I'm a person with AIDS; I'm HIV positive.'"[30] It is improbable that Daniel actually stated that he had been openly gay when he was a guerrilla fighter, but Leite's apparent memory slip reveals how the myth about Daniel's past surrounded him. She continued: "I'll never forget. He was chubby, short, there up in front. He raised his hand, and he talked about his life. It really moved me, and it was then that I got involved in the AIDS movement."

The Montreal conference injected renewed energy into the activities of its Brazilian participants, and Daniel returned to Rio to encourage the establishment of a national network. GAPA had already organized five nationwide inter-GAPA meetings between 1987 and 1989, and Daniel's proposal entailed including as many of the fifty AIDS groups in the network.[31] A first meeting of the AIDS NGOs within the Brazilian Network of Solidarity took place in Belo Horizonte immediately after delegates returned from Montreal, with representatives from fourteen organizations. A follow-up meeting was scheduled for October with thirty-eight groups in attendance.[32] The organizers of the event read a letter of support from Dr. Jonathan Mann, the director of the World Health Organization's Global Program on AIDS, and the body approved two important documents: "A Statement of Principles of the Network" and "A Declaration of Basic Rights of People with the AIDS Virus," which Daniel had elaborated.[33] A third meeting took place in Santos, São Paulo, in April 1990 in which sharp political differences led to the network's demise.

At least one scholar argues that the tensions within the network were due to the divisions between some of the gay rights groups, which worked on AIDS (among other activities) and were resource poor, and ABIA and its allies, which were well funded.[34] In ABIA's own historical accounts of the period, the division is explained as being between the politically minded (*políticos*), including ABIA and Pela VIDDA, and service-oriented associations (*assistencialistas*) and gay rights–focused organizations.[35] Another scholar points to tensions between those activists, such as Daniel, who were reluctant to trust any ongoing collaboration with the government and those who favored working closely with officials on AIDS.[36] Cristina Bastos, who did research at ABIA during this period, has argued that these differences were secondary to the larger international shifts that were taking place in AIDS work, including a redirection of global priorities toward Africa and a drop in funding for organized national and international networks.[37]

All of these explanations considered together seem to account for the discord, and Daniel was at the center of the on-the-ground controversy that revolved around whether or not to support the government's AIDS educational campaigns. The polarization provoked a sharp debate between Luiz Mott of GGB and ABIA/Pela VIDDA, regarding the government's approach encapsulated in the slogan "*AIDS mata*" (AIDS kills).[38] Mott argued the term had an educational value because it scared people who were misinformed and uneducated into learning about the AIDS virus and taking precautions.[39] Daniel countered that the statement AIDS = DEATH (which was different from ACT UP's slogan SILENCE = DEATH that pointed to governments' indifference) needed to be inverted to focus on how to live with AIDS. "This gives us a completely original perspective in dealing with the epidemic. It ranges from the modification of the use of therapies, which acknowledges that while it is not possible to remove the virus from the body, it is a treatable disease (rather than an incurable illness), to the integration of HIV positive people, sick or not, into society. The carrier of the virus is a citizen, not a burden or a provisional encumbrance."[40] To this day, Mott remains critical of Daniel's positions.[41] In many of his writings Daniel insisted that "the cure is hope. The vaccine is called solidarity." Mott has retorted: "Pure rhetoric, which wasn't enough for him to resist [getting] AIDS. Hope and solidarity are marvelous sentiments, but they are incapable of controlling the AIDS pandemic. The correct [slogan] is: Information is the AIDS's [sic] vaccine, and prevention is its cure."[42] In Daniel's writings, he always emphasized the importance of disseminating proper information in the efforts at AIDS prevention. His call for solidarity, however, was meant to humanize those affected by the disease. It was at the center of the campaign and had mobilized support to combat both discrimination and the disease itself.[43]

At the same time that Daniel confronted his political opponents in the AIDS movement, he played a leading role in direct-action campaigns designed to draw media attention and provoke public discussion. On December 1, 1988, International AIDS Day, ABIA unfurled a long banner with the word "Solidarity" printed on it in bold red letters at the bottom of the ninety-eight-foot-tall statue of Christ the Redeemer that towers over Rio. After Daniel returned from Montreal, ABIA, Pela VIDDA, and other groups organized a campaign against VARIG Airlines, which was testing its employees for the AIDS virus and then firing those who were HIV-positive.[44] The publicity around the campaign forced the airlines to rescind that policy.[45] The following year, ABIA, Pela VIDDA, and other groups carried out raucous picketing in front of the offices of the State Secretary of Health to protest the government's inaction on AIDS issues, and in 1991, activists covered a large obelisk-like statue in downtown Rio de Janeiro with a gigantic condom as part of a campaign to promote a state law requiring hotels to provide each guest with three free condoms in order to encourage safer-sex practices.[46]

Because of Daniel's openness about living with AIDS, the press constantly sought him out.[47] When Monica Teixeira read his *Jornal do Brasil* article "News from Another Life," it moved her profoundly. She was a journalist, who recently had been hired by TV Manchete to produce documentary programs, and she immediately contacted Daniel to do a story about living with AIDS.[48] She filmed for two months and the documentary aired at the end of the year with a large viewership. Teixeira recalled: "The report contains at least two conversations. One is about AIDS, and the other is about being a homosexual. These two topics were very new for Brazilian television."[49]

The program begins with a close-up shot of Daniel that focuses on his full, round face and wire-rimmed glasses. "I am a writer, homosexual, and sick with AIDS," he declares serenely.[50] The forty-five-minute television special features in-depth interviews with Daniel and Cláudio, in which the two speak openly about their love for each other, their eighteen-year relationship, and their thoughts about homosexuality, AIDS, and death. Cláudio describes the gay men's practice of seeking sexual partners in the beachfront Aterro Park, and he expresses fears about how he will survive when

Daniel is gone. Daniel explains how he decided to live his life after he found out that he had AIDS and details the social discrimination that forces people to hide their personal relations from others. His calmness in talking about his HIV status, the ways he came to understand death, and the tenderness of his relationship with Cláudio no doubt touched the audience profoundly.

Prior to this show, Brazilian media had not dealt with homosexuality and AIDS in such a positive, open, and nonsensationalist way. Teixeira recalled: "Saying that these two people live together was repeated several times. Being a partner, a lifetime partner." Márcio José Villard, who was in the process of accepting his homosexuality, remembers the program's impact: "When I watched it at home, the reaction was one of surprise, of something new, because we weren't living a time in Brazil of a totally open debate, and the question of homosexuality wasn't a prominent issue. Everything was camouflaged and hidden."[51] Daniel's candidness about his sexuality was a novelty, and the frank way he discussed living with AIDS was something that few Brazilians had heard or seen before. The program reached 11 percent of the viewing audience, a sizable segment, and was re-aired at least once. As a result of the filming, Daniel and Teixeira became close friends. She visited him every time she traveled to Rio from São Paulo, and she was with him the day he died.

The intimate relationship between Daniel and Cláudio, captured on television, remained steadfast throughout the next two and a half years. Although their sexual life together had waned in the early 1980s, if not earlier, the two remained inseparably bound. In the documentary *Homens* (Men), completed after Daniel's death, Cláudio explains that when their sexual desire dissipated and then disappeared, the relationship "took on another dimension. . . . Sexuality initiated our relationship without becoming its axis. It wasn't the most important or basic thing."

Throughout the 1980s, Elaine Maciel observed the couple close at hand and noted that Daniel was jealous about Cláudio's multiple sexual partners. "But at the same time he let him be free, as if he were saying: 'You want to. Go. But you will return because I'm the one who keeps things together.' So it was that way, you know, that is, there was jealousy, but he never prohibited Cláudio from doing anything."[52] According to Ângela Pezzuti, her sister Carmela (Ângelo's mother) characterized Cláudio and Daniel's arrangement as symbiotic; each one depended on the other.[53] In that regard, they remained a loving couple in spite of Cláudio's sexual escapades.

They also considered adopting a child. According to Ângela Pezzuti, it was mainly Cláudio's idea. "The daughter of a maid of a friend of mine was pregnant and didn't want the child. Cláudio came here [to Belo Horizonte] to get to know her, and she said that she would give the child up for adoption. He prepared the paperwork. . . . He offered her all the assistance [that she needed]."⁵⁴ But when Cláudio went to the hospital to sign the adoption papers, the mother had changed her mind. Eliane Maciel remembers other details of the story. According to her recollections, a religious relative of the young mother convinced her to keep her baby, who was born weak with many health problems and ended up dying. This devastated Cláudio and Daniel as they wondered whether or not their intention to adopt the child somehow might have provoked the mother's premature labor and the birth of a sick baby.⁵⁵

When the couple's adoption plans were foiled by tragically bad luck, the two immersed themselves in their respective passions. In 1987, Daniel had completed another novel, this one about AIDS: *Alegres e irresponsáveis abacaxis americanos* (Gay and irresponsible American suffering). The subtitle, translated as "images of days of fear" (incidentally, days [*dias*] is an anagram for AIDS), communicated the novel's theme, namely, an examination of the social prejudice, pain, and suffering of people dealing with the disease.⁵⁶ In the book, Daniel addresses many of the criticisms about the association of AIDS with death that he later articulates in the ABIA bulletins and in his activism as the president of Pela VIDDA.⁵⁷

Cláudio continued to work as a freelance graphic designer, and he eventually set up his own company with Beatriz Salgueiro dos Santos, known as A 4 Mãos (Four hands). Salgueiro loved working with Cláudio. "He was captivating, easy to deal with, generous, and fun."⁵⁸ ABIA and Pela VIDDA ended up contracting A 4 Mãos for graphic services to produce posters, pamphlets, and other publications, including a comic book directed toward youth, and another written for sailors and merchant marines.⁵⁹

The dynamic political situation in 1989 also drew Daniel back into politics. The 1988 constitution provided for the first democratic presidential elections since 1960. Twenty-two parties were poised to present candidates. Initially, there was an attempt to negotiate a coalition ticket, composed of Luiz Inácio Lula da Silva of the PT as the presidential candidate and Fernando Gabeira from the PV as his running mate. In mid-1989, when PT forces rejected Gabeira's nomination in favor of a more traditional politician, the Green Party decided to run its own candidate in order to promote the party's program and visibility nationwide. They chose Herbert Daniel as their standard-bearer.⁶⁰

In a statement announcing his nomination, Daniel recognizes that the Green Party was still in its early stages of growth: "It's a party of the future that we are going to begin to create, to establish, in the next decade."⁶¹

Daniel explains that the color green symbolizes life. He also insists that seriously tackling environmental problems is a matter of life or death for civilization as a whole, and it requires "dreaming" rather than merely presenting technical solutions. "We have to look toward a utopia, to a dream, to our desire to change the world, and we will succeed," he argues. His speech's idealistic language is reminiscent of the sentiments that had driven his commitment to the revolution two decades previously. Although supporters of the Green Party were few in number, a grasp of the larger context and the willingness to fight for clear goals would ensure a certain victory.

Daniel described his candidacy as symbolic, as the Green Party had just taken root in Brazil and was barely known to a wider public. It was a bold move to launch a figure who had openly declared his HIV status and proudly assumed his homosexuality, especially since most of the Left, along with the vast majority of Brazilian society, still held conservative ideas about same-sex sexuality. In an interview Daniel comments, "I want to discuss the absurdity that people don't let, for example, homosexuals be candidates. It is as if a sexual option qualifies or disqualifies someone. Whereas people who hide their sexuality can be candidates for anything."[62]

His candidacy, however, would not last long. Some Green Party members had reservations about whether Daniel would be an effective candidate because of his ongoing medical problems. He ended up withdrawing his candidacy. Gabeira, who then replaced him, received less than 1 percent of the vote in the first round.

During his brief time as a candidate, Daniel used his HIV status for political ends. In an open letter addressed to Fidel Castro, Daniel criticized Cuba's AIDS policy, which included forced testing and the quarantining of people who were HIV positive. Daniel evoked his own revolutionary past as one of the reasons for his missive to the Cuba leader: "I want to speak to you as if we had met along one of the paths of the Latin American Revolution of the 1960s, feet still grimy with mud, with hope arming the guns in our hands and our spirits full of your words telling us that it was possible to transform the world, to make it more beautiful."[63] Daniel explained that his illness led him to accept the nomination as the symbolic Green Party presidential candidate "in order to alert the Brazilian society about fundamental issues in the construction of democracy, a system in which everyone fully exercises the right to individual differences in the permanent struggle against all social inequalities." After criticizing actions by the Cuban government that isolated and stigmatized those with HIV/AIDS, whom Daniel called political prisoners, he ended his open letter with an appeal: "I ask you, compañero Fidel, to change the Cuban AIDS program. First, it is necessary to free those political prisoners. Second, it is necessary to implement a program based on the revolutionary principle of solidarity. I simply hope that Cuba will not permit itself to be defeated by prejudice."

Jorge A. Bolaños Suárez, the Cuban ambassador in Brasília, answered Daniel's letter, arguing that the Cubans in detention centers had agreed to their isolation. In Daniel's response, he questioned whether they freely consented to their internment and insisted that Cuba's approach to the disease was widely discouraged by international public health specialists and human rights activists. He suggested that Cuba should hold a seminar on the current scientific investigations about AIDS through the Global AIDS project of the World Health Organization. He also reiterated his appeal that people with HIV/AIDS be freed and treated with dignity and respect.[64]

While this interchange with a representative of the Cuban government didn't get widespread coverage in Brazil, it marked Daniel's definitive break with the tendency of many on the Left to retain a mythical idealization of the Cuban Revolution, years after the demise of the armed struggle in Brazil. Daniel admits in his letter to Fidel Castro that he had been "a sincere follower of Che Guevara."[65] The Cuban government had received many of his comrades in after they were released from prison, and there remained an aura about the infallibility of the Cuban Revolution. During the 1960s, there doesn't seem to have been a debate in Brazil among the Left about Cuba's antigay policies, and there is no indication that Daniel was aware of them, when he embraced the ideas of Castro and Guevara. Exile, his experience in engaging in political work as Brazil slowly inched toward democracy, and his HIV/AIDS status reshaped previously held assumptions about the revolutionary models that had inspired his activities in the 1960s and early 1970s. While he remained committed to radical social change, he insisted that it must be combined with forms of democracy that respected individuals' uniqueness.

Daniel's intransigent defense of people with AIDS in Cuba had echoes in Brazil in a different context. In 1989, three months after Daniel received the news from his doctor, the immensely popular young singer and songwriter Agenor Miranda Araújo Neto, known as Cazuza, admitted to the press he had AIDS.[66] Cazuza's story shocked and moved the entire nation. The announcement of his illness acted as a catalyst that humanized people with HIV/AIDS and made the public recognize the disease. Unlike Daniel, however, Cazuza skirted questions about his sexuality and didn't lend his support to a new LGBT movement, which was emerging from a period of relative weakness. Nor did he reach out to any AIDS groups. Nonetheless, Daniel sharply criticized ways the media had treated the topic of AIDS among Brazilian celebrities: "Every individual has the right to say whether or not he [or she] has AIDS. . . . I think that the rumors that circulate about this or that person are criminal because, at the end of the day, this tittle-tattle pries into the sexuality of a human being."[67] Cazuza died the following July, and his mother later set up the Viva Cazuza Society to care for children with AIDS. With Cazuza's death, Daniel became the most visible Brazilian public figure who openly talked about his experiences of living with AIDS.

Daniel's own bouts with the disease increased throughout 1990 and into 1991. He nevertheless tried to keep up with the pace he had set in 1989. He continued to produce the ABIA bulletin. He played a leadership role in ABIA and guided the expansion of Pela VIDDA to other cities. In May 1990, he attended the Fourth International Conference of People Living with AIDS in Madrid.[68] The next year, he joined the Global AIDS Policy Coalition, led by Dr. Jonathan Mann at the Harvard School of Public Health. (Mann had headed the World Health Organization's AIDS program, but had left that post in 1990 because of inadequate UN action on AIDS.)[69] Mann's invitation recognized Daniel's importance as an international activist. Daniel also attended a meeting on human rights, organized by the International Court of Justice in The Hague, that focused on AIDS. He closed his comments to the gathering with these words: "We all live with AIDS. Let's make life on our planet an inventory of uncountable beauty. Together let's raise a cry of exaltation and hope whose echo will be heard around the world and for all time. Long live life!"[70]

Daniel continued the campaign of criticizing the Brazilian government for its inaction throughout 1990 and 1991.[71] "The government's AIDS campaign is immoral, unjust and cowardly. It doesn't explain the disease and offends those who are sick," he proclaims in one newspaper interview.[72] "The Brazilian government has acted with indifference regarding AIDS, with a negligence that is criminal. The campaigns have been irresponsible. They don't provide information, and they should be radically modified. What is happening in Brazil is a disgrace, and it will increase prejudice." In the interview Daniel is relentless: "Imagine a sick person who turns on the television and hears the government say that there is no cure and the person is going to die."

Daniel's tirades against the government reflected the frustrations that many activists felt at the slow-paced official response to the disease. Fernando Collor de Mello (1990–92), Brazil's first democratically elected president in three decades, promised to eliminate wasteful government spending and control the economy, but he was unable to contain rampant inflation that reached 1,783 percent in 1990 and destabilized people's everyday lives. Cautious policies on the part of the National AIDS program also frustrated activists. Veriano Terto remembers, "People were dying at the door of hospitals, people were refused admission, there weren't beds, there were no drugs, only neglect, especially in Rio."[73]

At the same time that Daniel and others launched sharp criticisms against government inaction, ABIA faced an internal crisis. The organization had grown dramatically through outside funding, starting with the Ford Foundation, which had allowed Sílvia Ramos to hire Daniel.[74] By 1990, ABIA employed twelve full-time staff members and had outgrown its original financial and organizational model. Herbert de Souza (Betinho) remained the ABIA president but had relinquished any day-to-day involvement. Changes in the organization and other professional goals led Ramos and others to leave ABIA in 1991. Daniel ended up assuming the role of executive director. However, his health was declining dramatically, and it became increasingly difficult for him to carry out any administrative tasks. He needed additional help to sustain ABIA, so he called on Richard Parker, a U.S. anthropologist who worked on Brazilian sexuality, to see if he was willing to seek additional funds for the organization.

In 1990, Daniel and Parker had worked together on an edited collection published as AIDS, a terceira epidemia (AIDS, the third epidemic), whose title referred to the social, cultural, economic, and political reactions to AIDS. "In 1991, we published the book, and then he was hospitalized. He called me to the hospital room. He was really sick. . . . He explained the internal dynamics of ABIA. . . . He would stay as the vice president; Betinho would continue as the president. Betinho had total confidence in him, he explained, and wanted him to continue as vice president, but he [Daniel] was sick and couldn't really do what needed to be done, and he needed to raise money."[75] Parker agreed to step in, and a large MacArthur grant helped solve ABIA's financial problems.

Throughout 1991, Daniel was constantly in and out of the hospital. When Daniel became seriously ill, Cláudio would stop going to the office and stay at home to take care of him. Between washing, feeding, and nursing Daniel, he would work at his drawing board.[76] As Dona Geny remembered, Cláudio took amazingly tender care of him.

In December, Daniel and Cláudio decided to travel to Belo Horizonte to see Daniel's family. It was a bittersweet reunion, because his health was clearly declining. Yet the couple joked and played with Daniel's nieces and nephews. They enjoyed the traditional holiday foods and festivities, while Daniel reassured his mother that he was fine.

FIGURE 17.2 Cláudio and Daniel, with his brother Hamilton's son, Vâner, and daughter, Raquel, in Belo Horizonte, Christmas 1981. COURTESY OF GENY BRUNELLI DE CARVALHO.

After Daniel and Cláudio returned to Rio in January 1992, his health deteriorated even further, and he slowly lost his mental capacities.[77] Dilma Rousseff, and her daughter Paula, visited Daniel during this period. Although he was tired and frail, they talked for hours, reminiscing about old times and old friends. "He told me about the nightclub, and said that he had made up for everything that he had repressed," she recalled. "We had very different personalities, but we accepted each other.... We didn't judge each other."[78]

As Daniel grew weaker and lost more weight, he wasn't able to walk, so Cláudio took him out in a wheelchair. However, the bumpy sidewalks bothered him, and so they stopped going out.[79] He also lost his motor control, and even eating a spoonful of soup became a major production.[80] Monica Teixeira believes that his health had declined so much that at one point he simply stopped thinking. "Everything went at the same time. He wasn't the kind of person who dies with a weakened body and a mind that is working. He lost intellectual vitality.... He might even have lost it before he lost his physical abilities."[81]

Dona Geny traveled to Rio in February to help Cláudio nurse her beloved son. "I took care of him, cooked, and cleaned the house while Cláudio was at work," she recalled.⁸² Ângela and Carmela Pezzuti also made a point of visiting him, because Cláudio had warned them that Daniel's end was near. Ângela recalled: "The last time I saw Herbert was the week he died.... When we arrived at the apartment, Cláudio received us.... We talked a bit and then went into Herbert's room. He was really weak."⁸³ Carmela became really upset at the sight of Daniel's feeble body and sat down at the foot of the bed to talk with Dona Geny and calm herself down. Ângela approached Daniel and heard him explain faintly: "Today I dreamed about Ângelo and Juares. Ângelo was a little boy and Juares was an adult. And we began to talk like little children." He then drifted into a deep sleep, and Cláudio ushered the visitors out of the room.

While it's presumptuous to interpret one of Daniel's last dreams, Ângelo Pezzuti and Juares Guimarães de Brito and later Carlos Lamarca were three men who had played important roles in his life. Ângelo became his closest confidant while at the university. Juares had been an important political mentor. In spite of Lamarca's defection from the VPR, Daniel remained immensely loyal to his comandante. All had passed away while relatively young. Like Daniel, they had lived their lives with passion, and Daniel greatly admired them. He survived them all by two decades, constantly adapting to the changes around him and reinventing himself in the process. Yet they remained on his mind during his last moments.

In late March, Dona Geny returned to Belo Horizonte at Cláudio's insistence. "The bills had to be paid," she explained. "We didn't have automatic machines like you have today."⁸⁴ The next day, Cláudio summoned some of Daniel's closest friends to their apartment on Rua Toneleiros in Copacabana. On March 29, 1992, a Sunday afternoon, Herbert Eustáquio de Carvalho, known as Herbert Daniel, passed away, with Cláudio Mesquita, his loving partner, by his side.

EPILOGUE

Remnants

> Love and struggle, those are the two words that best define his personality.
>
> — CLÁUDIO MESQUITA

Daniel's death devastated Cláudio. He had remained HIV negative throughout his partner's illness. In fact, people found it ironic that Cláudio had been much more promiscuous than Daniel, yet he hadn't become infected. Then, in a self-destructive act of mourning after the departure of his lifetime companion, he purposely infected himself. Beatriz Salgueiro, the co-owner of his graphic design company, remembered that "he thought it was unfair that Daniel, who was more romantic, had the bad luck to be infected. And so he started seeking out relationships where he put himself at risk."[1] Cláudio's sister, Magaly, recalled the day he got back his test results, a year after Daniel had died. She paraphrased what Cláudio told her: "I've got AIDS because I wanted to. I had [unprotected] sex with people who were HIV positive to get AIDS because I don't want to live anymore."[2] Cláudio's father had died of a heart attack, and Monica Teixeira remembers that once, when he visited him after Daniel's death, he boasted, quite seriously, that he was eating a lot of butter in the morning to see if he would die. "Daniel's death killed Cláudio," she recalled.³

In the video *Homens* (Men), produced by ABIA in 1993 and featuring three people living with AIDS, Cláudio describes his sorrow: "You see when you close one eye. But the world is different. Each eye sees in a certain way, and the two images complement each other, making one image. I think our life was a little like that. I'm feeling blind in one eye when I see the world. My future is a new learning experience; that is, I have to get around in the world with only one eye." In 1991, Daniel had offered an optimistic assessment of himself as he lived with AIDS. "I always say we are all going to die. No one is going to be able to escape it. The important thing is not to die but to live. Every life should be lived with such intensity, with such beauty, that when the person dies, we commemorate their life and not just their death. I learned this my whole life and AIDS emphasized it."⁴ Cláudio repeats something similar in the *Homens* documentary: "You are not dead the moment that you discover that you have AIDS. You die the moment you die. And the most concrete proof of this was the three years of Daniel's life with AIDS. Knowing that he had AIDS, they were the most productive three years of his life."

Daniel had been scheduled to speak at the Eighth International AIDS Conference in Amsterdam in July 1992. Cláudio went in his place and read the text "The Soul of a Citizen," which Daniel had prepared.⁵ After evoking the message about living every day to the fullest, he quoted Daniel: "The only possible eternity is the interchange of light between each of the human actors who comes on stage: this act of transmission is what we call *solidarity!* . . . Our passage through time is the heart that regulates small and fundamental things—since the planet, our planet, which has the exact dimensions of our humanity, beats like a heart. Life does not win. It happens."⁶

Less than a year after Daniel died, Cláudio wrote a short essay in which he lamented that he was unable to enjoy that year's Carnival celebrations because Daniel was not there to share the experience with him. "When I knew he was sick, I was right to state that after his death Carnival would never be the same for me. Nor would life or the world. And they aren't. Nevertheless, things go on as usual, but I see them differently, in solitude."⁷

In spite of all his efforts, including finding a new boyfriend with whom he lived for a while, they weren't enough to avert the deep depression that overcame Cláudio. According to Veriano Terto, a close friend of the couple, "He lost all of his vitality. Cláudio was a very exuberant person, a handsome man. I saw him very withdrawn."⁸ Cláudio simply couldn't heed his beloved partner's advice about how to go on living. As he had hoped, Cláudio suffered a heart attack and passed away on October 30, 1994.

When Daniel died, Brazil had only recently seen the end of military rule. The country was still in the first stages of forging a democratic ethos that respected differences. In that process, Daniel pushed the boundaries of the Left far beyond its comfortable limits, challenging people to rethink ossified assumptions and age-old suppositions. His discussions of citizenship in relationship to AIDS were a call for democratic tolerance, empathy, and compassion.

Dr. Jonathan Mann, the visionary and universally acclaimed trailblazer in the global fight against AIDS, dedicated a hefty thousand-page tome, *AIDS in the World*, published in 1992, to Herbert Daniel. In his homage, he quotes a section of the essay that Cláudio had read at the Amsterdam conference: "I hope that one day, when death finally comes by chance or by any infection caused by the virus, nobody says that I was defeated by AIDS. I have succeeded in living with AIDS. AIDS has not defeated me." In a gesture that endorsed Daniel's farsighted approach to thinking about how to confront the disease, Mann wrote, "To Herbert Daniel and the many others who have died and who live, undefeated by AIDS."[9] There could be no greater recognition of Daniel's contribution to the global discussion about how to combat the disease and support those living with AIDS.

Two years later, the city of Belo Horizonte honored Daniel, along with other former revolutionaries, by naming a short street after him: Rua Herbert Eustáquio de Carvalho. It is near the city airport and not too far from the Pamploma Park, where some of Brazil's first modernist structures were built. A decade later the city government recognized Daniel posthumously with the Tribute to Utopia Award. They also republished a short biography by Cláudio about Daniel, which tells the story of his struggle with his sexuality, his feelings about his body, and the homophobia within the Left. Cláudio notes that paradoxically Daniel had published six books to critical acclaim but sold few copies. The seventh book, *Vida antes da morte / Life before Death*, a treatise about AIDS, his shortest and most successful, was published in five languages.[10]

To recognize Daniel's legacy, in 2007 the Brazilian Green Party established the Herbert Daniel Green Foundation, a nonprofit entity with the mission to carry out actions, projects, and programs; organize seminars, debates and symposia; and conduct research and studies related to culture, politics, and the environment. Although the current politics of the Greens have drifted away from the program and practices of its early years when Daniel was an active member, in honoring his memory, the foundation's

FIGURE E.1 Herbert and Dona Geny, December 1981. COURTESY OF GENY BRUNELLI DE CARVALHO.

site hosts a six-minute video recording of the speech Daniel gave explaining why he was a presidential candidate in 1989.[11]

This volume begins with my first meeting with Daniel's mother, and so it seems appropriate to end it with some brief comments by Dona Geny about her son. Dona Geny had a hard life. She experienced childhood poverty, followed by a happy early marriage that suddenly turned into a series of nursing duties: first taking care of her chronically infirm mother-in-law, then her father-in-law, and finally her husband. She did all this while being a devoted mother to her three sons and a loving grandmother. The toll it took was written on her wrinkled brow. Yet every time she bid me farewell after a visit to her tidy house, she had a happy twinkle in her eye. If one can inherit or acquire characteristics from one's parents, then certainly Daniel had his father's quick wit and wry humor and his mother's determination to persist. Both Daniel and his younger sibling Hamilton had a sense of obligation and destiny imbued in them by their mother. Though life took Hamilton in a different direction from that of his older brother, Dona Geny insisted on maintaining a united family, and the degree of love and respect that Hamilton and his other younger brother, Hélder, and their families hold for Daniel is notable.

Throughout our conversations, Dona Geny offered many different explanations about why her son's life took its fateful course. Although she recognized that Cláudio had taken care of her son Herbert in a loving and tender manner when he became ill, as far as she was concerned Cláudio had lured her son into homosexuality. Similarly, according to Dona Geny's reading of her son's past, Lamarca was the cause of his subversive activities, though the truth is that Daniel had been involved in underground left-wing politics three years before he met the revolutionary captain. As she recalled to me, "I said, 'My son, you don't even know how to change a light bulb. How are you going to confront the world?' I didn't think he would."[12]

While it is easy to disagree with Dona Geny's version of events about her son, it is, after all, a mother's prerogative to defend her child no matter what others say. In a way, though, and perhaps unintentionally, she noted something crucial. Daniel's trajectory reveals the power of the historical forces that shaped his life and that of so many other youth, who came of age under the military regime, sought diverse ways to challenge the dictatorship, and then later radically rethought the politics of power, sexuality, and the body in late twentieth-century Brazil. Although Daniel seems to be a rather unique and unusual personality, how he chose to live his life captures the spirit of a generation in all its contradictions and complexities.

CHRONOLOGY

1946	DECEMBER 14	Herbert Eustáquio de Carvalho is born in Bom Despacho, Minas Gerais, to Geny Brunelli de Carvalho and Geraldo Feliciano de Carvalho.
1949	JANUARY 14	Hamilton Brunelli de Carvalho is born in Belo Horizonte.
	JUNE 17	Cláudio Mesquita is born in Poço de Caldas, Minas Gerais.
1952		Herbert begins primary school at Escola Chopin.
1960	SEPTEMBER 29	Hélder Nazareno de Carvalho is born in Belo Horizonte.
1961	FEBRUARY	POLOP is founded. Herbert begins Colégio Tiradentes.
	AUGUST 25	President Jânio Quadro resigns from office.
	SEPTEMBER 7	Vice President João Goulart assumes the presidency.

1964	APRIL 1	With support of conservative civilian forces, the majority of the armed forces overthrow the government of João Goulart.
1965	MARCH	Herbert enters medical school at the UFMG.
1967	MARCH 28	Herbert joins a dissident group within POLOP.
	SEPTEMBER	During the Fourth National Congress of POLOP, those supporting armed struggle split off to form a new organization.
1968	MARCH	VPR founded in São Paulo.
	MARCH 28	The death of a high school student, Edson Luís, in Rio de Janeiro ignites nationwide student demonstrations.
	APRIL	POLOP dissidents from Minas Gerais form a new group that they refer to as "the O."
	MAY 4	Herbert is arrested and quickly released during the student occupation of the School of Medicine.
	JULY	The O. elects its first national command, with Herbert subsequently incorporated into the leadership.
	OCTOBER	The O. becomes Comandos de Libertação Nacional (COLINA).
	DECEMBER 12	President Costa e Silva issues Institutional Act No. 5, shutting down Congress, expanding executive powers, and eliminating habeas corpus.

1969	JANUARY 14	Herbert participates in a double bank robbery in Sabará, Minas Gerais.
	FEBRUARY 2	Herbert goes underground and flees to Rio de Janeiro, eventually assuming the nom de guerre Daniel.
	JUNE	VPR, COLINA, and other militants fuse to form VAR-Palmares.
	JULY 18	In Rio de Janeiro, VAR-Palmares seizes the safe of the former São Paulo governor Ademar de Barros; the safe contains US$2,600,000.
	SEPTEMBER–OCTOBER	At a clandestine congress of VAR-Palmares, Daniel and others split to refound VPR.
1970	FEBRUARY	Daniel joins the VPR leader Carlos Lamarca and seventeen others in a guerrilla-training encampment in rural São Paulo.
	APRIL 20	The Vale do Ribeira rural training encampment is discovered; Herbert avoids arrest and flees to Rio de Janeiro.
	JUNE 11–16	Daniel participates in the abduction of the German ambassador, which leads to the release of forty political prisoners, who are flown to Algeria.
	JUNE OR JULY	Daniel and Inês Etienne join Carlos Lamarca in the VPR national command.
	DECEMBER 7	Daniel helps to abduct the Swiss ambassador and stays in the house where he is hidden.

1971	JANUARY 13	The Swiss ambassador is freed in exchange for the release of seventy political prisoners, who are flown to Santiago, Chile.
	FEBRUARY	A doctor erroneously diagnoses Daniel with leukemia.
	AUGUST	Zenaide Machado and Daniel write a declaration announcing both the demobilization of the VPR and a call for a Congress abroad.
	NOVEMBER	Hiding in Niterói, Rio de Janeiro, Daniel meets Cláudio Mesquita.
1972		Daniel, Cláudio, and Cláudio's sister Magaly run a publicity firm in Rio de Janeiro.
1973	MARCH 2	During Carnival, Daniel and Cláudio flee Rio de Janeiro.
	MARCH 7	Daniel arrives in Barbacena, Minas Gerais, and hides in his aunt's house.
	JUNE	Daniel and Cláudio open the Dinosaurus discotheque in Minas Gerais.
1974	SEPTEMBER 7	With false passports, Daniel and Cláudio slip out of Brazil to Argentina then fly to Paris.
	OCTOBER 21	Daniel, Cláudio, and friends move to Portugal.
	NOVEMBER 15	MDB, the opposition political party, wins a landslide victory in Brazil's congressional elections.

1975	MAY 24		Daniel and Cláudio have sex for the first time.
	SEPTEMBER 11		Ângelo Pezzuti dies in a motorcycle crash in France.
1976	JANUARY 8		Daniel and Cláudio leave Lisbon and move to Paris.
	SEPTEMBER		Daniel begins work at the Continental, a luxury bathhouse.
1977	JANUARY		Daniel gets a job at Tilt, a gay sauna, where he writes his memoir.
1978	APRIL		*Lampião da Esquina*, Brazil's first commercial gay newspaper, is published.
1979	FEBRUARY 8		Members of Somos, Brazil's first gay and lesbian rights organization, participate in a public debate at the University of São Paulo.
	MAY 29		Daniel speaks about homosexuality with the exiled community at the Casa do Brasil in Paris.
	AUGUST 29		The Brazilian Congress passes the amnesty law that frees most political prisoners and allows most exiles to return to Brazil.
	OCTOBER 26		Daniel writes an open letter about exiles who are not covered by the amnesty law.
1980	MARCH		*Lampião da Esquina* reprints Daniel's open letter.

CHRONOLOGY 269

1981	SEPTEMBER 3	*Jornal do Brasil* publishes the first article in Brazil about AIDS.
	OCTOBER 9	Daniel arrives in Rio de Janeiro after seven years in exile.
1982	MARCH	Daniel publishes *Passagem para o próximo sonho*.
	NOVEMBER	Liszt Vieira is elected to the Rio de Janeiro state legislature on the Workers' Party ticket.
1983		Daniel publishes *A fêmea sintética*.
	OCTOBER	Daniel copublishes *Jacarés e lobisomens* with Leila Míccolis.
1984	AUGUST	Daniel publishes *Meu corpo daria um romance*.
	NOVEMBER	Daniel directs *As três moças do sabonete: Uma apologia sobre os anos Médici*.
1985	MAY	*Cegonha? . . . Que cegonha?* is produced in Rio de Janeiro.
1986	NOVEMBER 15	Herbert Daniel gets 5,485 votes in the race for the Rio de Janeiro State Assembly but does not win a seat.
	DECEMBER 21	ABIA is founded in Rio de Janeiro.
1987	DECEMBER	Daniel begins working at ABIA.
1988	JUNE	The Constituent Assembly passes provisions requiring blood screening.
	DECEMBER 1	On World AIDS Day, Daniel and others organize an action at the Christ the Redeemer statue in Rio de Janeiro.

1989	JANUARY 8	Daniel learns he is infected with HIV.
	MAY	Daniel founds Grupo Pela VIDDA.
	JUNE	Daniel participates in the Fifth International Conference on AIDS in Montreal.
		ABIA publishes *Vida antes da morte / Life before Death*.
1990		Daniel becomes executive director of ABIA.
1991		Daniel and Richard Parker publish *AIDS, a terceira epidemia*.
1992	MARCH 29	Herbert Eustáquio de Carvalho (Herbert Daniel) dies in Rio de Janeiro.
1994	OCTOBER 30	Cláudio Mesquita dies of a heart attack in Rio de Janeiro.

NOTES

ABBREVIATIONS

AA	Author's archives
ABIA	Associação Brasileira Interdisciplinar de AIDS
AEL	Arquivo Edgard Leuenroth, Universidade Estadual de Campinas
AERJ	Arquivo Público do Estado do Rio de Janeiro
AESI/UFMG	Assessoria Especial de Segurança e Informação, Universidade Federal de Minas Gerais
AESP/DEOPS	Departamento Estadual de Ordem Político e Social, Arquivo Público do Estado de São Paulo
AN	National Archive, Rio de Janeiro
APM	Arquivo Público Mineiro, Belo Horizonte
BDIC	La Bibliothèque de Documentation Internationale Contemporaine, l'Université de Paris Ouest Nanterre
BNM	Brasil Nunca Mais Digital Archives
DOPS/MG	Departamento de Ordem Política e Social, Minas Gerais
MAI	Ministério de Assuntos Internos, Torre de Tombo, Lisbon
TRC	Triânglo Rosa Collection, AEL
UNICAMP	Universidade Estadual de Campinas

INTRODUCTION

Epigraph: Rousseff, interview with Carvalho. Dilma Rousseff (the Brazilian president from 2011 to 2016) and Herbert Daniel were members of the same revolutionary organizations.

1. Daniel, "O que é isso, companheiros?," 10.
2. Daniel, "O que é isso, companheiros?," 10.
3. Green, "Desire and Revolution."

4. Green, "Who Is the Macho Who Wants to Kill Me?"
5. The term "Dona" shows respect for an older woman.
6. Borim, "Daniel, Herbert"; Fitch, "Life before Death"; Da Silva, *Os escritores da guerrilha urbana*; Pereira, "Herbert Daniel e suas escrituras de memória"; Martins, "AIDS, vida e morte no romance *Alegres e irresponsáveis abacaxis americanos*; Dias, "A trajetória soropositiva de Herbert Daniel."
7. I would like to thank Marycarolyn G. France, Moshé Sluhovsky, and the anonymous readers from Duke University Press for their contributions in helping me reshape the final version of the introduction.

CHAPTER 1. DARE TO STRUGGLE, DARE TO WIN (1992)

Epigraph: "AIDS mata aos 45 o escritor Herbert Daniel," *Folha de São Paulo*, March 31, 1992. José Stalin Pedroso was an AIDS activist.

1. Geny Carvalho, interview no. 1.
2. "Enterro," *O Globo*, April 1, 1992.
3. "Enterro," *O Globo*, April 1, 1992.
4. "AIDS mata ao 45 o escritor Herbert Daniel"; "Escritor aos 45 anos more de AIDS," *Folha da Tarde*, March 31, 1992; "Morre Herbert Eustáquio de Carvalho," *Veja*; "Enterro"; Marcos Barros Pinto, "Morrer com todas as letras," *O Globo*, April 8, 1992.
5. Geny Carvalho, interview no. 1.

CHAPTER 2. HE LOVED TO READ (1946–1964)

Epigraph: Geny Carvalho, interview no. 1. Other quotations are from this interview unless otherwise indicated.

1. Hamilton Carvalho, interview no. 1. Other quotations are from the same interview.
2. Santos, interview. Other quotations are from the same interview.
3. Daniel, *Passagem*, 25.
4. Hélder Carvalho, interview.
5. Herminio Prates, "Gê de Carvalho, o talento a serviço da emoção e do riso," *Jornal Minas Gerais*, November 17, 1987.
6. Pereira, interview no. 1. Other quotations are from the same interview unless otherwise indicated.
7. Elaine Espíndola, interview. All other quotations are from the same interview.
8. Nilton Espíndola, interview.
9. Daniel, *Meu corpo*, 124.
10. Calvacanti, "Ele vive de bicos" *Veja* (July 1, 1980): 26.
11. Daniel, *Meu corpo*, 121.
12. Daniel, *Meu corpo*, 121
13. Daniel, *Meu corpo*, 119.
14. Daniel, *Meu corpo*, 156.
15. Pereira, interview no. 2.

16. Morando, *Paraíso das Maravilhas*.
17. Morando, "Por baixo dos panos."
18. *Diário da Tarde*, September 14, 1964, quoted in Morando, "Por baixo dos panos," 57.
19. Daniel, *Passagem*, 25.
20. Skidmore, *Politics in Brazil*; Green, *We Cannot Remain Silent*, chapter 1.

CHAPTER 3. MEDICAL SCHOOL (1965–1967)

Epigraph: Jorge Nahas was Herbert Daniel's classmate and a member of the same revolutionary organization. Jorge Nahas, interview. Other quotations are from the same interview.

1. Silva, "Ideário do movimento estudantil."
2. Comissão Especial, *Direito à memória e à verdade*, 30.
3. Reis Filho, "Classe operária, partido de quadros e revolução socialista," 55.
4. Green, *We Cannot Remain Silent*; Leacock, *Requiem for Revolution*, 120–35.
5. Gorender, *Combate nas trevas*, 37–39.
6. Badaró, "Em busca da revolução socialista"; Oliveira, "POLOP."
7. Gorender, *Combate nas trevas*, 41; Ridenti, "Ação Popular."
8. Antônio Nahas, *A queda*, 41–76; Leite, "Comandos de libertação nacional."
9. Martins Filho, *Movimento estudantil e ditadura militar*, 75–109; Langland, *Speaking of Flowers*.
10. Geny Carvalho, interview with author.
11. Lisboa, interview. Other quotations in this chapter are from the same interview.
12. Guia, interview with Machado.
13. Jorge Nahas, interview with Ridenti.
14. Maria José Nahas, interview.
15. Pereira, interview no. 2.
16. Lisboa, interview.
17. Maria José Nahas, interview with Garcia, Leite, and Biagini.
18. Chacel, *Seu amigo esteve aqui*.
19. Lisboa, interview.
20. Lisboa, interview.
21. "Histórico escolar de Herbert Eustáquio de Carvalho," October 15, 1969, Acervo AESI/UFMG, Pasta 11, APM.
22. Pereira, interview no. 1.
23. Hamilton Carvalho, interview no 1.
24. "Histórico escolar de Herbert Eustáquio de Carvalho."
25. Daniel, *Passagem*, 86.
26. Daniel, *Passagem*, 86.
27. Daniel, *Passagem*, 86.
28. Daniel, *Passagem*, 87.
29. Garibaldi, interview.
30. Daniel, *Passagem*, 26.
31. Jorge Nahas, interview.

32. Dângelo and Machado, *O humor do show medicina*, 3–7.
33. Filgueiras, "Nos bastidores."
34. Sousa Neto, "Show medicina."
35. Program for the Show Medicina, Belo Horizonte, 1967, AA. The phrase was a pun, as *caro* means both expensive and dear.
36. Elaine Espíndola, interview; Pereira, interview no. 2.
37. Sousa Neto, "Show medicina," 12–13.
38. Sousa Neto, "Show medicina," 12–13.

CHAPTER 4. THE O. (1967–1968)

Epigraph: Erwin Duarte was a medical student and a member of the same revolutionary organization to which Herbert belonged. Duarte, interview. Other quotations are from the same interview.

1. Maria José Nahas, interview. Other quotations are from the same interview.
2. Garibaldi, interview. Other quotations are from the same interview.
3. Maria José Nahas, interview.
4. Daniel, *Meu corpo*, 128–31.
5. Rousseff, interview.
6. Huebra, interview.
7. Cowan, *Securing Sex*; Green, *Beyond Carnival*; Green, "Who Is the Macho Who Wants to Kill Me?"; Baiardi, "O homossexualismo e a militância revolucionária."
8. Lumsden, *Machos, Maricones and Gays*.
9. Huebra, interview.
10. Rousseff, interview.
11. In 1965, Ângelo penned an article about female virginity with an underlying tone suggesting that women's sexual liberation would offer more sexual possibilities for men, making the article both conservative and avant-garde. Silva, "O tabu da virginidade."
12. Daniel, *Passagem*, 96.
13. Pimentel, interview with Ridenti.
14. Debray, *Revolution within the Revolution?*
15. Rousseff, interview; Lisboa, interview; Jorge Nahas, interview.
16. Rousseff, interview; Lisboa, interview; Jorge Nahas, interview.
17. Política Operária, "Program Socialista para o Brasil," September 1967, AA.
18. Reis Filho and Sá, *Imagens da revolução*, 114–48.
19. Chacel, *Seu amigo esteve aqui*, 64.
20. Os revolucionários que rompem com a POLOP, "Carta Aberta aos Revolucionários," September 1967, AA.
21. Daniel, *Passagem*, 94.
22. Daniel, *Passagem*, 26.
23. In 1967, Herbert only passed one of six courses. Leite, "'Apurando a subversão,'" 154.
24. Hamilton Carvalho, interview no. 1.

25. Gurgel, *A rebelião dos estudantes*; Langland, *Speaking of Flowers*; Martins Filho, *A rebelião estudantil*; Ventura, *1968: A ano que não terminou*.
26. Serbin, *Needs of the Heart*.
27. Delgado, "Carlos Lacerda."
28. Martins Filho, *Movimento estudantil e ditadura militar*, 122–26; Alves, *Grain of Mustard Seed*; Ferrer, *68: a geração que queria mudar o mundo*; Araújo, *Memórias estudantis*; Fico and Araújo, *1968: 40 anos depois*.
29. Alves, *68 mudou o mundo*, 145–68.
30. Tavares de Almeida and Weis, "Carro-zero e pau-de-arara"; Ventura, *1968: O ano que não terminou*.
31. Cardoso de Mello and Novais, "Captialismo tardio e sociabilidade moderna." For military reaction to changes, see Cowan, *Securing Sex*.
32. Dunn, *Brutality Garden*; Dunn, *Contracultura*; Carli and Ramos, *Tropicália*.
33. Basualdo, *Tropicália*; Leu, *Brazilian Popular Music*; Veloso, *Verdade tropical*.
34. Hamilton Carvalho, interview no. 1.
35. See his biographical sketch on the Fundação Verde Herbert Daniel website, http://www.fvhd.org.br/page/herbert-daniel. He is not mentioned in the list of student movement leaders in political police archives: "Relação de estudantes universitários relacionados as esquemas da esquerda," 2, Acervo DOPS/MG, Pasta 4180, Rolo 055, February 1967–November 1968, APM.
36. Rousseff, interview.
37. "Protestos em todo o Brasil," *O Piquete*, 4, no. 65, April 1, 1968, Acervo DOPS/MG, Pasta 16, subpasta 12, APM.
38. Chacel, *Seu amigo esteve aqui*, 60–72.
39. Rousseff, interview.
40. Amaral, *A vida quer é coragem*, 43–53; Rousseff, interview.
41. Pimentel, interview with Ridenti.
42. Paiva, *O sonho exilado*, 15–32.
43. The dedication—"For Ângelo, because he saw. But didn't live to see this."—suggests Ângelo's formative role in Herbert's life story.

CHAPTER 5. ÂNGELO (1968)

Epigraph: Maria José Nahas was a classmante of Herbert's in the medical school and a member of the COLINA expropriations unit. Maria José Nahas, interview.

1. Pezzuti, interview no. 1.
2. Ratton, interview.
3. Garibaldi, interview.
4. Chacel, *Seu amigo esteve aqui*, 72. Dilma Rousseff doesn't recall such a sharp rivalry between them. Rousseff, interview.
5. Reis Filho and Sá, *Imagens da revolução*, 134–59.
6. Reis Filho and Sá, *Imagens da revolução*, 137.
7. Oliveira, "Conflito social, memória e experiência"; Grossi, "As greves de Contagem"; Neves, *Trabalho e cidadania*.

8. Castello Branco, "A história contada pelos protagonistas," 17.
9. Miranda, "A cidade operária símbolo," 24.
10. Skidmore, *Politics of Military Rule*, 70.
11. Rousseff, interview.
12. Amaral, *A vida quer é coragem*, 48; Paiva, *Companheira Carmela*, 27.
13. Miranda, "A cidade operária símbolo," 24.
14. Castello Branco, "A história contada pelos protagonistas," 17.
15. Ibrahim and Barreto, "Manifesto de balance da greve de julho"; Ramalho, "Sinais de mudança no sindicalismo brasileiro"; Santana, "Trabalhadores, sindicatos e ditadura militar."
16. "O primeiro de maio," Acervo DOPS/MG, Pasta 250, APM.
17. "Conflito da rua em Minas," *O Globo*, May 2, 1968.
18. "Estudantes prendem director na escola," *Correio da Manhã*, May 3, 1968.
19. Antônio Nahas, *A queda*, 187–98.
20. "Estudantes pressionam mestres para obter sua solidariedade," *Estado de Minas*, May 4, 1968.
21. Pereira, interview no. 2.
22. Herbert Eustáquio de Carvalho, "Antecedentes," Acervo DOPS/MG, Pasta 943, Rolo 24, October 1969 to June 1971, APM.
23. "Ferido Sodré no comício em São Paulo," *Última Hora*, May 2, 1968.
24. Vianna, *Uma tempestade*, 48.
25. Chacel, *Seu amigo esteve aqui*, 69–70.
26. Chacel, *Seu amigo esteve aqui*, 68; Paiva, *Companheira Carmela*, 26–27.
27. Maria José Nahas, interview with Garcia, Leite, and Biagini.
28. Maria José Nahas, interview with Leite.
29. Maria José Nahas, interview with Garcia, Leite, and Biagini.
30. "Homens com metralhadores atacam banco e levam 20 milhões," *Estado de Minas*, August 27, 1968.
31. "Bancários contam como foi o assalto," *Estado de Minas*, August 28, 1968.
32. Daniel, *Passagem*, 18.
33. "Informação No. 041: Colina," April 1969, Acervo DOPS/MG, Pasta 15, p. 24, APM.
34. "Homens com metralhadores"; "Bancários contam como foi o assalto."
35. "Interventor assina acordo na Justiça para aumento de 27% a metalúrigicos," *Estado de Minas*, October 4, 1968.
36. "Informação No. 041: Colina," p. 24.
37. Untitled document, October 1968, Acervo DOPS/MG, Pasta 22, pp. 9–24, APM.
38. Reis Filho and Sá, *Imagens da revolução*, 158.
39. Rousseff, interview.
40. "Informação No. 041: Colina," p. 22.
41. Daniel, *Meu corpo*, 131–34.
42. Daniel, *Passagem*, 97–98.

CHAPTER 6. UNDERGROUND (1969)

Epigraph: Ladislau Dowbor was a leader of the Vanguarda Popular Revolucionária and a roommate of Daniel's at some point in 1969 while they were living underground. Dowbor, interview with author.

1. COLINA, "Informe Nacional," January 1969, AA.
2. Daniel, *Passagem*, 16.
3. Daniel, *Passagem*, 16–17.
4. Case no. 158, p. 353, BNM.
5. Maria José Nahas, interview.
6. Langland, "Birth Control Pills and Molotov Cocktails."
7. "Ladrões com metralhadoras assaltam bancos em Sabará e levam 60 milhões," *Estado de Minas*, January 15, 1969.
8. Maciel, *O capitão Lamarca e a VPR*; Langland, "Birth Control Pills and Molotov Cocktails."
9. Daniel, *Passagem*, 38.
10. Daniel, *Passagem*, 38.
11. Ridenti, *O fantasma da revolução brasileira*, 197.
12. Maria José Carvalho Nahas, conversation with author, May 29, 2009, notes.
13. Ratton, interview.
14. Garibaldi, interview. Other quotations are from the same interview.
15. Duarte, interview.
16. "Pedro Paulo Bretas," Acervo DOPS/MG, Pasta 802, APM.
17. "Quadrilha confessa assaltos a bancos, drogaria e boate," *Estado de Minas*, January 31, 1969; Paiva, *O sonho exilado*, 36–39.
18. Chacel, *Seu amigo esteve aqui*, 74.
19. Garibaldi, interview; Huebra, interview.
20. Amaral, *A vida quer é coragem*, 54.
21. Ratton, interview.
22. Geny Carvalho, interview no. 1.
23. Hamilton Carvalho, interview no. 1.
24. Acervo DOPS/MG, Pasta 943, Rolo 24, October 1969–June 1971, APM.
25. "COLINA," Acervo DOPS/MG, Pasta 15, Rolo 1, April 1969–March 1975, APM.
26. Daniel, *Passagem*, 126.
27. Daniel, *Passagem*, 43–44.
28. Daniel, *Meu corpo*, 188.
29. Brito, interview no. 2; Osawa, interview.
30. Durão, interview.
31. Garibaldi, interview.
32. Rousseff, interview.
33. Dowbor, interview with author.
34. Daniel, interview with Patarra.
35. Rousseff, interview.
36. Lisboa, interview.
37. Ratton, interview.

38. Brito, interview no. 1.
39. Rousseff, interview.
40. Lisboa, interview.
41. Brito, interview no. 1.
42. Sirkis, interview.
43. Polari, *Em busca do tesouro*, 134.
44. Gradel, interview.
45. Cachapuz, interview.
46. Garibaldi, interview.

CHAPTER 7. UNITY AND DISUNITY (1969)

Epigraph: Alfredo Sirkis joined the VPR in 1969 and was the interpreter for the German and Swiss ambassadors who were held to obtain the release of political prisoners in exchange for their freedom. Sirkis, interview. Other quotations are from the same interview.

1. Skidmore, *The Politics of Military Rule*, 138–44.
2. Sirkis, *Os carbonários*, 139.
3. Fonseca, *Caminhas da história ensinada*, 39.
4. Polari, *Em busca do tesouro*, 81.
5. Sirkis, *Os carbonários*, 146–48.
6. Sirkis, *Os carbonários*, 144.
7. Carlos Franklin Paixão Araújo, "Resumo das declarações prestadas," September 28, 1970, 50-Z-9-14842, AESP/DEOPS.
8. Huebra, interview.
9. Vianna, *Uma tempestade*, 52.
10. Deposition of José Ibrahim in Caso, *A esquerda armada no Brasil*, 49–85.
11. Gorender, *Combate nas trevas*, 144.
12. José and Miranda, *Lamarca*.
13. Pedroso, *Sargento Darcy*, 51–53.
14. "Ele assalta em nome do terror," *Veja*, May 21, 1969, 37.
15. Gorender, *Combate nas trevas*, 145–47.
16. In *O fantasma da revolução brasileira*, Ridenti extracted statistics from the Supreme Military Court appeals and tallied 3,698 revolutionaries (p. 277), but this still underestimates the total.
17. Gorender, *Combate nas trevas*, 103–10; Magalhães, *Marighella*.
18. Espinosa, interview; Chachel, *Seu amigo esteve aqui*, 74–75; Gorender, *Combate nas trevas*, 147; Vianna, *Uma tempestade*, 52.
19. Carlos Franklin Paixão Araújo, "Depoimento," September 20, 1970, 50-Z-9-14840, AESP/DEOPS.
20. Daniel, *Meu corpo*, 21.
21. Daniel, *Passagem*, 49.
22. Gomes, *Palmares*.
23. Durão, interview.

24. Espinosa, interview.
25. Patarra, *Iara*, 79–115.
26. Chacel, *Seu amigo esteve aqui*, 74.
27. Dowbor, interview with Patarra.
28. Espinosa, interview with Patarra.
29. Rousseff, interview with Patarra.
30. Rodrigues, interview with Patarra; Rodrigues, interview.
31. Cardoso, *O cofre do Dr. Rui*.
32. Daniel, *Passagem*, 50–51.
33. Gorender, *Combate nas trevas*, 149; Espinosa, interview.
34. Jamil Rodriques (Ladislau Dowbor), "Os caminhos da vanguarda," October 1969, AERJ; Chagas, "A vanguarda popular revolucionária."
35. Espinosa, interview with Patarra.
36. Gorender, *Combate nas trevas*, 148.
37. Sirkis, *Os carbonários*, 170.
38. Espinosa, interview with Patarra.
39. Pedroso, *Sargento Darcy*, 120.
40. Chacel, *Seu amigo esteve aqui*, 86–94; Daniel, *Passagem*, 52; Vianna, *Uma tempestade*, 61–62.
41. Brito, interview no. 2; Osawa, interview; Vieira, *A busca*, 53.
42. Lisboa, interview.
43. Rousseff, interview.
44. Lafoz, interview.
45. Vieira, interview no. 1.
46. Cachapuz, interview.
47. Sirkis, *Os carbonários*, 191.
48. Sirkis, interview.
49. Cachapuz, interview.
50. Magalhães, *Marighella*.
51. Vianna, *Uma tempestade*, 64–65.
52. Vianna, *Uma tempestade*, 61.
53. Vianna, *Uma tempestade*, 61.
54. Cachapuz, interview.
55. Sirkis, *Os carbonários*, 194.
56. Polari, *Em busco do tesouro*, 134–35.

CHAPTER 8. TO THE COUNTRYSIDE! (1970)

Epigraph: Darcy Rodrigues was a sergeant who left the army with Carlos Lamarca in 1968 in order to join the VPR. Rodrigues, interview.

1. Rodrigues, interview; Daniel, interview with Patarra.
2. Chacel, *Seu amigo esteve aqui*, 70; Duarte, interview.
3. Nossa, *Mata!*; Portela and Genoino Neto, *Guerra de guerrilhas no Brasil*.
4. Pedroso, *Sargento Darcy*, 82.

5. Dowbor, interview with Ridenti.
6. Vianna, *Uma tempestade*, 62.
7. Daniel, *Passagem*, 53.
8. Rodrigues, interview.
9. Lungaretti, *Náufrago da Utopia*, 123.
10. Lungaretti, interview.
11. José and Miranda, *Lamarca*, 64.
12. Vianna, *Uma tempestade*, 62.
13. Daniel, *Passagem*, 53.
14. Rodrigues, interview with Patarra.
15. Pedroso, *Sargento Darcy*, 129.
16. Menkes, "Ribeiro," 332.
17. Daniel, *Meu corpo*, 29.
18. Comissão de Familiares, *Dossiê ditadura*, 155–59.
19. Souza, interview.
20. Comissão de Familiares, *Dossiê ditadura*, 141–42.
21. Lafoz, interview.
22. Pedroso, *Sargento Darcy*, 129.
23. Menkes, "Ribeiro," 332.
24. Patarra, *Iara*, 365–71.
25. Daniel, *Passagem*, 219.
26. Daniel, interview with Patarra.
27. Rodrigues, interview with Patarra.
28. Rodrigues, interview.
29. Rodrigues, interview.
30. Daniel, interview with Patarra.
31. Rodrigues, interview; Menkes, "Ribeiro," 334.
32. Daniel, *Meu corpo*, 31.
33. Daniel, *Passagem*, 28.
34. Rosa, *Devil to Pay in the Backlands*, 123–24.
35. Menkes, "Ribeiro," 335.
36. Rodrigues, interview; Daniel, interview with Patarra.
37. Daniel, *Passagem*, 220. Neither Darcy Rodrigues nor Ubiratan de Souza remembered the discussion about the crisis and potential split. Rodrigues, interview; Souza, interview.
38. Daniel, *Passagem*, 221.
39. Rodrigues, interview.
40. Sirkis, interview. Sirkis remembered it this way: "Two *viados* were in a deserted place, one fucking the other. Suddenly someone passes by, sees the two, and says, 'This is absurd, disgusting.' And so one says, 'Pull it out, Jorge.' And Jorge pulls it out. 'Sir, is this park yours?' 'No.' 'Sir, is this city yours?' 'No.' 'Sir, is Jorge yours?' 'No.' 'Then put it back in, Jorge.'"
41. Daniel and Míccolis, *Jacarés e lobisomens*, 29–45.
42. Rodrigues, interview.
43. Gorender, *Combate nas trevas*, 210; Okuchi, *O sequestro do diplomata*.

44. Vieira, *A busca*, 15.
45. Dowbor, interview.
46. Patarra, *Iara*, 377–80.
47. Rodrigues, interview.
48. Lungaretti, interview.
49. Pedroso, *Sargento Darcy*, 134.
50. Vianna, *Uma tempestade*, 81–96.
51. Rodrigues, interview.
52. Daniel, *Passagem*, 53–54.
53. Rodrigues, interview.
54. "Relatório da Operação Registro," July 24, 1970, BR-DRANBAB-V8-AC-ACE-RES-15755-70.SNI, AN.
55. Vigna, Onça, and Viana, "Napalm no Vale do Ribeira."
56. Gaspari, *A ditadura escancarada*, 196–220; "Relatório da Operação Registro."
57. Pedroso, *Sargento Darcy*, 137–47. Both were later released through negotiations following the abduction of the German ambassador in June 1970.
58. José and Miranda, *Lamarca*, 80.
59. Vanguarda Popular Revolucionária, "Manifesto da Vanguarda Popular Revolucionária (VPR) sobre a experiência guerrilheira no Vale do Ribeira," September 1970, AA.
60. Vanguarda Popular Revolucionária, "Manifesto da Vanguarda Popular Revolucionária."
61. Carlos Lamarca, "Entrevista de Carlos Lamarca aos jornais europeus," June 1970, AA.
62. Lamarca, "Entrevista."
63. Daniel, *Passagem*, 57.
64. Nossa, *Mata!*; Portela and Genoino Neto, *Guerra de guerrilhas no Brasil*.
65. Daniel, *Passagem*, 54–55.

CHAPTER 9. 40 + 70 = 110 (1970–1971)

Epigraph: Zenaide Machado de Oliveira was a member of the VPR in Rio. Oliveira, interview no. 1.

1. Cachapuz, interview.
2. Sirkis, interview.
3. Daniel, interview with Patarra.
4. In Cuba, Lamarca sent VPR militants a communication stating that Daniel was a rising intellectual leader. Jorge Nahas, interview.
5. Daniel, interview with Patarra.
6. Maria do Carmo Brito, "Declaração prestada," May 4, 1970, 50-Z-9-13852, AESP/DEOPS.
7. Vianna, *Uma tempestade*, 68; Sirkis, *Os carbonários*, 215; Patarra, *Iara*, 379.
8. Patarra, *Iara*, 383; Sirkis, *Os carbonários*, 242.
9. Oliveira, interview no. 1.

10. Zenaide Machado de Oliveira, conversation with author, May 14, 2009, notes.
11. Oliveira, interview no. 1.
12. Muniz, interview.
13. Daniel, *Passagem*, 127–28; Skidmore, *Politics of Military Rule*, 138–44; Gaspari, *A ditadura escancarada*, 207–21.
14. See Fico, *Reinventando o otimismo*; Schneider, *Brazilian Propaganda*; Skidmore, *Politics of Military Rule*, 107; Médici, *O jogo da verdade*, 10.
15. Romeu, interview with Patarra.
16. Daniel, *Passagem*, 101–3; Sirkis, *Os carbonários*, 239–76; Seixas, interview.
17. Gradel, interview.
18. Daniel, *Passagem*, 112–14.
19. Alves, *Torturas e torturados*.
20. Green, *We Cannot Remain Silent*.
21. Pezzuti, interview no. 2.
22. Amnesty International, *Report on Allegations of Torture in Brazil*; Wipfler, "Price of 'Progress' in Brazil"; Wipfler, "'Progress' in Brazil Revisited."
23. Daniel, *Passagem*, 39–40.
24. Daniel, *Passagem*, 57.
25. Muniz, interview.
26. Sirkis, interview.
27. Daniel, *Passagem*, 29.
28. Daniel, interview with Patarra.
29. Two examples of the positive images of the VPR that circulated internationally are given in Gramont, "How One Pleasant, Scholarly Young Man from Brazil"; and Truskier, "Politics of Violence."
30. "Cabo Anselmo," in *Dicionário Histórico Biográfico Brasileiro*, 258–59; Dos Santos, *Cabo Anselmo*, 144.
31. Borba, *Cabo Anselmo*, 20; Daniel, *Passagem*, 67; Ribeiro, *Por que eu traí*, 59–66.
32. Patarra, *Iara*, 426; Romeu, "Relatório Inês."
33. Oliveira, interview no. 2; Brito, interview no. 2; Osawa, interview.
34. Comissão de Familiares, *Dossiê ditadura*, 210–12.
35. Ribeiro, *Por que eu traí*, 59–66; Dos Santos, *Cabo Anselmo*, 163–67.
36. Dos Santos, *Cabo Anselmo*, 163–67.
37. Daniel, *Passagem*, 58.
38. Gorender, *Combate nas trevas*, 217–18.
39. ALN, MR-8, VPR, MRT, "Manifesto contra a farsa eleitoral ao povo brasileiro," 20-Z-160-301, October 1970, AESP/DEOPS.
40. Muniz, interview.
41. "O pesadelo dos votos brancos e nulos," 23; Alencastro, "O golpe de 1964 e o voto popular," 7.
42. Gorender, *Combate nas trevas*, 220.
43. Ângelo, interview no. 1.
44. Ângelo, interview no. 1; Daniel, interview with Patarra.
45. Barreira, "Espero o meu irmão para a ceia de Natal"; "Bucher"; "O terror desafiado."
46. Ângelo, interview no. 1.

47. Alfredo Buzaid, "Nota da Ministério da Justiça," December 21, 1971, RIO.TT.OMCP.AVU.79, AN.
48. Daniel, *Passagem*, 116; Romeu, interview with Patarra.
49. Daniel, *Passagem*, 117; Daniel, interview with Patarra; Sirkis, *Os carbonários*, 373.
50. Daniel, interview with Patarra; Brito and Osawa, interview with Patarra.
51. Alfredo Buzaid, "Nota da Ministério da Justiça," n.d., TT.O.MCP.AVU.79.UP 45, AN.
52. For a recent documentary featuring some of the political prisoners released as a result of the Swiss ambassador's abduction, see *Sesenta* (2013), directed by Emilia Silveira.
53. "O misterioso cativeiro de Bucher," *Manchete*, no. 980, January 30, 1971.
54. Sirkis, *Os carbonários*, 349.
55. Daniel, interview with Patarra.
56. Ângelo, interview no. 1.
57. Daniel, interview with Patarra.

CHAPTER 10. FALLING APART (1971)

Epigraph: Paulo Brandi de Barros Cachapuz was a supporter of the VPR. Cachapuz, interview.

1. Daniel, *Passagem*, 31.
2. Daniel, interview with Patarra.
3. Cachapuz, interview.
4. Daniel, interview with Patarra.
5. Daniel, *Passagem*, 64.
6. Alfredo Sirkis, "O caminho para a propaganda armada," December 28, 1970, AA.
7. Alfredo Sirkis, "Sequestro x propaganda armada," n.d., AA.
8. Carlos Lamarca, "Propaganda armada vinculada," n.d., AA.
9. Case 581, case no. 39,560 of the Superior Tribunal Military, BNM; Sirkis, *Os carbonários*, 403–10.
10. Sirkis, *Os carbonários*, 424–59.
11. Daniel, *Passagem*, 60–61.
12. Daniel, *Passagem*, 109.
13. Daniel, interview with Patarra.
14. Daniel, *Passagem*, 21.
15. Romeu, interview with Patarra; Zenaide Oliveira, interview no. 2.
16. Sirkis, *Os carbonários*, 447–51; Muniz, interview.
17. Zenaide Oliveira, interview no. 2.
18. Daniel, interview with Patarra.
19. Velloso, interview no. 1.
20. Romeu, interview with Patarra.
21. Commisão de Familiares, *Dossiê ditadura*, 235–36.
22. Velloso, interview no. 1.
23. Velloso, interview no. 1; Daniel, interview with Patarra; Romeu, interview with Patarra.

24. Cláudio (Carlos Lamarca), "Ao Comando da VPR," March 22, 1971, 30-Z-160-10043, p. 1, AESP/DEOPS.
25. Polari, *Em busca do tesouro*, 238–39.
26. Souza, interview.
27. Velloso, interview no. 1.
28. Daniel, *Passagem*, 64.
29. Romeu, "Relatório Inês," 4.
30. Sérgio Ferreira, interview; Daniel, interview with Patarra.
31. Ângelo, interview no. 1.
32. Comissão de Familiares, *Dossiê ditadura*, 251–52.
33. Polari, *Em busca do tesouro*.
34. Velloso, interview no. 1.
35. Comissão de Familiares, *Dossiê ditadura*, 248–49.
36. Ângelo, interview no. 1.
37. Velloso, interview no. 1.
38. Cachapuz, interview.
39. Cachapuz, interview.
40. Forin, "Confluências do teatro," 140–41; Veloso, *Verdade tropical*, 456.
41. Cachapuz, interview.
42. Comissão de Familiares, *Dossiê ditadura*, 265–66.
43. Velloso, interview no. 2.
44. Zenaide Machado de Oliveira, conversation with author, May 19, 2010, notes.
45. "Comunicados No. 1–3" [do Comando da VPR], Terrorismo, 12, fl. 85–88, AERJ.
46. Oliveira, interview no. 2. Tereza Ângelo concurred with this assessment. Ângelo, interview no. 1.
47. Martins Filho, "Segredos de estado," chapters 12 and 13.
48. Velloso, interview no. 1.
49. Daniel, letter to Lúcia Velloso, June 7, 1975, AA.
50. Daniel, letter to Velloso, June 7, 1975.
51. Iava Iavelberg's family and human rights activists believe that the police killed her. See the documentary *Em busca de Iara*, written and produced by her niece, Mariana Pamplona.
52. Fiúza, interview; Sousa, interview.
53. Daniel, *Meu corpo*, 22–23.
54. Daniel, *Meu corpo*, 232.
55. Daniel, letter to Velloso, June 7, 1975.
56. Daniel, letter to Velloso, June 7, 1975.

CHAPTER 11. CLÁUDIO (1972–1974)

Epigraph: Maria Elisalva Oliveira Joué was Cláudio Mesquita's second wife. Joué, interview.

1. *Homens*; Mesquita, interview no. 2.
2. *Homens*.

3. *Homens.*
4. *Homens*; Joué, interview; Mesquita, interview no. 1.
5. Joué, interview.
6. *Homens.*
7. Mesquita, interview no. 1.
8. *Homens.*
9. Joué, interview.
10. Joué, interview.
11. Joué, interview.
12. Joué, interview.
13. Daniel, *Meu corpo*, 19.
14. Daniel, *Meu corpo*, 19.
15. Daniel, *Passagem*, 36.
16. Daniel, letter to Lúcia Velloso, June 7, 1975, AA.
17. Daniel, letter to Velloso, June 7, 1975.
18. Daniel, *Meu corpo*, 22.
19. Daniel, *Meu corpo*, 18.
20. Daniel, *Meu corpo*, 18.
21. Daniel, *Passagem*, 97.
22. Joué, interview.
23. Maria José Nahas, interview.
24. Pereira, interview no. 2.
25. Brito, interview no. 1.
26. Sirkis, interview.
27. Velloso, interview no. 2.
28. Dunn, "*Desbunde* and Its Discontents."
29. Daniel, *Passagem*, 34.
30. Comissão de Familiares, *Dossiê ditadura*, 235–36; Daniel, letter to Velloso, June 7, 1975.
31. Daniel, letter to Velloso, June 7, 1975.
32. Ministério do Exército, I Exército, DOI no. 94/73, interrogation of Antonio de Morais Mesplé, AERJ.
33. Joué, interview.
34. Daniel, *Passagem*, 41.
35. Daniel, *Passagem*, 118.
36. Pereira, interview no. 1; Campos, interview; Maria José Nahas, interview.
37. Daniel, *Passagem*, 41; Prado and Earp, "O 'milagre' brasileiro."
38. Vianna, *Uma tempestade*, 117.
39. Vianna, *Uma tempestade*, 118.
40. Vianna, *Uma tempestade*, 125–27.
41. Vianna, *Uma tempestade*, 119–23; Daniel, *Passagem*, 66–68; Daniel, "Anselmo."
42. Romeu, "Relatório Inês."
43. Romeu, "Relatório Inês."
44. Silva, interview with Daniel, 10–11.
45. Vianna, *Uma tempestade*, 120–22.
46. Silva, interview with Daniel, 10–11.

47. Mota, *Soledad no Recife*.
48. Comissão de Familiares, *Dossiê ditadura*, 410–18.
49. Case no. 75, pp. 19–24, BNM.
50. Joué, interview; case no. 75, 2083, BNM.
51. Joué, interview.
52. Mesquita, interview no. 1.
53. Joué, interview; Mesquita, interview no. 1.
54. Daniel, letter to Velloso, June 7, 1975.
55. Joué, interview.
56. Daniel, letter to Velloso, June 7, 1975.
57. Daniel, *Passagem*, 129; Daniel, letter to Velloso, June 7, 1975.
58. Geny Carvalho, interview no. 1; Hamilton Carvalho, interview no. 1; Hamilton Carvalho, interview no. 3.
59. Daniel, letter to Velloso, June 7, 1975.
60. Caldas, interview.
61. Caldas, interview.
62. Caldas, interview.
63. Hamilton Carvalho, interview no. 2; Geny Carvalho, interview no. 3.
64. Hamilton Carvalho, interview no. 2; Geny Carvalho, interview no. 3.
65. Geny Carvalho, interview no. 3.
66. Caldas, interview.
67. Geny Carvalho, interview no. 3.
68. Von der Weid, interview; Rollemberg, *Exílio*, 178–79.
69. Vianna, *Uma tempestade*, 129–37.
70. Sousa, interview.
71. Pezzuti, interview no. 2.
72. Lenice Carvalho, interview.
73. Daniel, *Passagem*, 143.

CHAPTER 12. RED CARNATIONS (1974–1975)

Epigraph: Daniel, *Passagem*, 144.
1. Cases 42, 47, 75, and 158, BNM.
2. Teles, *Mortos e desaparecidos políticos*.
3. Couto, *História indiscreta da ditadura*; Kuczinski, *Abertura*.
4. Skidmore, *Politics of Military Rule*, 178–80; Street, "Coping with Energy Shocks."
5. Power and Roberts, "Compulsory Voting."
6. Kinzo, *Oposição e autoritarismo*, 153–63.
7. Jordão, *Dossiê Herzog*.
8. Pomar, *Massacre na Lapa*.
9. Daniel, letter to Lúcia Velloso, June 7, 1975, AA.
10. Daniel, *Passagem*, 143–44.
11. Tejo, interview. Other quotations are from the same interview.
12. Freire, "Ecos da estação Lisboa."

13. Chilcote, *Portuguese Revolution*; Ferreira and Marshall, *Portugal's Revolution*; Hammond, *Building Popular Power*, Maxwell, *Making of Portuguese Democracy*.
14. Tejo, interview.
15. Brito, interview no. 2.
16. Daniel, *Passagem*, 144.
17. Lúcia Velloso, letter to Daniel, June 30, 1975, AA.
18. Daniel, letter to Velloso, June 7, 1975.
19. Brito, interview no. 2; Osawa, interview; Sirkis, interview; Vieira, interview no. 1.
20. Minc, interview.
21. Caldas, interview.
22. Daniel, *Meu corpo*, 242–43.
23. Brito, interview no. 2; Osawa, interview.
24. Daniel, *Passagem*, 74.
25. Daniel, letter to Lúcia Velloso, September 7, 1975, AA.
26. Green, "Who Is the Macho Who Wants to Kill Me?," 450–51.
27. Minc, interview.
28. Tejo, interview.
29. Daniel, letter to Velloso, September 7, 1975.
30. Fiadeiro, interview with Ramalho.
31. Daniel, letter to Velloso, June 7, 1975.
32. Fiadeiro, interview with Ramalho.
33. "Herbert Eustáquio de Carvalho," Ministério de Assuntos Internos, ACL.MAI GM SE 007.12 CX 0544, MAI.
34. Daniel, *Passagem*, 151–52.
35. Daniel, *Passagem*, 148.
36. [Daniel], "O tempo que eu passei no útero da minha mãe."
37. [Daniel], "Aborto clandestine é crime."
38. [Daniel], "Ausência de dor não é saúde."
39. [Daniel], "O trabalho do descanço"; "Bilheteira no subsolo"; "Fazer deporte"; "Racismo."
40. [Daniel], "30 dias de mulheres pelo mundo."
41. [Daniel], "Conferência de México."
42. [Daniel], "Marilyn Monroe."
43. Castillo and Rechy, "Interview with John Rechy," 122; Dyer, *Heavenly Bodies*.
44. See, for example, Mulvey, "Visual Pleasure and Narrative Cinema."
45. Daniel, letter to Velloso, June 7, 1975.
46. Fiadeiro, interview with Ramalho.
47. Daniel, letter to Lúcia Velloso, December 28, 1975.
48. Daniel, letter to Velloso, September 7, 1975.
49. Daniel, letter to Velloso, December 28, 1975.
50. Daniel, letter to Velloso, December 28, 1975.
51. Brito, interview no. 2; Osawa, interview.
52. Advisa, interview.
53. Daniel, *Passagem*, 145.
54. Tejo, interview.

55. Vianna, *Uma tempestade*, 149.
56. Daniel, *Meu corpo*, 248.
57. Daniel, *Passagem*, 148–49.

CHAPTER 13. MARGINALIA (1976–1981)

Epigraph: Von der Weid was the president of the National Union of Students and one of the seventy people released after the abduction of the Swiss ambassador. Von der Weid, interview. Other quotations of Von der Weid are from the same interview.

1. Daniel, *Passagem*, 151–53.
2. Daniel, *Passagem*, 147.
3. Tejo, interview. Other quotations are from the same interview.
4. Mesquita, interview no. 2.
5. Daniel, *Meu corpo*, 249.
6. Sabalis, interview; Daniel, *Passagem*, 155.
7. Daniel, *Passagem*, 161.
8. Daniel, *Passagem*, 153.
9. Daniel, *Passagem*, 154.
10. Daniel, *Passagem*, 155.
11. Girard, *Le movement homosexuel en France*, 81–111.
12. Girard, *Le movement homosexuel en France*, 21.
13. D'Emilio, *Sexual Politics, Sexual Communities*; Chauncey, *Gay New York*; Green, *Beyond Carnival*.
14. Daniel, *Passagem*, 178.
15. Gunther, *Elastic Closet*, 77; Girard, *Le movement homosexuel en France*, 127–48.
16. Sabalis, interview.
17. Martel, *Pink and the Black*, 13.
18. Hocquenghem, *Homosexual Desire*, 55.
19. Daniel, *Passagem*, 173.
20. Daniel, *Passagem*, 173.
21. Daniel, *Passagem*, 173.
22. Daniel, *Passagem*, 173.
23. Le Bitoux, "Construction of a Political and Media Presence," 256.
24. Le Bitoux, "Construction of a Political and Media Presence," 256.
25. Daniel, *Passagem*, 145.
26. Gliochi, interview.
27. Silva, *A luta pela anistia*.
28. Kuczinski, *Jornalistas e revolucionários*.
29. Green, "Liberalization on Trial."
30. Alvarez, *Engendering Democracy*; Hanchard and Ribeiro, *Orfeu e o poder*.
31. Editors, "Saindo do Gueto," 2.
32. Editors, "Saindo do Gueto," 2.

33. Green, "Emergence of the Brazilian Gay Liberation Movement"; MacRae, "Homosexual Identities in Transitional Brazilian Politics"; Trevisan, *Perverts in Paradise*, 133–154; Simões and Facchini, *Na trilha do arco-íris*; and Green, "O Grupo SOMOS, a esquerda e a resistência à ditadura."
34. Dantas, "Negros, mulheres, homossexuais e índios nos debates da USP," 9.
35. Dantas, "Negros, mulheres, homossexuais e índios nos debates da USP," 9.
36. Von der Weid, interview.
37. Rollemberg, *Exílio*, chapter 7.
38. Rollemberg, *Exílio*, 208.
39. Glória Ferreira quoted in Rollemberg, *Exílio*, 208.
40. Von der Weid, interview.
41. Glória Ferreira, interview.
42. Daniel, *Passagem*, 214.
43. Von der Weid, interview.
44. Daniel, letter to Lúcia Velloso, May 28, 1979, AA.
45. Daniel, "Homossexual: Defesa dos interesses?"
46. Daniel, letter to Velloso, May 28, 1979.
47. Glória Ferreira, interview. Other quotes are from the same interview.
48. Daniel, *Passagem*, 213.
49. Rollemberg, *Exílio*, 223–35.
50. Interview with Glória Ferreira, quoted in Rollemberg, *Exílio*, 225.
51. Daniel, *Passagem*, 217.
52. Daniel, *Passagem*, 218.
53. Grossi, interview.
54. Daniel, "Homossexual: Defesa dos interesses?"
55. Daniel, letter to Velloso, May 28, 1979.
56. Daniel, "Homossexual: Defesa dos interesses?," 18.
57. Daniel, "Homossexual: Defesa dos interesses?," 21.
58. Daniel, "Homossexual: Defesa dos interesses?," 21.
59. Green, "Who Is the Macho Who Wants to Kill Me?"; Green and Quinalha, *Ditadura e Homossexualidades*.
60. Lúcia Velloso, letter to Daniel, June 9, 1979, AA.
61. Presidência da República, Casa Civil, Subchefia para Assuntos Jurídicos, Lei no. 6.683, August 28, 1979, https://www.planalto.gov.br/ccivil_03/leis/l6683.htm.
62. Telles, "As disputas pela interpretação da lei de anistia de 1979."

CHAPTER 14. RETURNING TO RIO (1981–1982)

Epigraph: "Exilado chega de Paris e diz que não é o ultimo," *O Estado de São Paulo* (October 10, 1981).
1. Apelação ao Supremo Tribunal Militar, no. 39,544, BNM.
2. Daniel, "O que é isso, companheiros?," 10.
3. Daniel, "O que é isso, companheiros?," 10.

4. Daniel, *Passagem*, 229.
5. Daniel, *Passagem*.
6. Daniel, letter to Ana Maria Muller, March 4, 1980, AA.
7. Daniel, letter to Muller.
8. Daniel, *Passagem*, 146.
9. Daniel, letter to Lúcia Velloso, March 21, 1980, AA.
10. Daniel, *Meu corpo*, 285.
11. Daniel, letter to his family, April 24, 1981, AA.
12. Calvacanti, "Ele vive de bicos."
13. Schpun, "Le regard décalé de l'exilé sur le Brésil post-amnistie."
14. Daniel, letter to the editor of *Veja*.
15. Daniel, *Meu corpo*, 346.
16. Daniel, letter to Geny Brunelli de Carvalho, August 31, 1981, AA.
17. Daniel, *Meu corpo*, 346.
18. "Herbert Eustáquio de Carvalho," DEOPS Ficha, p. 3, AESP/DEOPS; "Comissão Brasileira de Anistia-Paris," circular no. 1, F 633 006 CBA Paris, BDIC.
19. Daniel, *Meu corpo*, 351.
20. "Exilado volta após sete anos," *Jornal do Brasil*, October 10, 1981; "A emoção no retorno do penúltimo exilado," *O Estado de São Paulo*, October 10, 1981.
21. See Green, "Who Is the Macho Who Wants to Kill Me?"
22. Gabeira, *Entradas e bandeiras*, 99; Gabeira, "Fernando Gabeira," 5–8; Coelho, *Os movimentos libertários em questão*; Da Silva, *Os escritores da guerrilha urbana*; Pellegrini, *Gavetas vazias*.
23. Daniel, *Meu corpo*, 352.
24. Daniel, *Meu corpo*, 285.
25. Terto, interview no. 1.
26. Sirkis, *Os carbonários*. Alex Polari's *Em busco do tesouro* alternates between the story of his revolutionary career and subsequent prison ordeals. It had a similar limited reception.
27. Daniel, *Passagem*, 22.
28. Daniel, *Passagem*, 243.
29. Nogueira, "Herbert Daniel pede passagem pelo sonho," 6.
30. "Gente."
31. Daniel, *Meu corpo*, 357.
32. Daniel, *Meu corpo*, 357.
33. Barbosa, interview; Freitas, interview.
34. Maciel, interview. Other quotes are from the same interview.
35. Maciel, *Com licença*.
36. Keck, *Workers' Party and Democratization in Brazil*.
37. Daniel, *Meu corpo*, 3.
38. Vieira, interview no. 1.
39. Nogueira, interview.
40. "Qualquer maneira de amor vale a pena," 1986, AA.
41. Kauchakje, "Solidariedade política e constituição de sujeitos."
42. Vieira, interview no. 2; Nogueira, interview.

CHAPTER 15. WORDS, WORDS, WORDS (1983–1985)

Epigraph: Montenegro, interview. Cristina Montenegro is an actor who worked with Daniel in Rio de Janeiro in the early 1980s.

1. Von Mettenheim, *Brazilian Voter*, 108–13.
2. Daniel, "Confissões de um eleitor semi-virgem"; Daniel, "Computa que partiu"; Daniel, "1983: Aquela que virá."
3. Daniel, "As vésperas de AI-5exo"; Daniel, "Os brotos invisíveis."
4. Daniel, *A fêmea sintética*, 1983.
5. Rousseff, interview.
6. Daniel, "Erasmus e a lenda do pequeno polegar."
7. Míccolis, interview. Other quotes are from the same interview.
8. Míccolis and Daniel, *Jacarés e lobisomens*.
9. Míccolis and Daniel, *Jacarés e lobisomens*, 10.
10. Míccolis and Daniel, *Jacarés e lobisomens*, 45.
11. Míccolis and Daniel, *Jacarés e lobisomens*, 48.
12. Green, "More Love and More Desire."
13. Green, "Desire and Militancy."
14. Míccolis and Daniel, *Jacarés e lobisomens*, 67.
15. "Pesquisa determina entre homossexuais quem tem 'câncer gay,'" *Jornal do Brasil*, June 9, 1983.
16. Míccolis and Daniel, *Jacarés e lobisomens*, 126.
17. Daniel, "O gueto desmistificado."
18. These ideas are further developed in a book review of Délcio M. de Lima's *Os homoeróticos* in *O Pasquim*, November 30, 1985; and Daniel, "Do tabu a tabuado."
19. Daniel, "O gueto desmistificado," 84.
20. Daniel, "O gueto desmistificado," 84.
21. Daniel, "O gueto desmistificado," 84.
22. Green, "Desire and Militancy."
23. Daniel, "O gueto desmistificado," 84.
24. Ribeiro, "A confissão do cabo"; Ribeiro, *Por que eu traí*.
25. The declassification of DEOPS archives has revealed extensive infiltration of left-wing groups by activists who have been "turned," beginning in the 1930s. While Anselmo's deception may have had particularly disastrous consequences, it was part of a larger pattern.
26. Delgado, "Diretas-Já"; Leonelli and Oliveira, *Diretas já*.
27. Silva, "Cabo Anselmo," 4.
28. Pezzuti, interview with Daniel, in Daniel, "Anselmo," 11.
29. Pezzuti, interview with Daniel, in Daniel, "Anselmo," 11.
30. In 1981, Marco Aurélio Borba wrote a short book entitled *Cabo Anselmo: A luta armada ferida por dentro*, published without footnotes or sources, alleging Anselmo had a long history of homosexual activities in the Navy, in the Mexican embassy where he sought political asylum in 1964, and in Cuba. See pages 22, 24, 59, 68.
31. Daniel, "Anselmo," 8.
32. Daniel, "Anselmo," 8.

33. Daniel, "Anselmo," 9.
34. Pezzuti, interview with Daniel, in Daniel, "Anselmo," 11.
35. Daniel, *Meu corpo*, 121.
36. Daniel, *Meu corpo*, 126.
37. Daniel, *Meu corpo*, 126–27.
38. Daniel, *Meu corpo*, 235–36.
39. Daniel, *Meu corpo*, 196.
40. Daniel, *Meu corpo*, 196–97.
41. Daniel, *Meu corpo*, 198.
42. Daniel, *As três moças do sabonete*.
43. Albuquerque, *Tentative Transgressions*, 35.
44. Martins, interview. Other quotes are from the same interview.
45. Daniel became the godfather of Vanja Freitas and Gustavo Barbosa's firstborn child, Lourenço, and took his role very seriously. Freitas, interview.
46. Martins, interview.
47. Albuquerque, *Tentative Transgressions*, 109–10.
48. Montenegro, interview; "Proposta detalhada da montagem," AA.
49. "O mito da cegonha, numa peça infantil," *O Globo*, May 28, 1985, 10.
50. Skidmore, *Politics of Military Rule*, 250–53.

CHAPTER 16. THE POLITICS OF PLEASURE (1986–1988)

Epigraph: Daniel, quoted in 1986 campaign material, AA.
1. Vieira, interview no. 2.
2. Pinho, interview.
3. Vieira, interview no. 2.
4. Alfredo Sirkis, quoted in D'Angelo, "Verdes desde o início."
5. Viola, "O movimento ecológico no Brasil."
6. Hochstetler and Keck, *Greening Brazil*, 83–89.
7. Rabóczkay, *Repensando o Partido Verde Brasileiro*, 52–54; Gabeira, "A idéia do Partido Verde no Brasil."
8. Gabeira, "A idéia do Partido Verde no Brasil," 154.
9. Maciel, interview.
10. Rabóczkay, *Repensando o Partido Verde Brasileiro*, 54.
11. Toledo, interview; Green, "Emergence of the Brazilian Gay Liberation Movement."
12. Belloq, interview; Terto, interview no. 1; Laurindo-Teodorescu and Teixeira, *Histórias da AIDS no Brasil*, vol. 2, 31–38.
13. MacRae, *A construção da igualdade*.
14. João Antônio Mascarenhas, "Carta circular," August 29, 1986, TRC/AEL; Mascarenhas, "Situation of Homosexuals in Brazil." n.d., TRC/AEL.
15. Green, *Beyond Carnival*, chapter 4.
16. Ramires, interview.
17. Howe, "João Antônio Mascarenhas," 294–96.

18. João Antônio Mascarenhas, "Letter to Gregory Siemenson," research coordinator for Amnesty International, London, December 3, 1986, TRC/AEL.
19. Mascarenhas, interview.
20. Cláudio Alves de Mesquita, letter to *Le Gai Pied*, July 29, 1986, TRC/AEL.
21. Grupo Gay da Bahia, "Nosso candidato Herbert Daniel," August 20, 1986, TRC/AEL.
22. Fernando Gabeira, letter to Triângulo Rosa, October 3, 1986, TRC/AEL.
23. Mascarenhas, "Os dois lados do Beijo," 1.
24. Mascarenhas, "Os dois lados do Beijo," 1.
25. Herbert Daniel, "Quase plataforma Herbert Daniel," *Deixa aflorar* (1986), 7, AA.
26. Green, "O Grupo Somos."
27. "Abertura ainda não chegou ao povo," *Folha de São Paulo*, September 28, 1981; Green, "Desire and Militancy."
28. Herbert Daniel, "Qualquer forma de amor vale a pena" (1986), AA.
29. Ramos, interview.
30. Campos, interview.
31. Maciel, interview; Montenegro, interview; Míccolis, interview.
32. Ramires, interview.
33. Ramires, interview. Other quotations are from the same interview.
34. Ramires, interview.
35. Gliochi, interview.
36. Ramires, interview.
37. Campos, interview.
38. Campos, interview.
39. Ramires, interview; Campos, interview.
40. *Recuperação da memória sonora e visual do Partido Verde*.
41. Carlos Minc received 24,641 votes. Minc, interview.
42. Mascarenhas, interview.
43. Mascarenhas, *A tríple conexão*; Câmara, *Cidadania e orientação sexual*.
44. Gabeira, interview.
45. Ramos, interview.
46. Soon after the electoral campaign, Daniel wrote a feature article about AIDS. Daniel, "Eu mudei os meus hábitos sexuais."
47. Laurindo-Teodorescu and Teixeira, *Histórias da AIDS no Brasil*, vol. 1, 42, 48.
48. Paulo Teixeira, interview; Nunn, *Politics and History of AIDS Treatment in Brazil*, 34–37.
49. Laurindo-Teodorescu and Teixeira, *Histórias da AIDS no Brasil*, vol. 2, 33–34, 41–42.
50. Mascarenhas, interview; Terto, interview no. 1; Laurindo-Teodorescu and Teixeira, *Histórias da AIDS no Brasil*, vol. 2, 60–61.
51. Fico, *Ibase*; Souza and Sader, *No fio da navalha*.
52. Laurindo-Teodorescu and Teixeira, *Histórias da AIDS no Brasil*, vol. 2, 65–67.
53. Laurindo-Teodorescu and Teixeira, *Histórias da AIDS no Brasil*, vol. 2, 67–68; Parker and Terto, *Solidariedade*, 13–20; Ramos, interview.
54. Ramos, interview.
55. [Daniel], "Pra início do vôo."

56. [Daniel], "Quem semeia pânico, colhe epidemia."
57. [Daniel], "Onze críticas a uma campanha desgovernada."
58. [Daniel], "E como fica o Pinto Fernandes."
59. [Daniel], "E como fica o Pinto Fernandes."
60. [Daniel], "Sangue novo."
61. *Boletim* ABIA, no. 2 (April 1988): 17–18.

CHAPTER 17. FORTY SECONDS (1989–1992)

Epigraph: Daniel. "Quarenta segundas de AIDS." *Boletim* ABIA 6 (February 1989): 4.

1. Daniel, Quarenta segundas de AIDS." *Boletim* ABIA 6 (February 1989): 4.
2. *Viva a vida*.
3. Dias, "A trajetória soropositiva de Herbert Daniel."
4. Daniel, "Quarenta segundas de AIDS," 4; Daniel, "Noite da ronda da morte."
5. Daniel, "Quarenta segundas de AIDS," 4.
6. Daniel, "Notícias de outro mundo," 4.
7. Daniel, "Notícias de outro mundo," 4.
8. Laurindo-Teodorescu and Teixeira, *Histórias da AIDS no Brasil*, vol. 2, 78n65.
9. Daniel, *Vida antes da morte*.
10. The term *doente com AIDS* (sick with AIDS) was soon replaced by "living with AIDS."
11. Villard, interview.
12. Terto, interview no. 2.
13. Gaspar, quoted in Laurindo-Teodorescu and Teixeira, *Histórias da AIDS no Brasil*, vol. 2, 50.
14. Castilho, Chequer, and Struchiner, "A Epidemiologia da AIDS no Brasil," 60–63.
15. "Projecto Pela VIDDA," n.d., 1, ABIA.
16. Braiterman, "Fighting AIDS in Brazil."
17. "Projecto Pela VIDDA," n.d., 5.
18. "Projecto Pela VIDDA," n.d., 4.
19. "Projecto Pela VIDDA," n.d., 4.
20. "Projecto Pela VIDDA," n.d., 1.
21. Villard, interview.
22. [Daniel], "Solidariedade em Rede," 1.
23. [Daniel], "Solidariedade em Rede," 2.
24. Terto, interview no. 2.
25. Parker and Terto, *Solidariedade*, 26–27.
26. V. International AIDS Conference, *Program*, 253, AA.
27. *Boletim* ABIA, no. 8 (August 1989): 25.
28. Goldberg, "When PWAs First Sat at the High Table."
29. Hale, "After Montreal," 144–46; Kallings and McClur, *20 Years of the International AIDS Society*, 16.
30. Leite, quoted in Laurindo-Teodorescu and Teixeira, *Histórias da AIDS no Brasil*, vol. 2, 77.
31. Solano Vianna, "AIDS no Brasil," 12.

32. Bastos, *Global Responses to* AIDS, 68–95; Parker and Terto, *Solidariedade*, 27.
33. Galvão, "AIDS e ativismo."
34. Luiz Mott, letter to the president of ABIA, September 15, 1989, ABIA.
35. Parker and Terto, *Solidariedade*, 27.
36. Parker, "Public Policy, Political Activism, and AIDS."
37. Bastos, *Global Responses to* AIDS, 80–83.
38. Laurindo-Teodorescu and Teixeira, *Histórias da* AIDS *no Brasil*, vol. 2, 126.
39. Mott, letter to the president of ABIA.
40. [Daniel], "A vida e o direito à vida," 3.
41. Mott, email correspondence with author, July 16, 2013, AA.
42. Mott, *Boletim do Grupo Gay da Bahia*, 426.
43. Daniel, "O primeiro AZT a gente nunca esquece"; Accioli, "Betinho e Herbert Daniel"; Daniel, "We Are All People Living with AIDS."
44. [Daniel], "Grupo Pela VIDDA."
45. Veriano Terto, conversation with author, June 17, 2016, notes.
46. Parker and Terto, *Solidariedade*, 30; Minc, interview.
47. See Miguez, "Escrito com AIDS lidera combate à doença."
48. Monica Teixeira, interview no. 1.
49. Monica Teixeira, interview no. 2.
50. *Viva a vida*.
51. Villard, interview.
52. Maciel, interview.
53. Pezzuti, interview no. 2.
54. Pezzuti, interview no. 2.
55. Maciel, interview.
56. Daniel, *Alegres e irresponsáveis abacaxis americanos*.
57. Martins, "AIDS, vida e morte."
58. Salgueiro, interview.
59. The comic book was Mesquita, *Que qui é esta tal de* AIDS; the material for sailors was Mesquita, *Qual é o porto seguro contra* AIDS?
60. Gabeira, interview.
61. *Herbert Daniel*.
62. Reis, "Tenho AIDS, mas continuo vivo," 11.
63. Daniel, "Letters to the Editor: AIDS in Cuba"; Daniel, "Carta aberta a Fidel Castro."
64. Daniel, letter to Jorge A. Bolaños Suárez, August 21, 1989, ABIA.
65. Daniel, "Carta aberta a Fidel Castro."
66. Araújo and Echeverria, *Cazuza*.
67. "A luta em público contra a AIDS."
68. *Boletim* ABIA, no. 11 (July 1990): 34.
69. "Coalizão Global de Políticas Contra a AIDS," *Boletim* ABIA, no. 15 (December 1991): 4-5.
70. Ortells, "Brazil."
71. Daniel, "Trégua para tristes tigres sem trigo"; Daniel, "AZT"; Daniel, "Viviendo e aprendendo com AIDS."
72. Silva, "O governo não cumpre o seu papel."

73. Terto, quoted in Laurindo-Teodorescu and Teixeira, *Histórias da* AIDS *no Brasil*, vol. 1, 172.
74. Fry, interview.
75. Parker, interview.
76. Salgueiro, interview.
77. Salgueiro, interview.
78. Rousseff, interview.
79. Parker, interview.
80. Salgueiro, interview.
81. Monica Teixeira, interview no. 2.
82. Geny Carvalho, interview no. 2.
83. Pezzuti, interview no. 2.
84. Geny Carvalho, interview no. 2.

EPILOGUE. REMNANTS

   Epigraph: Mesquita, statement made at Herbert Daniel's funeral, AA.
1. Salgueiro, interview.
2. Mesquita, interview no. 1.
3. Monica Teixeira, interview no. 2.
4. Silva, "O governo não cumpre o seu papel," 5.
5. In Daniel and Parker, AIDS *in Another World?*, 154–57.
6. Daniel and Parker, AIDS *in Another World?*, 154.
7. Mesquita, "Legado."
8. Terto, interview no. 2.
9. Mann, Tarantola, and Netter, AIDS *in the World*.
10. Cláudio Mesquita, "Herbert Eustáquio de Carvalho."
11. *Herbert Daniel*.
12. Geny Carvalho, interview no. 1.

BIBLIOGRAPHY

ARTICLES BY HERBERT DANIEL IN CHRONOLOGICAL ORDER

"O tempo que eu passei no útero da minha mãe." *Modas e Bordados* 3298 (April 30, 1975): 7–10.
"Ausência de dor não é saúde." *Modas e Bordado* 3300 (May 14, 1975): 9–10.
"Racismo: Doença social, racista: Doente mental." *Modas e Bordados* 3302 (May 28, 1975): 11–12.
"O trabalho do descanço." *Modas e Bordados* 3303 (June 4, 1975): 9–11.
"Aborto clandestine é crime." *Modas e Bordados* 3306 (June 25, 1975): 10–11.
"Marilyn Monroe." *Modas e Bordados* 3311 (July 30, 1975): 15–16.
"30 dias de mulheres pelo mundo." *Modas e Bordados* 3311 (July 30, 1975): 46–47.
"Conferência de México." *Modas e Bordados* 3315 (August 27, 1975): 46–47.
"Bilheteira no subsolo." *Modas e Bordados* 3319 (September 24, 1975): 42–43.
"Fazer deporte." *Modas e Bordados* 3320 (October 1, 1975): 13–16.
"Homossexual: Defesa dos interesses?" *Notas Marginais* 3 (1979). Reprinted in *Niterói* 8, no. 2 (1st semester 2008): 15–21.
"O que é isso, companheiros?" *Lampião da Esquina* 2, no. 22 (March 1980): 10.
Letter to the editor of *Veja*, dated July 7, 1981. *O Pasquim* 632 (August 6, 1981): 25.
"As vésperas de AI-5exo." *Luta & Prazer* (Rio de Janeiro) 8 (April/May 1982): 2.
"Os brotos invisíveis." *Luta & Prazer* (Rio de Janeiro) 12 (September 1982): 6–7.
"Confissões de um eleitor semi-virgem." *Luta & Prazer* (Rio de Janeiro) 13 (October 1982): 7.
"Computa que partiu." *Luta & Prazer* (Rio de Janeiro) 15 (December 1982): 3–4.
"1983: Aquela que virá." *Luta & Prazer* (Rio de Janeiro) 16 (January 1983): 6.
"Anselmo: De cabo a rabo." *O Pasquim* 14, no. 774 (April 26, 1984): 8–11.
"Erasmus e a lenda do pequeno polegar." *O Pasquim* 15, no. 783 (July 5, 1984): 7.
"Do tabu a tabuado." *O Pasquim* 15, no. 852 (November 24, 1985).
"*Os homoeróticos* por Délcio M. de Lima." *O Pasquim* 16, no. 853 (November 30, 1985).
"Eu mudei os meus hábitos sexuais." *Jornal do Brasil* (January 11, 1987): section B-7.

"Pra início do vôo." *Boletim ABIA* [Associação Brasileira Interdisciplinar de AIDS] 1 (January 1988): 1.

"Quem semeia pânico, colhe epidemia." *Boletim ABIA* 2 (April 1988): 1.

"Onze críticas a uma campanha desgovernada." *Boletim ABIA* 2 (April 1988): 3–5.

"Sangue novo." *Boletim ABIA* 4 (September 1988): 1–2.

"E como fica o Pinto Fernandes." *Boletim ABIA* 5 (November 1988): 1.

"Quarenta segundas de AIDS." *Boletim ABIA* 6 (February 1989): 4.

"Notícias de outro mundo." *Jornal do Brasil* (March 5, 1989): section B-1: 4–5.

"Solidariedade em Rede." *Boletim ABIA* 7 (June 1989): 1–2.

"Grupo Pela VIDDA—Uma experiência." *Boletim ABIA* 8 (August 1989): 6–7.

"Carta aberta a Fidel Castro." *Boletim ABIA* 8 (August 1989): 29–30.

"Letters to the Editor: AIDS in Cuba." *New York Review of Books* (October 6, 1989): 68.

"A vida e o direito à vida." *Boletim ABIA* 11 (July 1990): 3.

"O primeiro AZT a gente nunca esquece." *Jornal do Brasil* (September 30, 1990): 8–9.

"Trégua para tristes tigres sem trigo." *Jornal do Brasil* (February 25, 1991): 11.

"AZT: O preço da omissão." *Última Hora* (Rio de Janeiro) (March 2, 1991).

"Vivendo e aprendendo com AIDS." *Universidade Aberta do Nordeste* (Fortaleza) 1 (September 27, 1991): 7.

"We Are All People Living with AIDS: Myths and Realities of AIDS in Brazil." *International Journal of Health Services* 21, no. 3 (1991): 539–51.

"Noite da ronda da morte." *O Globo* (Rio de Janeiro) (April 8, 1992): section 2, p. 1.

"The Soul of a Citizen." In *AIDS in Another World? Sexuality, Politics, and AIDS in Brazil*, edited by Herbert Daniel and Richard Parker, 154–57. London: Falmer Press, 1993.

BOOKS AND PLAYS BY HERBERT EUSTÁQUIO DE CARVALHO (HERBERT DANIEL) IN CHRONOLOGICAL ORDER

Passagem para o próximo sonho: Um possível romance autocrítico. Rio de Janeiro: Codecri, 1982.

A fêmea sintética. Rio de Janeiro: Codecri, 1983.

Jacarés e lobisomens: Dois ensaios sobe a homossexualidade. With Leila Míccolis. Rio de Janeiro: Achiamé, 1983. *As três moças do sabonete: Uma apologia sobre os anos Médici*. Rio de Janeiro: Rocco, 1984.

Meu corpo daria um romance. Rio de Janeiro: Rocco, 1984.

Alegres e irresponsáveis abacaxis americanos. Rio de Janeiro: Espaço e Tempo, 1987.

Vida antes da morte / Life before Death. Rio de Janeiro: Jaboti, 1989.

AIDS, a terceira epidemia: Ensaios e tentativas. With Richard Parker. São Paulo: Iglu, 1991.

AIDS in Another World? Sexuality, Politics, and AIDS in Brazil. Edited with Richard Parker. London: Falmer Press, 1993.

INTERVIEWS WITH HERBERT DANIEL IN CHRONOLOGICAL ORDER

Nogueira, Giselle. "Herbert Daniel pede passagem pelo sonho." *Estado de Minas* (April 1, 1982): 6.

Castello, José. "O gueto desmistificado: Preconceito e machismo entre os homossexuais." *Isto É* (July 27, 1983): 82–84.

Mascarenhas, João Antônio. "Os dois lados do beijo: O do candidato a deputado estadual e do amigo Herbert Daniel a João Antônio Mascarenhas." *Okzinho* (Rio de Janeiro) 3, no. 5 (June 3, 1986): 1–2.

Miguez, Ana Cristina. "Escrito com AIDS lidera combate à doença." *O Dia* (April 4, 1989): 10.

Reis, Cláudia. "Tenho AIDS, mas continuo vivo." *Afinal* (August 1, 1989): 9–11.

Braiterman, Jared. "Fighting AIDS in Brazil." *Gay Community News* (New York) 17, no. 39 (April 15–21, 1990): 10–11.

Silva, Paulo César S. "O governo não cumpre o seu papel." *Tribuna da Imprensa* (July 8, 1991): 5.

BIOGRAPHIES AND MEMOIRS

Amaral, Ricardo Batista. *A vida quer é coragem. Trajetória de Dilma Rousseff—a primeira presidenta do Brasil*. Rio de Janeiro: Primeira Pessoa, 2011.

Borba, Marco Aurélio. *Cabo Anselmo: A luta armada ferido por dentro*. 2nd ed. São Paulo: Global Editora, 1984.

Dos Santos, José Anselmo. *Cabo Anselmo: Minha verdade, autobiografia*. São Paulo: Matrix, 2015.

Gabeira, Fernando. *Entradas e bandeiras*. Rio de Janeiro: Codecri, 1981.

Gabeira, Fernando. *O que é isso, companheiro? Depoimento*. Rio de Janeiro: Codecri, 1979.

Green, James N. "Desire and Revolution: Socialists and the Brazilian Gay Liberation Movement in the 1970s." In *Human Rights and Transnational Solidarity in Cold War Latin America*, edited by Jessica Stites Mor, 239–67. Madison: University of Wisconsin Press, 2013.

José, Emiliano, and Oklack Miranda. *Lamarca: O capitão da guerrilha*. São Paulo: Global, 1989.

Lungaretti, Celso. *Náufrago da utopia: Vencer ou morrer na guerrilha. Aos 18 anos*. São Paulo: Geração Editorial, 2005.

Maciel, Eliane. *Com licença eu vou à luta (é illegal ser menor?)*. Rio de Janeiro: Codecri, 1982.

Magalhães, Mário. *Marighella: O guerrilheiro que incendiou o mundo*. São Paulo: Companhia das Letras, 2012.

Menkes, Roberto. "Ribeiro." In *68: a geração que queria mudra o mundo: Relatos*, edited by Eliete Ferrer, 332–36. Brasília: Ministério da Justiça, Comissão de Anistia, 2011.

Paiva, Maurício. *Companheira Carmela: A história de Carmela Pezzuti e seus dois filhos na resistencia ao regime militar e no exílio*. Rio de Janeiro: Mauad, 1996.

Paiva, Maurício. *O sonho exilado*. 2nd ed. Rio de Janeiro: Mauad, 2004.

Patarra, Judith Lieblich. *Iara: Reportage biográfica*. Rio de Janeiro: Rosas dos Tempos, 1992.

Pedroso, Antonio, Jr. *Sargento Darcy, lugar tenente de Lamarca*. Baurú: Centro de Estudos Sociais, Políticos e de Preservação da História, 2003.

Polari, Alex. *Em busca do tesouro: Uma ficção política vivida*. Rio de Janeiro: Editora Codecri, 1982.

Ribeiro, Otávio. *Por que eu traí: Confissões de Cabo Anselmo*. São Paulo: Globo, 1984.
Sirkis, Alfredo. *Os carbonários: Memórias da guerrilha perdida*. Rio de Janeiro: BestBolsa, 2008.
Vianna, Martha. *Uma tempestade como a sua memória: A história de Lia, Maria do Carmo Brito*. Rio de Janeiro: Record, 2003.
Vieira, Liszt. *A busca: Memória da resistência*. São Paulo: Editora Hucitec, 2008.

FILMS AND DVDS

Bonnie and Clyde, directed by Arthur Penn. Warner Bros.–Seven Arts, 1967.
Em busca de Iara, directed by Flávio Frederico. Kinoscópio Cinematográfica, 2013.
Herbert Daniel, created by Fundação Herbert Daniel Partido Verde, 1989. http://www.fvhd.org.br/video/video/show?id=3115145:Video:1145.
Homens, directed by Alfredo Alves. Grupo Pela/RJ, Grupo Pela VIDDA/SP, IBASE, 1993.
O que é isso, companheiro?, directed by Bruno Barreto. Columbia TriStar, 1997.
Recuperação da memória sonora e visual do Partido Verde, created by Fundação Herbert Daniel Partido Verde. Videorecording, two discs, 2008.
Sesenta, directed by Emilia Silveira, Empresa Produtora, 2013.
Viva a vida, Herbert Daniel, o amor e a AIDS nos anos 80, directed by Monica Texeira. TV Manchete, 1989.

INTERVIEWS CONDUCTED BY THE AUTHOR

Advisa, Maria Luisa. July 11, 2009. Paris.
Ângelo, Tereza. No. 1. May 24, 2009. Belo Horizonte.
Ângelo, Tereza. No. 2. May 19, 2010. Belo Horizonte.
Barbosa, Gustavo. November 23, 2010. Rio de Janeiro.
Bastos, Cristiana. August 24, 2010. Florienópolis.
Belloq, Jorge. June 20, 1995. São Paulo.
Brito, Maria do Carmo. No. 1. November 21, 2008. Rio de Janeiro.
Brito, Maria do Carmo. No. 2. August 16, 2010. Rio de Janeiro.
Cachapuz, Paulo Brandi de Barros. August 10, 2010. Rio de Janeiro.
Caldas, Cleide Brunelli. June 27, 2009. Barbacena, Minas Gerais.
Campos, André Luis Vieira de. June 15, 2016. Rio de Janeiro.
Carvalho, Geny Brunelli de. No. 1. June 3, 2008. Belo Horizonte.
Carvalho, Geny Brunelli de. No. 2. June 8, 2008. Belo Horizonte.
Carvalho, Geny Brunelli de. No. 3. August 6, 2010. Belo Horizonte.
Carvalho, Hamilton Brunelli de. No. 1. June 3, 2009. Belo Horizonte.
Carvalho, Hamilton Brunelli de. No. 2. June 8, 2009. Belo Horizonte.
Carvalho, Hamilton Brunelli de. No. 3. August 6, 2010. Belo Horizonte.
Carvalho, Hélder Nazareno de. June 8, 2008. Belo Horizonte.
Carvalho, Lenice Leandro de. June 3, 2009. Belo Horizonte.
Dowbor, Ladislau. July 27, 2010. São Paulo.

Duarte, Erwin Resende. June 5, 2008. Belo Horizonte.
Durão, Carlos Eduardo Saavedra. June 23, 2011. Rio de Janeiro.
Espíndola, Elaine de Mourão Costa. June 6, 2009. Belo Horizonte.
Espíndola, Nilton. June 6, 2009. Belo Horizonte.
Espinosa, Antonio Roberto. November 29, 2010. São Paulo.
Ferreira, Glória. August 13, 2010. Rio de Janeiro.
Ferreira, Sérgio Xavier. May 10, 2010. Rio de Janeiro.
Fiúza, Cleto José Praia. September 8, 2010. Rio de Janeiro.
Freitas, Vanja. November 23, 2010. Rio de Janeiro.
Fry, Peter. October 23, 2010. Rio de Janeiro.
Gabeira, Fernando. June 29, 2016. Rio de Janeiro.
Garibaldi, Aretuza. June 9, 2009. Rio de Janeiro.
Gliochi, Sheila Gomes. May 27, 2010. Rio de Janeiro.
Gradel, José. May 15, 2010. Rio de Janeiro.
Grossi, Míriam. August 24, 2010. Florienópolis.
Huebra, Vera Lígia. June 23, 2011. Rio de Janeiro.
Joué, Maria Elisalva Oliveira. July 8, 2010. Skype interview.
Lafoz, Sônia. May 21, 2010. Skype interview.
Lisboa, Apolo Herlinger. June 24, 2008. Belo Horizonte.
Lungaretti, Celso. July 15, 2011. São Paulo.
Maciel, Eliane. August 14, 2010. Petrópolis.
Martins, Almir. July 21, 2011. São Carlos.
Mascarenhas, João Antônio. July 29, 1995. Rio de Janeiro.
Mesquita, Magaly. No. 1. June 25, 2011. Rio de Janeiro.
Mesquita, Magaly. No. 2. November 25, 2015. Rio de Janeiro.
Míccolis, Leila. December 10, 2010. Rio de Janeiro.
Minc, Carlos. June 30, 2016. Rio de Janeiro.
Montenegro, Cristina. August 9, 2010. Rio de Janeiro.
Muniz, Carlos. November 24, 2015. Rio de Janeiro.
Nahas, Jorge. May 20, 2009. Belo Horizonte.
Nahas, Maria José de Carvalho. May 21, 2009. Belo Horizonte.
Nogueira da Costa, Fernando. October 25, 2010. Campinas.
Oliveira, Zenaide Machado de. No. 1. September 26, 2004. São Paulo.
Oliveira, Zenaide Machado de. No. 2. May 19, 2010. Campinas.
Osawa, Shizuo (Mário Japa). August 16, 2010. Rio de Janeiro.
Parker, Richard. September 30, 2010. New York City.
Pereira, Laís Soares. No. 1. January 6, 2008. Belo Horizonte.
Pereira, Laís Soares. No. 2. June 6, 2009. Belo Horizonte.
Pezzuti, Ângela. No. 1. July 6, 2006. Belo Horizonte.
Pezzuti, Ângela. No. 2. May 19, 2009. Belo Horizonte.
Pinho, Sérgio. November 25, 2010. Rio de Janeiro.
Ramires, Lula. July 21, 2011. São Paulo.
Ramos, Sílvia. October 14, 2010. Rio de Janeiro.
Ratton, Helvécio. August 7, 2010. Belo Horizonte.
Rodrigues, Darcy. July 21, 2011. Bauru, São Paulo.

Rousseff, Dilma. July 21, 2016. Brasília.
Sabalis, Michael. January 10, 2013. Paris, France, notes.
Salgueiro, Beatriz. June 24, 2009. Rio de Janeiro.
Santos, Pitágoras dos. June 5, 2009. Belo Horizonte.
Seixas, Ivan. October 27, 2010. São Paulo.
Sirkis, Alfredo. May 16, 2009. Rio de Janeiro.
Sousa, João Belisário de. June 23, 2011. Rio de Janeiro.
Souza, Ubiratan de. June 16, 2011. Porto Alegre.
Teixeira, Monica. No. 1. July 28, 2010. São Paulo.
Teixeira, Monica. No. 2. October 30, 2010. São Paulo.
Teixeira, Paulo. June 15, 1995. São Paulo.
Tejo, Maria Helena. October 14, 2010. Rio de Janeiro.
Terto, Veriano, Júnior. No. 1. July 24, 1995. Rio de Janeiro.
Terto, Veriano, Júnior. No. 2. June 26, 2009. Rio de Janeiro.
Toledo, Eduardo. September 18, 1993. São Paulo.
Velloso, Lúcia. No. 1. May 25, 2010. Rio de Janeiro.
Velloso, Lúcia. No. 2. June 22, 2013. Rio de Janeiro.
Vieira, Liszt. No. 1. June 28, 2006. Rio de Janeiro.
Vieira, Liszt. No. 2. November 22, 2010. Rio de Janeiro.
Villard, Márcio José. October 15, 2010. Rio de Janeiro.
Von der Weid, Jean Marc. August 13, 2010. Rio de Janeiro.

INTERVIEWS CONDUCTED BY OTHERS

Brito, Maria do Carmo, and Shizuo Osawa. Interview with Judith Patarra. N.d. AEL/UNICAMP.
Daniel, Herbert. Interview with Judith Patarra. N.d. AEL/UNICAMP.
Dowbor, Ladislau. Interview with Judith Patarra. N.d. AEL/UNICAMP.
Dowbor, Ladislau. Interview with Marcelo Ridenti. February 20, 1986. AEL/UNICAMP.
Espinosa, Antonio Roberto. Interview with Judith Patarra. N.d. AEL/UNICAMP.
Fiadeiro, Maria António. Interview with António J. Ramalho. May 6, 2013. Lisbon, Portugal.
Gaspar, Júlio. Interview with Lindinalva Laurindo-Teodorescu and Paulo Roberto Teixeira. In *Histórias da AIDS no Brasil, 1983–2003*. Vol. II: *A sociedade civil se organiza pela luta contra a AIDS*. Brasília: Ministério da Saúde, Secretaria de Vigilância em Saúde, Departamento de DST, AIDS e Hepatites Virais, 2015.
Guia, João Batista Mares. Interview with Otávio Luiz Machado. December 28, 2001. Deposition collected by the Laboratório de Pesquisa Histórica do Instituto de Ciências Humanas e Sociais / Universidade Federal de Ouro Preto, Belo Horizonte.
Leite, Gabriela. Interview with Lindinalva Laurindo-Teodorescu and Paulo Roberto Teixeira. In *Histórias da AIDS no Brasil, 1983–2003*. Vol. II: *A sociedade civil se organiza pela luta contra a AIDS*. Brasília: Ministério da Saúde, Secretaria de Vigilância em Saúde, Departamento de DST, aids e Hepatites Virais, 2015.
Nahas, Jorge. Interview with Marcelo Ridenti. July 15, 1985. Militância Política e Luta Armada no Brasil Collection, AEL/UNICAMP.

Nahas, Maria José de Carvalho. Interview with Lígia Garcia, Isabel Leite, and Rodrigo Biagini. January 11, 2003. Belo Horizonte.
Nahas, Maria José de Carvalho. Interview with Isabel Leite. April 2, 2005. Belo Horizonte.
Pimentel, Fernando de Matos. Interview with Marcelo Ridenti. July 16, 1985. Militância Política e Luta Armada no Brasil Collection, AEL/UNICAMP.
Rodrigues, Darcy. Interview with Judith Patarra. N.d. AEL/UNICAMP.
Romeu, Inês Etienne. Interview with Judith Patarra. N.d. AEL/UNICAMP.
Rousseff, Dilma. Interview with Judith Patarra. N.d. AEL/UNICAMP.
Rousseff, Dilma. Interview with Luiz Maklouf Carvalho. In "Dilma diz ter orgulho de ideais da guerrilha," *Folha de São Paulo*, June 21, 2005.
Silva, Ângelo Pezzuti de. Interview with Herbert Daniel. In "Cabo Anselmo: A desmoralização da verdade." *O Pasquim* 14, no. 773 (April 19, 1984): 4–5.
Silva, Otavino Alves da. Interview with Valter Pomar. In "Memória: Entrevista Otavino Alves da Silva." *Teoria e Debate*, no. 24 (March/April/May 1994).
Terto, Veriano, Júnior. Interview with Lindinalva Laurindo-Teodorescu, and Paulo Roberto Teixeira. In *Histórias da AIDS no Brasil, 1983–2003*. Vol. I: *As respostas governmentais à epidemia de AIDS*. Brasília: Ministério da Saúde, Secretaria de Vigilância em Saúde, Departamento de DST, AIDS e Hepatites Virais, 2015.

NEWSPAPERS CONSULTED

Estado de Minas
Estado de São Paulo
Folha da Tarde (São Paulo)
Folha de São Paulo
Jornal do Brasil (Rio de Janeiro)
Jornal Minas Gerais
O Globo (Rio de Janeiro)
Tribuna da Imprensa (Rio de Janeiro)

PERIODICALS, BULLETINS, AND NEWSLETTERS

Accioli, Cláudio. "Betinho e Herbert Daniel." *Manchete* 1943 (July 15, 1989).
Barreira, Roberto. "Espero o meu irmão para a ceia de Natal." *Manchete* 973 (December 12, 1970): 12–13.
"Bucher: o 4° alvo do terror." *O Cruzeiro* 42, no. 52 (December 22, 1970): 22.
Calvacanti, Pedro. "Ele vive de bicos: 'Sebá' existe e é porteiro de uma sauna em Paris." *Veja* (July 1, 1980): 26.
Dantas, Eduardo. "Negros, mulheres, homossexuais e índios nos debates da USP." *Lampião da Esquina* 10 (March 1979): 9.
Editors. "Saindo do Gueto." *Lampião da Esquina*, no. 0 (April 1978): 2.
"Ele assalta em nome do terror." *Veja* (May 21, 1969): 37.
Filgueiras, Mauro. "Nos bastidores de um sucesso." *O Debate* (December 1965): n.p.

Gabeira, Fernando. "Fernando Gabeira fala, aqui e agora, diretamente dos anos 80." *Lampião da Esquina* 2, no. 18 (November 1979): 5–8.

"Gente." *Veja*, no. 705 (March 10, 1982): 81.

Goldberg, Ron. "When PWAs First Sat at the High Table." *Poz* (July 1998).

Gramont, Sanche de. "How One Pleasant, Scholarly Young Man from Brazil Became a Kidnapping, Gun-Toting, Bombing Revolutionary." *New York Times Magazine* (November 15, 1970): 43–45, 136–53.

"A luta em público contra a AIDS. Abatido aos poucos pela doença, o compositor Cazuza conta como resiste em nome da vida e da carreira." *Veja* (April 26, 1989): 80–87.

Mesquita, Cláudio. "Legado." *Boletim Pela VIDDA* 15 (1993): 3.

Mott, Luiz, ed. *Bulletim do Grupo Gay da Bahia, 1981–2001*. Salvador: Grupo Gay da Bahia, 2011.

"O misterioso cativeiro de Bucher," *Manchete*, no. 980 (January 30, 1971).

"O pesadelo dos votos brancos e nulos." *Veja*, no. 116 (November 25, 1970): 23.

Ribeiro, Otávio. "A confissão do cabo." *Isto É* (March 28, 1984): 24–38.

Romeu, Inês Etienne. "Relatório Inês: Dossiê da tortura." *O Pasquim* 607 (February 12–18, 1981): 4–5, 26.

Silva, Ângelo Pezzuti da. "O tabu da virginidade em nosso contexto cultural." PH-7 19, no. 3 (December 1965): 12.

"O terror desafiado." *Veja*, no. 119 (December 16, 1970): 22–25.

Truskier, Andy. "Politics of Violence: The Urban Guerrilla in Brazil." *Ramparts* 9, no. 4 (October 1970): 30–34, 39.

Vigna, Anne, Luciano Onça, and Natalia Viana. "Napalm no Vale do Ribeira." *Agencia Pública* (August 2014).

SECONDARY SOURCES

Albuquerque, Severino J. *Tentative Transgressions: Homosexuality, AIDS and the Theater in Brazil*. Madison: University of Wisconsin Press, 2004.

Alencastro, Luiz Felipe de. "O golpe de 1964 e o voto popular," *Novo Estudos—CEBRAP*, no. 98 (March 2014): 5–11.

Alvarez, Sonia E. *Engendering Democracy in Brazil: Women's Movements in Transitional Politics*. Princeton, NJ: Princeton University Press, 1990.

Alves, Márcio Moreira. *A Grain of Mustard Seed: The Awakening of the Brazilian Revolution*. Garden City, NY: Anchor, 1973.

Alves, Márcio Moreira. *Torturas e torturado*. 2nd ed. Rio de Janeiro: P.N., 1967.

Alves, Márcio Moreira. *68 mudou o mundo*. 2nd ed. Rio de Janeiro: Nova Fronteira, 1993.

Alves, Maria Helena Moreira. *State and Opposition in Military Brazil*. Austin: University of Texas Press, 1985.

Amnesty International. *Report on Allegations of Torture in Brazil*. Palo Alto, CA: West Coast Office, Amnesty International, 1973.

Araújo, Lucinha, and Regina Echeverria. *Cazuza: Só as mães são felizes*. São Paulo: Editora Globo, 1997.

Araújo, Maria Paula. *Memórias estudantis: Da fundação da* UNE *aos nossos dias*. Rio de Janeiro: Relume Dumara; Fundação Roberto Marinho, 2007.

Badaró, Marcelo. "Em busca da revolução socialista: A trajetória da POLOP (1961–1967)." In *História do Marxismo no Brasil*, vol. V, *Partidos e organizações dos anos 20 aos 60*, edited by Marcelo Ridenti and Daniel Aarão Reis Filho, 185–212. Campinas: Editora da UNICAMP, 2002.

Baiardi, Amílcar. "O homossexualismo e a militância revolucionária." *Recôncavos: Revista do Centro de Artes, Humanidades e Letras* 1, no. 2 (2008): 5–12.

Bastos, Cristiana. *Global Responses to* AIDS. Bloomington: Indiana University Press, 1999.

Basualdo, Carlos, ed. *Tropicália: Uma revolução na cultural brasileira*. São Paulo: Cosac Naify, 2007.

Borim, Dário, Jr. "Daniel, Herbert (Brazil: 1946–1992)." In *Latin American Writers on Gay and Lesbian Themes: A Bio-Critical Sourcebook*, edited by David William Foster, 129–35. Westport, CT: Greenwood, 1994.

Câmara, Cristina. *Cidadania e orientação sexual: A trajetória do grupo Triângulo Rosa*. Rio de Janeiro: Academia Avançada, 2002.

Cardoso, Tom. *O cofre do Dr. Rui: Como a* VAR-*Palmares de Dilma Rousseff realizou o maior assalto da luta armada brasileira*. Rio de Janeiro: Civilização Brasileira, 2011.

Cardoso de Mello, João Manuel, and Fernando A. Novais. "Capitalismo tardio e sociabilidade moderna." In *História da vida privada no Brasil*, vol. 4, edited by Lilia Moritz Schwarz, 559–658. São Paulo: Companhia das Letras, 1998.

Carli, Ana Mery Sehbe de, and Flávia Brocchetto Ramos. *Tropicália: Gêneros, identidades, repertórios e linguagens*. Caxia do Sul: EDUCS, 2008.

Caso, Antonio. *A esquerda armada no Brasil: 1967–1971*. Lisbon: Editora Moraes, 1976.

Castello Branco, Andréa. "A história contada pelos protagonistas." *Teoria e Debate Especial 1968* (May 2008): 15–20.

Castilho, Euclides, Pedro Chequer, and Cláudio Struchiner. "A Epidemiologia da AIDS no Brasil." In *A* AIDS *no Brasil*, edited by Richard Parker, Cristiana Bastos, Jane Galvão, and José Stalin Pedroso, 59–67. Rio de Janeiro: Associação Brasileira Interdisciplinar de AIDS, Instituto de Medicina Social da Universidade Estadual do Rio de Janeiro, Relume Dumará, 1994.

Castillo, Debra, and John Rechy. "Interview with John Rechy." *Diacritics* 25, no. 1 (Spring 1995): 113–25.

Chacel, Cristina. *Seu amigo esteve aqui: A história do desaparecidos político Carlos Alberto Soares de Freitas, assasinado na Casa da Morte*. Rio de Janeiro: Zahar, 2012.

Chagas, Fábio André Gonçalves das. "A vanguarda popular revolucionária: Dilemas e perspectivas da luta armada no Brasil (1968–1971)." M.A. thesis, Universidade Estadual Paulista, Franca, 2000.

Chauncey, George. *Gay New York: Gender, Urban Culture, and the Making of the Gay Male World, 1890–1940*. New York: Basic Books, 1994.

Chilcote, Ronald H. *The Portuguese Revolution: State and Class in the Transition to Democracy*. Lanham, MD: Rowman and Littlefield, 2010.

Coelho, Cláudio Novaes Pinto. *Os movimentos libertários em questão: A política e a cultura nas memórias de Fernando Gabeira*. Petrópolis: Vozes, 1987.

Comissão de Familiares de Mortos e Desaparecidos Políticos, Instituto de Estudos sobre a Violência do Estado. *Dossiê ditadura: Mortos e desaparecidos poíticos no Brasil (1964–85)*, 2nd ed., revised and enlarged. São Paulo: Instituto de Estudo sobre a Violência do Estado, Imprensa Oficial, 2009.

Comissão Especial sobre Mortos e Desaparecidos Políticos. *Direito à memória e à verdade*. Brasília: Secretaria Especial dos Direitos Humanos, 2007.

Couto, Ronaldo Costa. *História indiscreta da ditadura e da abertura: Brasil, 1964–1985*. 3rd ed. Rio de Janeiro: Editora Record, 1999.

Cowan, Benjamin. *Securing Sex: Morality and Repression in the Making of Cold War Brazil*. Chapel Hill: University of North Carolina Press, 2016.

D'Angelo, Ana Cristina. "Verdes desde o início." *Página 22* (September 10, 2010).

Dângelo, Jota, and Angelo Machado. *O humor do show medicina*. Rio de Janeiro: Livraria Atheneu Editora, 1999.

Da Silva, Mário Augusto Medeiros. *Os escritores da guerrilha urbana: Literatura de testamunho, ambivalência e transição política (1977–1984)*. São Paulo: Annablume, 2008.

Debray, Régis. *Revolution within the Revolution? Armed Struggle and Political Struggle in Latin America*. New York: MR Press, 1967.

Delgado, Lúcilia de Almeida Neves. "Diretas-Já: Vozes das cidades." In *Revolução e democracia*, edited by Jorge Ferreira and Daniel Aarão Reis, 409–27. Rio de Janeiro: Civilização Brasileira, 2007.

Delgado, Márcio de Paiva. "Carlos Lacerda, Juscelino Kubitschek, João Goulart e a Frente Ampla de oposição ao Regime Militar (1966–1968)." In *Veredas da História*, Ano III, Ed. 2, 2010.

D'Emilio, John. *Sexual Politics, Sexual Communities: The Making of a Homosexual Minority in the United States, 1940–1970*. Chicago: University of Chicago Press, 1983.

Dias, Cláudio José Piotrovski. "A trajetória soropositiva de Herbert Daniel (1989–1992)." M.A. thesis in History of Science, Fundação Oswaldo Cruz, Casa de Oswaldo Cruz, 2012.

Dicionário histórico biográfico Brasileiro pós 1930. 2nd ed. Rio de Janeiro: Ed. FGV, 2001.

Dunn, Christopher. *Brutality Garden: Tropicália and the Emergence of a Brazilian Counterculture*. Chapel Hill: University of North Carolina Press, 2001.

Dunn, Christopher. *Contracultura: Alternative Arts and Social Transformation in Authoritarian Brazil*. Chapel Hill: University of North Carolina Press, 2017.

Dunn, Christopher. "*Desbunde* and Its Discontents: Counterculture and Authoritarian Modernization in Brazil, 1968–1974." *Americas* 70, no. 3 (January 29, 2014): 429–58.

Dyer, Richard. *Heavenly Bodies: Film Stars and Society*. 2nd ed. New York: Routledge, 1986.

Ferreira, Hugo Gil, and Michael W. Marshall. *Portugal's Revolution: Ten Years On*. Cambridge: Cambridge University Press, 1986.

Ferrer, Eliete, ed. *68: A geração que queria mudra o mundo: Relatos*. Brasília: Ministério da Justiça, Comissão de Anistia, 2011.

Fico, Carlos. *Ibase: Usina de idéias e cidadania*. Rio de Janeiro: Garamon, 1999.

Fico, Carlos. *Reinventando o otimismo: Ditadura, propaganda e imaginário social no Brasil*. Rio de Janeiro: Fundação Getulio Vargas, 1997.

Fico, Carlos, and Maria Paulo Araújo, eds. *1968: 40 anos depois: História e memória*. Rio de Janeiro: 7Letras, 2009.

Fitch, Melissa A. "Life before Death: Homophobia in Two Works by Activist-Author Herbert Daniel." *Luso-Brazilian Review* 43, no. 2 (2006): 103–18.

Fonseca, Selva Guimarães. *Caminhas da história ensinada.* Campinas: Papirus, 1993.

Forin, Renato, Jr. "Confluências do teatro e da música popular no espetáculo de Maria Bethânia." *Moringa: Artes do espetáculo* (João Pessoa) 4, no. 2 (July–December 2013): 131–49.

Freire, Américo. "Ecos da estação Lisboa: O exilio das esquerdas brasileiras em Portugal." *Sociologia: Problemas e práticas* 64 (2010): 37–57.

Gabeira, Fernando. "A idéia do Partido Verde no Brasil." In *Ecologia e política no Brasil*, edited by José Augusto Padua, 163–80. Rio de Janeiro: Espaço e Tempo / Instituto Universitário de Pesquisas do Rio de Janeiro, 1987.

Galvão, Jane. "AIDS e ativismo: O surgimento e a construção de novas formas de solidariedade." Paper presented to the seminar "AIDS e Ativismo Social e Político." Instituto de Medicina Social do Estado do Rio de Janeiro, Rio de Janeiro, 1992.

Gaspari, Elio. *A ditadura escancarada.* São Paulo: Companhia das Letras, 2002.

Girard, Jacques. *Le movement homosexuel en France, 1945–1880.* Paris: Syros, 1981.

Gomes, Flávio dos Santos. *Palmares: Escravidão e liberdade no Atlântico Sul.* São Paulo: Contexto, 2005.

Gorender, Jacob. *Combate nas trevas.* São Paulo: Editora Ática, 1998.

Green, James N. *Beyond Carnival: Male Homosexuality in Twentieth-Century Brazil.* Chicago: University of Chicago Press, 1999.

Green, James N. "Desire and Militancy: Lesbians, Gays, and the Brazilian Workers' Party. In *Different Rainbow: Same-Sex Sexuality and Popular Struggles in the Third World*, edited by Peter Drucker, 57–70. London: Gay Men's Press, 2000.

Green, James N. "The Emergence of the Brazilian Gay Liberation Movement, 1977–81." *Latin American Perspectives* 21, no. 1 (Winter 1994): 38–55.

Green, James N. "O Grupo Somos, a esquerda e a resistência à ditadura." In *Homossexualidade e a ditadura brasileira: Opressão, resistencia e a busca da verdade*, edited by James N. Green and Renan Quinalha, 177–200. São Carlos: Editora da Universidade Federal de São Carlos, 2014.

Green, James N. "Liberalization on Trial: The Brazilian Workers' Movement." *North American Congress on Latin America's Report on the Americas* 13, no. 3 (May–June 1979): 15–25.

Green, James N. "More Love and More Desire: The Building of the Brazilian Movement." In *The Global Emergence of Gay and Lesbian Politics: National Imprints of a Worldwide Movement*, edited by Barry Adam, Jan Willem Duyvendak, and André Krouwel, 91–109. Philadelphia: Temple University Press, 1999.

Green, James N. *We Cannot Remain Silent: Opposition to the Brazilian Military Dictatorship.* Durham: Duke University Press, 2010.

Green, James N. "'Who Is the Macho Who Wants to Kill Me?' Male Homosexuality, Revolutionary Masculinity, and the Brazilian Armed Struggle of the 1960s and '70s." *Hispanic American Historical Review* 92, no. 3 (August 2012): 437–69.

Green, James N., and Renan Quinalha, eds. *Ditadura e Homossexualidades: Repressão, resistência e a busca da verdade.* São Carlos: Editora da Universidade Federal de São Carlos, 2014.

Grossi, Yonne de Souza. "As greves de Contagem—1968: Notas para uma revião crítica." *Cadernos Movimentos Populares Urbanos* 1 (1979): 3–54.

Gunther, Scott. *The Elastic Closet: A History of Homosexuality in France, 1942–Present.* Houndmills, UK: Palgrave Macmillan, 2009.

Gurgel, Antonio de Padua. *A rebelião dos estudantes, Brasília, 1968.* Brasília: Editora Universidade de Brasília, 2002.

Hale, James. "After Montreal, International AIDS Conferences Will Never Be the Same." *Canadian Medical Association Journal* 141 (July 15, 1989): 144–46.

Hammond, John L. *Building Popular Power: Workers' and Neighborhood Movements in the Portuguese Revolution.* New York: Monthly Review Press, 1988.

Hanchard, Michael George, and Vera Ribeiro. *Orfeu e o poder: O Movimento Negro no Rio de Janeiro e São Paulo (1945–1988).* Rio de Janeiro: Editora da Universidade Estadual do Rio de Janeiro, 2001.

Hochstetler, Kathryn, and Margaret E. Keck. *Greening Brazil: Environmental Activism in State and Society.* Durham: Duke University Press, 2007.

Hocquenghem, Guy. *Homosexual Desire.* Durham: Duke University Press, 1993.

Howe, Robert. "João Antônio Mascarenhas (1927–1998): Pioneiro do ativismo homossexual no Brasil." In *Homosexualidade: Sociedade, movimento e lutas,* edited by James N. Green and Sonia Maluf, 291–309. *Cadernos AEL* 10, no. 18–19 (2003).

Ibrahim, José, and José Campos Barreto. "Manfiesto de balance da greve de julho." In *A esquerda e o movmento operário, 1964–84,* vol. 1, edited by Celso Frederico, 180–92. São Paulo: Editora Novos Rumos, 1987.

Jordão, Fernando. *Dossiê Herzog: Prisão, tortura e morte no Brasil.* São Paulo: Globo Editora, 2005.

Kallings, Lars, and Craig McClur. *20 Years of the International AIDS Society: HIV Professionals Working Together to Fight AIDS.* Geneva: International AIDS Society, 2008.

Kauchakje, Samira. "Solidariedade política e constituição de sujeitos: A atualidade dos movimentos sociais." *Sociedade e Estado* (Brasília) 23, no. 3 (September–December 2008): 667–96.

Keck, Margaret E. *The Workers' Party and Democratization in Brazil.* New Haven, CT: Yale University Press, 1992.

Kinzo, Maria D'Alva Gil. *Oposição e autoritarismo: Gênese e trajetória do MDB (1966–1979).* São Paulo: Editora Revista dos Tribunais, 1988.

Kuczinski, Bernardo. *Abertura, a história de uma crise.* São Paulo: Brasil Debates, 1982.

Kuczinski, Bernardo. *Jornalistas e revolucionários nos tempos da imprensa alternativa.* São Paulo: Página Aberta, 1991.

Langland, Victoria. "Birth Control Pills and Molotov Cocktails: Reading Sex and Revolution in 1968 Brazil." In *In From the Cold: Latin America's New Encounter with the Cold War,* edited by Gilbert M. Joseph and Daniela Spenser, 308–49. Durham: Duke University Press, 2008.

Langland, Victoria. *Speaking of Flowers: Student Movements and the Making and Remembering of 1968 in Military Brazil.* Durham: Duke University Press, 2013.

Laurindo-Teodorescu, Lindinalva, and Paulo Roberto Teixeira. *Histórias da AIDS no Brasil, 1983–2003.* Vol. 1. *As respostas governmentais à epidemia de AIDS.* Brasília: Ministério da Saúde, Secretaria de Vigilância em Saúde, Departamento de DST, AIDS e Hepatites Virais, 2015.

Laurindo-Teodorescu, Lindinalva, and Paulo Roberto Teixeira. *Histórias da AIDS no Brasil, 1983–2003*. Vol. 2. *A sociedade civil se organiza pela luta contra a AIDS*. Brasília: Ministério da Saúde, Secretaria de Vigilância em Saúde, Departamento de DST, AIDS e Hepatites Virais, 2015.

Leacock, Ruth. *Requiem for Revolution: The United States and Brazil, 1961–1969*. Kent, OH: Kent State University Press, 1990.

Le Bitoux, Jean. "The Construction of a Political and Media Presence: The Homosexual Liberation Groups in France between 1975 and 1978." In *Homosexuality in French History and Culture*, edited by Jeffrey Merrick and Michael Sibalis. *Journal of Homosexuality* 41, no. 3/4 (2001): 249–80.

Leite, Isabel Cristina. "'Apurando a subversão': Um estudo de caso sobre repressão na universidade pelos arquivos da AESI/UFMG." *Temporalidades—Revista Discente do Programa de Pós-graduação em História da UFMG* 2, no. 1 (January–July 2010): 148–56.

Leite, Isabel Cristina. "Comandos de libertação nacional: Oposição armada à ditadura em Minas Gerais (1967–1969)." M.A. thesis in History, Federal University of Minas Gerais, 2009.

Leonelli, Domingos, and Dante Oliveira. *Diretas já: 15 meses que abalaram a ditadura*. Rio de Janeiro: Record, 2004.

Leu, Lorraine. *Brazilian Popular Music: Caetano Veloso and the Regeneration of Tradition*. Burlington, VT: Ashgate, 2006.

Lumsden, Ian. *Machos, Maricones, and Gays: Cuba and Homosexuality*. Philadelphia: Temple University Press, 1996.

Maciel, Wilma Antunes. *O capitão Lamarca e a VPR: Repressão judicial no Brasil*. São Paulo: Almada, 2006.

MacRae, Edward. *A construção da igualdade: Identidade sexual e política no Brasil da "abertura."* Campinas: Editora da Universidade Estadual de Campinas, 1990.

MacRae, Edward. "Homosexual Identities in Transitional Brazilian Politics." In *The Making of Social Movements in Latin America: Identity, Strategy and Democracy*, edited by Arturo Escobar and Sonia E. Alvarez, 185–203. Boulder, CO: Westview, 1992.

Mann, Jonathan M., Daniel J. M. Tarontola, and Thomas W. Netter, eds. *AIDS in the World: The Global AIDS Policy Coalition*. Cambridge, MA: Harvard University Press, 1992.

Martel, Fréderic. *The Pink and the Black: Homosexuals in France since 1968*. Translated by Jane Marie Todd. Stanford, CA: Stanford University Press, 1999.

Martins, Antonio Carlos Borges. "AIDS, vida e morte no romance *Alegres e irresponsáveis abacaxis americanos* de Herbert Daniel." M.A. thesis in Literature, Centro do Ensino Superior de Juiz de Fora, 2005.

Martins Filho, João Roberto. *Movimento estudantil e ditadura militar, 1964–68*. Campinas: Papirus, 1987.

Martins Filho, João Roberto. *A rebelião estudantil: México, França, Brasil, 1968*. Campinas: Mercado de Letras, 1996.

Martins Filho, João Roberto. "Segretos de estado: O governo britânico e a tortura no Brasil (1969–1976)." Thesis for Full Professorship, Universidade Federal de São Carlos, 2015.

Mascarenhas, João Antônio de Souza. *A tríple conexão: Conservadorismo político, falso moralismo, machismo*. Rio de Janeiro: Planeta Gay, 1998.

Maxwell, Kenneth. *The Making of Portuguese Democracy*. New York: Cambridge University Press, 1995.

Médici, Emílio Garrastazu. *O jogo da verdade*. Brasília: Secretária da Imprensa da Presidência da República, 1970.

Mesquita, Cláudio. "Herbert Eustáquio de Carvalho." In *Rua Viva: Desenho a Utopia*, 2nd ed., edited by Betinha Duarte, 290–97. Ronã, Brazil: Belo Horizonte, 2004.

Mesquita, Cláudio. *Qual é o porto seguro contra AIDS?* Rio de Janeiro: Associação Brasileira Interdisciplinar de AIDS, 1988.

Mesquita, Cláudio. *Que qui é esta tal de AIDS*. Rio de Janeiro: Associação Brasileira Interdisciplinar de AIDS, 1989.

Miranda, Nilmário. "A cidade operária símbolo." *Teoria e Debate Especial 1968* (May 2008): 21–24.

Morando, Luiz. *Paraíso das Maravilhas: Uma história do Crime do Parque*. Belo Horizonte: Argumentum, 2008.

Morando, Luiz. "Por baixo dos panos: Repressão a gays e travestis em Belo Horizonte (1963–69)." In *Ditadura e homosexualidades: Repressão, resistência e a busca da verdade*, edited by James N. Green and Renan Quinalha, 53–82. São Carlos: Editora da Universidade Federal de São Carlos, 2015.

Mota, Urariano. *Soledad no Recife*. São Paulo: Boitempo, 2009.

Mulvey, Laura. "Visual Pleasure and Narrative Cinema," *Screen* 16, no. 3 (Autumn 1975): 6–18.

Nahas, Antônio, Júnior. *A queda: Rua Atacarambu, 120*. Belo Horizonte: Scriptum, 2015.

Neves, Magda de Almeida. *Trabalho e cidadania: As trabalhadores de Contagem*. Petrópolis: Vozes, 1995.

Nossa, Leonencio. *Mata! O Major Curió e as guerrilhas no Araguaia*. São Paulo: Companhia das Letras, 2012.

Nunn, Amy. *The Politics and History of AIDS Treatment in Brazil*. New York: Springer, 2009.

Okuchi, Nobuo. *O sequestro do diplomata: memórias*. São Paulo: Primus, 1991.

Oliveira, Edgard Leite de. "Conflito social, memória e experiência: As greves dos metalúrigocs de Contagem em 1968." M.A. thesis in Education, Universidade Federal de Minas Gerais, 2010.

Oliveira, Joelma Alves de. "POLOP: As origens, a coesão e a cisão de uma organização marxista (1961–1967)." M.A. thesis in Sociology, Universidade do Estado de São Paulo Araraquara, 2007.

Ortells, Pascual. "Brazil: A Model Response to AIDS." *Envio Digital* 254 (September 2002).

Parker, Richard. "Public Policy, Political Activism, and AIDS." In *Global AIDS Policy*, edited by Douglas Feldman, 28–46. Westport, CT: Bergin and Garvey, 1994.

Parker, Richard, and Veriano Terto Jr. *Solidariedade: A ABIA na virada do milênio*. Rio de Janeiro: Associação Brasileira Interdisciplinar de AIDS, 2001.

Pellegrini, Tania. *Gavetas vazias: Ficção e política nos anos 70*. São Carlos: Editora da Universidade Federal de São Carlos–Mercado de Letras, 1996.

Pereira, Rômulo Medeiros. "Herbert Daniel e suas escrituras de memória: Exercícios autobiográficos e traços estéticos de uma existência (1967–1984)." M.A. thesis in History, Universidade Federal da Paraíba, 2013.

Pomar, Pedro Estevan da Rocha. *Massacre na Lapa: Como o exército liquidou o Comitê Central do PC do B*. São Paulo: Busca Vida, 1987.

Portela, Fernando, and José Genoino Neto. *Guerra de guerrilhas no Brasil: A saga de Araguaia*. São Paulo: Terceiro Nome, 2002.

Power, Timothy J., and J. Timmons Roberts. "Compulsory Voting, Invalid Ballots, and Abstention in Brazil." *Political Research Quarterly* 48, no. 4 (December 1995): 795–826.

Prado, Luiz Carlos Delorme, and Fábio Sá Earp. "O 'milagre' brasileiro: Crescimento acelerado, integração internacional e concentração de renda (1967–73)." In *O tempo da ditadura: Regime militar e movimentos socais em fins do século XX*, edited by Jorge Ferreira and Lucilia de Almeida Neves Delgado, 207–42. *O Brasil Republicano*, vol. 4. Rio de Janeiro: Civilização Brasileira, 2003.

Rabóczkay, Tibor. *Repensando o Partido Verde Brasileiro*. Cotia: Ateliê Editorial, 2004.

Ramalho, José Ricardo. "Sinais de mudança no sindicalismo brasileiro: O significado das greves de 1968 em Contagem e Osasco." In *1968: 40 anos depois: História e memória*, edited by Carlos Fico and Maria Paula Araújo, 131–49. Rio de Janeiro: 7Letras, 2009.

Reis Filho, Daniel Aarão. "Classe operária, partido de quadros e revolução socialista. O itinerário da Política Operária—POLOP (1961–1986)." In *Revolução e democracia*, edited by Jorge Ferreira and Daniel Aarão Reis, 53–71. Rio de Janeiro: Civilização Brasileira, 2007.

Reis Filho, Daniel Aarão, and Jair Ferreira de Sá, eds. *Imagens da revolução: Documentos políticos das organizações clandestinas de esquerda dos anos 1961–71*. São Paulo: Expressão Popular, 2006.

Ridenti, Marcelo. "Ação Popular: Cristianismo e marxismo." In *História do Marxismo no Brasil, vol. V, Partidos e organizações dos anos 20 aos 60*, edited by Marcelo Ridenti and Daniel Aarão Reis Filho, 213–82. Campinas: Editora da Universidade do Estado de Campinas, 2002.

Ridenti, Marcelo. *O fantasma da revolução brasileira*. São Paulo: Editora da Universidade do Estado de São Paulo, 1993.

Rollemberg, Denise. *Exílio: Entre raízes e radares*. Rio de Janeiro: Record, 1999.

Rosa, João Guimarães. *The Devil to Pay in the Backlands*. Translated by James L. Taylor and Harriet de Onís. New York: Alfred A. Knopf, 1963.

Santana, Marco Aurélio. "Trabalhadores, sindicatos e ditadura militar." In *1968: 40 anos depois: História e memória*, edited by Carlos Fico and Maria Paula Araújo, 150–67. Rio de Janeiro: 7Letras, 2009.

Schneider, Nina. *Brazilian Propaganda: Legitimizing an Authoritarian Regime*. Gainesville: University of Florida Press, 2014.

Schpun, Mônica Raisa. "Le regard décalé de l'exilé sur le Brésil post-amnistie: Sebá, personnage de l'humoriste Jô Soares." In *L'Exil brésilien en France: Histoire et imaginaire*, edited by Idelette Muzart-Fonseca dos Santos and Denis Rolland, 365–74. Paris: l'Harmattan, 2008.

Serbin, Kenneth. *Needs of the Heart: A Social and Cultural History of Brazil's Clergy and Seminaries.* Notre Dame, IN: University of Notre Dame Press, 2006.

Silva, Heike R. Keber da, ed. *A luta pela anistia.* São Paulo: Editora da Universidade do Estado de São Paulo, 2009.

Silva, Maria Elizabeth Corrêa Campos e. "Ideário do movimento estudantil de Belo Horizonte entre 1964 e 1968: Utopias e desencantos." M.A. thesis in Social Sciences, Pontifícia Universidade Católica Minas, Belo Horizante, 2001.

Simões, Júlio Assis, and Regina Facchini. *Na trilha do arco-íris: Do moivmento homossexual ao LGBT.* São Paulo: Editora Fundação Perseu Abramo, 2009.

Skidmore, Thomas E. *Politics in Brazil, 1930–64: An Experiment in Democracy.* 2nd ed. New York: Oxford University Press, 2009.

Skidmore, Thomas E. *The Politics of Military Rule in Brazil, 1964–85.* New York: Oxford University Press, 1988.

Solano Vianna, Nelson. "AIDS no Brasil: Avaliando o passado e planejando o futuro." Paper delivered at the seminar "AIDS e Ativismo Político." Social Medicine Institute, State University of Rio de Janeiro, May 11–13, 1992.

Sousa Neto, Júlio Anselmo de. "Show medicina: 1962–1991." In *O humor do show medicina,* edited by Jota Dângelo and Angelo Machado, 9–16. Rio de Janeiro: Livraria Atheneu Editora, 1991.

Souza, Herbert José de, and Emir Sader, *No fio da navalha.* Rio de Janeiro: Editora Revan, 1996.

Street, James N. "Coping with Energy Shocks in Latin America: Three Responses." *Latin American Research Review* 17, no. 3 (1982): 128–47.

Tavares de Almeida, Maria Hermínia, and Luiz Weis. "Carro-zero e pau-de-arara: O cotidiano da oposição de classe média ao regime militar." In *História da vida privada no Brasil: Contrastes da intimidade contemporânea,* vol. IV, edited by Lilia Moritz Schwarcz, 319–409. São Paulo: Companhia das Letras, 1998.

Telles, Janaína de Almeida. "As disputas pela interpretação da lei de anistia de 1979." *Idéias* 1 (1st semester 2010): 71–93.

Telles, Janaína de Almeida, ed. *Mortos e desapareidos politicos: Reparação ou impunidade?* São Paulo: Humanitas- Faculdade de Filosofia, Letras e Ciências Humanas / Universidade de São Paulo, 2001.

Trevisan, João S. *Perverts in Paradise.* Translated by Martin Foreman. London: GMP Publishers, 1986.

Veloso, Caetano. *Verdade tropical.* São Paulo: Companhia das Letras, 1997.

Ventura, Zeunir. *1968: A ano que não terminou, a aventura de uma geração.* Rio de Janeiro: Editora Nova Fronteira, 1988.

Viola, Eduardo J. "O movimento ecológico no Brasil (1974–1986): Do ambientalismmo à ecopolítica." *Revista Brasileira de Ciencias Sociais* 3 (1993): 5–26.

Von Mettenheim, Kurt. *The Brazilian Voter: Mass Politics in Democratic Transition, 1974–1986.* Pittsburgh: University of Pittsburgh Press, 1995.

Wipfler, William L. "The Price of 'Progress' in Brazil." *Christianity and Crisis,* March 6, 1970, 44–48.

Wipfler, William L. "'Progress' in Brazil Revisited." *Christianity and Crisis,* October 6, 1986, 345–48.

INDEX

A 4 Mãos (Four hands), 252
Abduction, of diplomats: German ambassador, 1, 3, 9, 115–20, 182, 267; Japanese consul, 107, 115, 129; Swiss ambassador, 1, 3, 9, 106, 123–31, 133, 147, 152, 182, 267, 280, 285n52; U.S. ambassador, 29, 94, 117, 119, 125, 148, 182
Ação Libertadora Nacional (ALN), 88–89, 94, 96, 102, 116, 121–22, 136
Ação Popular (AP), 30, 46, 85, 125, 237
Advisa, Maria Elena, 152–53, 169
AIDS, 5–6, 7, 9, 195, 207–11, 229, 235–61, 270–71
AIDS, a terceira epidemia: Ensaios e tentativas, 256, 271
Alves, João Lucas, 46, 61, 83
Alegres e irresponsáveis abacaxis americanos, 252
Alencar, 216–17
Aliança Renovadora Nacional (ARENA), 94, 122, 155, 200
Ambassador, German, 1, 3, 9, 115–20, 182, 267
Ambassador, Swiss, 1, 3, 9, 106, 123–31, 133, 147, 152, 182, 267, 280, 285n52
América Latina, 51
Amnesty Law, 1–2, 179–82, 185–88, 191–93, 200, 237, 269

Ângelo, Tereza, 118, 123–27, 129, 133, 136
Anti-Vietnam War movement, 3, 32, 61
Antunes, Valneri Neves, 102, 184
Aparelho, 64, 70–73, 87, 91–92, 107, 116, 129–30, 144, 149
Araújo, Carlos Franklin Paixão de, 86, 90, 93, 95, 102
Araújo Neto, Agenor Miranda (Cazuza), 254
Araguaia, 100, 112
ARENA, 94, 122, 155, 200
armed struggle, women and, 71, 96, 102–3
Army Intelligence Center, 108–9
Army, Second, 108–13
Associação Brasileira Interdisciplinar de AIDS (ABIA), 235–52, 255–56, 260, 270–71
Asterix, 80
Ato Institucional Número 5 (AI-5), 67, 94, 116

Bandeirantes, Operação, 106–7
bank robber, blond, 69–71
bank robberies. *See* expropriations
Bankworkers' Union, Belo Horizonte, 53, 65, 73
Barbacena, Minas Gerais, 12, 74, 150–51, 157, 159, 176, 268

Barbosa, Gustavo, 198, 219
Barcelos, Maria Auxiliadora Lara (Dodora), 31, 38, 43, 51, 125
Barros, Ademar de, 92, 148
Bastos, Cristiana, 249
Belgo-Mineira Iron and Steel Company, 57–58
Belo Horizonte: bank robberies in 68–70; Brazilian Network of Solidarity meeting in, 248; Carvalho family in everyday life in, 12–20; gay life in, 22–24; Herbert Daniel's burial in 9; Herbert Daniel's escape from, 73–74; Herbert Daniel hiding in, 153; Herbert Daniel's return to, 195, 256–58; labor strike near, 58–65; Pezzuti family in, 55–56, 153; Rua Herbert Eustáquio de Carvalho in, 261; student life in, 27–28; student movement in, 31–34, 52–53, 55, 67–69
Betânia, Maria, 134–35
Black Power, U.S., 32, 38
Boletim ABIA, 235, 238–39, 242, 244
Bonnie and Clyde, 70
Brazilian Women's Circle, 181
Breno (Carlos Alberto Soares de Freitas), 32, 34, 46, 52, 54, 56, 58, 61–64, 71, 76, 78–79, 86, 90–93, 95, 99
Brito, Maria do Carmo, 61–62, 73–74, 76, 78–79, 81, 86, 90, 92–97, 107–8, 113, 115, 119–20, 147, 153, 213
Brito, Juares Guimarães de, 61–62, 74, 76, 78–79, 81, 86, 90, 92, 97, 107–8, 113, 115, 120, 147, 258
Brunelli, Adolpho, 12, 17
Brunelli, Carmelita Delben, 12
Bucher, Giovanni, 123–29

Cabo Anselmo. *See* Santos, José Anselmo dos
Canada, 237, 238
Capriglione, Ana Benchimol, 92
Cachapuz, Paulo Brandi de Barros, 82, 96–98, 113–14, 133–35, 137
Caldas, Cleide Brunelli, 150–51, 159

Campos, André Luis Vieira de, 231–32
Carvalho, Geny Brunelli de, 4, 7–9, 11–18, 73–74, 150–52, 193, 207, 256–58, 262–63, 265
Carvalho, Geraldo Feliciano de, 7, 9, 12–13, 15, 17–19, 25, 34, 74, 150, 152, 192, 262, 265
Carvalho, Hamilton Brunelli de, 4, 7, 9, 15–17, 19, 24–25, 35, 74, 150, 153, 257, 262, 265
Carvalho, Hélder Nazareno de, 7, 18, 24, 195, 262, 265
Carvalho, Herbert Eustáquio. *See* Herbert Daniel
Carvalho, Lenice Leandro de, 153
Casa do Brasil, 183–85, 197, 269
Castro, Fidel, 38, 46, 253–54
Castroism: The Long March of Latin America (Debray), 46
Cegonha . . . Que cegonha?, 220–21, 270
Censorship, 37, 40, 47, 49, 67, 85, 125, 155, 178, 184
Centro de Estudos de Medicina (CEM), 32, 38
Chacara São Bento, Massacre of, 149
Chandler, Charles, 87
Chauí, Marilena, 233
Chile, ix, 3, 124–26, 130, 135, 142, 146, 147–49, 152–53, 156, 169–71, 181, 213, 237, 271
Church, Catholic, 11, 20, 27, 30–31, 38, 49, 60, 141, 200, 224, 231
Colégio Tiradentes, 17–19, 24
Collor de Mello, President Fernando, 255
Colon, Serverino Viana, 79
Comando de Estudantes Secundaristas (COSEC), 86
Comandos de Libertação Nacional (COLINA), 3, 9, 65–69, 73, 81, 83, 86, 90–95, 100, 102–3, 114, 116–17, 119, 125, 147, 217, 266–67
Comitê Brasileiro de Anistia (CBA), 2, 180–82, 186, 188, 192
Conference, Eighth International AIDS, 260

Consul, Japanese, 107, 115, 129
Contagem, 56–59, 64, 87
Costa e Silva, Athos Magno, 53
Costa e Silva, President General Artur, 58, 67, 94, 154, 266
Costa, José Raimundo, 95, 121, 129, 135
Coup d'état (1964), 25, 27–28, 30, 32, 34, 37, 48, 57, 61–62, 84, 86, 90, 117, 120, 129, 205, 207, 212, 237, 266
Cuba, 29, 32, 34, 46, 87, 88, 100, 120, 131, 133, 147–49, 212, 214, 253–54
Cuban AIDS policy, 253, 54
Cuban Revolution, 29, 32, 34, 43, 45–46, 57, 62, 66, 88, 111, 193

Dângelo, José Geraldo, 37, 40, 217
Daniel, Herbert: and AIDS, 9, 195, 207–11, 226, 229, 235–61; anonymous sexual encounters of, 22–23, 26, 35, 172–77; assumed names of 36, 51, 74, 151; death of, 7–10, 258–61; first exile of, 23; and Colégio Tiradentes, 17–19; and Escola Chopin, 17; family relationships of, 7–25, 34–35, 74, 150–53, 192, 195, 256–58, 262–63, 265; friendship with Laís Pereira, 4, 19–25, 32, 37–38, 40, 43, 51, 60, 144; funeral of, 7–10; in love with Erwin Duarte, 41–43, 51, 215–16; and jokes about gays, 106, 209, 282n40; and leukemia, 128; and military training, 3, 16, 69, 98, 99–111, 114–15, 128–29, 142, 160, 184; medical training of, 3, 9, 24–40, 48–50, 60, 63, 99, 103, 162–63, 169, 191, 197, 210, 240; as movie critic, 20, 26, 34, 51, 207; and Municipal Park of Belo Horizonte, 22–23, 26, 35; and participation in bank robberies, 17, 69, 71; and physical activities, 16, 21, 99; in Portugal, 156–70, 173, 207, 216, 232; and primary school, 17–18; and radio scripts, 26, 34, 51; repression of homosexuality, 22–23, 26, 35, 42–43, 47–48, 50, 76, 79, 85, 105–6, 143, 160–61, 175–76, 184–85, 196, 215–17, 257; School of Medicine strike, 48, 60; and sports, 16, 21; as playwright, 38–40, 207, 218–20; as theater director, 40, 51, 217, 220; and Vale do Ribeira, 99–109, 112, 114, 119–21, 128, 142, 160, 184
death, civil, 243
Debray, Régis, 45–46, 57, 103
Delizoikov, Eremias, 102
Deslocados, 74
Dias, Ivan Mota, 132–33
Dinosaurus, 151
Dissidence of the Dissidence (DDD), 86
Dissidência de VAR-Palmares (DVP). *See* Vanguarda Armada Revolucionária—Palmares (VAR-Palmares)
Dowbor, Ladislau, 78, 90, 93, 96–97, 100, 108, 113, 119
Duarte, Erwin Resende, 41–43, 51, 62, 71, 82, 215–16
Duarte, Marilda, 41

"Economic Miracle," 84–85, 115–16, 155
elections: 1965, 28, 122; 1966, 122; 1970, 122; 1974, 200, 268; 1978, 200; 1982, 201–7, 210, 226; 1985, 224–25; 1986, 225–35, 246; 1989, 252
exile, the last, 190–93
expropriations (bank robberies), 17, 62–65, 68–71, 87, 91, 96, 103, 113, 119, 129, 145, 267
Expropriations Unit, 63–64, 68, 71–73, 97, 103
Espíndola, Elaine de Mourão Costa, 20–21
Espíndola, Nilton, 20–21
Espinosa, Antonio Roberto, 86, 90, 93, 95, 114

Fatal, Paulo, 236
Faria Lima, Giberto, 75, 102
Father Eustáquio, 13
A fêmea sintética, 207–8, 270
Feminine Committee for Amnesty, 178
feminism, 3, 165–67, 174, 178, 181, 194, 197, 205–8, 244
Fensterseifer, Delci, 102, 105

Ferreira, Aluísio Palhano Pedreira, 133
Ferreira, Glória, 181–83
Ferreira, Joaquim Câmara, 138
Ferreira, Manoel Henrique, 120
Fiadeiro, Maria Antónia, 163
Figueiredo, President General João Batista, 185–86
Filgueiras, Mauro, 37–40
Fleury, Sérgio, 106–7
Foco theory, 46
"Forty Seconds of AIDS," 242
Foundation, Herbert Daniel Green, 261–62
Foundation, Ford, 237, 256
Franco, Moreira, 234
Fujimore, Yoshitame, 102, 121
France, 2–5, 10, 61, 153, 155–59, 165, 169–92, 195, 197, 210, 213, 216, 232, 268–69
Freitas, Carlos Alberto Soares. *See* Breno
Freitas, Vanja, 219
Front homosexuel d'action révolutionnarie (FHAR), 174–77
funeral, of Herbert Daniel, 8–9

Gabeira, Fernando, 194–95, 225–28, 234–35, 252–53
Garibaldi, Aretuza, 36, 41, 56, 71, 73, 77, 82
Gaspar, Júlio, 245
Gai Pied, 175–76
Gê de Carvalho. *See* Carvalho, Geraldo Feliciano de
Geisel, President General Ernesto, 154–55, 178, 200
Gelli, Guido, 225
Gil, Gilberto, 85, 234
Gliochi, Sheila Gomes, 232
Gonçalves, Adair, 136
Gonçalves, Milton, 220
Gondim, José Carlos de Medeiros, 140
Göpfert, Edmauro, 102, 119
Gordon, Lincoln, 29
Goulart, Diana, 140
Goulart, João, 24–30, 38, 86, 120, 265–66

Gradel, José, 82, 116, 120
Grande Sertão Veredas, 104–5
Greco, Helena, 9
Green Party. *See* Partido Verde
Grossi, Míriam, 184
Groupe de libération homosexuelle—Politique & Quotidien (GLH—P&Q), 177
Grupo de Apoio a Prevenção à AIDS (GAPA), 236, 248
Grupo Gay da Bahia (GGB), 227, 239, 249
Grupo Pela VIDDA (Valorização, Integração e Dignidade do Doente de Aids), 243–52, 271
Guevara, Che, 46–47, 57, 94, 254
guerrillas: rural, 3, 5, 32, 45–47, 56–57, 62–65, 87–95, 99–112; urban, 64, 69–71, 81, 86–89, 113–38, 195–96, 235. *See also* Ação Libertadora Nacional; Comandos de Libertação Nacional; Movimento Revolucionário 8 de Outubro; Movimento Revolucionário Tiradentes; Vanguarda Armada Revolucionária; Vanguarda Popular Revolucionária

Henfil. *See* Souza Filho, Henrique de
Herzog, Vladimir, 155
heteronormativity, 6, 21–22, 36, 44–45, 50, 79–81, 106, 140, 144, 161, 184, 215, 228
Hocquenghem, Guy, 175–76
Holanda, Chico Buarque de, 85
Homens (Men), 251, 260
"Homosexual: Defense of Interests?" 83–84
Homosexual Desire, 175
homosexual movement, 2–3, 178–79, 226–28, 233–36, 239, 246, 249
homosexuality: revolutionary left and, 3, 6, 35–36, 43–45, 78–79, 106, 159–62, 169, 191–85, 191–92; social discrimination, 21–23, 43–44, 139–40, 143–44, 191–92, 202–5, 218–20, 227–30, 232–36, 242, 246, 250–53

"Homosexuality and Politics," 183
Human Rights Commission, Belo Horizonte City Council, 9
Huebra, Vera Lígia, 44, 73, 77

Iavelberg, Iara, 77–78, 90–93, 97, 102–7, 120–21, 129–32, 137, 148
Ibrahim, José, 86, 94
Institutional Act, 28
Institutional Act No. 2, 28
Institutional Act No. 5, 67, 94, 116, 266

Jacarés e lobisomens: Dois ensaios sobe a homossexualidade, 106, 208, 211, 235, 270
Jacomoni, Carmen Moneiro, 102–8, 120
Japa, Mário, 93, 95, 97, 106–7, 111, 147, 152–53, 157–59, 169–70
Jonjoca (João Belisário de Souza), 142, 145, 149, 153, 157–58
Joué, Maria Elisalva Oliveira, 140–43, 146, 149–50

Kubitschek, President Jucelino, 25, 38

Lacerda, Carlos, 38, 48
Lafoz, Sônia, 95–96, 103, 120
Lamarca, Carlos, 87–116, 119–32, 135–37, 142, 148, 191, 224, 258, 263, 267
Lampião da Esquina, 2, 179–80, 188, 194, 208, 210, 227, 236
Lavecchia, José, 101–2, 119
Leite, Afonso Celso Lana, 59
Leite, Eduardo, 116, 118
Leite, Gabriela, 248
Lieshout, Humberto van (Father Eustáquio), 12–13
Linhares, Cláudio Galeno Magalhães, 52–53, 63
Lisboa, Apolo Herlinger, 9, 32, 34, 38, 46, 52–53, 59, 61, 63, 75, 78–80, 95, 102, 121, 137
Lisbon, 154–70, 268–69
Lungaretti, Celso, 107–8

Machado, Ângelo, 37
Maciel, Eliane, 199–200, 226, 231, 251–52
Magalhães, Vera Sílvia, 182
Mann, Dr. Jonathan, 248–49, 255
Mariani, José, 87
Maoism, 30, 46, 80–81, 85
March of 100,000, 52
Martins, Almir, 219–20
Marxist-Leninist Group, 85–86
Mascarenhas, João Antônio, 227, 235–36
May Day rally: Belo Horizonte (1968), 48, 59–60; São Paulo (1968), 60; São Bernardo (1980), 229–30
Melo, Reinaldo José de, 62
Mendes, Lieutenant Alberto, 109–10
Menkes, Roberto, 101–2, 105, 108, 120
Mesquita Filho, Cláudio Alves de: adoption of a child, 251–52; as designer, 141, 146, 172, 183, 195, 202–5, 207, 220, 235, 252, 259; care of Herbert Daniel, 7–8, 256, 258–60; death of, 261; early life of, 138–41; Carvalho family and, 7–9, 150–52, 256–57; Herbert Daniel and, 2, 7–9, 138, 160–63, 168–72, 177–78, 189–98, 215–16, 219, 223, 250–51; marriages of, 140–41; Movement of Popular Resistance and, 141–42
Mesquita, Magaly, 140, 142, 146, 259, 268
Mesquita, Mercedes, 142, 146
Meu corpo daria um romance, 22, 215–17, 230, 270
Mexico, 3, 94, 107, 116–19, 124, 166, 237
Míccolis, Leila, 208–10, 216, 231–32, 270
Military Police Academy, 25
Minc, Carlos, 85, 96, 159, 225, 234, 245
Modas e Bordados, 163, 166–69
Monroe, Marilyn, 81, 144, 166–68, 209, 232
Montenegro, Cristina, 220, 231
Montreal AIDS Conference, 244, 247–50
Mott, Luiz, 227, 239, 249–50
Movimento das Forças Armadas (MFA), 156–57, 167–68

Movimento Democrático Brasileiro (MDB), 122, 155, 200, 205, 268
Movimento de Resistencia Popular (MRP), 137, 142, 145
Movimento Revolucionário 8 de Outubro (MR-8), 94, 120, 122, 125, 131–32, 225
Movimento Revolucionário Tiradentes (MRT), 107, 116, 122
Muller, Ana Maria, 188, 192

Nahas, Jorge, 31–32, 37, 41, 51, 53, 63, 69, 71, 73, 119
Nahas, Maria José de Carvalho (Zezé), 31, 41, 63, 103, 119
National Security Act, 1, 50, 64, 74, 154
National Union of Students (União Nacional de Estudantes), 28, 102, 125
Neves, President-elect Tancredo, 220, 222
Niterói, 82, 127, 142, 145–46, 149, 216, 232, 268
Nóbrega, José Araújo, 95, 102, 119
Nogueira da Costa, Fernando, 202

Okuchi, Nobuo, 107, 115, 129
Okzinho, 228–29
Olímpio. *See* Herbert Daniel, assumed names of
Oliveira, Ariston Lucena, 102
Oliveira, Gerson Theodoro de, 118, 123–25, 129, 131–32, 145
Oliveira, Tercina Dias de, 101, 107, 119
Oliveira, Zenaide Machado de, 115, 124, 131–37, 268
Organização Revolucionária Marxista—Política Operária (POLOP), 30–47, 52–61, 73, 85–86, 90, 93, 265
The Organization. *See* The O.
Osawa, Shizuo (Mário Japa), 93, 95, 97, 106–7, 111, 147, 152–53, 157–59, 169–70

Paiva, Maurício, 53, 119
Palla, Maria Antónia, 163
Palmeira, Vladimir, 205, 234
Paris, 2–5, 10, 61, 153, 155–59, 165, 169–92, 195, 197, 210, 213, 216, 232, 268–69

Parker, Richard, 256, 271
Partido Comunista Brasileira (PCB), 29, 36, 155
Partido Comunista do Brasil, 100, 112
Partido Democrático Social (PDS), 222
Partido Democrático Trabalhista (PDT), 205–6, 226
Partido do Movimento Democrático Brasileiro (PMDB), 206, 234
Partido dos Trabalhadores (PT), 197, 200–5, 211, 215, 224–24, 228, 230–31, 234, 270
Partido Trabalhista Brasileira (PTB), 29
Partido Verde (PV), 225–26, 235, 244, 252–53, 261
O Pasquim, 191, 212–14
Passagem para o próximo sonho: Um possível romance autocrítico, 4–5, 54, 175, 177, 188–89, 195–97, 207, 216–17, 230, 237, 270
People's Republic of China, 29
Pereira, Laís Soares, 4, 19–25, 32, 37–38, 40, 43, 51, 60, 144
Pezzuti, Ângela, 56, 153, 251, 258
Pezzuti, Ângelo, 35–37, 41, 43–44, 46, 48, 51, 53–67, 69, 71–72, 82, 117, 119, 147–49, 151, 153, 155–56, 169–70, 213–14, 217, 251, 258, 269
Pezzuti, Carmela, 44, 55, 63, 71, 170, 251, 258
Pinho, Sérgio, 224
Pinto, Onofre, 87, 94, 100, 148, 213–14
O Piquete, 51–53, 58–59, 65
Polari, Alex, 81–82, 96, 98, 114, 129, 131–34, 144, 159
Pontos, 76–78, 80–82, 133
Portugal, 154–70, 268–69
propaganda, nationalist, 116
Public Publicity, 146, 149

Ramires, Lula, 231–35
Ramos, Sílvia, 231, 235–38, 256
Ratton, Helvécio, 56, 73, 79
Régi, Irlando de Souza, 116–17

Resende, José Roberto Gonçalves de, 133
Resistência Democrática (REDE), 102, 107
Revollo, Mário Bejar, 102, 108
Revolution, Carnation, 154–70
Revolution within the Revolution (Debray), 46
Ribeiro, Cláudio de Souza, 90, 94–95
Rio D'Ouro, 120–21
Rocha, Guido, 52, 58, 63
Rocha, Maria Nazareth Cunha da, 76
Rodrigues, Darcy, 87, 91, 95, 99, 101, 114, 119
Romeu, Inês Etienne, 53, 73, 93, 116, 119, 121, 128–29, 131–33, 147–48, 267
Rosa dos Ventos: O Show Encantado, 134–35
Rosas, João Guimarães
Rousseff, Dilma, 43–44, 46, 51–53, 58, 65, 73, 77–78, 80–81, 86, 90, 93, 95, 207, 257

Sachs, Eric, 30, 46
Salgueiro, Beatriz, 252, 259
Santos, José Anselmo dos, 120–21, 132–33, 148–49, 212–14
Santos, Lucélia, 225
Santos, Pitágoras dos, 17–18
Sarney, President José, 222, 239
sauna, gay, 4, 172–77, 189, 197, 269
Schiller, Gustavo Buarque, 92
School of Medicine, Federal University of Minas Gerais, 24–27, 31–41, 48, 51, 53, 59–64, 266
Sebá, 189–91
Show Medicina, 37–40, 45, 47, 51, 217
Silva, Aguinaldo, 2, 179, 188
Silva, Luiz Inácio Lula da, 200, 230, 252
Silva, Murilo da, 55–58, 65, 119
Silva, Roberto das Chagas e, 120
Silva, Roque Apareido da, 86
Silva, Theofredo Pinto da, 55
Silveira, Maurício Guilherme da, 131
Sirkis, Alfredo, 81–82, 85, 94, 96, 98, 106, 114, 118–19, 124–26, 129–31, 144, 158–59, 195, 224–25

Social Democratic Party (PDS), 222
Socialist Convergence, 221
Somos-Rio, 236, 245
Somos: Grupo de Afirmação Homossexual (Somos), ix, 179, 229–30, 236, 269
Soto, Jesus Paredes
Sousa, João Belisário de (Jonjoca), 142, 145, 149, 153, 157–58
Souza, Chico Mário de, 237
Souza, Diógenes Sabrosa de, 102
Souza, Herbert de, 5, 237, 256
Souza, Ubiratan de, 102, 132, 282f37
Souza Filho, Henrique de (Henfil), 191, 195, 237
Support Group for AIDS Prevention. *See* Grupo de Apoio a Prevenção à AIDS
"Syndrome of Prejudice," 210–11, 239

Teixeira, Monica, 250–51, 257, 259–60
Teixeira, Paulo, 236
Tejo, Maria Helena, 156–63, 169–72
Teresópolis, Congress in, 193–97, 114
terrorism, 9, 65, 68, 70, 74, 113, 117, 129, 146, 151, 163, 186, 194
Terto, Veriano, 245, 256, 260
The O., 41–66
torture, 71, 73, 77, 82–83, 96, 106–9, 117, 132–33, 148–49, 155–56, 186; denunciation of, 49; *geladeira*, 136
Triângulo Rosa, 228, 233–36
Turma OK, 228–29
Tupamaros, 89

underground, living, 3–6, 9, 13, 21–22, 36, 64, 68–83, 117, 133, 141–42, 144–48, 161
União Nacional de Estudantes (UNE), 28, 102, 125
Universidade Federal de Minas Gerais (UFMG) 26–30

Vale do Ribeira, 99–121, 128, 132, 142, 160, 184, 267
Valentini, Leonardo, 137–38, 141–43, 145, 149–50

Vanguarda Armada Revolucionária—
  Palmares (VAR-Palmares), 89–97, 100,
  102, 111, 114, 116, 119, 125, 129, 137,
  156, 159, 217, 224, 267
Vanguarda Popular Revolucionária (VPR),
  2, 67, 86–90, 92–97, 100–36, 142, 145,
  147–49, 153, 157, 195, 209, 212–14, 225,
  234, 258, 256–58
Velloso, Lúcia, 131–37, 142, 144–45, 150,
  158–59, 162–63, 168–69, 182–83, 185,
  189
Veloso, Caetano, 50, 85, 134, 202, 234
Vida antes da morte / Life before Death,
  261, 271
Videma, Soledad Barret, 148–49
Vieira, Liszt, 95, 159, 163, 171, 201–7, 211,
  222–23, 226, 234, 270
Vieira, Válber, 8
Villard, Márcio José, 247, 251
Von der Weid, Jean Marc, 125, 152,
  182–84
Von Holleben, Ehrenfried, 116

wanted posters, 9, 74–75, 113, 146–47
World Cup, 116

Zanirato, Carlos Roberto, 102
Zerbini, Terezinha, 178

www.ingramcontent.com/pod-product-compliance
Lightning Source LLC
Chambersburg PA
CBHW070750230426
43665CB00017B/2312